Laboratory Manual
Networking Fundamentals

Second Edition

Richard M. Roberts

Publisher
The Goodheart-Willcox Company, Inc.
Tinley Park, Illinois
www.g-w.com

Table of Contents

Chapter 7   Microsoft Network Operating Systems

Chapter 8   UNIX/Linux Operating Systems

Chapter 9   Introduction to the Server

Chapter 10   TCP/IP Fundamentals

Chapter 11   Subnetting

Chapter 12   Multimedia Transmission

Chapter 13 Web Servers and Services

Chapter 14 Remote Access and Long-Distance Communications

Chapter 15 Network Security

Chapter 16 A Closer Look at the OSI Model

Chapter 17 Maintaining the Network

Chapter 18 Fundamentals of Troubleshooting the Network

Chapter 19   Designing and Installing a New Network

Chapter 20   Network+ Certification Exam Preparation

Chapter 21   Employment in the Field of Networking Technology

Introduction

This *Laboratory Manual* complements the *Networking Fundamentals* textbook and classroom-related studies. The laboratory activities in this manual are designed with the novice or entry-level student in mind as well as the new professional. The activities provide the valuable skills needed to obtain or retain a job in the networking environment.

Laboratory activities should be an essential part of your training because they link the concepts and related knowledge presented in the *Networking Fundamentals* textbook to on-the-job performance. A network technician cannot be trained simply through textbooks, lectures, and demonstrations. The following Chinese proverb best describes the importance of laboratory activities.

Tell me, and I forget;
Show me, and I remember;
Let me do, and I understand.
Chinese Proverb

Many of the laboratory activities are designed to use a minimum of equipment. Whenever possible, you should perform the laboratory activities at home to reinforce what you have learned in class or to catch up if you fall behind. Check with your instructor to determine which activities you can perform at home. Some activities may be beyond your scope of expertise at that given time and may result in disastrous consequences to your home computer.

It is strongly advised that serious students of networking technology build or buy two computers to connect as a simple network. The computers do not need to be expensive, especially the workstation. Check with your instructor for some suggestions and check www.RMRoberts.com for information about setting up a home network. (This site also contains help in the form of quizzes, practice tests, more laboratory activities, and up-to-date information to supplement your studies.)

In most lab settings, the equipment is used by more than one student. Your instructor may wish you to make a restore point before every laboratory activity on the computer you are using. Always leave the computer in working order for the next student to use.

The typical networking fundamentals student is assumed to have basic knowledge of standard desktop operating systems obtained through a CompTIA A+ type of classroom instruction or by completing coursework using the *Computer Service and Repair* textbook. Since not all students will have completed a CompTIA A+ course, many key topics are presented in this manual that should have been covered or mastered during the study of computer service and repair. Some critical topics, such as installing a network adapter card, setting up a peer-to-peer network, and installing network shares, are included in this *Laboratory Manual* to ensure that students have the required basic skills necessary to complete the course.

I would like to take this opportunity to wish you every success in your studies of networking fundamentals.

Best wishes!

Richard M. Roberts

Using This Manual

Each laboratory activity begins with a number of learning objectives. These are the goals you should accomplish while working through the activity. In addition to the objectives, each laboratory activity contains an *Introduction* section, which presents a brief description of the activity and, in some cases, an overview of the required theory.

Following the *Introduction* is an *Equipment and Materials* list. The list provides general guidelines for the material required for the activity. A graphic in the upper right-hand corner of each laboratory activity indicates the operating system required. For example, if a laboratory activity requires a particular operating system such as Windows Server 2008, the name of that operating system appears in the graphic. A laboratory activity that requires a Windows Server or the openSUSE Linux operating system may also require a Windows Vista or later workstation. Check the *Equipment and Materials* list first before beginning the activity to see if a Windows Vista or later workstation is needed. Laboratory activities that are unlabeled can be completed with any available operating system.

The *Procedure* section provides step-by-step instructions for completing the activity. You should read through the entire laboratory activity, including the *Procedure* section, before beginning an activity. If you have any questions about the requirements or procedures involved with the activity, ask your instructor for help. Some laboratory activities require you to enter information in the *Equipment and Materials* list or *Procedure* section. These are not test questions, but simply opportunities to record information about the computer you are using. Often, this information will be required in later steps in the activity.

The final part of each laboratory activity is the *Review Questions*. The *Review Questions* are designed to reinforce the concepts critical to each lesson and to closely match the CompTIA Network+ Certification objectives. Not all questions can be answered simply by reading through the laboratory activity. Some questions require you to deduce the answer using the knowledge you have gained from working through the exercise. Other questions require you to consult outside sources. Such questions force you to use your new knowledge, and thus, reinforce the new knowledge. You should complete all review questions and then routinely review the questions to better prepare for Network+ Certification exam and classroom exams.

As you read this text, you will notice that certain words or phrases stand out. File names, such as notepad.exe and student.txt appear in roman sans-serif typeface. In this manual, any time you direct the computer to perform a function, whether by entering a line of text at the command prompt or clicking an element in the GUI, it is considered a command. Commands, such as **dir C:** or **Start | All Programs | Accessories | System Tools**, are set in bold sans-serif typeface. Internet addresses appear in roman sans-serif typeface, such as www.g-w.com.

Be sure to read any Notes or Warnings that you encounter. Such features may alert you to an act that may damage your computer or yourself. Losing all of your data is the most common danger you will encounter with computers. But, you may also encounter some dangerous voltages, especially when dealing with monitors. Those repairs should be left to special technicians.

The laboratory activities that appeared in the *Networking Fundamentals* textbook are reprinted in this manual in write-in form. These laboratory activities are nearly identical to their counterparts in the textbook. The following is a list of the end-of-chapter laboratories in the textbook and the corresponding laboratory activity in this manual.

Lab Name	Textbook	Lab Manual
Identifying a Workstation's IP Configuration Settings	Chapter 1	Laboratory Activity 2
Making a Cat 6 Straight-Through Patch Cable	Chapter 2	Laboratory Activity 3
Fiber-Optic Connector Identification	Chapter 3	Laboratory Activity 10
Installing a USB Network Adapter and Configuring a Wireless Router	Chapter 4	Laboratory Activity 17
Introduction to Wireshark	Chapter 5	Laboratory Activity 20
Using the ARP Command	Chapter 6	Laboratory Activity 22
Adding Users to Window Server 2008	Chapter 7	Laboratory Activity 31
Installing openSUSE 11 Linux	Chapter 8	Laboratory Activity 36
Using the DiskPart Command Interpreter	Chapter 9	Laboratory Activity 43
Configuring a Static IPv6 Address	Chapter 10	Laboratory Activity 46
Subnet Mask Calculator	Chapter 11	Laboratory Activity 54
Windows Meeting Space	Chapter 12	Laboratory Activity 56
Installing Internet Information Services (IIS)	Chapter 13	Laboratory Activity 58
Routing and Remote Access Service (RRAS)	Chapter 14	Laboratory Activity 66
Security Event Monitoring	Chapter 15	Laboratory Activity 72
Wireshark OSI Model Exploration	Chapter 16	Laboratory Activity 80
LANguard Network Security Scanner	Chapter 17	Laboratory Activity 82
Using the Netstat Command	Chapter 18	Laboratory Activity 91
Designing a Small Network	Chapter 19	Laboratory Activity 95

General Safety Procedures

1. Before opening a computer's case, turn off all power to the PC and accessories and unplug the power cord from the outlet.

2. Before working on the computer, discharge static electricity by touching an unpainted, metallic surface. Paint is an insulator, and may prevent a static discharge from the body.

3. Do not touch pin connectors on chips or other components. Pins can be easily bent. Also, when a person touches something, the oils in the person's skin leave a residue, which can hinder a low-voltage electrical connection.

4. Leave parts in their antistatic bags until the parts are needed. When you are done with the parts, return them to the antistatic bags. Do not leave parts on work surfaces or on the PC case.

5. Do not touch connection pins or the conductive edge of any electronic component, such as network interface cards.

6. Never unplug or connect any device while power is applied to the PC. Unplugging a device, such as the hard disk drive or network adapter card, while power is applied can seriously damage the device.

7. Never open a monitor. A typical monitor can hold an electrical charge in excess of 25,000 volts, even long after the power to the unit has been cut off. In general, a PC technician does not service any parts found inside a computer monitor.

Laboratory Activity

1

Name_____ Date _____

Class/Instructor _____

Introduction to the CompTIA Network+ Examination Objectives

After completing this laboratory activity, you will be able to:
- Use the Internet to locate and download the Network+ Examination Objectives.
- Identify required knowledge associated with the Network+ Certification exam.

Introduction

The CompTIA organization provides a blueprint of the areas or objectives tested for on the CompTIA Network+ Certification exam. This laboratory activity will familiarize you with these objectives. Becoming familiar with the Network+ Examination Objectives will help you concentrate on the required knowledge associated with the exam as you proceed through this course.

The Network+ Examination Objectives are revised periodically. While every effort has been made to keep the course content up-to-date, it is recommended that you check the CompTIA Web site (www.comptia.org) periodically throughout this course for additional changes. You may also wish to check the www.RMRoberts.com Web site for notices about changes in the objectives.

However, do not lose focus on the intent of this networking fundamentals course. You are not in this course to simply pass the CompTIA Network+ Certification exam. You are in this course to learn networking fundamentals. You can prepare for the Network+ Certification exam by memorizing facts and figures, but memorization of facts and figures will not prepare you to be a successful network technician. To be a successful network technician, you need a combination of textbook readings, classroom lecture and discussion, lab activities, and most importantly, a desire to learn the subject. The laboratory activities can provide you with a wealth of experiences that cannot be obtained through textbook readings and classroom lectures.

Equipment and Materials

❑   PC with Internet access.

Note
This laboratory activity may be performed at home.

Procedure

1. _____   Report to your assigned workstation for this activity.

2. _____   Boot the PC and access the CompTIA Web site at www.comptia.org. (Note that the Web site domain address ends in "org," not "com."

3. _____ Navigate the Web site until you locate the CompTIA Network+ page. At the time of this writing, the CompTIA Network+ page can be accessed through the Certifications & Exams link on the home page.

4. _____ Once you have found the CompTIA Network+ page, navigate to the certification objectives download page. As of this writing, it is located under the How to Study link. If you have difficulty locating the certification objectives download page, you can conduct a Google search using the key words "CompTIA Network+ objectives."

You must provide an e-mail address and your name and country before being allowed to download a PDF file of the test objectives. You may be presented with several variations of the test objectives. Be sure to download the very latest version. Also, be aware that CompTIA provides a short set of sample test questions so that you will have an idea of the difficulty level of the questions and insight of what to expect on the test.

5. _____ After you have completed the download, look at the objectives and fill in the domain areas and the percentage that each domain represents in the following chart.

CompTIA Network+ Certification Domain Areas	Percent of Examination
Total	100%

Based on the CompTIA Network+ 2009 objectives.

6. _____ Scan through the Domain 1.0 contents, noticing the many acronyms listed in the objectives. There are hundreds of acronyms used in the network technology industry. The last few pages of the Network+ Examination Objectives list the common acronyms associated with the test. Scan the last few pages of the objectives to see how the acronyms are presented.

7. _____ Scan Domain 2.0 through Domain 6.0. You will see many more acronyms.

8. _____ Look through the entire list of Network+ Examination Objectives to see if you can locate which network operating system will be covered. See if you can locate operating system terms such as Novell, Microsoft, and Linux.

Did you see any of these terms? Yes _____ No _____

You should have not located any terms specific to the three major operating systems. The Network+ Certification exam is vender neutral, which means it does not align specifically with any one vender's network operating system.

As you progress through the course you will become familiar with the various operating systems and you will see that the terminology is very similar, especially those acronyms. The test measures basic networking technology, not vender-specific operating system knowledge. Vender-specific certifications are more advanced than the Network+ Certification, but mastering networking fundamentals is a must before mastering vender-specific skills.

9. _____ Keep a copy of the CompTIA Network+ Certification exam objectives in your notebook for reference. As you progress through your course, check off items listed in the objectives as you learn them. By the time you finish the course, you should have covered each and every objective.

10. _____ Use your copy of the Network+ Examination Objectives to answer the review questions.

Review Questions

1. What does it take to become a successful network technician? _____

_____

2. What network topologies are you required to identify by description or diagram? _____

_____

3. Which network address formats are identified in Domain 1.3? _____

_____

4. What is the main topic in the first section of Domain 4.0? _____

5. What do the two acronyms "Mbps" and "MBps" represent? _____

_____

Name_____ Date _____

Class/Instructor _____

Identifying a Workstation's IP Configuration Settings

After completing this laboratory activity, you will be able to:

■ Use the **ipconfig** command to determine the IP configuration settings of a workstation.

■ Summarize the function of each IP configuration setting.

Introduction

This laboratory activity is extremely important because it provides you with the information necessary to reconfigure the network adapter properties assigned to your workstation. You will learn to quickly check the network configuration properties using the **ipconfig** command with and without the **/all** switch.

This lab activity does not require an in-depth understanding of the configuration properties or an in-depth understanding of the **ipconfig** command and associated switches. You will simply learn to use the command to quickly identify specific information.

On a separate sheet of paper, record your assigned user name, password, the number or name of your assigned workstation, and the server you are logged on to. You will most likely need to record the server name if there is more than one server for students to log on to. The default server specified in the logon box could be different than the server used for the Networking Fundamentals class, or there may not be any server specified at all. Your instructor will provide you with all required pertinent information, such as your user name and password, the workstation number or name and the server name.

To access the workstation IP configuration, you will issue an **ipconfig** command from the command prompt. The following image is a typical display provided by the **ipconfig** command issued from Windows Vista.

```
C:\Windows\system32\cmd.exe                                          _ □ X
Microsoft Windows [Version 6.0.6002]
Copyright (c) 2006 Microsoft Corporation.  All rights reserved.

C:\Users\Richard>ipconfig

Windows IP Configuration

Wireless LAN adapter Wireless Network Connection:

   Connection-specific DNS Suffix  . : hsd1.fl.comcast.net.
   Link-local IPv6 Address . . . . . : fe80::8c62:b6aa:704d:22b1%10
   IPv4 Address. . . . . . . . . . . : 192.168.1.104
   Subnet Mask . . . . . . . . . . . : 255.255.255.0
   Default Gateway . . . . . . . . . : 192.168.1.1

Tunnel adapter Local Area Connection* 6:

   Media State . . . . . . . . . . . : Media disconnected
   Connection-specific DNS Suffix  . : hsd1.fl.comcast.net.

Tunnel adapter Local Area Connection* 9:

   Connection-specific DNS Suffix  . :
   IPv6 Address. . . . . . . . . . . : 2001:0:4137:9e50:34a2:3f47:3f57:fe97
   Link-local IPv6 Address . . . . . : fe80::34a2:3f47:3f57:fe97%9
   Default Gateway . . . . . . . . . : ::

C:\Users\Richard>_
```

When the **ipconfig** command is issued, important information about the network connection is revealed. For this particular lab activity, you are interested in the IPv4 address, the subnet mask, and the default gateway. You can ignore the IPv6 address at this time. The IPv6 address will be covered in greater detail in a later lab activity. A TCP/IP network system uses the IPv4 assigned IP address to identify each device on the network. Every computer on the local area network must have a unique IP address. Each computer must also have a subnet mask to go with the assigned IPv4 address. The subnet mask is a set of four numbers separated by a period, such as 255.255.255.000. The subnet mask identifies the network portion of the address. There will be much more about subnet masks later in the course.

The default gateway is typically the device that is used to connect through to another network, such as the Internet. The gateway can be a device such as a router, a server, or another computer. Again, there will be much more about the function of a gateway later in the course.

When the **ipconfig** command is issued with the **/all** switch, much more detailed information is revealed about the connection configuration. Look at the following screen capture to see a sample of what is displayed after issuing the **ipconfig/all** command.

Additional information is displayed, such as the physical address of the network adapter, IPv6 address of the DNS servers, if the adapter is DHCP enabled, the assigned address of the DHCP server, and if the adapter is configured to use NetBIOS over TCP/IP. Please note that the physical address is another name for the MAC address. The additional detailed information can be of great importance when troubleshooting a networking problem. For now, all this information is most likely overwhelming you. Be patient and you will learn all the details of the network adapter connection configuration. For now, just be familiar with how to issue the **ipconfig** and **ipconfig/all** commands.

IPv6 is automatically configured and first appeared by default in Windows Vista. IPv6 is intended to replace IPv4 in the near future. As of this writing, IPv6 is only used to communicate on the local area network, not on the Internet. IPv4 is used for both the local area network and the Internet. IPv4 requires a subnet mask; IPv6 does not.

IPv4 addresses can be assigned manually or automatically. The network device responsible for issuing unique IPv4 addresses automatically to workstations is called the *DHCP server*. Many times the same network device is responsible for more than one task such as acting as a gateway and as a DHCP server.

Equipment and Materials

❑ Assigned computer with Windows Vista or Windows 7 installed. The computer must be installed as part of a network or have a direct connection to the Internet for the lab activity to work correctly.

❑ The following information from your instructor:

User name: _____

Password: _____

Workstation number or name: _____

Server name: _____

Note
You will need administrator privileges to access and run **ipconfig**.

Procedure

1. _____ Report to your assigned workstation for this activity.

2. _____ Boot the computer and look for the logon screen. There may or may not be a logon screen for your computer, depending on how it is configured in a network system. You will use your assigned user name and password to log on to the network if required.

3. _____ In the **Search** box located on the **Start** menu, type **cmd** and wait for a moment. You will see "cmd" listed at the top of the **Search** list under **Programs**. If you pressed [Enter] after typing **cmd** in the **Search** box, the command prompt automatically appeared on the screen in its own dialog box.

   The command prompt can also be accessed in Windows Vista or Windows 7 by following the path **Start | All Programs | Accessories | Command Prompt**.

4. _____ At the command prompt, type and enter the **ipconfig** command. On a separate sheet of paper, record the follow information:

   IPv4 address: _____

   Subnet mask: _____

   Default gateway: _____

   IPv6 address: _____

5. _____ At the command prompt, type and enter **ipconfig/all**. On a separate sheet of paper, record the follow information:

   Physical address (MAC): _____

   DHCP enabled (Yes/No): _____

DHCP server address: _____

DNS server addresses (2): _____

_____

6. _____ After recording the information, answer the review questions.

7. _____ When you have finished the review questions, shut down your workstation and return all materials to their proper storage area.

Review Questions

1. What is the purpose of the IPv4 address? _____

_____

2. What is the purpose of the IPv4 subnet mask? _____

_____

3. What command is issued from the command prompt to reveal the assigned IP address? _____

_____

4. What is another name for the physical address? _____

5. Does IPv6 require a subnet mask? _____

6. What is the purpose of the gateway? _____

_____

7. Which operating system first used IPv6 by default? _____

8. What is the purpose of a DHCP server? _____

_____

9. What is the path used to access the command prompt in Windows Vista and Windows 7? _____

_____

Name _____ Date _____

Class/Instructor _____

Making a Cat 6 Straight-Through Patch Cable

After completing this laboratory activity, you will be able to:

■ Construct a Category 6 or Category 6e patch cable following the 568A or 568B standards.

■ Explain the difference between the 568A and 568B wiring standard.

■ Test a patch cable.

Introduction

In this laboratory activity, you will make a Category 6 or Category 6e straight-through patch cable. The following illustration shows the basic parts associated with a Category 6 connector: the boot, RJ-45 connector (8P8C), and load bar.

Note

Category 6 and Category 6e typically use the same type of RJ-45 connector. Category 6a connectors, however, are not the same as Category 6 or Category 6e connectors and are generally not compatible. Check with the cable connector manufacturer's Web site for more information about compatibility issues.

Not all Category 6 connector manufacturers use a load bar. A load bar helps arrange the conductors in their proper color sequence prior to insertion into the RJ-45 connector body. Category 6 cable uses a plastic spine to improve cable pair data-rate performance. The cable spine is a major design improvement over Category 5 and Category 5e cable. The plastic spine adds further separation distance between conductor pairs, thus allowing for high frequencies to be carried by each set of cable pairs. Notice the plastic spine located in the center of the cable in the following illustration.

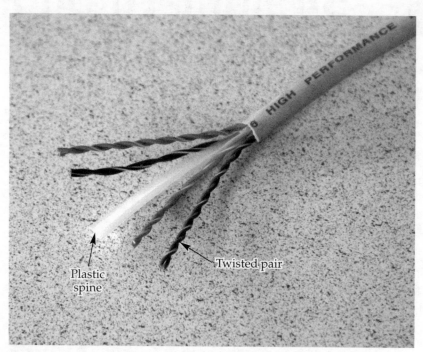

Plastic spine

Twisted pair

You will use the following 568A and 568B color code illustration to assist you in the lab activity. Notice that the main difference between the 568A and 568B standard is the position of the orange and green pairs. The blue and brown pairs remain in the same locations. If you use the 568A color standard on one end and the 568B standard on the opposite end, you will create a crossover cable rather than a straight-through cable.

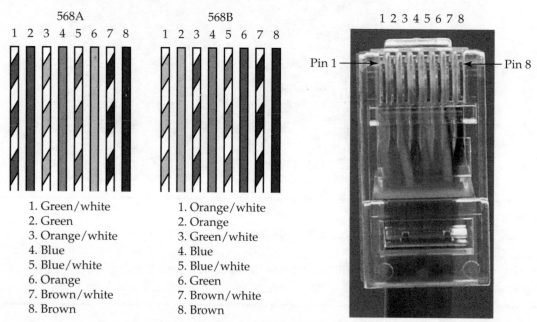

568A
1 2 3 4 5 6 7 8

1. Green/white
2. Green
3. Orange/white
4. Blue
5. Blue/white
6. Orange
7. Brown/white
8. Brown

568B
1 2 3 4 5 6 7 8

1. Orange/white
2. Orange
3. Green/white
4. Blue
5. Blue/white
6. Green
7. Brown/white
8. Brown

1 2 3 4 5 6 7 8

Pin 1 —→ ←— Pin 8

The two standards produce equal performance, and there is no real difference other than the color code. Most cable testers come with a copy of the 568A and 568B standard printed on the tester. Look at the following illustration of a cable tester.

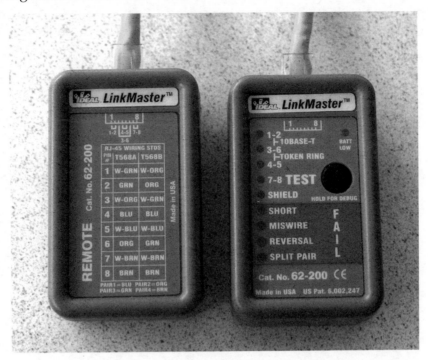

The cable tester you use in the lab activity will not necessarily match the one in the illustration, but it will be similar in design. You simply plug each end of the finished cable into the two cable tester modules and then press the "TEST" button. Faults will be indicated by a light.

Early 10BaseT and 100BaseTX cables only used two of the four pairs of conductors to transmit and receive. The two pairs corresponded with cable pins 1, 2, 3, and 6. High-speed cable, such as for 1000BaseT, still follow the 568A and 568B wire map but use all four pairs of conductors.

Stranded wire is preferred for patch cables because the cable needs to be flexible. Solid wire is flexible, but it tends to break at the connector if flexed excessively. Solid wire is typically used for horizontal runs. Horizontal runs are the network cable runs inside building walls. Because the horizontal run is installed inside building walls, the cable is not required to be as flexible as stranded wire.

Equipment and Materials

❑ Category 6 crimping tool.
❑ Cable cutter. (May be part of the cable crimping tool.)
❑ UTP cable jacket stripper. (May be part of the cable crimping tool.)
❑ Two Category 6 RJ-45 connectors, load bars, and boots.
❑ Length of Category 6 or Category 6e cable as indicated by your instructor.
❑ Cable tester.
❑ The following information provided by your instructor:

Cable length: _____

Cable color code (568A or 568B) to follow: _____

Procedure

1. _____ After gathering all required materials, report to your assigned workstation.

2. _____ Cut the cable to the desired length as indicated by your instructor. If you plan to use a cable boot to protect the finished connector, install the cable boot now. (You will need one boot for each end of the cable.)

3. _____ Remove approximately 1 1/2″ to 2″ of cable insulating jacket.

4. _____ Separate the cable pairs. Bend the end of each pair to a 90° angle to help the conductor pair untwist easily.

5. _____ Bend the conductors out of the way and cut off the cable center spine as close as possible to the end of the insulating jacket.

Right angle bend

6. _____ Arrange individual conductors into the color order (568A or 568B) indicated by your instructor. Keep the conductors as straight as possible.

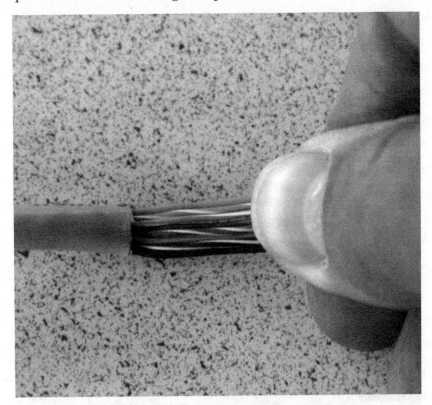

7. _____ If using a load bar, cut the conductors at slight angle. Cutting the conductors at an angle will make it easier to insert the conductors into the load bar. If using an RJ-45 without a load bar, cut the conductors at a right angle.

Laboratory Activity 3   23

8. _____ If using a load bar, insert the conductors into the load bar and then slide the load bar down as close as possible to the cable jacket end.

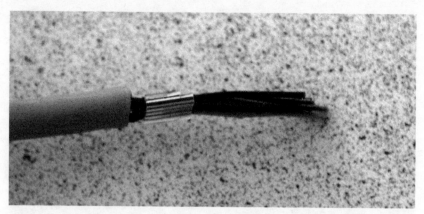

9. _____ Check the color code arrangement one more time.

10. _____ If using a load bar, cut the conductors off at approximately 1/4" past the load bar.

11. _____ Insert the conductors and load bar into the RJ-45 connector. Do *not* leave conductors exposed before the connector, as this may result in crosstalk.

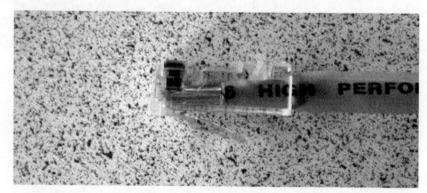

12. _____ Crimp the RJ-45 connector by squeezing the handles of the crimper firmly.

13. _____ Have your instructor inspect the connector before sliding the boot down.

14. _____ Repeat the installation operation for the other end of the cable.

15. _____ Use the cable tester to ensure the cable has been properly made. Demonstrate the results using the cable tester for your instructor. Simply plug both ends into the tester and then press the "Test" button. The LEDs will indicate the condition of the cable.

16. _____ Clean your workstation and return all tools and supplies to the proper storage area.

Review Questions

1. What physical feature improves the performance of Category 6 cable when compared with Category 5 cable? _____

2. What is the purpose of a load bar? _____
   _____

3. What is the difference between the 568A and 568B color code? _____
   _____

4. What will happen if you make one end of a patch cable according to the 568A standard and the opposite end according to the 568B standard? _____
   _____

5. What cable fault may occur if conductors are exposed before the connector? _____
   _____

6. How many pairs of conductors are used to communicate on a 10BaseT or 100BaseT network?
   _____
   _____

7. How many pairs of conductors are used to communicate on a 1000BaseT network? _____
   _____

8. Why is stranded core cable preferred for patch cables? _____
   _____

9. What is a horizontal run? _____
   _____

10. What type of copper conductor (solid or stranded) is typically used for horizontal runs? _____
    _____

Name_____ Date _____

Class/Instructor _____

Making a Crossover Cable

After completing this laboratory activity, you will be able to:

■ Construct an Ethernet crossover cable.

■ Differentiate a crossover cable from a straight-through cable.

■ Recall where a crossover cable might be used.

Introduction

In this laboratory activity, you will make an Ethernet crossover cable from two RJ-45 connectors and a one three-foot length of Category 5e cable. Crossover cables are typically used for connecting two workstations together without the use of a hub. They are also used for connecting some network equipment together, such as hubs, that do not have a cable select feature. A cable select feature allows the equipment to automatically set up a specific connection port for use with either a straight-through cable or a crossover cable.

The crossover cable is made by reversing pin connections 1, 2, 3, and 6 at one end of the cable. Look at the following wire map.

```
1 ——————╲           ╱—————— 1
2 ——————╲╲         ╱╱—————— 2
3 ——————————╲——╱——————————— 3
4 ——————————————————————————— 4
5 ——————————————————————————— 5
6 ——————————╳——————————————— 6
7 ——————————————————————————— 7
8 ——————————————————————————— 8
```

The wire map indicates that pin 1 connects to pin 3 and pin 2 connects to pin 6. A crossover cable can be made easily by wiring an RJ-45 connector at one end of the cable following the 568A standard and wiring the RJ-45 connector at the other end of the cable following the 568B standard.

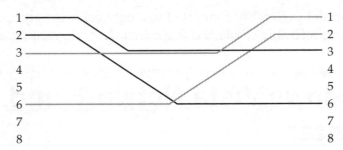

	568A			568B
Pin #	Color		Pin #	Color
1	Green striped		1	Orange striped
2	Green		2	Orange
3	Orange striped		3	Green striped
4	Blue		4	Blue
5	Blue striped		5	Blue striped
6	Orange		6	Green
7	Brown striped		7	Brown striped
8	Brown		8	Brown

Equipment and Materials

❑ Two or more RJ-45 connectors. (Additional connectors may be required for mistakes.)
❑ Standard RJ-45 crimping tool.
❑ UTP cable stripper. (Some crimping tools incorporate a striping tool as part of the assembly.)
❑ 3-foot length of Category 5e UTP cable.
❑ Cable tester.
❑ Paper and pencil or pen to make drawing of the cable assembly color code.

Procedure

1. _____ Gather all required materials and report to your assigned workstation.

2. _____ Make a chart representing the color sequence for each end of the cable based on the 568A and 568B standards. Have the instructor approve the chart before you proceed.

3. _____ Remove approximately 1 1/2″ to 2″ of outer jacket from one end of the UTP cable.

4. _____ Arrange the conductors into the 568A color-code sequence. Trim the conductors so that approximately 1/2″ protrudes from the outer jacket.

5. _____ Carefully insert the conductors into the RJ-45 connector and then crimp the connector.

6. _____ Repeat steps 3 through 5 using the 568B color-code sequence instead of the 568A color-code sequence.

7. _____ Test the cable using a standard cable test tool. If required, set the tool to test for a crossover cable.

8. _____ Have your instructor check your project.

9. _____ Clean up your workstation and then return all materials and equipment to their proper storage area.

10. _____ Answer the review questions.

Note
Save this cable. It will be used in a later laboratory activity to connect two workstations.

Review Questions

1. Where would you use a crossover cable? _____

_____

_____

_____

2. How does a crossover cable differ from a straight-through cable? _____

_____

_____

_____

3. Which pin assignments are changed for a crossover cable? _____

_____

Laboratory Activity

5

Name_____ Date _____

Class/Instructor _____

Viewing Network Connection Status and Properties (Part I)

After completing this laboratory activity, you will be able to:

■ Check the status of a network connection in Windows XP.

■ Check the properties of a network connection in Windows XP.

■ Recall the values associated with the status of a network connection.

■ Recall the values associated with the properties of a network connection.

Introduction

In this laboratory activity, you will view the status dialog box and properties dialog box associated with a particular network connection. You will need to access these locations throughout the course and throughout your career as a network technician or administrator. The purpose of this laboratory activity is to show you the location of and general features associated with these dialog boxes in Windows XP. You will use them often to inspect and modify the network connection. You will need to practice locating, opening, and viewing the contents until you are confident that you will be able to locate these items in future laboratory activities and on the job.

To view the network connections associated with the workstation, right-click **My Network Places** located in the **Start** menu or on the desktop. Select **Properties** from the shortcut menu. A window similar to the following will display.

The **Network Connections** window displays all connections associated with the workstation. It also provides a list of common network administrative activities such as **Create a new connection, Setup a home or small office network, Change Windows Firewall settings, Disable this network device, Repair this connection, Rename this connection, View status of this connection**, and **Change settings of this connection**. Also, notice the **Details** box listed at the bottom of the left-hand pane. When a connection is selected, details for this connection display in this area.

In the previous screen capture, you can see the Local Area Network connection and a connection called StratoNet. The Local Area Connection is the local LAN connection through the Ethernet network adapter. The StratoNet connection is a telephone modem connection used to access the StratoNet ISP.

The default name of a network connection is Local Area Connection. When more than one network connection is configured for a workstation, the next default name is Local Area Connection2. Each additional network connection is given the next sequential number. Administrators typically rename connections so that their function can be easily identified. For example, a workstation could have a telephone modem, a LAN connection through a network adapter, and a wireless connection using a wireless network adapter. The default names would be confusing and difficult to determine for which connection each is used. The connections can be renamed for easy identification. To rename a connection, right-click the connection and then select **Rename** from the shortcut menu.

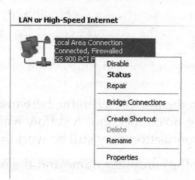

Two other important shortcut menu options are **Status** and **Properties**. When the **Status** option is selected, a dialog box similar to the following displays.

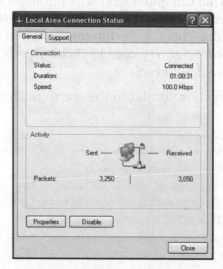

Name _____

The **Local Area Connection Status** dialog box provides a summary of the network connection status. In the following screen capture, you can see that the Local Area Connection is connected and has been connected for 1 hour and 31 seconds. The connection speed is 100 Megabits per second (Mbps) and has sent and received over 3,000 packets. Also take notice of the two buttons at the bottom of the dialog box: **Properties** and **Disable**. You can view the connection properties or disable the connection. Selecting the **Support** tab produces a dialog box similar to the following.

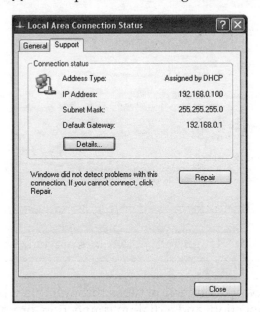

Information about the IP address is revealed. You can also perform a connection repair from this dialog box by selecting the **Repair** button. The **Repair** button activates a software utility that performs some general tasks in an attempt to repair the connection. These tasks can also be performed from the command prompt, such as releasing the network connection and reissuing the IP address. Selecting the **Details** button reveals a screen similar to the following.

This dialog box displays detailed information about the network connection. It replaces the need to use the command prompt to gather information about the connection.

Another dialog box that is often used is the **Local Area Connection Properties** dialog box. It is accessed by right-clicking the **Local Area Connection** icon and selecting **Properties** from the shortcut menu. This dialog box provides information about the connection, protocols, authentication, and advanced features. An entire laboratory activity is devoted to exploring the features associated with this dialog box. For now, be able to locate it and understand that this is where you add and remove protocols associated with a particular network adapter in Windows XP.

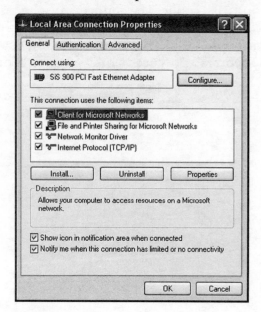

Equipment and Materials

❑ Windows XP computer connected to a network.

Procedure

1. _____ Report to your assigned workstation.

2. _____ Boot the computer and verify it is in working order.

3. _____ Open the **Network Connections** window by right-clicking the **My Network Places** icon on the desktop or from the **Start** menu and selecting **Properties** from the shortcut menu. A network connection should display.

Note
A network connection must exist for a network connection to display in the **Network Connections** window.

---

4. _____ Close the **Network Connections** window and then disconnect the network cable.

5. _____ Open the **Network Connections** window. You should no longer see the network connection.

6. _____ Close the **Network Connections** window and then reconnect the network cable.

7. _____ Open the **Network Connections** window. The network connection should display.

8. _____ Access the **Local Area Connection Status** dialog box by right-clicking the network connection and selecting **Status** from the shortcut menu. Inspect the information available. What information is displayed? Use the space provided to describe the information.

_____

_____

_____

9. _____ Select the **Support** tab and view the information displayed. List the information in the space provided.

_____

_____

_____

_____

10. _____ Select the **Details** button. What additional information is displayed? List the information in the space provided.

_____

_____

_____

_____

11. _____ Close the **Local Area Connection Status** dialog box and open it again.

12. _____ Select the **Repair** button and then observe the activity.

13. _____ Close the **Network Connection Status** dialog box and **Network Connections** window and practice opening the **Network Connection Status** dialog box starting from the **Start** menu.

14. _____ Now, access the **Local Area Connection Properties** dialog box by right-clicking **My Network Places** and selecting **Properties** from the shortcut menu. When the **Network Connections** window displays, right-click the **Local Area Connection** icon and select **Properties** from the shortcut menu. You should see a list of items such as Client for Microsoft Networks, File and Printer Sharing for Microsoft Networks, and Internet Protocol (TCP/IP).

15. _____ Open the **Internet Protocol (TCP/IP) Properties** dialog box by selecting **Internet Protocol (TCP/IP)** and then clicking the **Properties** button.

16. _____ Practice locating and opening the **Network Connections** window and the dialog boxes presented in this laboratory activity until you feel confident that you can open or locate them in the future.

17. _____ Answer the review questions.

18. _____ Shut down the workstation.

Review Questions

1. How is the **Network Connections** window accessed in Windows XP? _____

_____

_____

2. Which dialog box provides a feature to repair a connection? _____

_____

3. What information does the **Local Area Connection Status** dialog box provide? _____

_____

_____

4. What information does the **Local Area Connection Status** dialog box under the **Support** tab provide? _____

_____

_____

5. What additional information is revealed in the **Local Area Connection Status** dialog box after the **Details** button is selected? _____

_____

_____

6. What would be a reason for a network connection not displaying in the **Network Connections** window? _____

_____

_____

Viewing Network Connection Status and Properties (Part II)

After completing this laboratory activity, you will be able to:

- Check the network connection status in Windows Vista and Windows 7.
- Evaluate information about the network adapter configuration in Windows Vista and Windows 7.
- Carry out a diagnostic test of the network connection using Windows Vista and Windows 7.
- Compare and contrast network status dialog box options for Windows Vista and Windows 7.
- Summarize how to enable or disable featured items in the **Local Area Connection Dialog** box.

Introduction

In this laboratory activity, you will explore the **Local Area Connection Status** dialog box similar to the one in the following screen caption.

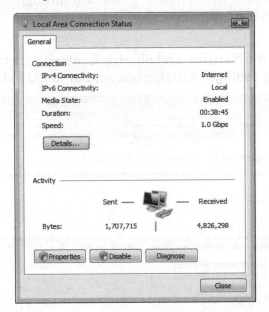

The **Local Area Connection Status** dialog box is very similar in Windows XP, Windows Vista, and Windows 7 as well as in all Windows Server operating systems. This dialog box is where you would go to quickly inspect the status of the network connection and verify that network packets are being sent and received. Be sure to practice accessing this dialog box and the features presented in this lab activity.

Equipment and Materials

❑ Windows Vista or Windows 7 computer connected to a network.

Procedure

1. _____ Report to your assigned workstation.

2. _____ Boot the computer and verify it is in working order.

3. _____ Open the **Network and Sharing Center**. To do this, simply type "net" into the **Search** box and then select **Network and Sharing Center** from the generated search list.

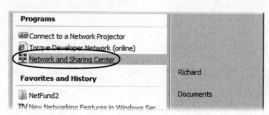

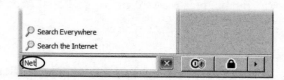

You can also access the **Network and Sharing Center** through the **Network** icon in the notification area of the taskbar.

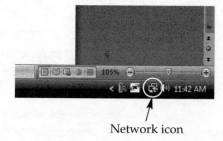

Network icon

Right-clicking the **Network** icon in Windows Vista will present you with options such as **Diagnose and repair** and **Networking and Sharing Center**. Windows 7 provides only two options: **Troubleshooting problems** and **Open Network and Sharing Center**.

As you can see, there are many different ways to access the Network and Sharing Center. Practice each method before moving to step 4. After selecting **Network and Sharing Center**, you should see the familiar Network and Sharing Center similar to the one in the following screen capture.

Name _____

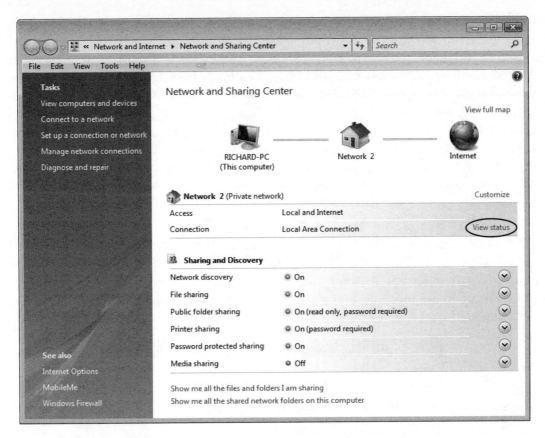

4. _____ In Windows Vista, select **View Status** in the Network and Sharing Center as shown in the previous screen capture. In Windows 7, select **Local Area Connection** to view the status of the local area connection as shown in the following screen capture.

The **Local Area Connection Status** dialog box will display and look similar to the following.

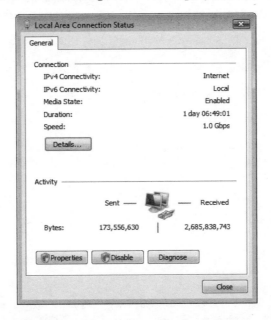

The **Local Area Connection Status** dialog box has a similar appearance in Windows XP, Windows Vista, and Windows 7. It provides information about the network adapter that is being used for the local area network connection. In the **Connection** section of this dialog box, you can see that IPv4 is being used for the Internet. IPv6 is being used for the local network. The **Media State** option is enabled. The duration of the connection in days, hours, minutes, and seconds is displayed as well as the speed of the connection.

The **Activity** section shows the number of bytes sent and received from the network connection. This is where you would check if the network adapter is functioning properly. If these numbers are very low, for example 100 or less for the received bytes, the connection has a problem. The first thing you should do is click the **Diagnose** button. The **Diagnose** button will reset the network adapter. That means it will disable the connection and then enable the connection.

5. _____ Click the **Diagnose** button for practice. The operating system will complete a set of automatic diagnostic tests on the connection to see if there is a problem and then will recommend a course of action. Since the connection is working, there will not be a recommendation.

There is a slight difference in the options presented in Windows Vista and Windows 7. In Windows Vista you are presented with two options: **Send a report to Microsoft** and **Reset the network adapter "Local Area Connection"**.

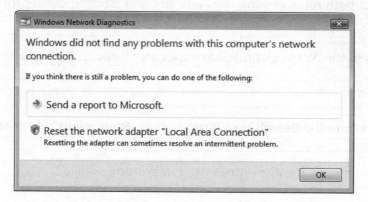

When you select **Reset the network adapter "Local Area Connection"**, the network adapter releases the assigned IP addresses and then has the DHCP server reissue an IP address. This can usually solve some problems with a network connection.

In Windows 7, the diagnostic dialog box presents you with a different set of options: **Explore additional options**, **Close the troubleshooter**, and **View detailed information**.

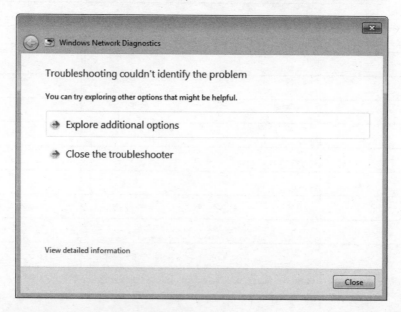

Selecting **View detailed information** will display a screen similar to the following.

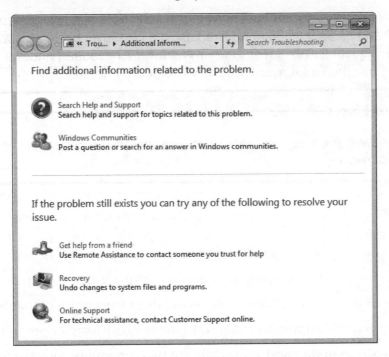

As you can see, Windows 7 provides you with many more options than Windows Vista. Pay particular attention to the three bottom options: **Get help from a friend**, **Recovery**, and **Online Support**.

Get help from a friend sets up a Remote Assistance session with another user. There will be more about this in future lab activities.

Recovery allows you to roll back or reset your computer to a previous system restore point.

Online Support allows you to get support for your problem by exploring resources such as TechNet and Microsoft Answers Web site. It also allows you to set up a Remote Assistance session just like in the first option.

6. _____ Close the diagnostic dialog box for the appropriate operating system to return to the **Local Area Connection Status** dialog box.

7. _____ Click the **Details** button. You should see a dialog box similar to the following. The **Network Connection Details** dialog box is similar for Windows Vista and Windows 7.

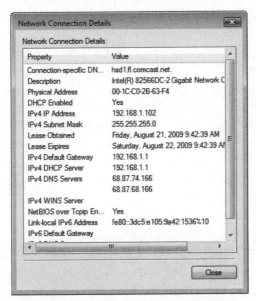

8. _____ Write the information that is revealed about your computer's network connection in the space provided. Do *not* use the information from the screen capture.

Connection-specific DNS Suffix: _____

Description: _____

Physical Address: _____

DHCP Enabled (Yes or No?): _____

IPv4 Address: _____

IPv4 Subnet Mask: _____

Lease Obtained: _____

Lease Expires: _____

IPv4 Default Gateway: _____

IPv4 DHCP Server: _____

IPv4 DNS Servers: _____

_____

IPv4 WINS Server: _____

NetBIOS over Tcpip Enabled (Yes or No?): _____

Link-local IPv6 Address: _____

IPv6 Default Gateway: _____

IPv6 DNS Server: _____

In most cases, the **WINS Server** property will be blank because there will most likely not be a WINS server in your network. Also, the **IPv6 Default Gateway** and **IPv6 DNS Server** will most likely be blank if there is no IPv6 gateway or DNS server. Also note that Windows XP does not have an IPv6 address by default; only IPv4.

You will learn more about these configuration properties as you progress through the textbook and additional lab activities. For now, be sure you know how to access the various network information dialog boxes. You will be using them a lot during your study of networking fundamentals.

9. _____ Close the **Network Connection Details** dialog box to return to the **Local Area Connection Status** dialog box.

10. _____ Click the **Properties** button. You should see a dialog box similar to the following.

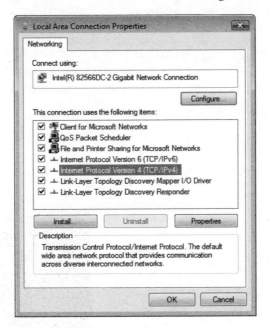

This dialog box is similar in all Microsoft Windows operating systems, both desktop and server versions. You will be accessing this dialog box quite a lot as a network technician. This dialog box will allow you to change many of the configuration options you were viewing in the **Network Connection Details** dialog box.

You can enable or disable network property items by simply selecting the check boxes with the mouse. A check mark means the item has been enabled. No check mark means the item is disabled.

11. _____ Take a few minutes to practice accessing the **Network and Sharing Center** and viewing the network connection status and network connection details.

Note

In future labs, the exact step-by-step method of accessing these features will be intentionally left out to force you to learn how to access them. For example, the lab activity may simple say, "Open the **Local Area Connection Properties** dialog box, and then disable the IPv6 protocol."

---

12. _____ Complete the review questions, and then return the computer to its original order. Return all materials to their proper storage area.

Review Questions

1. Which option would you select in Windows Vista **Network and Sharing Center** to view the status of the network adapter? _____

2. Which option would you select in Windows 7 **Network and Sharing Center** to view the status of the network adapter? _____

3. What items of information is immediately displayed in the **Local Area Connection Status** dialog box for Windows Vista? _____

_____

_____

4. Which button in the Windows Vista or Windows 7 **Local Area Connection Status** dialog box would you select to see detailed information about the network adapter? _____

_____

5. How do you enable or disable IPv4 and IPv6 protocols in the **Local Area Connection Properties** dialog box? _____

_____

WINDOWS VISTA AND WINDOWS 7

Name_____ Date _____

Class/Instructor _____

Network and Sharing Center

After completing this laboratory activity, you will be able to:

■ Use the Network and Sharing Center.

■ Recall the various options available through the Network and Sharing Center.

■ Differentiate between the Windows Vista and Windows 7 Network and Sharing Center.

Introduction

In this laboratory activity, you will explore the Network and Sharing Center of the Windows Vista and Windows 7 operating systems. As a network technician, you will constantly be required to inspect and modify network configurations. Because the task is so common, you need to be extremely familiar with the Network and Sharing Center for both Windows Vista and Windows 7.

The Network and Sharing Center was first introduced as part of the Windows Vista operating system and became part of Windows 7 and Windows Server 2008. The Windows Server 2008 Network and Sharing Center looks most similar to the Windows Vista Network and Sharing Center. The Network and Sharing Center is similar in function in all three Windows operating systems. It provides a centralized dialog box to handle the most common networking configuration options and networking status. The following are screen captures of the Network and Sharing Center in Windows 7 and Windows Vista.

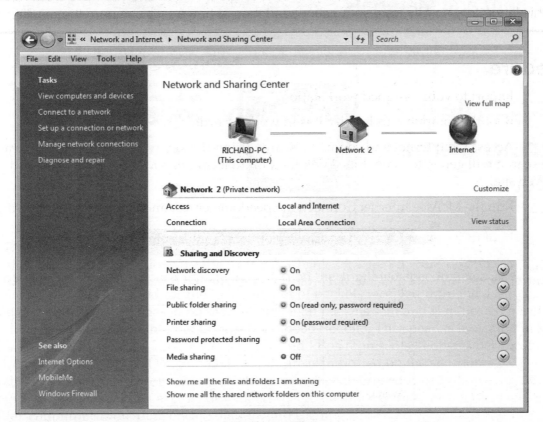

Windows Vista

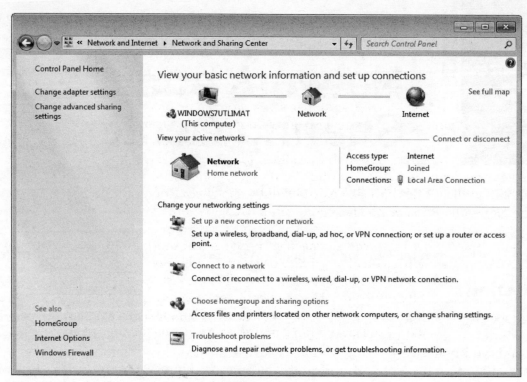

Windows 7

As you can see, there are some subtle differences in the presentation of options. Microsoft often changes the location of various configuration options whenever they design a new operating system.

Equipment and Materials

❑ Windows Vista computer preferably connected to a network workgroup. (Part I)
❑ Windows 7 computer preferably connected to a network workgroup. (Part II)

Part I—Windows Vista Network and Sharing Center

Procedure

1. _____ Report to your assigned workstation.

2. _____ Boot to Windows Vista and verify that the computer is in working order.

3. _____ Access the Network and Sharing Center through Control Panel. Follow the path **Start | Control Panel | Network and Internet | Network and Sharing Center**. After the Networking and Sharing Center opens, close it.

4. _____ Right-click the **Network** icon located in the notification area of the taskbar and then select **Network and Sharing Center** from the shortcut menu. The following screen captures show the Windows Vista and Windows 7 **Network** icons.

Windows Vista   **Windows 7**

Note

In Windows 7, the Network icon shortcut menu will display two options: **Troubleshooting problems** and **Open Network and Sharing Center**.

---

5. _____ Close the Network and Sharing Center.

6. _____ Type "net" into the **Search** box located off the **Start** menu. You should see "Network and Sharing Center" listed under **Programs**. Simply select the "Network and Sharing Center" entry using the mouse.

7. _____ Look at the following partial screen capture, which shows the name of the computer, the name of the network, and if the network has access to the Internet. This information is displayed at the top of the Network and Sharing Center.

Network and Sharing Center

View full map

RICHARD-PC
(This computer)

Network 2

Internet

When there is no Internet access, the line between the network and Internet in the illustration will have a large red X indicating no connection. A yellow warning icon indicates a possible configuration problem, but the connection may still be working.

In the space provided below, list the computer name and the network name.

Computer name: _____

Network name: _____

8. _____ Double-clicking the **This Computer** icon will automatically open the view of the computer hard drive and storage devices. Double-clicking the **Network** icon will produce a view of network devices. Double-clicking the **Internet** icon will automatically open an Internet connection using the default browser. Try double-clicking each of the icons one by one and then closing the dialog box associated with each.

9. _____ Look at the **Network** section similar to the one in the following screen capture.

Network 2 (Private network)		Customize
Access	Local and Internet	
Connection	Local Area Connection	View status

10. _____ Click **Customize**. The **Set Network Location** dialog box similar to the following will display.

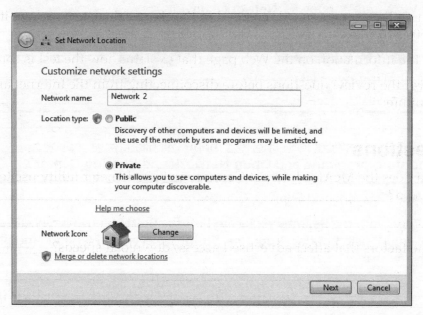

You can select the type of network location from "public" or "private." Selecting the **Public** option will automatically turn off the Network Discovery feature. You can also change the name of the network using this dialog box.

11. _____ Close the **Set Network Location** dialog box to return to Network and Sharing Center.

12. _____ Click **View status**. The **Local Area Connection Status** dialog box similar to the following will display.

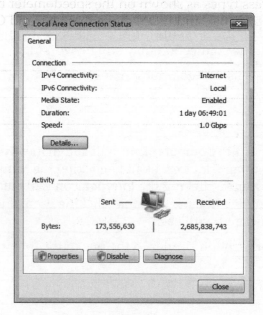

The **Local Area Connection Status** dialog box presents general information about the network connection. For detailed information you can click the **Details** button, which will provide you with information such as the MAC, IPv4 and IPv6 addresses; default gateway address, DHCP server address; DNS servers addresses; and more. To view the network adapter properties to see which protocols and services are assigned to the network adapter, simply click the **Properties** button.

13. _____ Close the **Local Area Connection Status** dialog box to return to the Network and Sharing Center.

14. _____ Look carefully at the options listed in the **Sharing and Discovery** section. Open each option and read the information provided. Do *not* change the default settings during this lab activity. The following is an explanation of each of these options.

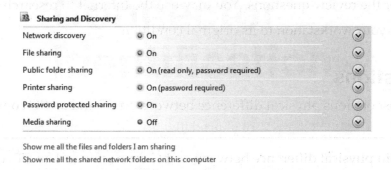

In the **Sharing and Discovery** section, you directly control specific aspects of a network, such as enabling or disabling the Network Discovery feature, file sharing, public folder sharing, printer sharing, password protected sharing, and media sharing. The following is a description of the options listed in this section.

Network Discovery—When enabled, allows you to see other computers and devices on the local area network. The Network Discovery feature works quickly when all devices and computers are part of the same workgroup.

File sharing—When enabled, files and printers shared by this computer can be accessed by others on the local area network.

Public folder sharing—When enabled, people on the network can access the Public folder. There will be more about this feature in later lab activities.

Password protected sharing—When enabled, only persons with a user account and password created on this computer can access shared files, printers, and the Public folder. This allows you to select the local area network users by name rather than let all local area network users have access. The user must provide a name and password to access the shared file, folder, public folder, or printer.

Media sharing—When enabled, allows local area network users to access media such as music, photos, and videos. When enabled it also allows this computer to locate the same media resources on other computers located on the local area network.

15. _____ Now look at the **Tasks** list on the left side of the Network and Sharing Center. Tasks commonly associated with networking are listed in this section.

View computers and devices shows all computers and devices connected to the local area network. If a device does not have the Network Discovery feature enabled, it will not appear.

Connect to a network allows you to make a connection to a different network if one exists.

Set up a connection or network starts the Set Up a Connection or Network wizard. Look at the following screen capture.

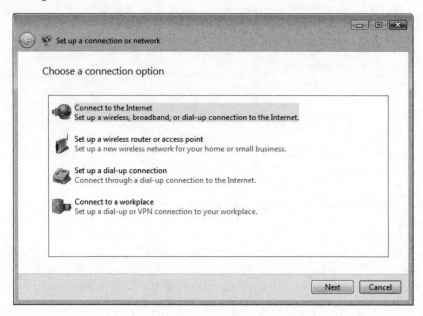

You can set up various network connection types through this wizard, such as an Internet connection, a wireless connection, and a dial-up connection, or you can connect to your workplace using a virtual private network (VPN) connection. There will be much more about VPN in later lab activities.

Manage network connections provides access to the network connection(s) available for this computer and allows you to view information about the connection and modify the configuration.

Diagnose and repair allows you to diagnose the status of the network connection and possibly automatically repair the connection. The repair simply drops the assigned IP address and requests a new IP address from the DHCP.

Take a few minutes to explore the tasks but do *not* change the network connection configuration. Do *not* run the Set Up Connection or Network wizard, but you may view the first dialog box to see the options.

16. _____ Close the Network and Sharing Center. Take a few minutes to practice accessing the Network and Sharing Center.

17. _____ Go on to "Part II—Windows 7 Network and Sharing Center."

Part II—Windows 7 Network and Sharing Center

Procedure

1. _____ Report to your assigned workstation.

2. _____ Boot to Windows 7 and verify that the computer is in working order.

3. _____ Open the Network and Sharing Center by typing "net" into the **Search** box located off the **Start** menu.

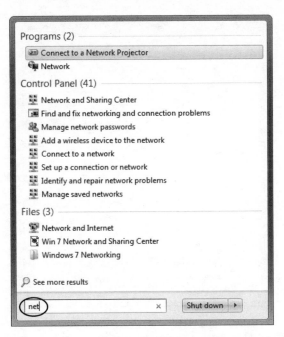

The search results are different for Windows 7 when compared with Windows Vista. "Network and Sharing Center" is listed under the **Control Panel** section not the **Programs** section as in Windows Vista. Also, the search results generate more network-related results of various programs, such as "Add a wireless device to a network," "Connect to a network," and "Set up a connection or network."

4. _____ Close the Network and Sharing Center. Open it once more by going through Control Panel: **Start | Control Panel | Network and Internet | Network and Sharing Center.**

5. _____ At the top of the Network and Sharing Center is a graphic similar to that in Windows Vista.

Click each of the three icons (**This computer, Network,** and **Internet**) and view the results. Again, this is very similar to Windows Vista. Close all the dialog boxes and return to the Network and Sharing Center.

6. _____ Look at the **View your active networks** section in the Network and Sharing Center.

Notice that there is a link besides the **Connections** property named **Local Area Connection**. This link produces the same results as the Windows Vista **View Status** link—it opens the **Local Area Connection Status** dialog box.

7. _____ Click the **Local Area Connection Status** link that is next to the **Connections** property. The **Local Area Connection** dialog box will display similar to the following.

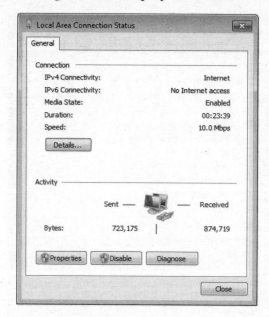

8. _____ Close the **Local Area Connection Status** dialog box to return to the Network and Sharing Center.

9. _____ Click the **Joined** link located next to the **HomeGroup** property in the **View your active networks** section. You will see a dialog box similar to the following.

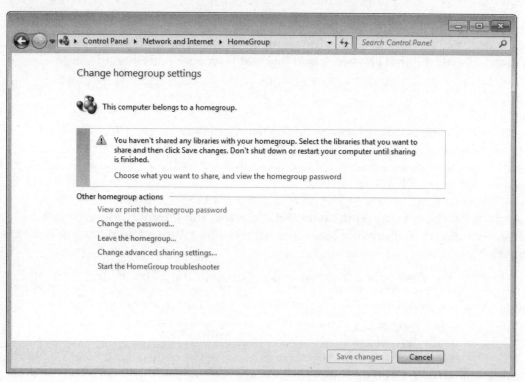

The HomeGroup feature is new in Windows 7. It is especially designed as an easy way for home users to share files and media securely on a home network. There will be more about the HomeGroup feature in a later lab activity. You can take a few seconds to briefly look at the options presented. When finished, use the arrow at the top left to return to the Network and Sharing Center.

10. _____ Now, look at the section labeled **Change your networking settings**.

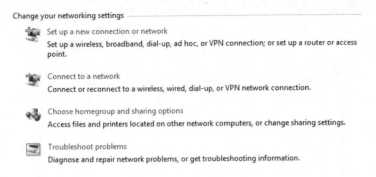

The **Change your networking settings** section in Windows 7 is drastically different than the Windows Vista **Sharing and Discovery** section. Microsoft moved many of the **Sharing and Discovery** options to the **Change advanced sharing settings** dialog box, which is accessed from the left-side of the Network and Sharing Center.

11. _____ In the **Change your networking settings** section, click the **Set up a new connection or network** option. The **Set Up a Connection or Network** dialog box similar to the following will display.

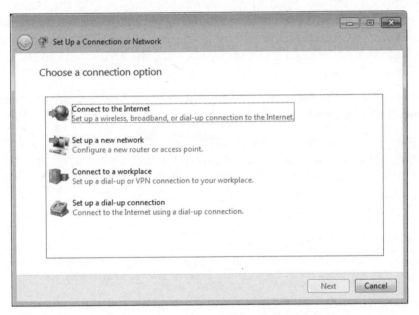

As you can see, this dialog box is similar to the **Set up a connection or network** dialog box in Windows Vista. There will be more about these featured options in later lab activities. Simply take a few seconds to briefly look at the available options and then click **Cancel** to return to the Network and Sharing Center.

12. _____ In the **Change your networking settings** section, look at the **Connect to a network** option. Clicking this option will only verify that you are presently connected to a network or it will take you to the Network and Sharing Center. There is no need to select this option at this time.

13. _____ In the Network and Sharing Center **Change your networking settings** section, look at the **Choose homegroup and sharing** option. This option will produce the same dialog box as in step 9. Again, there is no need to select this particular option at this time.

14. _____ In the **Change your networking settings** section, click the **Troubleshooting problems** option. A dialog box similar to the following will display.

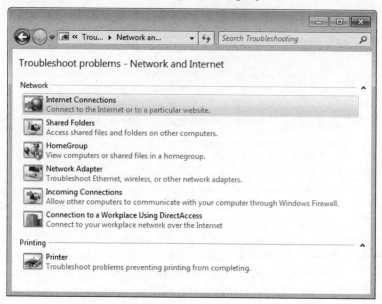

This is a new feature in Windows 7 and quite an improvement over the previous troubleshooting feature in Windows Vista. In Windows 7, you can specifically target a problem area such as that with the Internet connection, a shared folder, and the HomeGroup. When you determine in which major area your networking problem is located, you simply select the appropriate link. A wizard will start and guide you through the troubleshooting process. Return to the Network and Sharing Center by clicking the arrow icon in the upper-left corner of the screen.

15. _____ In the left side of the Network and Sharing Center under **Control Panel Home**, click **Change advanced sharing settings**. A dialog box similar to the following will display.

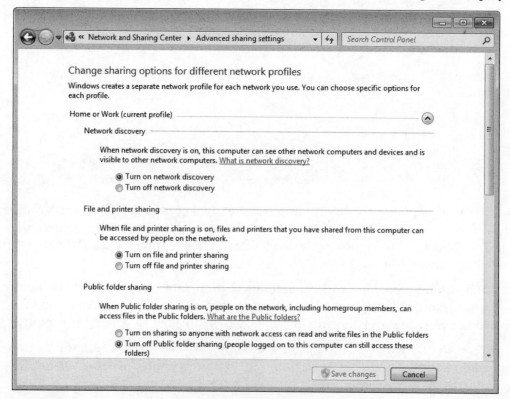

The **Advanced sharing and settings** dialog box contains the options to configure the Network Discovery feature, file and printer sharing, Public folder sharing, and more. The advanced sharing settings will be explored in greater detail in a later lab activity. For now, just take a few seconds to look at the various options available. Many of these options were made available in Windows Vista Network and Sharing Center under the **Sharing and Discovery** section.

By now, you can see that all the features that were available in Windows Vista are still available in Windows 7, but that many of the options have been relocated or redesigned. There are also many new options and features in Windows 7, such as the HomeGroup feature and a more detailed troubleshooting interface.

16. _____ Take a few minutes to review the entire lab activity before completing the review questions. Go back to the introduction and compare the two screen captures of Network and Sharing Center.

17. _____ Return the computer to its original condition and then answer the review questions.

Review Questions

1. What is the correct path for accessing the Network and Sharing Center through Control Panel?

_____

2. How can you access the Network and Sharing Center through the taskbar in Windows Vista and Windows 7? _____

_____

3. What can you type into the **Search** box located on the **Start** menu to access the Network and Sharing Center? _____

4. What are the two network locations presented in Windows Vista? _____

_____

5. Which network location will disable the Network Discovery feature: public or private?

_____

6. Which Windows operating system uses HomeGroup as a networking feature? _____

Name_____ Date _____

Class/Instructor _____

Connecting Two Computers Using a Crossover Cable

After completing this laboratory activity, you will be able to:

■ Use a crossover cable to connect two workstations.

■ Identify the IPv4 APIPA address range.

■ Summarize the purpose for using APIPA.

■ Check if the DHCP service has failed.

Introduction

In this laboratory activity, you will connect two workstations using a crossover cable and running the same operating system such as Windows Vista or Windows 7. This is a very easy task because Windows Vista and Windows 7 automatically detect a network connection and then automatically assign an IPv4 address and an IPv6 address. The IPv4 address will be a special type of IPv4 address known as an *Automatic Private IP Address (APIPA)*. The APIPA address is automatically generated by the host computer when it is configured to receive a DHCP address but fails to receive a DHCP-assigned IPv4 address. The two most common reasons for failure are that a connection to the DHCP service device has failed or the DHCP service device has failed.

A workstation must be assigned an IP address to be able to communicate with other computers on an Ethernet network. When you connect two computers together using a crossover cable, you will have eliminated the DHCP server. Each computer will automatically generate a random IPv4 address in the range from 169.254.0.1 to 169.254.255.254 with a subnet mask of 255.255.000.000.

The IPv4 address is divided into four sets of numbers separated by a period. When an APIPA is assigned, the first two sets of numbers are always 169.254. This is a good way to tell if the DHCP service has failed when troubleshooting a network problem.

Note

You may not need a crossover cable if both computers are equipped with a Gigabit Ethernet network adapter. The Gigabit Ethernet standard requires that the network card be capable of automatically switching the transmit and receive cable pairs at the connection. This feature, called *Auto-MDIX*, automatically negotiates the connection, thus eliminating the need for a crossover cable.

Equipment and Materials

❑ Two workstations running either Windows Vista or Windows 7.

❑ Crossover cable. (You may be able to use a straight-through cable if both computers are using a network adapter with Auto-MDIX capabilities. Most Gigabit Ethernet network adapters have the Auto-MDIX feature.)

Note

Do *not* use Windows XP or an earlier Windows edition for this assignment. While Windows XP and earlier can be connected using a crossover cable, Windows XP will not automatically detect Windows Vista or Windows 7 because Windows XP and earlier do not use the Link-Layer Discovery Protocol by default.

Note

You may perform this lab activity with another student, each using one of the two required workstations.

Procedure

1. _____ Report to your assigned workstation(s).

2. _____ Boot the computers and verify they are in working order.

3. _____ Shut down the two computers. Disconnect them from any existing network system.

4. _____ Plug one end of the crossover cable into the network adapter port on each computer.

5. _____ Reboot each computer and wait while the two computers detect each other.

6. _____ At one of the two computers, open the Network and Sharing Center: **Start | Control Panel | Network and Internet | Network and Sharing Center**. You can also type "net" into the **Search** box located on the **Start** menu, and then select "Network and Sharing Center" from the list. When the Network and Sharing Center opens, you should see an unidentified network in the map area, similar to the one in the following screen capture.

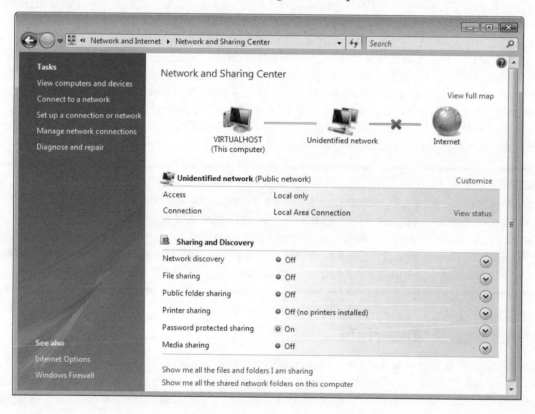

Notice that there will be no Internet connection as indicated by the red *X*. Also, the name for the crossover cable network is "Unidentified network."

7. _____ Select **View full map** to map the crossover cable network. The mapping will fail if the **Network discovery** and **File sharing** options are turned off or the network is set to "Public network." To map the two computers, each should be set to "Private network" and each should have the **Network discovery** and **File sharing** options turned on.

8. _____ The map should look similar to the following screen capture. As you can see in the map, the two computers are connected directly together. Although a hub appears in the map, it is not connected between the two computers.

> Control Panel ▶ Network and Internet ▶ Network Map

Tasks
View computers and devices
Diagnose and repair
Why are some computers and devices missing?

VirtualHost

Windows7Utlimat

Hub

9. _____ After you have successfully displayed the map of the two computers, call your instructor to inspect your lab activity.

10. _____ Open the **Local Area Connection Status** dialog box and then click the **Details** button to inspect the assigned IPv4 address. Record the assigned IPv4 address in the space provided below.

Assigned IPv4 address: _____

11. _____ Shut down both computers. Disconnect the crossover cable. If the computers were part of a network, reconnect both computers.

12. _____ Reboot both computers and verify they are working correctly. If they are part of a network, inspect the assigned IPv4 address once more.

13. _____ Return all materials to the proper storage area and then answer the review questions.

Review Questions

1. What does the acronym APIPA represent? _____

2. What is the numeric value for the first two numerical octets of an APIPA address? _____

_____

3. What is the entire range of IPv4 addresses used for APIPA? _____

4. What is the subnet mask equal to for APIPA? _____

5. What must you do if you cannot generate a map of the two crossover cable connected computers?

_____

_____

6. What are the two most common reasons for DHCP failure? _____

_____

Name_____ Date _____

Class/Instructor _____

Testing Internet Connection Speeds

After completing this laboratory activity, you will be able to:

■ Check Internet download speed using the McAfee Internet Connection Speedometer utility.

■ Give examples of factors that affect advertised access/download speeds.

Introduction

In this laboratory activity, you will test the speed of your Internet connection with the McAfee Internet Connection Speedometer utility. This is a free utility that can be run directly from the McAfee Web site. You will search for this utility using the key words *McAfee* and *speedometer*. These words will produce many hits because McAfee Internet Connection Speedometer is popular and free and can be accessed at many Web sites. To avoid using a Web site that requires you to register your e-mail address and possibly other information, look for McAfee in the URL. This will provide you with a connection directly to the McAfee Web site.

After accessing the McAfee Internet Connection Speedometer utility, you will see a screen similar to the following. To test the speed of your Internet connection, select **Click Here to Test Now**.

Your Internet connection speed will be indicated on the animated speedometer. The speedometer indicates the speed for the total number of packets received from the destination. The calculated download speed is based on the average of all packets sent and is indicated beside the bright red text that reads **Your Internet Connection Speed Results**. The speed is indicated in kbps and kBps. The kbps represents kilobits per second, and kBps represents kilobytes per second.

Notice the 56 k modem, ISDN, and DSL/Cable areas indicated on the speedometer. The speeds listed in these areas represent common, advertised speeds. Advertised speeds, however, can be deceiving. Several factors affect access/download speed: network traffic, control messages sent in half-duplex communication, data encapsulation, and caching.

A high amount of traffic on the network (local and Internet) can slow transmission. Transmission over the Internet may be forced to take a longer, alternate route because of congestion or downed routers. Control messages sent to and from the destination and source can also slow transmission. For example, after several blocks of data are received, a message is sent to the source verifying the data was received. Since most Internet connections are half-duplex, the download sequence must stop in order to send an acknowledgement that the data sent so far has been received. A half-duplex system can only transmit in one direction at a time; therefore, the source and destination must take turns transmitting.

Data encapsulation also affects speed. A single block of data transmitted across the network contains the desired data plus information such as the IP address, MAC address, and assorted information required by the protocol to properly function. The desired data accounts for only a portion of the entire block of data. You will learn more about data encapsulation in later laboratory activities.

Another factor that affects speed is the operating system's browser cache. A copy of a frequently accessed Web page is stored in a cache so that it can be instantly displayed the next time the page is requested. Proxy servers cache Web pages to reduce network traffic, and many ISP providers run proxy servers to provide faster access. The McAfee Internet Connection utility does not test Internet connection speeds by drawing information from a cache. Therefore, the indicated speed will be lower than if the Web page was drawn from the cache.

Equipment and Materials

❑   Computer with Internet access.

Note

If you have a different type of Internet access than your school, you may want to perform this laboratory activity from your home and compare the results with that obtained at school. For example, if your school has a T1 line and you have DSL, run this laboratory activity from your school and then at home and compare the results.

Procedure

1. _____ Report to your assigned workstation.

2. _____ Boot the computer and verify it is in working order.

3. _____ Access the Internet and conduct a search using the key words *McAfee* and *Speedometer*. The search will generate many hits. Look for a hit that contains *McAfee* in the URL and access its Web site.

4. _____ Run the McAfee Internet Connection Speedometer test and complete the following chart.

Test #	Speed in kbps
1	
2	
3	
4	
5	
Average	

5. _____ After running five tests, calculate and record the average speed. To calculate the average speed, add the five speeds together and divide by five.

6. _____ Based on the average speed recorded in the chart, calculate how long it would take to download a 500 MB file.

7. _____ Read the information on the Web page that explains how the test is conducted.

8. _____ Answer the review questions before disconnecting from the Internet and shutting down the computer.

Review Questions

1. What formula does the McAfee Internet Connection Speedometer utility use to test the connection speed? _____

   _____

2. What are some factors that affect advertised access/download speeds? _____

   _____

   _____

   _____

3. Why do results of each test vary? (Answer can be found on the McAfee Internet Connection Speedometer utility page.) _____

   _____

   _____

4. Rank the four Internet access types as shown on the speedometer by indicating the dial speed for each: 56 k Modem, DSL/Cable, and ISDN. Note that DSL and Cable Internet access types are ranked the same.

   a. Slowest = _____

   b. Midrange = _____

   c. Fastest = _____

Name_____ Date _____

Class/Instructor _____

Fiber-Optic Connector Identification

After completing this laboratory activity, you will be able to:

- Identify common fiber-optic connector types.
- Distinguish between common fiber-optic connectors by physical traits.

Introduction

This laboratory activity will familiarize you with various fiber-optic cable, connectors, and venders. You will search the Internet for images of common, fiber-optic connectors. Once located, you will copy the images and paste them into a word processing document and then label the image with the appropriate acronym.

To copy a Web page image, right-click the image and then select **Copy** from the shortcut menu. To insert the image into a word processing document, right-click a blank area of the document page and click **Paste**. When you have finished copying the images specified in the laboratory activity, you will print two copies of the assignment, one for your reference and the other to turn in to your instructor.

Some fiber-optic cable manufacturers and distributors include the following: Ortronics, Siemon, Belden, Black Box, Agilent, Fluke, and 3Com. You may wish to visit their Web sites for information about various fiber-optic cables and connectors.

Equipment and Materials

- ❑ Computer with Internet access and word processing software, such as Microsoft WordPad. (WordPad is included in all Microsoft operating systems.)
- ❑ Printer access.

Procedure

1. _____ Report to your assigned workstation.
2. _____ Boot the computer and verify it is in working order.
3. _____ Open Internet Explorer.
4. _____ Conduct a search for fiber-optic connectors. Use the following phrases in your search:

- Fiber-optic connectors.
- Fiber optic connectors.
- Fiber-optic cable connectors.
- Fiber optic cable connectors.

5. _____ After locating images of fiber-optic connectors, copy each image from the Web page and paste it into a word processing document. Be sure to label each example. Use the following labels, one for each connector type: Biconic, ESCON, FC, FDDI, MTRJ, SC, SC Duplex, SMA, and ST.

6. _____ When you are finished, print out two copies of your document.

7. _____ Answer the review questions. You may use the Internet to research the answers.

8. _____ Return your workstation to its original condition.

Review Questions

1. What is the most obvious physical difference between an ST and an SC connector? _____
   _____

2. What is the main physical difference between an LC connector and an ST connector? _____
   _____

3. How many fiber-optic cores are typically associated with an FDDI connector? _____

4. How many fiber-optic cores are typically associated with an MTRJ connector? _____

5. How many fiber-optic cores are typically associated with an ST connector? _____

6. What does the acronym ESCON represent? _____
   _____

7. What does the acronym FDDI represent? _____
   _____

8. In general, what does the term *duplex* mean when referring to fiber-optic connectors? _____
   _____
   _____

Laboratory Activity

11

Name_____ Date _____

Class/Instructor _____

Installing and Configuring a PCI Network Adapter

After completing this laboratory activity, you will be able to:

- Carry out proper procedures for installing and configuring a PCI network adapter card.
- Give examples of common problems associated with installing a network adapter card.
- Use Device Manager to confirm the proper installation of the network adapter card.
- Carry out proper procedures to disable or uninstall a network adapter card for troubleshooting purposes.
- Use the **Controller Properties** dialog box to identify system resources assigned to the network adapter card.

Introduction

In this laboratory activity, you will install a PCI network adapter card. A network adapter card is commonly referred to as a *NIC*. While most network adapter cards are automatically configured through Plug and Play technology, there are many times when technician intervention is required. This most commonly happens when the network card and the operating system are from two different eras. For example, when installing a dated network adapter into a computer running the latest operating system, a driver may need to be installed manually.

You should check the Microsoft Hardware Compatibility List (HCL) prior to purchasing a network adapter. Purchase a card that is on the list. Cards not on the HCL may present a problem during installation. When using a network adapter not previously tested and approved by Microsoft, a warning message may appear. The message will inform you that the drivers are not digitally signed and will advise you not to install the card. You may ignore the warning and continue with the installation process. Most times, the network adapter will install properly, but you will most likely need to supply the driver disk during the installation process.

All network adapters require driver software. When a Plug and Play network adapter is detected by the operating system, the driver is typically automatically installed and no further intervention is required from the technician. Occasionally, a network adapter driver must be installed manually. When such an instance occurs, the next step in the installation process can vary depending on how much information about the network adapter was identified by the operating system. For example, the device may be identified as a network adapter, but the network driver software must be supplied by the technician. Or, the hardware device may not be identified by type of device and the network technician may need to identify the device as a network adapter and manually install the drivers. The operating system may not detect the new device at all. In such a case, the technician will need to start the process from **Control Panel | Add Hardware**.

Device Manager can be used to view the status of a hardware device installed in the computer. From Device Manager, the technician can uninstall, disable, scan for property changes, or update the network adapter driver. Device Manager can also be used to view the system resource assignments of hardware devices. Network adapters use three system resources: Interrupt Request (IRQ), I/O port, and RAM memory. Some network adapters also use Direct Memory Access (DMA). Device Manager usually detects conflicts between devices using the same system resource.

The Windows XP, Windows Vista, and Windows 7 operating systems install the TCP/IP protocol by default when a network adapter is installed. To verify that the TCP/IP protocol is installed, issue the **ping** command at the command prompt. If TCP/IP is not installed, you will not be able to use the **ping** command.

Note

When installing a network adapter into a computer that has a network port built into the motherboard, the motherboard network port usually needs to be disabled to prevent a conflict with the additional network adapter. The network port can be disabled through Device Manager.

Equipment and Materials

- ❏ Computer running Windows XP Professional, Windows Vista, or Windows 7.
- ❏ Patch cable.
- ❏ PCI Ethernet network adapter card and driver disc.
- ❏ Manufacturer's instructions for installing the network card and the device driver CD or floppy disk. (Your instructor may require you to download a copy of the network adapter card installation instructions and drivers from the manufacturer's Web site.)
- ❏ Hub.
- ❏ Screwdriver to match expansion slot screw.
- ❏ Antistatic wrist strap.

Procedure

1. _____ Gather all required materials and then report to your assigned workstation.

2. _____ Familiarize yourself with the manufacturer's installation instructions.

3. _____ Boot the computer and verify it is in working order.

4. _____ Shut down the computer and then unplug the power cord. Follow antistatic procedures as defined by your instructor.

5. _____ Remove the computer case cover and then check for an available PCI slot. Remove the slot cover associated with the chosen PCI slot. A small screw at the top of the slot cover typically retains the slot cover. Some slot covers do not use a screw to hold it in place. Slot covers without a screw usually must be bent back and forth several times to break free of the metal frame. Some computer cases use a simple latching mechanism to retain the slot cover. Check carefully before proceeding with the removal. If you are in doubt as to how to remove the slot cover, call your instructor.

6. _____ Position the network adapter over the PCI slot and then insert the card by applying firm, even pressure along the top edge of the card. Do *not* rock the card excessively.

7. _____ After the card has been fully inserted into the PCI slot, use the screw or appropriate mechanism to mount the card.

8. _____ Plug in the power cord and then boot the computer. The network adapter may or may not be automatically detected and configured. If it is not automatically detected and configured, you will need to configure the card manually. You will be prompted to identify the hardware device or to install the driver, or both. When prompted for installing the driver, click the **Have Disk** button.

Note

Be sure to read each screen carefully. Most installation problems are caused by failure to read the information presented.

---

9. _____ After the driver has been installed, open Device Manager to check the status of the network adapter. You can access Device Manager by right-clicking **My Computer** or **Computer** and selecting **Manage** from the shortcut menu.

In the Device Manager list, you should see **Network adapters**. Expand **Network adapters** by clicking the plus sign. Clicking the plus sign expands the device type network adapters and shows all network adapters installed in the computer.

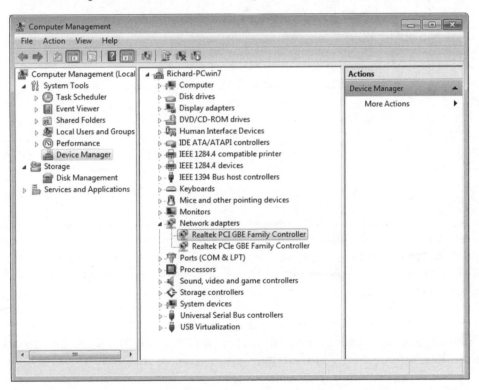

In the previous screen capture, two network adapters are identified. Both are in working order. No problems are indicated. Device Manager indicates a hardware device problem by inserting a symbol over the device name. A red X indicates the device is disabled. A black exclamation mark on a yellow field indicates the device is having a problem but may still be working. A blue i on white field indicates that the resources for the device were manually selected.

10. _____ Right-click the network adapter entry. A shortcut menu will appear with the following commands: **Update Driver Software**, **Disable**, **Uninstall**, **Scan for hardware changes**, and **Properties**.

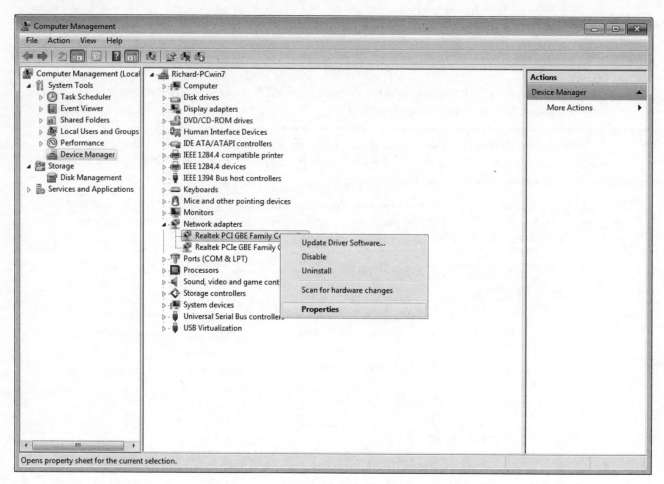

11. _____ Select **Disable** from the shortcut menu. Notice the effect on the appearance of the device. What symbol appeared over the network adapter to indicate that it is disabled? Record the answer in the space provided.

_____

12. _____ Enable the network adapter by right-clicking the network adapter entry and selecting **Enable** from the shortcut menu. The **Enable** option appears in the shortcut menu after the **Disable** command is selected.

13. _____ Right-click network adapter and select the **Uninstall** option.

Note

After uninstalling the network adapter using Device Manager, some versions of Windows will automatically detect and install the network device again. If the network adapter is not longer viewable in Device Manager, select **Action | Scan for hardware changes**.

---

14. _____ After the network adapter has been reinstalled, open Device Manager and select the network adapter once more. Right-click the network adapter entry and select **Properties** from the shortcut menu. A dialog box similar to the following will display. Notice that the **Device status** box indicates the network adapter is working properly.

15. _____ Select the **Advanced** tab. This area of the dialog box will allow you to change various properties for the network adapter card.

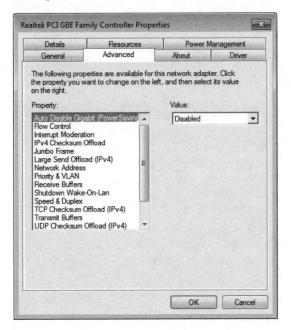

16. _____ Select the **Driver** tab. From this location, you can view driver details, update the driver, roll back the driver, and uninstall the driver. The **Driver Details** button reveals information about the manufacturer, where the driver is located, and if the driver was digitally signed. A digitally signed driver means Microsoft has approved the driver. The Roll Back Driver feature removes the last installed driver for the card. You would normally use this option in place of using the System Restore feature, which rolls back all changes to the computer since the last restore point was created. Rolling back all changes since the last restore point was created can undo many changes that you wish to retain. The Roll Back Driver feature is the best choice for uninstalling a driver.

17. _____ Select the **Resources** tab. A dialog box similar to the following will appear and will display system resources assigned to the network adapter.

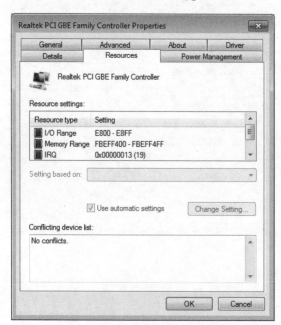

18. _____ Record in the spaces provided the resources assigned to your network adapter.

I/O range: _____

Memory range: _____

IRQ: _____

19. _____ Select the **Power Management** tab. This area of the dialog box displays several options related to power saving features available for the network adapter. Typically, you will not need to access this tab or the other tabs mentioned in this laboratory activity. Also, be aware that the type of information as well as the appearance of the information presented in a dialog box can change by card manufacturer. Manufacturers have access to Windows programming information. They often change the way a dialog box appears to match the capabilities of their network adapters.

20. _____ Practice accessing and opening the menu items and dialog boxes presented in this laboratory activity. After you have practiced, answer the review questions.

21. _____ Return all materials to their proper storage area.

Review Questions

1. What does the acronym HCL represent? _____

2. What does the acronym NIC represent? _____

3. What symbol is used to indicate a device is disabled in Device Manager? _____

4. What symbol is used to indicate a problem with a device in Device Manager? _____

_____

5. What three system resources are assigned to a network adapter? _____

_____

6. What four options are available from the **Driver** tab? _____

_____

_____

7. Why is the Roll Back Driver feature the preferred way to remove a network adapter driver
rather than using the System Restore feature? _____

_____

_____

Laboratory Activity

12

Name_____ Date _____

Class/Instructor _____

Creating a Windows XP Peer-to-Peer Network

After completing this laboratory activity, you will be able to:

■ Install and configure a peer-to-peer network.

■ Explain the major Network Setup Wizard steps.

■ Select the correct Network Setup Wizard options for a specific network configuration.

■ Create a network setup disk for automatically configuring additional workstations.

Introduction

In this laboratory activity, you will install and configure a simple peer-to-peer network. A peer-to-peer network consists of two or more computers that have equal control over resources and security. Microsoft Windows peer-to-peer networks are often referred to as *workgroups*. In a peer-to-peer network, the security is not centralized. Each workstation in the peer-to-peer network must have a user account for each user intending to access its resources.

A client/server network consists of computers connected to one or more servers. In a client/server network, security is centralized. A server in a Microsoft Windows client/server network, called a *domain controller*, controls all resources and security. The domain controller provides a centralized security system for user authentication by name and password. Windows XP Professional and Windows XP Home Edition can be used to create a workgroup, but only Windows XP Professional can be used to join a domain.

All computers in a Microsoft peer-to-peer network should have the same workgroup name, such as *workgroup* or *home*. The default workgroup name for Windows XP Professional is *WORKGROUP*. Each workstation in the workgroup must have a unique name—for example, *station1*, *station2*, and *station3*.

Note

There is a lot of misinformation concerning the default workgroup name for the Windows XP edition. When performing a clean installation of the operating system, the default workgroup name for Windows XP Professional is *WORKGROUP*, and for Windows XP Home Edition it is *MSHOME*. Also, note that when the Network Setup Wizard is run in either the Professional or Home Edition, the default suggested workgroup name is *MSHOME*.

Microsoft Windows XP provides a wizard for automatically setting up and configuring a network. The wizard gives you an option to create a setup disk for automatically configuring the other workstations. The option to create a setup disk is provided to make configuring a home- or small-office network as easy as possible.

Windows XP Home Edition is designed for home use, whereas Windows XP Professional is designed for client/server environments. Windows XP Home Edition will not connect to a domain. It will only serve as a member of a workgroup. Windows XP Professional can serve as a member of a workgroup or connect to a domain. When a Windows XP Professional workstation serves as a member of a workgroup, up to ten workstations can connect to it simultaneously. Windows XP Home Edition allows up to five simultaneous connections.

If you encounter a problem while attempting to view other workstations in the peer-to-peer network, try the following:

- Check the network cable connections.

- Check the TCP/IP configuration settings (IP address and subnet mask), computer name, and workgroup name.

- Reset the hub by powering it off and then on.

- Restart the workstation.

Be aware that most hubs have a port designated as an uplink connection. The uplink connection is used to connect to another hub or networking device and eliminates the need to use a crossover cable. Avoid using this port for workstation connections. If you must use this port, make sure it is not configured for use as an uplink. Some hubs have a push-button switch that is used to change the port uplink state.

A commonly encountered problem of a newly installed peer-to-peer network is the failure of a workstation to appear in **My Network Places**. This is especially true when using network adapters that are not on the hardware compatibility list or when using legacy network adapters. Also, if all configuration settings are correct and the station fails to appear, it is usually due to a malfunctioning network adapter. A network adapter that was not automatically detected as Plug and Play and automatically configured by the Windows XP operating system could be the source of the problem. If the network adapter was not properly detected and was configured manually, it is common for the host computer not to appear in **New Connection** or **My Network Places** when browsed. In this case, download an updated driver from the manufacturers' Web site and install it. This will typically correct the problem. Also, be aware that in some cases, the network adapter will still support sharing even if it does not appear in the browser. Additional reference material can be found in the following Microsoft Knowledge Base articles:

- 813936: How to Set Up a Small Network with Windows XP Home Edition (Part1)

- 813937: How to Set Up a Small Network with Windows XP Home Edition (Part 2)

- 813938: How to Set Up a Small Network with Windows XP Home Edition (Part 3)

- 813939: How to Set Up a Small Network with Windows XP Home Edition (Part 4)

- 813940: How to Set Up a Small Network with Windows XP Home Edition (Part 5)

- 814003: How to Set Up a Small Network with Windows XP Home Edition (Part 6)

- 814004: How to Set Up a Small Network with Windows XP Home Edition (Part 7)

- 814005: How to Set Up a Small Network with Windows XP Home Edition (Part 8)

Equipment and Materials

❑ Two workstations running Windows XP Professional. (You may use Windows XP Home Edition; however, not all screens will match the screen captures in this laboratory activity.) Each workstation should have a network adapter configured from previous laboratory activities.
❑ Two Ethernet network cables.
❑ Hub.

❑ Floppy disk.
❑ The following information:

Workstation names: _____
(Each workstation name must be unique.)

Workgroup name: _____
(The workgroup name must be the same for each workstation.)

User name: _____
(Create a user account on each workstation using the same user name and password.)

Password: _____

Procedure

1. _____ Gather the required materials and report to your assigned workstations.

2. _____ Boot the computers and verify they are in working order.

3. _____ Each workstation should have a network adapter configured from a previous laboratory activity. If not, install and configure the network adapters now.

4. _____ Using the Ethernet cables, connect each workstation to the hub. (One end of the Ethernet cable connects to the RJ-45 connection on the workstation and the other end connects to the RJ-45 port on the hub.) Check if the LED indicator lights on the network adapters and hub are lit. A green light typically indicates a connection has been established.

5. _____ Access the Network Setup Wizard through the following path: **Start | All Programs | Accessories | Communications | Network Setup Wizard**. A dialog box similar to the following will display, listing the common tasks a network can perform.

The wizard is designed to make configuring these tasks easy for even a novice user. Record these tasks in the spaces provided.

_____

_____

_____

_____

6. _____ Click **Next**. A dialog box similar to the following will display, prompting you to complete three things before continuing:

- ■ Install the network cards, modems, and cables.
- ■ Turn on all computers, printers, and external modems.
- ■ Connect to the Internet.

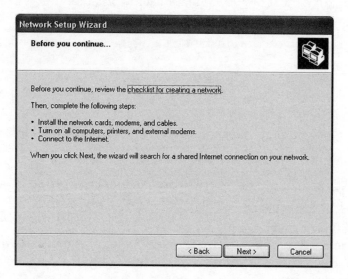

All hardware devices should be installed before continuing with the wizard, such as installing the network adapter, modems, and cables. You should turn on all printers and the external modem if one exists. You should also establish a connection to the Internet if Internet access is available. You do not, however, need to establish a connection to the Internet or have a printer connected or a modem installed to complete this laboratory activity.

Note

If Internet access is detected during the automatic configuration, screen presentations will not match the laboratory activity.

---

7. _____ Click **checklist for creating a network** and review the information about home and office networking and Internet access. If lab time is limited, review the material later or at home.

8. _____ Click **Next**. A dialog box similar to the following will display. Its appearance will vary depending on if you have Internet access. If you do not have an Internet connection, select **Other**.

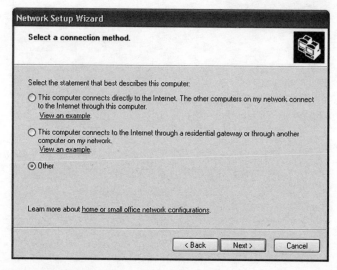

9. _____ Click **Next**. A dialog box similar to the following will display.

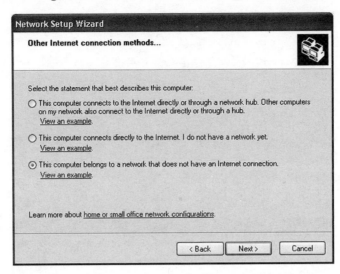

Click **View an example** for each option listed and study the illustrations. Then, select **Learn more about home or small office network configurations**. You will be directed to the Help and Support files located on the workstation. If there is not sufficient time to review all the information, you may review it at a later time or at home.

After viewing the information, select **This computer belongs to a network that does not have an Internet connection**.

10. _____ Click **Next**. A dialog box similar to the following will display, prompting you for a computer description and computer name.

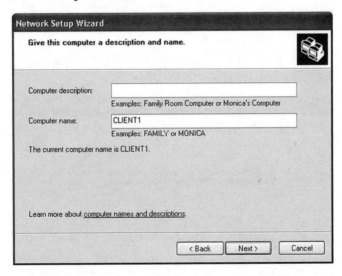

The description can be very important for identifying workstations. For example, **My Network Places** displays the description of the workstation, such as *Workstation in main office* or *Workstation12 in building C room 212*.

The computer name must also be unique. No two computers can have the same name on a network. Certain characters are not allowed in a computer name.

11. _____ Click **computer names and descriptions** and answer the following questions.

What is the maximum number of characters for the computer name? _____

Can the name contain spaces? _____

What symbols cannot be part of the computer name? _____

_____

What do certain ISP's require for naming a computer? _____

12. _____ Enter the computer name identified for this lab and a short description.

13. _____ Click **Next**. A dialog box similar to the following will display, prompting you to enter the network name. Notice the suggested default name *MSHOME*. Enter the workgroup name provided earlier in the lab. A workgroup name has the same restrictions as the computer name.

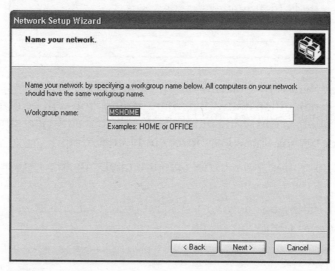

14. _____ Click **Next**. A dialog box similar to the following will display, prompting you to enable file and printer sharing.

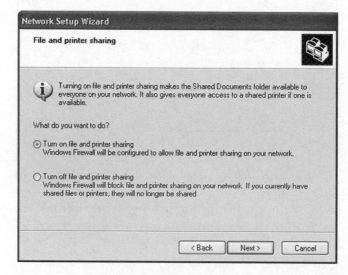

Many of the items, such as file and printer sharing, can be configured after running the wizard. The wizard simply groups together all the common networking tasks that are typically required.

15. _____ Select **Turn on file and printer sharing** and then click **Next**. A dialog box similar to the following will display, providing a review of the configuration. You can review the computer description, computer name, and workgroup name and check if the computer is configured for sharing files and a printer before performing the final configuration. You are given the opportunity to use the **Back** button to backtrack through the dialog boxes and make changes. You can also abandon the entire Network Setup Wizard configuration by clicking **Cancel**.

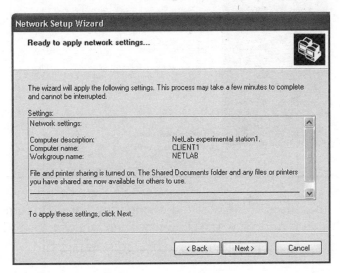

16. _____ Click **Next** to complete the Network Setup Wizard configuration. A dialog box similar to the following will display offering other options related to the network configuration.

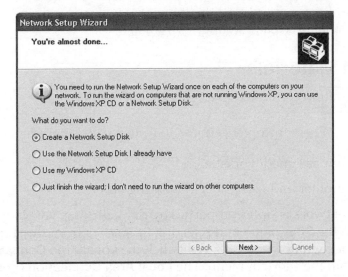

Four options are available: **Create a Network Setup Disk, Use the Network Disk I already have, Use my Windows XP CD, Just finish the Wizard; I don't need to run the wizard on other computers**.

17. _____ Insert a floppy disk into the floppy drive. Select **Create a Network Setup Disk** and then click **Next**.

18. _____ After creating the setup disk, a dialog box similar to the following will display.

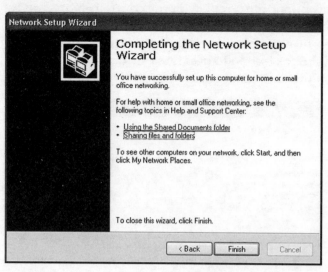

Notice the two Help and Support topics listed: **Using the Shared Documents folder** and **Sharing files and folders**. Click each and view the contents. Then, answer the following questions.

How are files and folders placed in the Shared Documents folder? _____

_____

When is the Shared Documents folder not available? _____

_____

What is the Microsoft definition of the term *workgroup*? _____

_____

_____

_____

19. _____ Click **Finish**. When prompted, choose to restart your computer at this time.

20. _____ Insert the network setup floppy disk into the floppy disk drive on the other workstation.

21. _____ Open the **Run** dialog box located off the **Start** menu and enter a:\netsetup. A message will appear that reads, "Welcome to the Network Setup Wizard. Before continuing, Windows must install some network support files on your computer and possibly restart your computer. If you are running Windows XP, the wizard will start immediately. Do you want to continue?"

22. _____ Select the appropriate response. The Network Wizard will begin. Follow the on-screen instructions just as you have done previously in this laboratory activity. Do *not* select to create a network setup floppy.

23. _____ After completing the Network Setup Wizard for the second workstation, open the **Internet Protocol (TCP/IP) Properties** dialog box for each workstation and verify the IP address and subnet mask. Make one workstation IP address 192.168.0.1 and the other 192.168.0.2. Enter the same subnet mask for each: 255.255.255.0.

If you are performing this laboratory activity with more than two workstations or as a group of students, continue the series of IP addresses by increasing the last number by one. For example, the next workstation to be added to the group will use IP address 192.168.0.3. Keep the subnet mask the same for all computers in the workgroup.

After the IP address configuration has been verified for all workstations, check for network connectivity by browsing My Network Places. To access My Network Places, right-click **My Network Places** from the **Start** menu or desktop and select **Explore** from the shortcut menu. A window similar to the following will display.

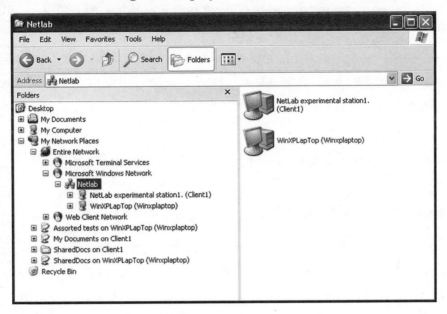

Notice that two workstations in the workgroup called *Netlab* appear. When you browse your peer-to-peer network, you should see all members of the workgroup. If not, check the items listed at the beginning of the laboratory activity that might prevent you from browsing your network. If you still cannot see all members of the workgroup, call your instructor for assistance.

24. _____ After successfully browsing your workgroup, expand the icons representing the workstations and see what files are shared. If you are unable to view any file shares, call your instructor for assistance.

25. _____ Disconnect the network cable from one of the workstations and observe the network adapter and hub LED indicator lights. Also, look for a message to display on the desktop informing you that a network cable has been disconnected.

26. _____ Perform this laboratory activity again. This time, do not create a network setup disk for use on the other workstation. Configure the IP configuration settings manually on the other workstation.

27. _____ Answer the review questions, and then shut down the workstations when you are finished.

Review Questions

1. Which edition of Windows XP can be used to create a peer-to-peer network? _____

   _____

2. Which edition of Windows XP can join a domain? _____

3. What is the suggested workgroup name supplied during the running of the Network Setup Wizard? _____

   _____

4. What is the default workgroup name for Windows XP during a clean installation of the operating system? _____

_____

5. How many simultaneous connections are supported by Windows XP Professional and Home Edition when connected as a peer-to-peer network? _____

_____

6. Which edition of Windows XP can be a member of a client/server network? _____

7. What two configuration settings are the same for each workstation in a peer-to-peer network?

_____

8. What two configuration settings must be unique in a peer-to-peer network? _____

_____

9. What four tasks are listed in the Welcome to the Network Setup Wizard opening dialog box?

_____

_____

_____

_____

10. What is the first thing you should check when there is a network connectivity problem? _____

_____

11. What is the uplink port on a hub used for? _____

_____

12. What type of connector is used for standard Ethernet cables? _____

13. What is the maximum number of characters used in the computer name? _____

14. What special symbols cannot be used as part of the computer name? _____

15. What is the maximum number of characters that can be used in a workgroup name? _____

_____

16. What symbols cannot be used in a workgroup name? _____

_____

17. What is the name of the network setup file on the network setup floppy? _____

Creating a Windows Vista and Windows 7 Peer-to-Peer Network

After completing this laboratory activity, you will be able to:

■ Carry out proper procedures for configuring a simple peer-to-peer network.

■ Carry out proper procedures to identify and change the default workgroup name.

■ Compare Windows XP, Windows 7 and Windows Vista basic networking configuration settings.

■ Compare the Windows Vista and Windows 7 **Set Network Location** dialog box.

■ Use the **net view** command to view local area network computers.

Introduction

In this laboratory activity, you will join two or more computers together as a peer-to-peer network. It is amazingly simple to connect Windows Vista or Windows 7 together as a peer-to-peer network when using the same operating system for all computers.

The first time you connect a Windows Vista or Windows 7 computer to a network, you will see a dialog box that will ask you to identify the network location. This usually takes place during the installation of the operating system. You will be asked to identify a home, public, or work location (domain). Any time after that, the computer will typically automatically configure itself as part of a peer-to-peer network. In this lab, you will simply connect a computer to a hub or switch using an Ethernet cable. The computer will automatically detect other computers and devices in the peer-to-peer network.

A hub or a switch may be used as the center connection of the peer-to-peer network. The main difference between a hub and a switch is a switch can limit network traffic by allowing packets to travel through the switch to only the designated computer.

Setting up Internet access is optional and not required for a peer-to-peer network. If you are going to set up a peer-to-peer network with Internet access, it is advisable to use a router as the center connection.

Running the Network Setup Wizard is only necessary for wireless adapters, not for a wired peer-to-peer network. A computer wired to a peer-to-peer network will automatically detect the other network devices and automatically configure the computer as part of the network.

Testing the Network Connection

Testing the network is easy. If you can view other computers, then you have successfully networked the computer(s). This does not mean that you have created sharing between the computers. You have simply created a network.

To see all devices connected in the peer-to-peer network, select **Start | User Name | Network**.

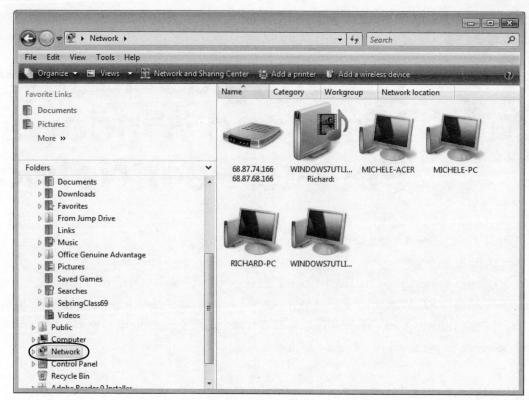

Windows Vista

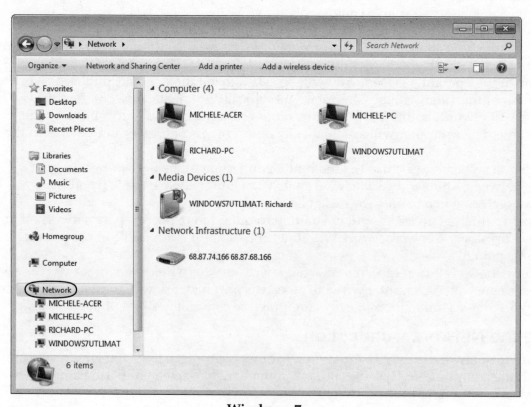

Windows 7

If you do not see the other computers and network devices, check if the Network Discovery feature has been enabled. You should be aware that older operating systems such as Windows XP and Windows 98 might take several minutes before appearing. This is because of the older network technology used by earlier systems. They typically do not broadcast their presence as often as Windows Vista or later operating systems. Also, be aware that some software programs such as antivirus suites may block the network discovery process, thus not allowing you to view other computers.

You can use the command prompt to view other computers and devices on the local area network or the peer-to-peer network. Simply open the command prompt and then enter the command **net view**. You will generate a list of devices that are presently connected and running on the local network. Look at the screen capture of the results of issuing the **net view** command. Note that the command consists of two words: *net* and *view*.

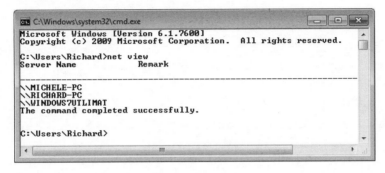

When setting up a peer-to-peer network that contains Windows XP or earlier computers, you should use the same workgroup name as the Windows XP computers. The default workgroup name is not the same for all versions of operating systems. Windows XP Home Edition uses *MSHome* for the default workgroup name.

Set Network Location Dialog Box

Both Windows Vista and Windows 7 have a dialog box called **Set Network Location**, which automatically changes the configuration of the Windows Firewall and shared files and devices. Look at the following screen captures of the Windows Vista and Windows 7 versions of the **Set Network Location** dialog box.

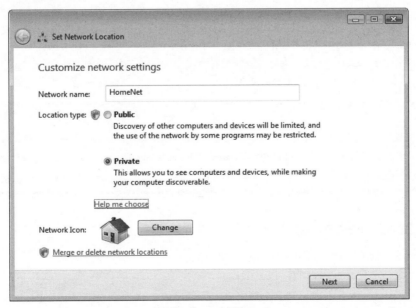

Windows Vista

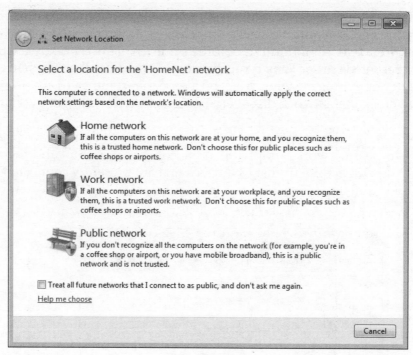

Windows 7

The main difference between the Windows Vista and Windows 7 versions of the **Set Network Location** dialog box is the number of locations identified. Windows Vista has two location options: **Public** and **Private**. Windows 7 has three network location options: **Home network**, **Work network**, and **Public network**. A short description accompanies each location type. The addition of the **Work network** location is to accommodate the new HomeGroup feature in Windows 7. The **Work network** option will allow you to view other computers and devices on the network but will not allow you to enable the Windows 7 HomeGroup feature used for sharing on a home network.

The network location providing the highest level of security is **Public** or **Public network**.

By default as a security measure, the Network Discovery feature and file sharing are not enabled. The theory is that if you cannot see a computer, you will not attempt to access the computer.

Check the following link to learn more about Windows networking: http://technet.microsoft.com/en-us/network/bb545868.aspx. You can also learn more through **Help and Support** located off of the **Start** menu. In the **Help and Support Search** box, type and enter "networking." This will generate a long list of networking topics that cover networking basics. You should take time to review the topics available in Windows Vista and Windows 7.

Note

When using lab computers that are used by multiple students, the default settings are often changed by other students. Never make assumptions about the network, network devices, or computer configuration.

Equipment and Materials

❏   Two computers running Windows Vista or Windows 7.
❏   Two Cat 5, Cat 5e, or Cat 6 Ethernet cables.
❏   Hub or switch.

Name _____

Procedure

1. _____ Gather the required materials and report to your assigned workstations.

2. _____ Boot the computers and verify they are in working order.

3. _____ After checking each computer, power them off.

4. _____ Connect each computer to the hub or switch using one of the Ethernet cables.

5. _____ Boot each computer and look at the hub or switch LED associated with each cable. The LED should be blinking to indicate network activity.

6. _____ To view all computers and network devices, select **Start | User Name | Network**. You should see both computers listed by assigned computer name. If you cannot see the other computer, check if the Network Discovery feature has been enabled.

   In Windows Vista, open the Network and Sharing Center and turn on the **Network discovery** option.

   In Windows 7, open the Network and Sharing Center, select **Change advanced sharing settings**, and then select **Turn on network discovery**.

Note

The two Windows Vista or Windows 7 computers do not need to be part of the same workgroup to be viewable. Only older computer systems, such as Windows XP or earlier, need to use the same workgroup name to be viewable.

7. _____ If you still cannot view the other computer, call your instructor for assistance. If you can view the other computer, call your instructor to inspect your lab activity as completed.

8. _____ Open the command prompt by entering **cmd** into the **Search** dialog box off of the **Start** menu. Use the **net view** command to view the other computer. Using the command prompt is an alternative way to view the local area network computers.

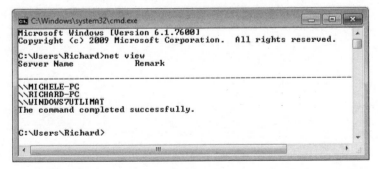

9. _____ Answer the review questions and return all materials to their proper storage area.

Review Questions

1. What is the default workgroup name for Windows Vista and Windows 7? _____

   _____

2. What are the two default workgroup names used by Windows XP? _____

3. Which version of Windows XP uses MSHOME for the workgroup name? _____

4. What should you check if the other computer does not appear when viewing the network?

   _____

5. Does the workgroup name need to be the same to view the other computer when using
   Windows Vista or Windows 7? _____

6. What are the two network locations associated with Windows Vista? _____

   _____

   _____

7. What are the three network locations associated with Windows 7? _____

   _____

8. Which network location provides the highest level of security? _____

   _____

9. What is the default network location for Windows Vista and Windows 7 when first installed?

   _____

10. What command issued from the command prompt will display a list of local area network
    computers? _____

Name_____ Date _____

Class/Instructor _____

HomeGroup

After completing this laboratory activity, you will be able to:

■ Use the Network and Sharing Center to create a homegroup.

■ Use the Network and Sharing Center to join a computer to a homegroup.

■ Use Computer to access resources on another member of the homegroup.

■ Use the **HomeGroup** dialog box to remove a computer from a homegroup.

■ Use the **HomeGroup** dialog box to recover a homegroup password.

Introduction

In this laboratory activity, you will explore the Windows 7 HomeGroup feature for sharing resources on a home or small network. HomeGroup was first introduced in Windows 7. Microsoft designed the HomeGroup feature to make it as easy as possible for the average computer user to automatically create a peer-to-peer network. The concept of workgroups and domains proved to be too difficult for the average computer user to comprehend. The HomeGroup feature is designed especially for home networking and is not intended for corporate applications found in a domain environment. The HomeGroup feature has been designed to easily and safely share pictures, videos, music, documents, and printers in a home network.

A homegroup is automatically created when you install Windows 7 on a computer. To participate in a homegroup, all computers must be running Windows 7. Any version of Windows 7 can join a homegroup, but only Windows 7 Home Premium, Professional, or Ultimate can create a homegroup.

Shared items in a homegroup are referred to as *libraries*. Only members of the same homegroup can view the contents of the libraries. If a computer is a member of a homegroup, it will be identified in the Network and Sharing Center. Look at the following partial screen capture.

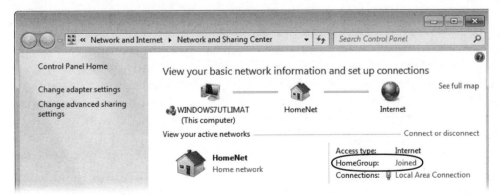

You can see that the computer has "joined" the homegroup as indicated in the Windows 7 Network and Sharing Center.

If the computer is not part of a homegroup, the Network and Sharing Center will appear similar to the one in the following partial screen caption. Notice the **Ready to create** link.

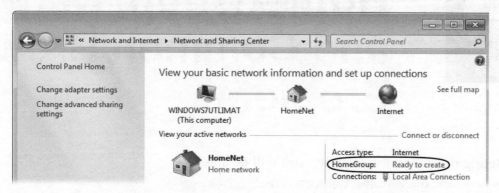

You can modify the HomeGroup configuration through the **HomeGroup** dialog box which will appear similar to the one in the following screen capture.

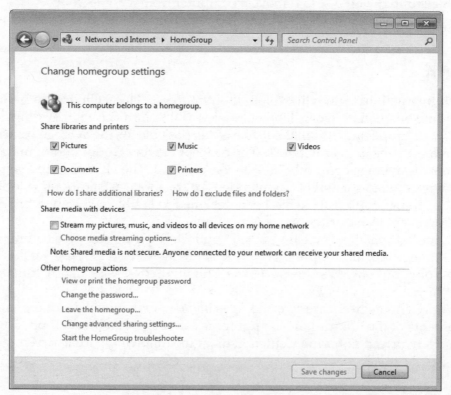

You select which items or libraries to share, such as pictures, music, videos, and documents. You can select the option to share your printer also. Pay particular attention to the options at the bottom of the screen in the **Other homegroup actions** section. The options listed here allow you to accomplish the most common tasks associated with HomeGroup. For example, if you forget what the password is, you can view a copy of the password here.

Equipment and Materials

❑ Two networked Windows 7 computers.

Note

You may perform this lab activity with a partner, each person using his or her own assigned networked computer.

Procedure

1. _____ Gather the required materials and report to your assigned workstations.

2. _____ Boot the computers and verify they are in working order.

3. _____ Open Network and Sharing Center to see if the computer is part of a homegroup. If the computer is not part of a homegroup, go to step 4 in the lab activity. If the computer is part of a HomeGroup, go to step 10.

4. _____ In the Network and Sharing Center, select the **Ready to create** link to start the HomeGroup wizard. The **HomeGroup** dialog box will appear similar to the following cropped screen capture.

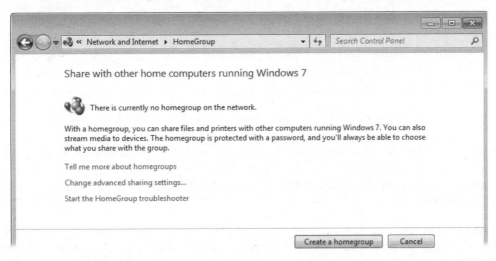

Notice that there are links to provide you with more information about homegroups and to allow you to perform routine tasks such as changing the advanced sharing settings. There is also a HomeGroup troubleshooter. Click the **Create a homegroup** button to create the new homegroup.

5. _____ The next dialog box to appear is similar to the following.

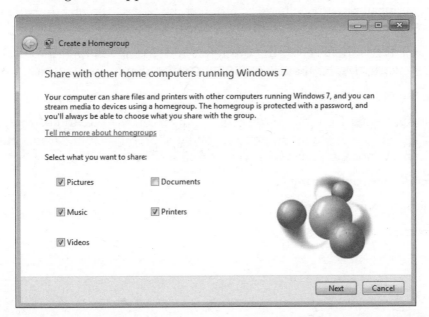

You can select which items or libraries you wish to share with other users. By default, all items except **Documents** are automatically selected. You can leave the default settings for this exercise. Click **Next** to continue.

6. _____ The next dialog box presents the homegroup password.

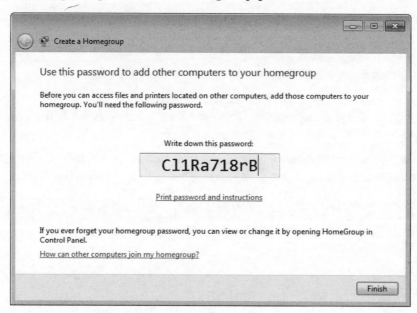

The password is automatically generated by the wizard. You can also create your own password by simply typing the desired password into the text box. You will use the homegroup password for each computer in the homegroup. The password must match at each computer to be able to access resources in the homegroup.

Notice that the password generated by the wizard follows the general guidelines for a secure password. The general guideline for secure passwords is the password should contain number and characters of the alphabet, both uppercase and lowercase letters. The password should also not be any word that would match a word in a dictionary. This is an example of a password that would be impossible to guess.

Record the password in the space provided so that you can use it later on another computer.

_____

7. _____ Click **Finish**. You have successfully created a homegroup.

8. _____ Open the Network and Sharing Center to verify that you have joined the homegroup as indicated by the word "Joined" beside the **HomeGroup** label.

9. _____ Close the Network and Sharing Center.

10. _____ Access **Computer** from the **Start** menu. You should see the **HomeGroup** icon listed on the left side of the screen and a list of libraries being shared by HomeGroup. Right-click the **HomeGroup** icon. A shortcut menu will appear that includes the following options:

- **Change the HomeGroup settings**.

- **View the HomeGroup password**.

- **Start the HomeGroup troubleshooter**.

11. _____ Take a few minutes to explore these three options. Look for and explore the links **How do I share additional libraries?** and **How do I exclude files and folders?**

12. _____ Call your instructor to check your lab activity.

Review Questions

1. What is the purpose of HomeGroup? _____

   _____

2. Which operating system first introduced the HomeGroup feature? _____

3. Can a Windows XP computer access HomeGroup shared resources? _____

4. What resources are shared? List five. _____

   _____

   _____

5. Which resource is not shared by default? _____

6. Can you share additional resource using HomeGroup? _____

7. What is another name for the shared resources in HomeGroup? _____

Name_____ Date _____

Class/Instructor _____

Exploring Network Adapter Configuration Settings

After completing this laboratory activity, you will be able to:

- Recall the purpose of typical network adapter settings.
- Recall the purpose of a DHCP server.
- Recall the purpose of a DNS server.
- Recall the purpose of a WINS server.

Introduction

In this laboratory activity, you will explore various network adapter configuration settings. An in-depth understanding of a vast array of networking topics is required to fully understand the purpose, function, and effect of these settings. The purpose of this laboratory activity, however, is only to familiarize you with the various options available and where they are located. As you progress though this course, you will gain an in-depth understanding of the networking topics mentioned in this lab.

The network adapter configuration settings can be accessed through the **Local Area Connection Properties** dialog box. This dialog box contains information specific to the network adapter configured for the local area network.

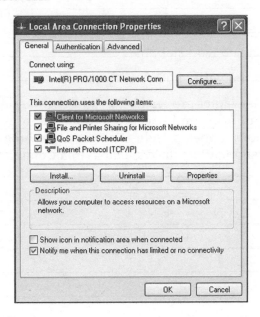

Configurations specific to the TCP/IP protocol can be accessed by highlighting **Internet Protocol (TCP/IP)** and clicking the **Properties** button. The **Internet Protocol (TCP/IP) Properties** dialog box will display.

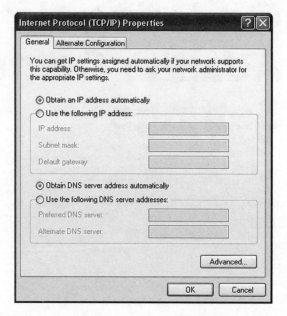

Through this dialog box, an entire set of options are made available for managing the TCP/IP properties, such as the method of IP address assignment, DNS settings, and WINS settings. We will briefly explore the meanings of these settings as you work through the lab. These settings will be revisited in later laboratory activities. At that time, you will gain a deeper understanding of the networking technology related to each setting.

Equipment and Materials

❑ Windows XP workstation connected to an Ethernet network.

Procedure

1. _____ Report to your assigned workstation.

2. _____ Boot the computer and verify it is in working order.

3. _____ Access the network adapter properties by right-clicking My Network Places either from the desktop or from the **Start** menu and selecting **Properties** from the shortcut menu. When the Network Connections window appears, right-click the **Local Area Connection** icon and then select **Properties** from the shortcut menu. The **Local Area Connection Properties** dialog box will display.

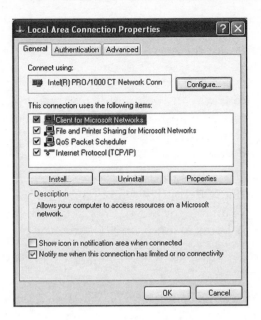

Notice that the network adapter for the LAN connection is identified in the **Connect using** text box. Record in the space provided the name or model number identified in your display.

_____

4. _____ Click **Configure**. Notice that the dialog box displayed allows you to change the network card configuration. Explore the various tabs and then record in the spaces provided the various items under each tab that can be changed.

General: _____

_____

Advanced: _____

_____

Driver: _____

_____

_____

Resources: _____

Power Management: _____

5. _____ Click **Cancel** to exit the network card's configuration dialog box. You will be returned to the **Network Connections** window.

6. _____ Right-click the **Local Area Connection** icon and then select **Properties** from the shortcut menu to return to the **Local Area Connection Properties** dialog box.

7. _____ Look at the items displayed in the **This connection uses the following items** text box. This is a list of installed services and protocols, such as Client for Microsoft Networks, File and Printer Sharing for Microsoft Networks, QoS Packet Scheduler, and Internet Protocol (TCP/IP). A check mark entered in the box on left of the item indicates the item is enabled. Removing the check mark only disables the item. It does not remove it. Use the information in the **Local Area Connection Properties** dialog box to answer the following questions.

What client is installed? _____

Is File and Printer Sharing for Microsoft Networks enabled? _____

What protocols are configured for the network adapter (i.e. NetBEUI, TCP/IP, and IPX/SPX)?

_____

8. _____ Notice the three buttons directly below this text box: **Install**, **Uninstall**, and **Properties**. These buttons are used to make changes to the installed services and protocols. For example, to view the properties of the Internet Protocol (TCP/IP), you would first select Internet Protocol (TCP/IP) and then click the **Properties** button.

Not all buttons are enabled for each of the items. For example, in Windows XP you cannot uninstall the Internet Protocol (TCP/IP). The **Uninstall** button will be shaded, indicating that the uninstall function is not available for the TCP/IP protocol. Highlight each item in the **This connection uses the following items** text box and observe the buttons.

9. _____ Disable the TCP/IP protocol. To do this, simply click the box to the left of the Internet Protocol (TCP/IP) entry.

10. _____ Attempt to uninstall the TCP/IP protocol. What happened? _____

_____

11. _____ Look at the two options at the bottom of the dialog box: **Show icon in notification area when connected** and **Notify me when this connection has limited or no connectivity**. The function of these options is to report the network state. This is done through an icon that represents a connection in the status area of the taskbar and a message notifying of network connection changes.

12. _____ Select the **Show icon in notification area when connected** option and then click **OK**. Record the result in the space provided.

_____

_____

13. _____ Reopen the **Local Area Connection Properties** dialog box and then click the **Authentication** tab. The **Authentication** tab reveals information about how the workstation authenticates itself to a network domain. The options on this page are explained in-depth later in the course and in related laboratory activities. For now, simply be aware that the settings in the **Authentication** dialog box control the way the network adapter is authenticated to a secure domain controller server.

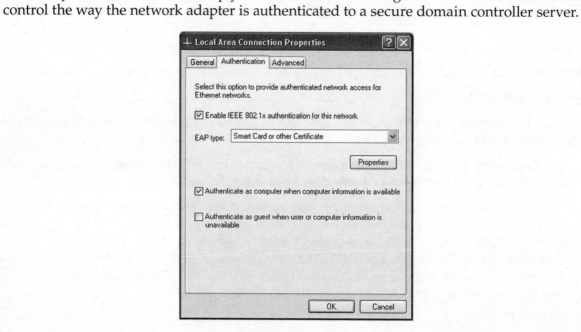

14. _____ Click the **Advanced** tab. The **Advanced** tab provides you with access to the Windows XP Firewall settings. The Microsoft Windows XP Firewall is covered in detail in a later laboratory activity. For now, simply be aware of how to access the firewall, and that the main function of the firewall is to prevent unauthorized access to the workstation.

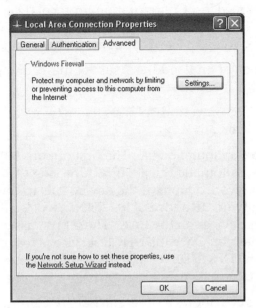

15. _____ Click the **Settings** button. Is the firewall enabled? _____

16. _____ Click **Cancel** to exit the **Windows Firewall** dialog box.

17. _____ Click the **General** tab to return to the **General** dialog box.

18. _____ Access the **Internet Protocol (TCP/IP) Properties** dialog box by highlighting the Internet Protocol (TCP/IP) entry and clicking **Properties**. The **Internet Protocol (TCP/IP) Properties** dialog box will display, allowing you to manage the TCP/IP properties.

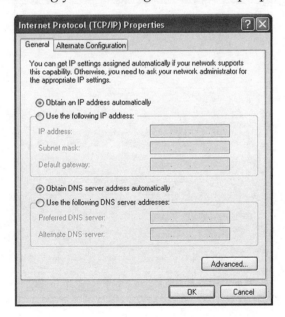

The **General** tab contains options for the way the network adapter is to obtain TCP/IP settings. During the installation of the Window XP operating system, the network adapter is configured for **Obtain an IP address automatically**. This means that the network adapter is configured to accept TCP/IP settings, such as an IP address, subnet mask, and default gateway address, automatically from a Dynamic Host Configuration Protocol (DHCP) server. This method of obtaining TCP/IP settings is called *dynamic IP addressing*. A DHCP server can be any server that provides the DHCP service. You will learn about the DHCP service later in this course.

An administrator can also enter an IP address, subnet mask, and gateway address manually in the text boxes provided. This is called *static IP addressing*.

19. _____ Look at the dialog box on your display. Is the network adapter configured to obtain an IP address dynamically or statically? _____

20. _____ Click the **Alternate Configuration** tab. The first option, **Automatic private IP address**, allows Microsoft to use the Automatic Private IP Addressing (APIPA) service to automatically assign an IP address to a network adapter if the device fails to connect to a DHCP server. APIPA assigns a Class B network IP address, 169.254.xxx.xxx, so the device can continue to communicate with other devices on the LAN. The APIPA assignment cannot be used to communicate across the Internet. Once the DHCP service is restored, the APIPA assigned IP address is discarded and the DHCP server assigns an IP address. APIPA and IP address classes are covered later in this course.

The **User configured** dialog box allows a different TCP/IP configuration to be set up for the network adapter. This is useful if the computer is a laptop that will be used at home and at work, since both locations typically require different TCP/IP settings. Configuring an alternate IP address is covered in a later laboratory activity.

21. _____ Click the **General** tab and then click the **Advanced** button. The **Advanced TCP/IP Settings** dialog box will display. Look at the four tabs available at the top of the dialog box: **IP Settings**, **DNS**, **WINS**, and **Options**.

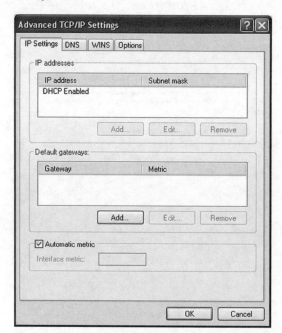

In the **IP Settings** dialog box, multihoming can be configured for the computer. When a computer is configured as a multihomed device, it is configured with two or more IP addresses to communicate with two or more subnets at the same time. This is not the same as Alternate Configuration presented earlier, which is used to connect to two or more networks, but not at the same time.

22. _____ Now, select the **DNS** tab. The **DNS** dialog box is used for configuring how the workstation will resolve the assigned computer name (host name) to an IP address. The Internet network system uses IP addresses to locate destinations, not host names or URLs. A Domain Name Service (DNS) server is used to resolve host and domain names to IP addresses. The IP addresses of DNS servers the workstation is to consult are entered in the **DNS Server Addresses, in order of use** text box. The DNS dialog box does not normally need to be configured when the network adapter has been configured for DHCP (dynamic IP addressing) because the DHCP server provides the required DNS server information.

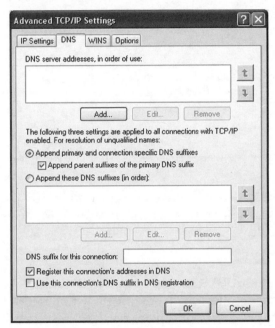

Look at the **DNS Server Addresses, in order of use** text box in your display. What address(s) have been entered for the DNS server? (If the network adapter has been configured to receive TCP/IP information dynamically, the DNS address section will be blank.)

_____

23. _____ Look through the rest of the options in the **DNS** dialog box. Notice that they make reference to a DNS suffix. The DNS suffix is part of the Fully Qualified Domain Name (FQDN). An FDQN is the name of the computer (host name) appended to the front of a domain name in which the workstation is installed. For example, an FQDN for a workstation called *Client1* installed in a domain called RMRoberts.com would be Client1.RMRoberts.com. The DNS suffix would be RMRoberts.com. There will be much more about DNS, FQDNs, and domains later in this course.

24. _____ Click the **WINS** tab. The Windows Internet Naming Service (WINS) is used to resolve NetBIOS names to IP addresses. A NetBIOS name is the name given to a computer during the Windows operating system installation process. The **WINS addresses, in order of use** text box is used to list the IP addresses of the WINS servers the workstation is to consult.

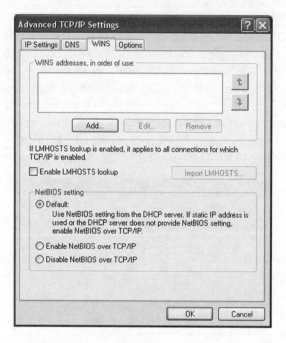

Look at the **WINS addresses, in order of use** text box on your display. What address(s) have been entered? (If the network adapter has been configured to receive TCP/IP information dynamically, the WINS address section will be blank.)

_____

25. _____ Notice the **Enable LMHOSTS lookup** option in the middle of the **WINS** dialog box. This option refers to the lmhosts text file, which contains a list of NetBIOS names and corresponding IP addresses. This file is typically used in place of a WINS server. If enabled, the computer automatically checks the lmhosts file when attempting to resolve NetBIOS names to IP addresses. All computers in the LAN, however, must have the same contents in their lmhosts file. When a computer communicates with a different computer, it will look in the lmhosts file to find the IP address of the destination computer.

Note
The function of the lmhosts file has been replaced by the use of DNS servers.

26. _____ Now, look at the **NetBIOS setting** options at the bottom of the dialog box. In earlier versions of Microsoft before Windows 2000, LANs communicated by broadcasting NetBIOS name information to all devices in the LAN. Starting with Windows 2000, it became optional to conform to NetBIOS naming standards and the methods used to resolve a NetBIOS name to an IP address. The earlier operating systems required a WINS server to be running WINS services to resolve NetBIOS names to IP addresses so that network devices could communicate over the Internet, which uses IP addresses, not NetBIOS names.

The **Default** option is automatically selected when the network adapter is configured to use a DHCP service. The other two options are for enabling or disabling NetBIOS over TCP/IP. If a network consists only of Windows 2000 or later computers, you can disable NetBIOS over

TCP/IP. If the network contains versions of Windows earlier than Windows 2000, enable NetBIOS over TCP/IP. Look at the NetBIOS settings on your display. What is the NetBIOS configuration for the network adapter? _____

_____

Note

WINS and DNS can coexist in a network system.

---

27. _____ Click the **Options** tab. The **Options** dialog box allows you to configure TCP/IP filtering. TCP/IP filtering prevents certain types of network connections or services from being run on the workstation. You will learn more about filtering later in this course.

28. _____ Answer the review questions before closing any dialog boxes and shutting down your workstation.

Review Questions

1. What are the two main ways IP addresses are assigned to a network adapter? _____

_____

2. What does the acronym DHCP represent? _____

3. What is the purpose of a DHCP server? _____

_____

4. What does the acronym DNS represent? _____

5. What is the purpose of a DNS server? _____

_____

6. What does the acronym WINS represent? _____

7. What is the purpose of a WINS server? _____

_____

8. What does the APIPA acronym represent? _____

9. How can you identify an Automatic Private IP Address? _____

_____

10. When is an APIPA address assigned to a network adapter? _____

_____

WINDOWS XP PROFFESIONAL

Name_____ Date _____

Class/Instructor _____

Browsing the Network and Common Browser Problems

After completing this laboratory activity, you will be able to:

■ Summarize the role of a master browser.

■ Summarize a server role in relation to a workgroup.

■ Use network browser utilities to view a network's workgroups, workgroup members, and shares.

■ Give examples of the error messages associated with common network browser problems.

Introduction

In this laboratory activity, you will recreate some of the most common network browser problems encountered by users and technicians. All versions of Windows contain network browser utilities capable of viewing workgroups, workgroup members, and shares. Examples of network browser utilities are My Network Places, Network Neighborhood, Computers Near Me, and Windows Explorer. The availability of these utilities varies by operating system.

The network browsing operation provides a display of local workgroup(s), shared resources, and connections to a shared resource. The browser system consists of a master browser and browser clients. The master browser is any workstation in the workgroup or workgroups designated as the master browser through what Microsoft refers to as an election process. An election process is based on a workstation's physical characteristics, such as amount of RAM, processor type, bus speed, connection speed, and workstation role. Elections happen periodically as workstations connect and disconnect from the LAN. Some large workgroups consisting of 32 or more clients also select a backup master browser. Look at the following illustration.

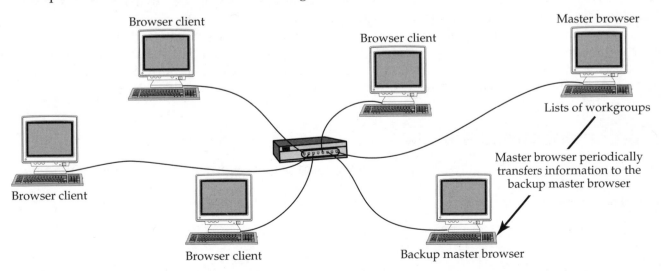

Browser client

Browser client

Master browser

Lists of workgroups

Master browser periodically transfers information to the backup master browser

Browser client

Browser client

Backup master browser

The master browser maintains a list of workgroups and workgroup members and provides information to browser clients when requested. It also periodically updates the backup master browser. In a client/server network environment, the domain controller functions as the master browser.

Browser clients do not maintain a list of workgroups and workgroup members but do maintain a list of shares. When the browser client accesses a share for the first time, a shortcut to the share is created. Each browser client depends on the master browser for workgroup information. The browser client is automatically configured on any computer that has Client for Microsoft Networks installed. In the Windows XP operating system, Client for Microsoft Networks is installed by default with the installation of a network adapter.

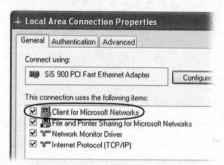

Three items are required to be able to view the network from a browser client: Client for Microsoft Networks, File and Printer Sharing for Microsoft Networks, and Internet Protocol (TCP/IP). Information about workgroups and shares are exchanged by broadcast messages on the network. By providing specialized roles, such as master browser, the total number of broadcasts is greatly reduced.

Note

Microsoft refers to workstations with shares connected in a peer-to-peer network as *servers*. They are referred to as *servers* because they provide shares, and providing shares is considered providing a service. Every client in a peer-to-peer has the ability to be a server.

Successful network browsing requires the master browser and browser client to operate in a coordinated manner. A browser that fails to operate in a coordinated manner causes problems when certain network operations are performed. Be aware that if you reassign a workstation to a different workgroup, it will no longer be able to access shares to which it was previously connected. You will need to delete the connection and reconnect as when connecting for the first time.

Many unique browser problems can occur when the workgroup consists of different Microsoft Windows operating systems. Also, be aware that the *Guest* account affects the sharing of Windows XP files in a workgroup. Nonmembers of the workgroup use the *Guest* account. This is standard. If the *Guest* account is not activated, users other than those with accounts on the computer will not be able to access the shares.

Equipment and Materials

❑ Three or more workstations configured as a peer-to-peer network. All workstations should be running Windows XP Professional.

❑ The following information:

Workgroup names: _____

_____

(Suggested workgroup names are *NETLAB1* and *NETLAB2*.)

Name _____

Workstation names: _____

_____

_____

(Suggested workstation names are *Client1*, *Client2*, and *Client3*.)

Note

The results for this laboratory activity may vary according to the service pack version installed. Also, be aware that certain software packages can affect results. For example, certain security software packages, such as antivirus software, affect the ability to view workgroups and shares.

Note

Some configuration changes you will make in this laboratory activity take a long time to display the results—typically 12 to 15 minutes. You can decrease the time it takes to display the results of a change by rebooting all workstations involved in the laboratory activity. Lab time is limited. Your instructor will provide you with more information about how long to wait for a change to take place.

Procedure

1. _____ Report to your assigned workstation(s).

2. _____ Boot the computers and verify they are in working order and are configured in a peer-to-peer network.

3. _____ Configure three (or more) computers with the workgroup names selected earlier. If using three workstations, configure two workstations with one workgroup name and the remaining workstation with the other workgroup name. For example, configure *Client1* and *Client2* as part of the *NETLAB1* workgroup and *Client3* as part of the *NETLAB2* workgroup.

4. _____ Open My Network Places and view the two workgroups (**Start | My Network Places | View workgroup computers**). Repeat this step at each of the workstations.

In the following screen capture, the workgroup *NETLAB1* is listed in the address bar. *Client1winxp* and *Gateway computer.(Client2)* are members of the *NETLAB1* workgroup. The third computer, *Client3*, is in the *NETLAB2* workgroup and is not displayed.

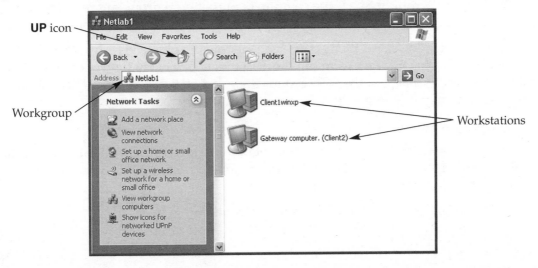

5. _____ To see the other workgroup, click the **Up** icon in the toolbar. The **Up** icon is represented by a folder with a green arrow pointing upward. Clicking this icon moves the view up one directory level. All workgroups using the same subnet mask will be displayed. Try it now. You should see the two workgroups. If not, call your instructor for assistance.

6. _____ Close the My Network Places window and then browse the network by opening Windows Explorer view of My Network Places. To access the Windows Explorer view, right-click the **My Network Places** icon and select **Explore** from the shortcut menu. To view the workgroups, click **Entire Network** and then click **Microsoft Windows Network**. Your display should look similar to the following.

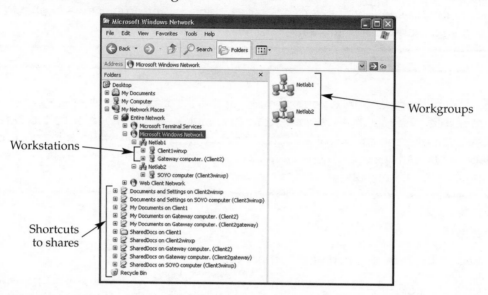

The Windows Explorer view provides a much more detailed view of the network than My Network Places. With this view you are able to see all workstations available in each workgroup and the shares associated with each workstation. Take note of the fact that all shares available for connection are also listed in the left-hand pane of the window.

Note

The easiest way to ensure a view and a connection to a different workgroup is to enable the Remote Desktop feature. The Remote Desktop feature can be accessed by right-clicking **My Computer**, selecting **Properties** from the shortcut menu, and selecting the **Remote** tab.

---

7. _____ Click a workgroup to see if the computers in that workgroup are revealed. Computers in each of the workgroups should be revealed. If not, call your instructor for assistance.

8. _____ Close all windows and then access the Windows Explorer view by right-clicking **My Computer** and selecting **Explore** from the shortcut menu. Select **My Network Places**. Notice that only the shares are visible, not the workgroups and workstations. You can click the **Up** icon to see the workstation and workgroups associated with the share.

9. _____ Close all windows.

10. _____ Change the name of one of the workstations. To do this, right-click **My Computer** and then select **Properties**. Select the **Computer Name** tab and then click the **Change** button. Enter a different workstation name.

11. _____ When prompted, select to restart the workstation.

12. _____ After the workstation has rebooted, open a network browser window and check the workgroup memberships. Specifically, check if the old computer name and the new computer name in the workgroup exists. Write your findings in the space provided.

_____

_____

13. _____ Double-click the icon with the old computer name. Record the error message in the space provided.

_____

_____

14. _____ Right-click the icon with the old computer name and select **Properties** from the shortcut menu. Then, do the same for the icon with the new computer name. Record the results in the space provided. _____

15. _____ Attempt to open each workstation's shares. Record the results in the space provided.

_____

_____

16. _____ The old workstation name will remain as a ghost workstation for a variable length of time before disappearing. It is common for the ghost image to remain 12 minutes or more. Wait for a period of time (approximately 15 minutes) until the image of the old workstation icon disappears from the workgroup. You may attempt the **Refresh** option located in the **View** menu to update the view.

17. _____ Change the name of one workstation to match the name of another workstation. For example, change *Client2* to *Client1* to create a duplicate in the same workgroup. Observe the error message and record it in the space provided.

_____

_____

18. _____ You will not be able to change the name, so simply click the **Cancel** button.

19. _____ Activate Windows Firewall on all workstations. If Service Pack 2 or later is installed, open Control Panel and then double-click the **Security Center** icon. Enable Windows Firewall. If the Service Pack 2 or later is not installed, right-click **My Network Places** and select **Properties** from the shortcut menu. Right-click the **Local Area Connection** and then select **Properties** from the shortcut menu. Select the **Advanced** tab and then click the **Settings** button. Enable Windows Firewall.

20. _____ After enabling Windows Firewall on all of the workstations, view the workstations from a network browser, such as **My Network Places**. Record your observations in the space provided.

_____

_____

Note

The Windows Firewall feature contains special settings to make exceptions for the local area network. When you turn the firewall feature on, the default settings take effect. There will be more about the Windows Firewall and the advanced settings later in this laboratory manual.

---

21. _____ Turn the Windows Firewall off on each workstation and attempt to view the network again. You should be able to see all workgroups and all workstations.

22. _____ Properly shut down a workstation and observe the action from another workstation. For example, properly shut down *Client1* while observing the action from *Client2*. After the workstation is shut down, attempt to access the workstation by double-clicking its icon in the network browser. Record your observations in the space provided. You may need to wait 12 to 15 minutes. To accelerate the process, shut down and restart all workstations in the workgroup.

_____

_____

23. _____ Boot the workstation and watch the network from another workstation. For example, boot *Client1* while viewing the network from *Client2*. Record your observations in the space provided.

_____

_____

24. _____ Record the IP address and subnet mask for one of the workstations.

IP Address: _____

Subnet mask: _____

25. _____ Change the IP address on that workstation from static to dynamic. Reboot the workstation and then observe the results in a network browser. Record your observations in the space provided.

_____

_____

26. _____ Change the workstation's IP configuration to its original settings.

27. _____ Open the network browser to view the network shares. Delete an existing share by right-clicking the share and then selecting the **Delete** option. The share will be deleted. The share will be recreated automatically the next time you access the workstation associated with that share.

28. _____ You can access and display shares on a computer through the **Run** dialog box off the **Start** menu. For example, to access *Client2* from *Client1*, open the **Run** dialog box on *Client1* and enter **\\Client2**. A view of all shares available on *Client1* will appear.

Note
The double backslash indicates the computer is a server.

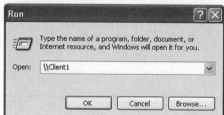

29. _____ Enter a nonexistent client, such as **\\ClientXYZ**, into the **Run** dialog box, and then observe and record the error message in the space provided.

_____

_____

30. _____ Answer the review questions.

31. _____ Restore the workstations to the state indicated by your instructor, and then return all materials to their proper storage area.

Review Questions

1. What is the role of the master browser? _____

_____

_____

2. Which computer is responsible for the role of master browser in a client/server type network?

_____

3. Approximately how long does the icon image of a workstation remain viewable before it disappears? _____

4. When is a backup browser configured on a LAN? _____

_____

5. You run a technical support operation for several small business peer-to-peer networks in the local community. A customer calls you about seeing several network shares that no longer exist in their network. How might they remove the nonexistent shares? _____

_____

6. Write the command you would enter to view the shares available on a workstation named *Station12* when using the **Run** dialog box. _____

_____

7. Can you view a workgroup workstation that has a different subnet mask? _____

_____

WINDOWS VISTA

Name_____ Date _____

Class/Instructor _____

Installing a USB Network Adapter and Configuring a Wireless Router

After completing this laboratory activity, you will be able to:

- Summarize the purpose of a Wireless Access Point (WAP).
- Recall typical wireless network configuration requirements.
- Summarize the purpose of an SSID.
- Summarize why wireless device default settings usually do not provide security.
- Carry out proper procedures to install an 802.11 USB network adapter.
- Carry out proper procedures to install an 802.11 wireless router/WAP.

Introduction

In this laboratory activity, you will install an 802.11 USB wireless network adapter and then install and configure a wireless router/WAP. Wireless devices fall into four categories as defined by the IEEE: 802.11a, 802.11b, 802.11g, and 802.11n.

IEEE Classification	Assigned Frequency	Maximum Data Rate	Comments
802.11a	5 GHz	54 Mbps	Not compatible with other wireless classifications. Obsolete at this time.
802.11b	2.4 GHz	11 Mbps	Compatible with 802.11g and 802.11n
802.11g	2.4 GHz	11 Mbps in 802.11b mode 54 Mbps in 802.11g mode	Some manufacturers exceed the 54 Mbps as defined in the IEEE standard and can support over 100 Mbps.
802.11n	2.4 GHz 5 GHz	300 Mbps in 802.11n mode 54 Mbps in 802.11a mode 11 Mbps in 802.11b mode 54 Mbps in 802.11g mode	A maximum data rate as high as 600 Mbps has been reported.

Note
The chart reflects maximum theoretical data rates as defined by the IEEE standard. Some manufacturers specify data rates that exceed the data rates defined by IEEE. However, the actual throughput will be considerably lower than the advertised rate.

Maximum data rates can only be experienced under ideal conditions. For best data rates, devices need to be in close proximity and in direct line of sight with no partitions or other objects blocking the radio waves. Radio waves can penetrate through solid objects such as wood or concrete but not through metallic objects such as metal building walls, metallic file cabinets, or some types of window tint that is derived from metallic substances.

New wireless device technologies are typically designed to be backward compatible with other earlier wireless device technologies. As you can see in the table, 802.11n is backward compatible with all earlier wireless standards.

Microsoft Windows XP was the first operating system released by Microsoft that came with generic drivers and applications to support and configure wireless devices. Wireless device manufacturers almost always recommend using its installation CD/DVD to install device drivers and applications before installing the wireless device. Microsoft operating systems such as Windows Vista will typically recognize a new device, such as a USB adapter, and automatically configure the wireless device without the need of the manufacturer CD/DVD. When installing a wireless router, it is best to install the router software before connecting the wireless router.

Wireless routers typically provide both wireless connectivity and wired connection ports. Look at the wireless router in the following illustration.

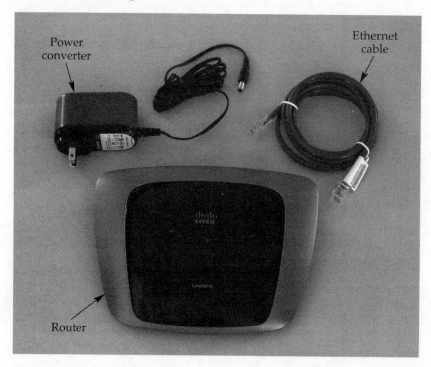

The router comes with an electrical power converter that changes the 120 volts AC to a much lower 12 volts DC. This particular router comes with one Ethernet cable to connect the router to the Internet modem or to a computer. The next illustration shows a close-up of typical router connections.

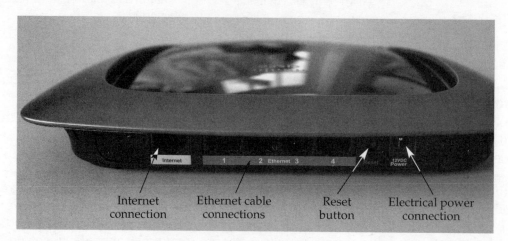

The Internet connection connects to the Cable or DSL modem, and the Ethernet cable connections connect to computers using network cable. The reset button is used to reset the router configuration to the default configuration set by the manufacturer. The electrical power connection connects to the electrical power converter.

Wireless routers are commonly encountered today and incorporate features such as Wireless Access Point (WAP) and Dynamic Host Configuration Protocol (DHCP). DHCP is a feature that automatically issues IP addresses to client devices.

Wireless devices can be configured in two different configurations: Ad hoc and infrastructure mode. In ad hoc mode, wireless devices are free to communicate with each other and all devices are considered equal. Ad hoc mode does not use a router or WAP to control the connections between devices. In infrastructure mode, a WAP is used to control communication between devices. Wireless routers incorporate the WAP feature. Thus, the router controls communication between wireless devices and wired devices connected to the same router. Wireless devices such as routers and WAPs are also referred to at times as *bridges* because they bridge the connection between two dissimilar media types: wireless and cable.

The Service Set Identifier (SSID) is the name used to identify the wireless network. Manufacturers assign a default SSID to their wireless devices. For example, D-Link uses "WLAN" or "Default," Netgear uses "Wireless" or "NETGEAR," Linksys uses "Linksys," and 3Com uses "WLAN" or "3Com." You can usually locate the default SSID as well as the default user name and password to access the wireless router setup program by conducting a search on the Internet. Because it is so easy to locate the default SSID and user name and password, the default values are considered an extreme security risk. You can actually perform a Google search for the default user name and password for most router devices. During or after the initial configuration, you should change the SSID to a name other than the default name. Wireless devices from the same manufacturer will automatically connect to other wireless devices using the same SSID unless they are encrypted or have password authentication configured. The default SSID, user name, and password can be reset to the original manufacturer's values by pressing the reset button on the router for approximately 15 seconds or more.

The default wireless channel, or dedicated frequency, also varies according to manufacturer. In the United States, the FCC has assigned 11 wireless channels for use with wireless devices. Each wireless device in the wireless network should be assigned the exact same channel. When wireless devices automatically configure themselves, they assign a specific channel to themselves. You can manually assign the wireless channel if need be. For example, a specific channel may be experiencing radio interference resulting in very low data speeds or not connecting at all. You can sometimes overcome the effects of the radio interference by changing the assigned channel.

The wireless router configuration can be changed remotely from a wireless laptop or wireless workstation. The router or WAP is typically accessed by using a browser and entering the assigned IP address of the wireless router into the browser's address bar. Typical default assigned IP addresses are 192.168.0.1 and 192.168.1.1. Check the wireless router documentation for the assigned default IP address. During the connection process, you will be prompted for a user name and password. Again, the default user name and password assigned by the manufacturer should be changed to make the wireless network more secure.

Equipment and Materials

- ❑ 802.11(g or n) USB wireless network adapter with installation CD/DVD and manual.
- ❑ 802.11(g or n) Wireless Access Point or wireless router with installation CD/DVD and manual.
- ❑ Patch cable (Cat 5, Cat 5e, or Cat 6).
- ❑ Paper clip. (Used to press the reset button if needed.)
- ❑ Computer (desktop or laptop) running Windows Vista.
- ❑ The following information provided by your instructor:

User name: _____

Password: _____

IP address: _____

Subnet mask: _____

Default gateway: _____

Wireless channel: _____

Wireless router: _____

IP address: _____

Subnet mask: _____

Default gateway: _____

User name: _____

User password: _____

Wireless channel: _____

SSID: _____

Note

Both wireless devices should be the same IEEE standard, either 802.11g or 802.11n, and should (but not required) be the same brand to allow for easier setup and configuration.

Note

Most modern routers and USB wireless network adapters will automatically configure most of the values using the default settings. Review the manufacturer's installation procedures before attempting to install any devices or running the installation CD/DVD.

Part I—Installing a USB Wireless Network Adapter

Procedure

1. _____ Gather all required materials and report to your assigned workstation.

2. _____ Boot the computer and verify it is in working order.

3. _____ Review the manufacturer's installation manual for the USB wireless network adapter. You may have a "Quick Start" guide or need to open the CD/DVD that came with the device to view the installation manual. Typically, you install the software for the wireless device before installing the device. A typical installation consists of inserting the device's CD/DVD and having the disc automatically detected and its installation program started. A series of windows will appear prompting you for information while the device drivers are automatically installed. At the end of the software installation process, you will be prompted to insert the USB wireless network adapter.

4. _____ Insert the USB wireless network adapter. It should automatically be detected and configured by the operating system.

5. _____ After successfully installing the USB network adapter, an icon should appear in the taskbar representing the wireless network device.

6. _____ Verify that the USB wireless adapter card has been installed successfully by opening Device Manager. If you see a red *X* or a yellow exclamation mark (!) beside the device, there is a problem. Some older wireless device drivers are not compatible with Windows Vista or Windows 7. If there is a problem, check the manufacturer's Web site for troubleshooting information. Also, check the manufacturer's Web site for the very latest drivers.

7. _____ Call your instructor to inspect your USB wireless network adapter installation.

Part II—Configuring a Wireless Network Router

The screen captures used in this portion of the lab activity are based on a Cisco Linksys router and may not necessarily match your router configuration screens. However, they will be somewhat similar.

The wireless router CD/DVD will have a wizard program to assist you in the automatic configuration of the router. Because of the discovery-type protocols widely used today, the router can not only discover information about your Internet provider, it can automatically configure your Internet connection in most cases. You will very seldom need to manually configure the wireless router, but you will still have the manual configuration option available to you.

Procedure

1. _____ Insert the router setup disc into the CD/DVD drive and wait for the installation program to open. A screen similar to the following will appear.

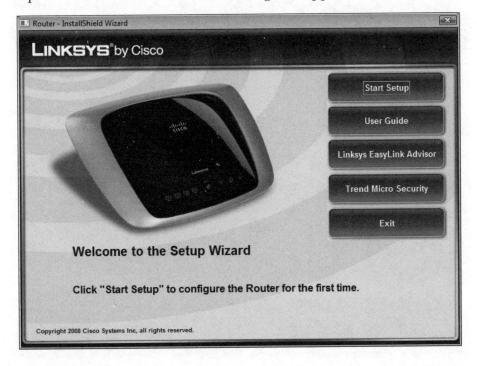

2. _____ Click the **Start Setup** button and then follow the instructions as presented in the setup wizard. The following is a series of some of the typical screens you will encounter while installing and configuring the router. These are not steps to perform but rather an overview of a typical wireless router configuration.

The setup wizard will automatically check for an Internet connection and install and configure the router. You may be asked to respond to some simple questions as the router is configured.

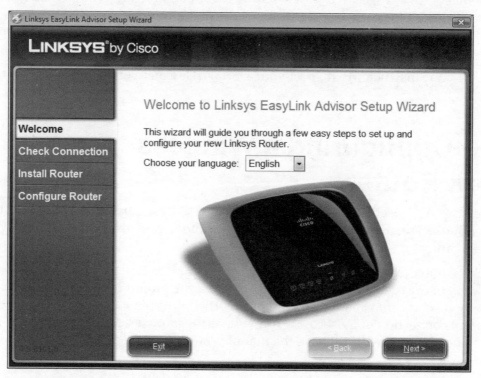

The installation wizard will even provide you with illustrations of how to connect your router to the Internet and to the computer.

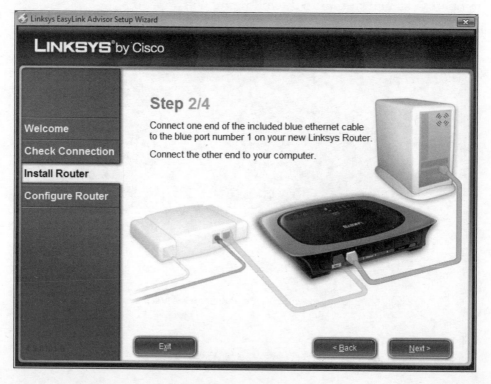

In the following screens, the setup wizard configures the router with minimal input from the user.

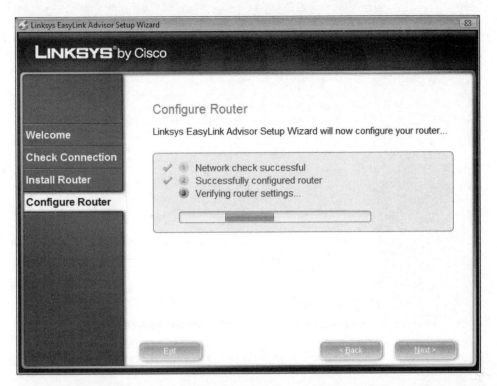

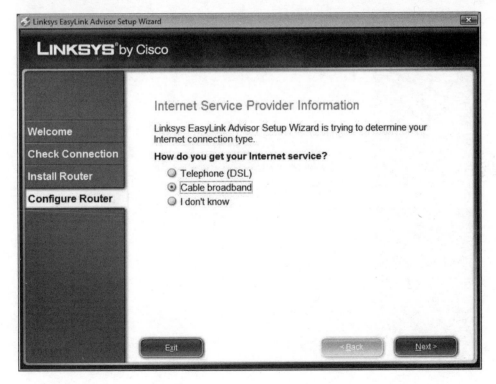

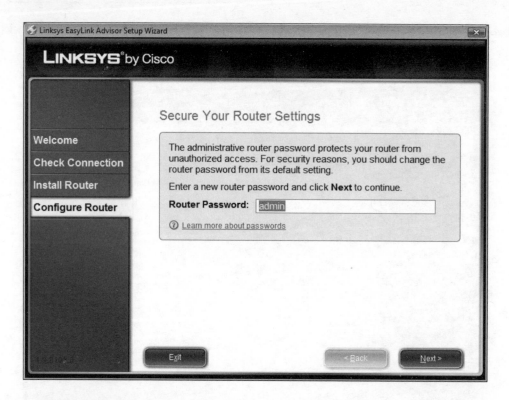

In the following two screens, notice the default SSID entry "linksys" has been replaced with the "HomeNet" SSID.

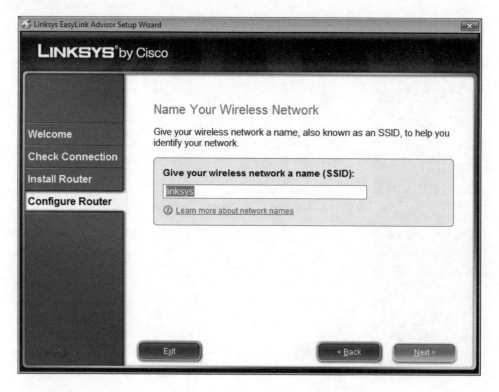

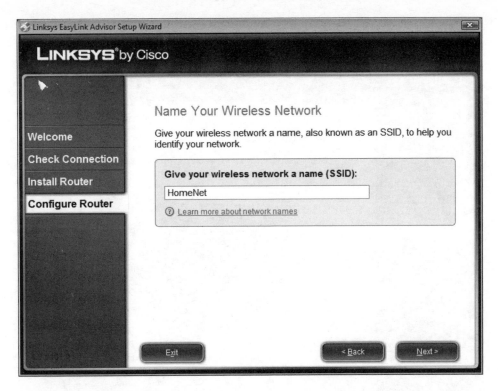

In the following screen, you are prompted to select the type of security you wish to configure.

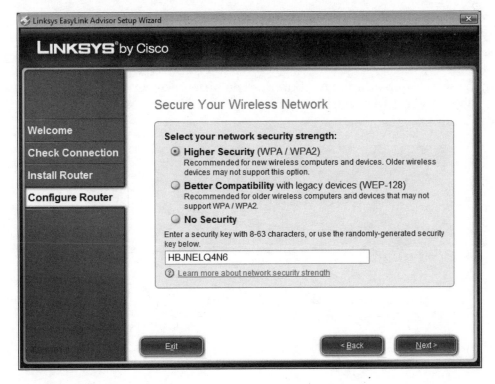

When the installation is finished, you should see a dialog box similar to the following.

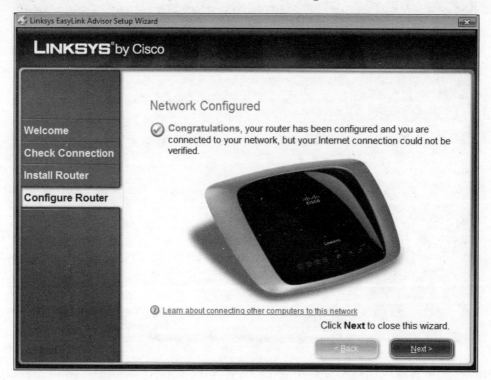

The Microsoft Vista operating system works in collaboration with the router when configuring the local area network. Security on the local area network is controlled by the Microsoft Vista operating system. As you can see in the following screen capture, you simply verify the network location, which is set to "Private" by default in the Network and Sharing Center. You may change the network location to "Public." The difference between public and private is the Network Discovery feature is enabled in a private location and Network Discovery is disabled in public locations.

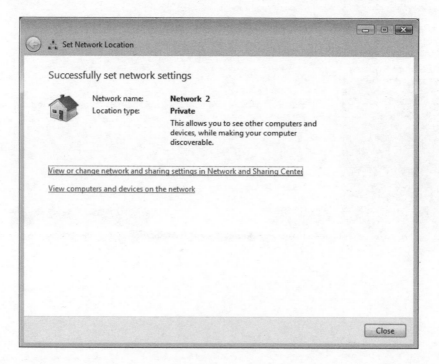

3. _____ After you have completed the configuration, open the network view to see all computers connected to the router. You can open the network view by selecting **Network** from the **Start** menu. You will have a view of all devices being served by the router, similar to that in the following screen capture. If you are performing the lab activity by yourself, you may have a view of only your computer. You can only view the devices if you have enabled the Network Discovery feature and have chosen the "Private" location. Network Discovery is disabled when the "Public" network setting is selected.

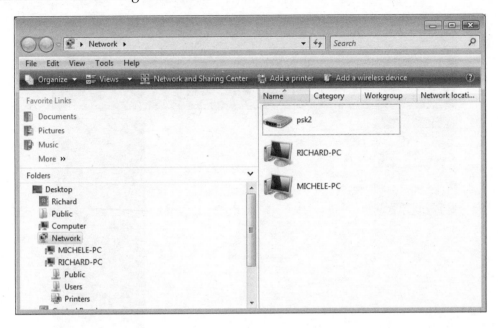

4. _____ To access the wireless router, you will need to type and enter the default IPv4 address of the router into the address bar of your Web browser. The default is typically 192.168.1.1, or very similar. Check the manufacturer's installation guide for the correct IPv4 address. You will be prompted for an administrator user name and a password. Again, check the manufacturer's information for the correct administrator user name and default password.

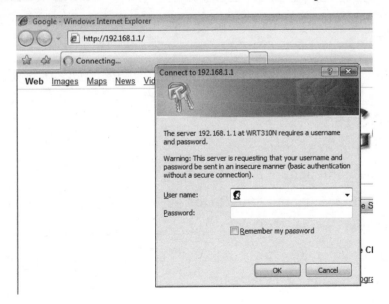

5. _____ After entering the administrator user name and password, you will see a user interface similar to the following. The user interface allows you to view and modify the router configuration. Take a few minutes to explore the various menu items and options, but do *not* change any settings at this time.

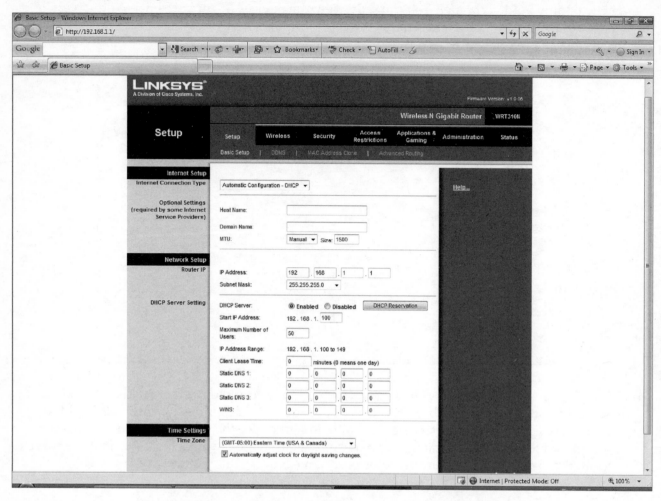

6. _____ Call your instructor to inspect this portion of your lab activity.

7. _____ Answer the review questions and then return all materials to their proper storage area.

Review Questions

1. What does the acronym WAP represent?_____

2. What is the maximum throughput for 802.11g? _____

3. What is the maximum throughput for 802.11b? _____

4. What is the maximum throughput for 802.11a?_____

5. What is the throughput for 802.11n? _____

6. What is the assigned frequency for 802.11b? _____

7. What is the assigned frequency for 802.11g? _____

8. What is the assigned frequency for 802.11a?_____

9. What is the assigned frequency for 802.11n? _____

10. With which standards are an 802.11g device backward compatible? _____

_____

11. What does the acronym SSID represent? _____

12. What are the two general wireless configurations? _____

_____

13. True *or* False? All wireless device manufacturers use the same SSID. _____

14. What is the purpose of the SSID? _____

_____

Laboratory Activity

18

Name_____ Date _____

Class/Instructor _____

Configuring and Troubleshooting Wireless Connections

After completing this laboratory activity, you will be able to:

■ Use the **Connect to a network** dialog box to select a preferred wireless network from several identified networks.

■ Evaluate a wireless network connection problem using the Network and Sharing Center.

■ Evaluate a wireless network connection using the **Wireless Network Connection Status** dialog box.

■ Evaluate a wireless network connection problem using the **Network Connection Details** dialog box.

■ Check if a wireless network is using security and what type of security is being used.

Introduction

In this laboratory activity, you will explore the features and options associated with making a new wireless network connection. The general configuration of a laptop computer will automatically make a wireless connection when the preferred wireless network is in range. When using a laptop, it is often reconfigured to connect to another wireless network when available, for example in an airport, a coffee shop, a hotel, a school, or another location.

When performing this lab activity in a school lab environment, you may have problems caused by the computer being used by a previous student. For example, once a wireless connection is made, it is often retained even after being disconnected. You may need to delete any existing wireless connection to fully benefit from this lab activity.

A computer equipped with a wireless adapter and not connected to a Wireless Access Point will appear in the Network and Sharing Center similar to that in the following screen capture.

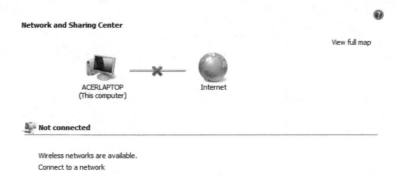

A red *X* indicates that there is no established wireless connection to any wireless devices. You will also see two links: **Wireless networks are available** and **Connect to a network**. After selecting the **Connect to a network** link, you will see a dialog box similar to the following.

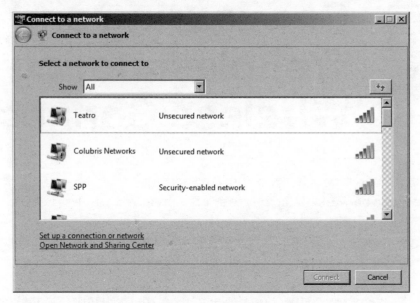

A list of all available wireless networks will be displayed. They will be listed in descending order with the strongest wireless signals at the top and the weakest wireless signals at the bottom. You will also see the strength of the wireless signal indicated by a green bar graph. The more green bars, the stronger the signal. "Secured-enable network" or "Unsecured network" is listed beside the name of the wireless network. An "Unsecured network" has not configured any security, such as WEP, WAP, and 802.11x. If the wireless network is labeled "Secured-enable network," you will need to know the security passphrase or encryption key to gain access.

You can view information about the type of security being used to protect the wireless connection by hovering the mouse over the "Security-enabled network" text. A message similar to the one in the following partial screen capture will appear.

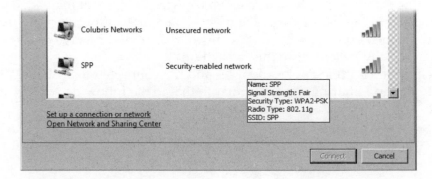

In the sample partial screen capture, you can see that the SPP network is using WAP2-PSK security method. You will need the passphrase or pre-shared key to access the network.

To make a connection to a wireless network location, you select the wireless network from the list and then click the **Connect** button. Even after connecting to a Wireless Access Point, you could still experience problems. Look at the following screen captures comparing a good connection to a connection experiencing problems.

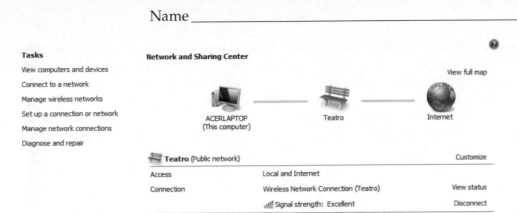

Good Connection to Teatro Wireless Access Point

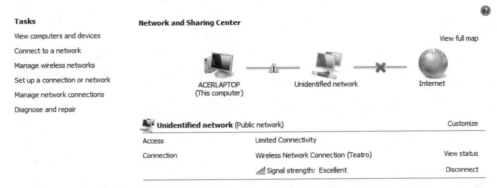

Problems with Teatro Wireless Access Point Indicated

The connection experiencing problems indicates a problem with the text "Unidentified network" and with a yellow triangle containing an exclamation mark. There is also a red *X* indicating no Internet connection. Even though there is a problem with the Wireless Access Point, the signal strength indicated is excellent and a connection to the wireless network connection known as (Teatro) has been indicated. This screen capture was taken from a network with a failed wireless router. The router could still broadcast a signal but could not support a connection to a computer, Internet access, or provide an IP address through its DHCP service. Look at the following screen captures comparing network status information.

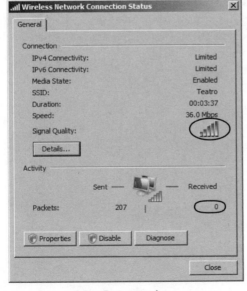

No Connection

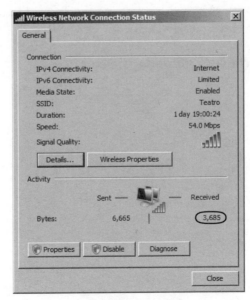

Good Connection

The good connection is recording packet activity for both "Sent" and "Received." The no connection example is only recording activity for "Sent" packets. There are no "Received" packets. You can also see the signal strength associated with the no connection example has excellent signal strength. The signal strength is more closely associated with the speed of the connection rated in Mbps. Poor signal strength will usually only support a very low data rate from 1 Mbps to 5 Mbps. Excellent signal strength will support a data rate of 36 Mbps to 54 Mps or higher, depending on the wireless standard design of the adapter, such as 802.11g or 802.11n.

Clicking the **Details** button will display the **Network Connection Details** dialog box, allowing you to view important details about the wireless adapter. Compare the following screen captures.

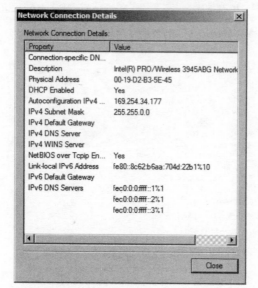

Failed Network Connection

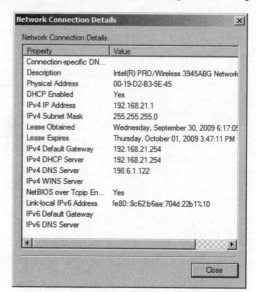

Completed Network Connection

When a connection fails, the computer is issued an APIPA IPv4 address that starts with 168.254. A good connection will have an IPv4 address other than an APIPA address. In the screen capture of the completed network connection, the IPv4 address starts with 192.168, which indicates a typical private IPv4 address, such as the type used by a home-office router or gateway. The connection could also have a different IPv4 address, but the most common default assigned IPv4 address starts with 169.254.

A wireless computer can be configured to automatically connect to more than one WAP or even to automatically connect to a WAP with the strongest signal. You can configure the wireless computer to connect to a WAP in a preferred order. Look at the following screen capture of the **Manage Wireless Networks** dialog box.

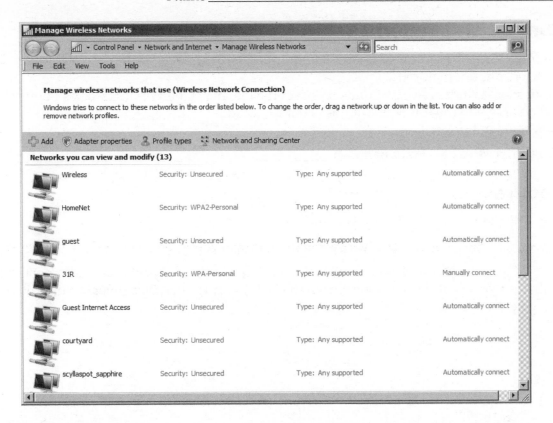

The **Manage Wireless Networks** dialog box contains a list of previously established wireless network connections. The wireless network listed at the top of the list is given the highest priority when the wireless computer comes in range of any of the listed networks. You can change the order by using the mouse to select and drag a wireless network to another place in the list. You can also add or delete network profiles using this dialog box.

In the previous figure, the wireless networks in the list have unique names. The names of the wireless networks are also their SSID. This is a good reason you should change the default name of a WAP to a descriptive name other than the default name. If all wireless networks used the same wireless router with the same default SSID, it would cause connection problems. A person using a laptop and changes physical locations to such a location as a hotel in a large city could have several WAPs in range of their room. The laptop would try to automatically connect to the strongest signal of the WAP with the same name. Because the WAP could be using a security method such as WEP, the user would not be able to connect to the WAP. The user would most likely not know the reason for the failure. All the typical user would know is that they cannot establish a connection to the desired WAP and it keeps prompting them for a password or such.

Always reassign a WAP SSID. Never leave the default SSID. The main reason is security. A hacker can easily obtain the default SSID of any wireless device by brand from the Internet and usually the default password as well. A hacker then can access and reconfigure the WAP to meet his or her own needs. Hacking a WAP is quite common if the technician has not changed the default SSID and the default administrative password.

You probably will not have more than one or two WAPs within reach of your lab computer. However, you will still be able to view the **Manage Wireless Networks** dialog box.

Equipment and Materials

❑ Windows Vista or Windows 7 computer equipped with a wireless adapter. A laptop is preferred, but not required.

❑ One or more Wireless Access Points set up in the lab area. One Wireless Access Points should provide access to the Internet, but this is not required.

❑ The following information:

SSID (Wireless Access Point name): _____

Procedure

1. _____ Report to your assigned workstation.

2. _____ Boot the computer and verify it is in working order.

3. _____ Open the Network and Sharing Center. If a wireless connection already exists, you will need to disconnect it. To disconnect from the WAP, simply click **Disconnect** as indicated in the following screen capture.

4. _____ Create a new instance of a wireless connection by selecting **Connect to a network** from the **Tasks** list displayed in the Networking and Sharing Center.

The **Connect to a network** dialog box will display, listing all wireless networks within range of the computer.

5. _____ Select the wireless network (SSID) that was set up for this lab activity. Some school lab environments may display many wireless networks. The wireless network inside the lab area will most likely produce the strongest signal and be displayed at the top of the list. Select the wireless network indicated in the list of materials for this lab. You will see a dialog box showing a progress bar until the connection is completed.

When the connection is successfully completed for the first time, a dialog box will appear requesting you select the type of network location.

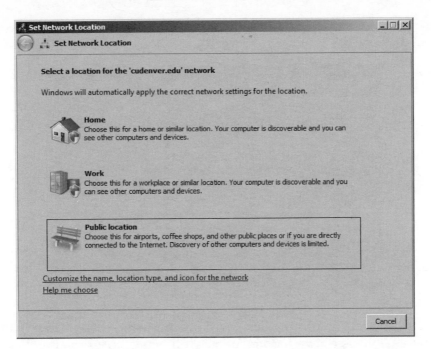

In Windows Vista, your choices are **Home**, **Work**, and **Public location**. In Windows 7, your choices are **Home network**, **Work network**, and **Public network**. If you cannot establish a connection, you will see a dialog box similar to the following informing you that you have an unsuccessful connection.

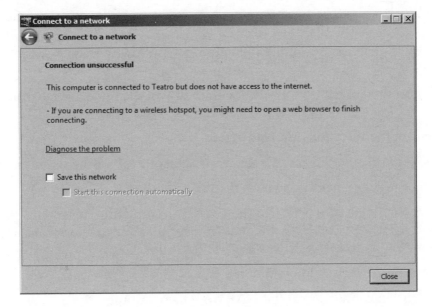

You can select the **Diagnose the problem** link to run automatic diagnostic tests. The following dialog box will display.

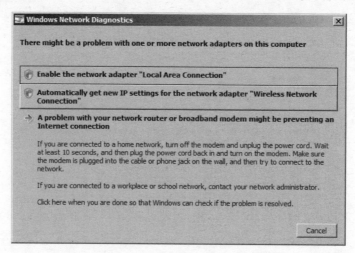

Normally, the appropriate option to select would be **Automatically get new IP settings for the network adapter "Wireless Network Connection"**. If this fails to fix the problem, then you would check if another computer is connected to the WAP. If another computer is connected wirelessly to the WAP, then the problem is your computer. If no one else can connect to the WAP, then the problem is most likely the WAP. You can reset the WAP and then try connecting.

6. _____ Have your instructor check your lab activity to verify a successful wireless connection.

7. _____ To gain some firsthand troubleshooting experience, disconnect the electrical power to the WAP. Open your computer's Network and Sharing Center after the power is disconnected from the WAP and view the information displayed about the wireless connection.

8. _____ Disconnect the cable that is used to establish the connection from the WAP to the Internet. Reconnect the power to the WAP with the Internet connection disconnected. Open the Network and Sharing Center to view the information displayed.

9. _____ Reconnect the WAP Internet connection.

10. _____ Open Network and Sharing Center. Click **Disconnect** for the wireless connection.

11. _____ Disconnect the electrical power to the WAP.

12. _____ Try establishing a connection to the WAP from the computer while the electrical power is disconnected from the WAP. View the dialog boxes that are generated and try to repair the connection with the options that appear in the dialog box.

13. _____ Reconnect the electrical power to the WAP.

14. _____ Reestablish a connection to the WAP from the computer.

15. _____ Open the Network and Sharing Center and select the **Manage Wireless Networks** option. View the information provided. Your lab activity might only have one wireless network to appear.

Look at the information provided, such as the type of security being used. The order in which the computer tries to connect to a wireless network starts at the top and descends to the bottom. You can change the order by simply selecting a preferred network connection and dragging it to the new position.

16. _____ Return all materials to their proper storage area and then answer the review questions.

Review Questions

1. How is a problem with a wireless connection between a computer and a WAP indicated in the Network and Sharing Center? _____

   _____

   _____

2. If the WAP has lost its connection to the Internet, how is it indicated in Network and Sharing Center? _____

3. What IPv4 address is used to indicate that the WAP such as a router has failed to issue a DHCP IPv4 address? _____

4. How can you determine or verify if a problem exist between the computer and the WAP by looking at the **Wireless Network Connection Status** dialog box? _____

   _____

   _____

5. Why should you change the default SSID of a WAP? _____

   _____

WINDOWS VISTA OR LATER

Name_____ Date _____

Class/Instructor _____

Wireless Throughput vs. Distance

After completing this laboratory activity, you will be able to:

■ Describe the relationship between distance and wireless network throughput.

■ Describe the effect of various objects on wireless network throughput.

Introduction

In this laboratory activity, you will explore the effects of distance in relation to wireless network throughput and the effect of placing objects in the direct line of sight of wireless devices. To observe the differences in throughput, you will transfer the contents of a large file. The file should be 20 MB or larger. One way to obtain a large file is to create one with Microsoft Paint. To increase the file size, increase the color depth and picture size until the desired file size is reached. Save the file as a bitmap file. A bitmap file has a BMP file extension. A bitmap does not employ compression techniques, and thus will not reduce the size of the file when saved. Do *not* use any other file format such as TIF or GIF.

Wireless LANs have become popular because of their reputation for being easy to install. Cables can be difficult to install through partitions and can be a hazard when run across the floor. Although wireless networks are easier to install, distance and building materials can adversely affect wireless LAN activity.

The type of material used to construct the wall and the angle through which the transmission travels through the wall affects transmission. For example, if the path between the source and destination computers runs directly through the wall, the affect of the building material on transmission will be less than if the path between the source and destination computers ran at an angle through the wall. The angled path has the same effect on transmission as does a thicker wall. Look at the following illustration.

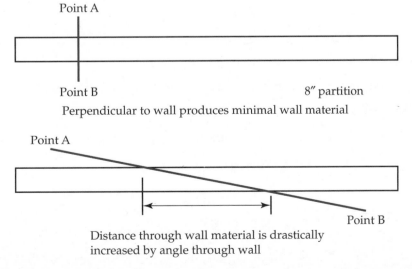

Point A

Point B   8″ partition

Perpendicular to wall produces minimal wall material

Point A

Point B

Distance through wall material is drastically increased by angle through wall

As you can see, when the transmission travels directly through the wall, the distance through the material is much shorter than when the transmission travels at an angle. The angle in the example would produce three times the effect of the 8" wall or approximately 24".

You can record throughput by measuring the amount of time it takes to transfer the file from source to destination. You can also observe the effects of throughput by looking at the signal strength indicator in the **Wireless Network Connection Status** dialog box. To access the **Wireless Network Connection Status** dialog box, open the Network and Sharing Center. Click **View Status** for the wireless network connection. A dialog box similar to the following will display.

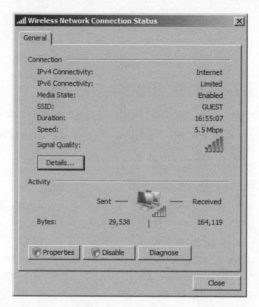

You will see the effects of signal strength in the bar graph. You will also see a change in the speed rating. As distance is increased, the speed will drop. The throughput of the signal will also decrease as the distance increases. Increasing the distance will cause the signal to become weaker at the receiving computer and become more susceptible to radio interference. Radio interference will corrupt packets and cause the packet to be resent. The overall effect is loss in throughput.

Equipment and Materials

❑ Windows Vista or Windows 7 computer configured with a wireless network adapter.
❑ Laptop configured with a wireless network adapter.
❑ Measuring device, such as a tape measure or yardstick, to measure distances.

Procedure

1. _____ Report to your assigned computers (laptop and PC).

2. _____ Boot the computers and verify they are in working order.

3. _____ Place the laptop 3' from the PC.

4. _____ Create a large bitmap file on one of the computers.

5. _____ Transfer the file to the other computer and record in the following chart the amount of time it takes. Repeat this step five times.

	File Size	Time	Throughput
1			
2			
3			
4			
5			
Average			

6. _____ Calculate the average time and average throughput.

7. _____ Increase the distance between computers to 25'.

8. _____ Transfer the file to the other computer and record in the following chart the amount of time it takes. Repeat this step five times.

	File Size	Time	Throughput
1			
2			
3			
4			
5			
Average			

9. _____ Calculate the average time and average throughput.

10. _____ Increase the distance between computers to 50'.

11. _____ Transfer the file to the other computer and record in the following chart the amount of time it takes. Repeat this step five times.

	File Size	Time	Throughput
1			
2			
3			
4			
5			
Average			

12. _____ Calculate the average time and average throughput.

13. _____ Test the effect of walls and doors on throughput. Use the **Wireless Network Connection Status** dialog box to observe the effects. First, test data transmission directly through the wall and then at an acute angle through the wall.

14. _____ Answer the review questions.

15. _____ Return all materials to their proper storage area.

Review Questions

1. Describe the effect on throughput in relationship to distance? _____

   _____

   _____

2. What is the major benefit of wireless LAN? _____

   _____

   _____

3. What are some concerns of wireless LAN throughput in relation to distance? _____

   _____

   _____

   _____

Wireshark Network Protocol Analyzer (Part I)

After completing this lab activity, you will be able to:

- Identify the common features of a network protocol analyzer.
- Recall the purpose of the WinPcap program.
- Differentiate between promiscuous and non-promiscuous mode as related to a network protocol analyzer.
- Use Wireshark to perform a simple capture.

Introduction

In this laboratory activity, you will download, install, and configure the network protocol analyzer program Wireshark previously known as *Ethereal* (pronounced "ether real").

Note
The name "Ethereal" was changed to "Wireshark" in 2006 because of a legal issue when its creator Gerald Combs changed employment.

There are many commercial network protocol analyzers available that cost a thousand dollars or more. Wireshark is a free, open source product developed under the GNU General Public License. While originally developed for Linux operating systems, it runs on all the latest versions of Windows. Many Linux operating systems incorporate a version of Ethereal or Wireshark as part of the administrative tools. Ethereal was originally written by Gerald Combs in 1998. Since that time, many programmers in the open source community have contributed to the development of Ethereal and now Wireshark.

You can still download a copy of the last version of Ethereal at www.ethereal.com or the very latest version called Wireshark at www.wireshark.org.

A network protocol analyzer captures network frames or packets and then displays details about the contents. Look at the following screen capture to see a sample Wireshark capture.

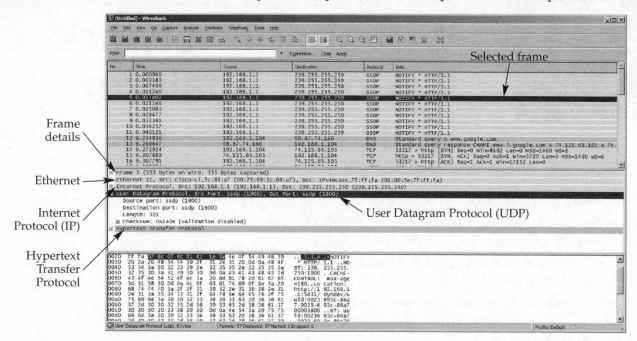

A frame is a collection of data transferred across a network as a single unit captured by the Wireshark protocol analyzer. The frame encapsulates protocol packets such as Ethernet, IP, UDP, and HTTP. All protocols that are part of the single transfer of data are collectively known as a *frame*.

There is a tremendous amount of information displayed in a Wireshark capture. Looking from left to right at the top half of the display, you will first see a number assigned to each frame starting with 1. The next column displays the exact amount of time from the start of Wireshark until the frame was captured. The next two columns display the source and destination IP addresses in IPv4 or IPv6 format, depending on which format is being used by the network operating system. In the fifth column, the protocol is identified such as ARP, DNS, DHCP, etc. Wireshark can identify approximately 700 different protocols—more protocols than you will ever normally need to monitor. The last column on the right provides a brief bit of information about each frame captured. Some examples of this information are a request to log on, DHCP information, and a response to another frame.

You can use Wireshark to study the protocols presented in your training course. You can either make your own captures or download sample captures of protocols that are available at the Wireshark Web link: http://wiki.wireshark.org/SampleCaptures.

You can also use Wireshark to conduct experiments such as watching the sequence of packets and protocols during the initial startup of a computer on a network. You can see how the booting computer sends out a series of frames to identify itself to other computers and devices on the local area network. You can also see it request an IP address from the DHCP server.

Conducting a protocol analysis will help you better understand how network systems operate. At first, Wireshark as any other protocol analyzer will be very intimidating, but the more you use it, the more comfortable you will be. Later, you will be able to use a protocol analyzer to inspect the network system and detect intruders, virus activities, and malfunctioning equipment.

Be sure to read the *Wireshark User's Guide* available at the Wireshark Web site (www.wireshark.org/docs/wsug_html_chunked). Look over the summary of features such as filtering, which allows you to capture only packets related to a particular protocol, a particular computer, or a group of computers identified by IP address.

A protocol analyzer is an extremely useful tool when it comes to network security. It will allow you to study how security protocols function and can be used to identify the source of an attack on a network system. If you are to become a true networking professional, you need to master how to use a protocol analyzer.

Note
Ethereal required that the WinPcap program be installed on a Windows operating system before installing the Ethereal program. WinPcap is a software program that must be installed to allow live packet captures on a Microsoft operating system. Wireshark will automatically detect any existing WinPcap version that might be already installed on the computer and will offer to install the latest version during the installation process.

Equipment and Materials

❑ Windows XP, Windows Vista, or Windows 7 computer.
❑ The location of where to store the Wireshark captures as indicated by your instructor.

Capture location: _____

Note
This lab activity is based on Wireshark version 1.2.1 and may be different but similar to the version you will be using.

Procedure

1. _____ Report to your assigned workstation.

2. _____ Boot the computer and verify it is in working order.

3. _____ Connect to the Internet and locate the Wireshark home page or the Wireshark download page (www.wireshark.org/download.html).

Note
Wireshark may already be installed on the workstation by a previous student. If Wireshark is installed, go to step 6.

---

4. _____ Read the instructions for installing Wireshark. Select the correct version of Wireshark matching your operating system (32-bit or 64-bit). Download Wireshark and install it, following the instructions for your particular operating system. The installation program is very intuitive and makes it very easy to install Wireshark. Be sure to select the **Install desktop shortcut** option during the installation process.

5. _____ After Wireshark is installed, look for the desktop icon similar to the following. If you cannot locate the icon, call your instructor for assistance.

6. _____ Start Wireshark by double-clicking the **Wireshark** icon. You can also start Wireshark by selecting it from the **Start | All Programs**. After Wireshark is started, you should see a page similar to the one in the following screen capture.

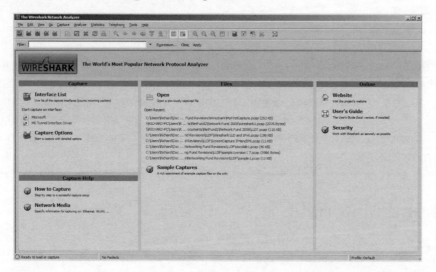

Take a few minutes to study the interface. Notice the **User's Guide** link in the right column. The *Wireshark User's Guide* provides a great deal of information on all topics related to Wireshark. Also, notice the **Sample Captures** link in the center column. The **Sample Captures** link will take you to a list of over 50 of the most common protocols encountered today. You will be making your own sample captures during this course.

7. _____ Wireshark must know which network interface to use before beginning a capture. Look at the following screen capture.

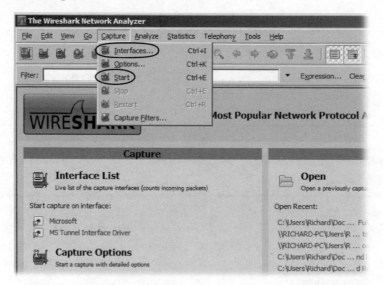

You must first select the network interface you will use for the capture. Some computers, especially laptops, have more than one network interface. They can have one or two network adapter cards that use an RJ-45 cable connector and may also have a wireless network card installed. A telephone modem also counts as a network interface. If you have more than one network interface, you will need to select the one you will be using. Look at the following screen captures to see a listing of interfaces on two different computers.

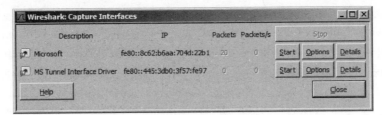

Laptop

Desktop

The first capture was taken from a Windows Vista laptop and the second from a Windows Vista desktop. The top capture used Wireshark version 1.0, and the second used Wireshark version 1.2.1. The version you are using may be even later, so there can be some differences between the screens in the captures and that on your computer.

Notice that the laptop (top screen capture) is using an IPv6 address and the desktop (bottom screen capture) is using an IPv4 address. You can use Control Panel to access the local area network adapter status and properties to help you identify the correct network adapter to use. Select the interface you will be using for this exercise. If you are not sure which one to use, ask your instructor.

8. _____ After choosing the interface, begin the capture series by selecting **Start** from the **Capture** menu. You may also use the shortcut keys [Ctrl] [E]. As the capture runs, you will see a display similar to the one in the following screen capture.

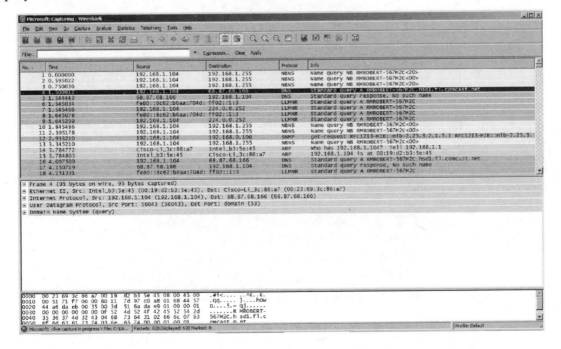

Wireshark will continue to capture frames until you stop the capture process. To stop the capture process, select **Stop** from the **Capture** menu or simply press [Ctrl] [E] once more. The keyboard combination [Ctrl] [E] not only starts a capture session, it also stops it.

After several packets have been captured, stop the capture process. If no packets have been captured, restart the capture and then access the Internet to start an exchange of packets. You should see a series of packets being captured similar to those in the previous screen capture. If not, call your instructor for assistance.

9. _____ Look closely at the capture. The columns are labeled left to right as follows: No., Time, Source, Destination, Protocol, and Info. You can rearrange the information in each column by simply clicking the top of the column in the area indicated in the following screen capture.

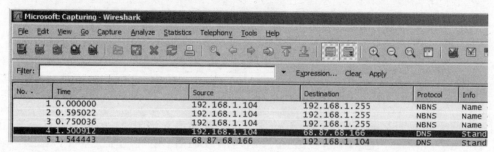

The frame numbers will change from ascending to descending order with a mouse click. You can also quickly sort other columns the same way. Click at the top of each column now to see how it affects the column contents.

10. _____ Select the **File** menu to see a list of menu items similar to those in the following screen capture.

The **Close** menu option will close the display of captured packets. You will be prompted to save the capture or to continue without saving the capture.

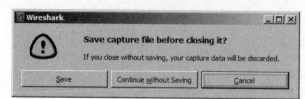

When you select the **Save** option, you will be prompted to select a location to which to save the contents of your capture. Look at the following screen capture of typical **Save file as** dialog box options.

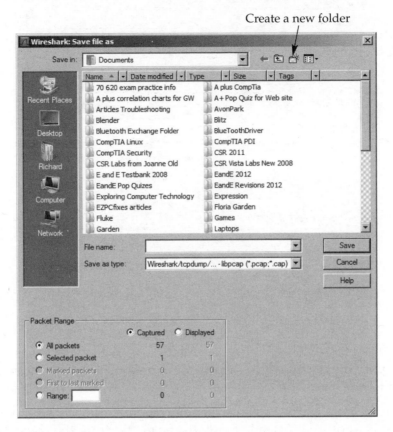

The operating system directory is presented. You will need to select a location and a file name for the capture. You can create a new folder to store your capture in by clicking the **Create New Folder** icon at the top of the dialog box. You can also navigate to a location other than Documents if you wish.

Also, notice that you are presented with options to save **All packets**, **Selected packet**, or a **Range** of packets.

Save your first capture to the location indicated by your instructor, and then call your instructor to inspect your lab.

11. _____ Select the **Capture** menu and then the **Options** menu item or use the keyboard combination [Ctrl] [K].

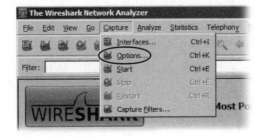

The **Wireshark Capture Options** dialog box will display and will look similar to that in the following screen capture.

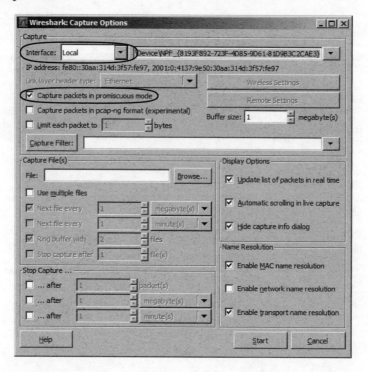

Here you can modify the default Wireshark capture options to meet your needs. The first option to look at is **Interface**, which indicates the default network adapter to use for the capture.

Another option is **Capture packets in promiscuous mode**. Promiscuous mode enables all network traffic to be captured instead of only traffic to and from the chosen network interface. Pay particular attention to the section labeled **Name Resolution** located in the lower, right corner of the dialog box. In this section, you can configure Wireshark to automatically resolve (present) names in the frame capture based on such items as the MAC address, network name, or transport name. For example, MAC name resolution converts the MAC address's first six numbers to the adapter manufacturer name, such as "Intel." Network resolution converts an IP address to its Fully Qualified Domain Name such as mailserver.mynetwork.com. Transport name resolution converts the port number to the equivalent protocol, such as port 110 to POP3.

Another feature is the **Capture Filter** option. As you will see, networks generate a great deal of traffic displayed as frames. In fact, thousands of frames can be generated in a very short time. The **Capture Filter** option allows you to limit the scope of the capture to a particular area of the total network data being collected. For example, you can filter by IP address, MAC address, protocol, port number, and several other options.

To learn all the possible options, refer to the *Wireshark User's Guide*. Also, check out the following Wireshark link: http://wiki.wireshark.org/CaptureSetup.

12. _____ Answer the review questions and then close the Wireshark protocol analyzer.

Review Questions

1. How much does Wireshark cost? _____

2. How many protocols can Wireshark capture and identify? _____

3. What is WinPcap? _____

_____

4. What is the difference between promiscuous and non-promiscuous mode? _____

_____

_____

5. How can the sequence order of packets be changed from ascending to descending? _____

_____

6. How can you sort protocols by type? _____

_____

7. What does the box with the plus sign mean at the beginning of an information line? _____

_____

Laboratory Activity

21

Name_____ Date _____

Class/Instructor _____

Wireshark Network Protocol Analyzer (Part II)

After completing this lab activity, you will be able to:

- Identify common encapsulation protocols.
- Interpret protocol details.
- Use Wireshark to open previously saved captures.
- Use Wireshark to save a capture.

Introduction

In an earlier laboratory activity, you were introduced to the Wireshark network protocol analyzer. In this laboratory activity, you will take a closer look at various Wireshark options. A complete understanding of all Wireshark options and functions cannot be covered in a single laboratory activity. This laboratory activity covers only what you need to know to get you started analyzing frame and packet contents. In future laboratory activities, you will use Wireshark to observe the following:

- How a workstation announces its presence to other workstations.
- How the network browser operates.
- How a workstation properly shuts down or disconnects from a network.
- How files are exchanged (shared).
- How information is retrieved from the Internet.
- How e-mail is transferred.
- How security is implemented during network logon.

Additional options and functions are presented in these upcoming laboratory activities. For now, only the options and functions needed to run elementary laboratory activities are covered.

In this lab activity, you will see how data is encapsulated. Encapsulation involves several different protocols, one encapsulated inside another. A Wireshark capture file is used in this laboratory exercise and will be provided by your instructor. The file name is Wireshark Sample 1. Using this file, you will look at the way a collection of protocols is assembled into a complete packet and frame. Pay particular attention to which protocol requires addressing information for the destination and source.

Note

Wireshark laboratory activities are based on Wireshark 1.2.1, which is the latest version at the time of this writing. Screen capture images and exact procedure steps may not exactly match this lab activity when using a newer version of Wireshark.

Equipment and Materials

❑ Two or more Windows XP, Windows Vista, or Windows 7 computers connected as a peer-to-peer network.
❑ USB storage device.
❑ Wireshark Sample 1 file.

Wireshark Sample 1 file location: _____

Note

Sample Wireshark files used in the lab activities can also be downloaded from www.RMRoberts.com.

Procedure

Note

Contents of a capture will vary according to what services are running at the time the capture was made as well as the type of devices and operating systems running in the network. When making captures, the use of a network hub is ideal. Networking devices such as switches, routers, and firewalls may limit the captures.

---

1. _____ Report to your assigned workstation(s).

2. _____ Boot the computers and make sure they are in working order.

3. _____ Open Wireshark from the **Start** menu (**Start | Wireshark**) or double-click the **Wireshark** icon on your desktop.

A screen similar to the following will display.

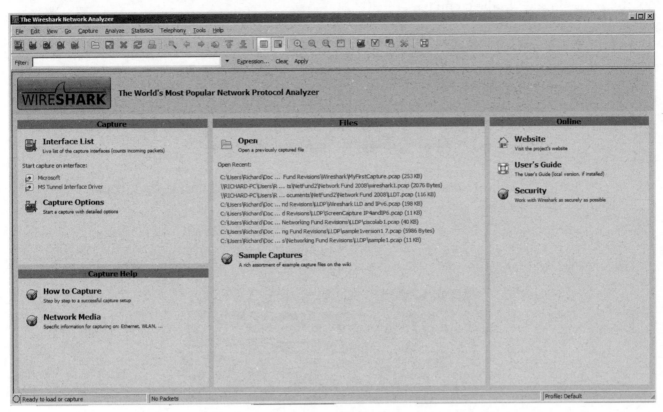

4. _____ Select **Capture | Interfaces**. The **Wireshark: Capture Interfaces** dialog box will display. Then, select the appropriate network adapter and click the **Start** button. You may also select the appropriate network adapter located in the **Capture** section of the screen under **Interface List**. The capture will automatically start when you select the interface.

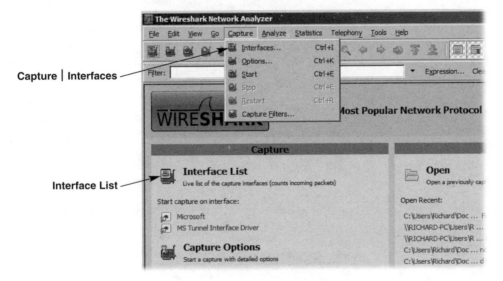

5. _____ After one or two minutes, stop the capture by selecting **Capture | Stop** or by clicking the **Stop** icon located in the menu bar.

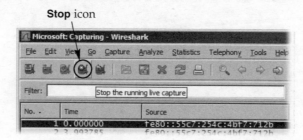

6. _____ After the capture is stopped, scroll through the captured frames and inspect the packets and protocols.

7. _____ Save the capture as a file on your computer or on a device such as USB storage device. If you try to start a new capture, Wireshark will automatically prompt you to save the file or discard it. The dialog box that will appear will look similar to the following.

You can also save a file from the main interface by selecting **File | Save** or **File | Save as**. Notice in the menu that you can also use the shortcut keys [Ctrl] [S] or [Shift] [Ctrl] [S].

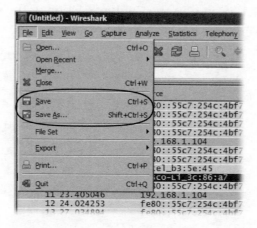

To save a capture, you can also click the **Save** icon, as shown in the following screen capture.

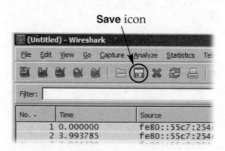

8. _____ After selecting any of the **Save** or **Save as** options, a dialog box similar to the following will display.

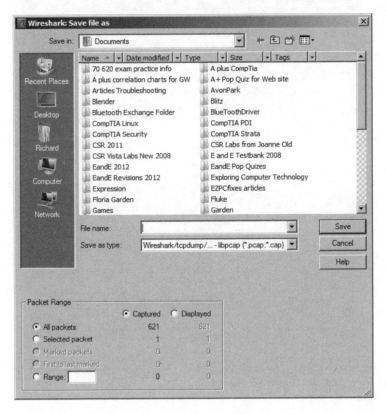

Use the dialog box to locate the folder/directory to which you want to save the capture. You must name the capture to save it. You should always use a meaningful name for the capture. For example, if you are studying the ARP protocol, you may wish to name the saved capture "ARP capture" or something similar. Also notice that in the **Packet Range** section, there are options that will allow you to save part of the capture. You can save a single frame or an entire range.

Note
Only save captures to the location indicated by your instructor.

For this exercise, save the capture you just created to your USB storage device if indicated by your instructor. Call your instructor to inspect your progress after saving the capture.

9. _____ Now, you will explore some of the configuration options. Open the **Wireshark: Capture Options** dialog box by selecting **Capture | Options** from the menu bar. You can also press the [Ctrl] [K] combination.

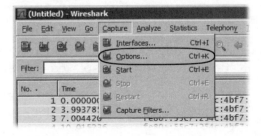

10. _____ After selecting **Options**, a dialog box similar to the following will display.

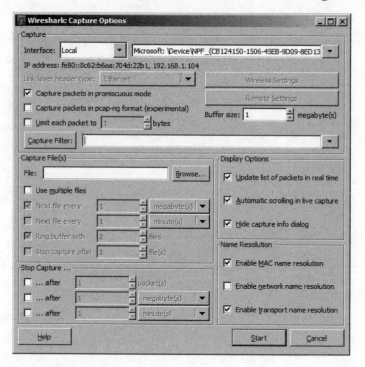

Look over the **Wireshark: Capture Options** dialog box carefully. Notice that there are five major sections for configuring capture options:

■ Capture.

■ Capture File(s).

■ Stop Capture.

■ Display Options.

■ Name Resolution.

The **Capture** section allows you to select a local or remote interface. **Capture packets in promiscuous mode** is selected by default. Yours may not be selected by default when the computer is shared by other students. Also, notice the **Capture Filter** button and text box, which will allow you to preselect specific types of captures based on protocol(s) or specific devices or locations.

The **Capture File(s)** section allows you to open a previously saved capture. You simply type in the path to the file location or click the **Browse** button to locate the path.

The **Stop Capture** section allows you to automatically stop a capture series after a specific lapse time, size of capture in megabytes, or a specific number of packets.

The **Display Options** section allows you to specify how you want to view packets while they are being captured.

The **Name Resolution** section is very handy for identifying items by name rather than by number. For example, the MAC manufacturer name can be displayed instead of the MAC address.

11. _____ Close the **Wireshark: Capture Options** dialog box and any other open Wireshark dialog boxes.

12. _____ Restart the Wireshark protocol analyzer and open the Wireshark Sample 1 file. To open a file, select the **File | Open** or use the [Ctrl] [O] key combination. Navigate to the location of the Wireshark Sample 1 file. Highlight the file and then click **Open**.

13. _____ Look at the protocols listed in the **Protocol** column. Notice that the protocols are displayed as acronyms. To see the full protocol name, select the packet with the desired protocol. The name of the protocol will appear in the middle pane.

14. _____ In the middle pane, notice the Ethernet II protocol. This protocol encapsulates all the other protocols. Looking at the Ethernet II section, you will see that the MAC address of the source and destination have been identified as Src: 00:0c:41:eb:89:df and Dst: 00:04:5a:4d:f1:0b. Expand the contents of the Ethernet II protocol by clicking the box with the plus sign (+) inside. You will see additional information.

15. _____ Look at the Internet Protocol section in the middle pane. The source and destination IP addresses are associated with this protocol. The source IP address is 192.168.0.3, and the destination IP address is 192.168.0.1.

16. _____ Now look at the next major protocol for frame 1: Transmission Control Protocol (TCP). Notice that the TCP protocol lists the ports associated with the protocol. The port for the source is 139, and the port for the destination is 1091. The complete address (MAC address, IP address, and the port number) of the source and destination is contained inside the three protocols: Ethernet II, IP, and TCP. This frame is an example of a connection-oriented transmission because all information for the source and destination is contained in the frame.

17. _____ Look at the bottom pane. It contains data from the packet selected in the top pane. The left side is displayed in hexadecimal, and the right side is a mixture of ASCII and indistinguishable characters that cannot be expressed in ASCII. Most of the time, this information will be meaningless. At other times, you will be able to read specific information, especially when the contents of the packet contain plain text files.

18. _____ Select the **Statistics | Summary**. You should see a dialog box similar to the one in the following screen capture. The **Statistics | Summary** dialog box provides you with a quick summary of statistics for the capture.

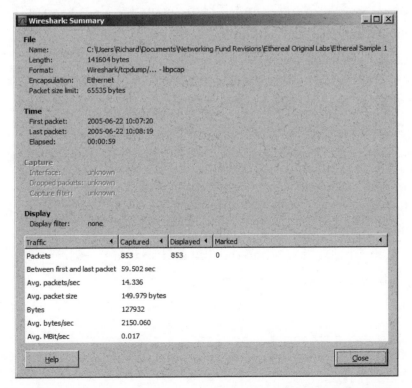

19. _____ Close the **Wireshark: Summary** dialog box and then select **Statistics I Protocol Hierarchy**. You should see a dialog box similar to the one in the screen capture.

Wireshark: Protocol Hierarchy Statistics							
Display filter: none							
Protocol	% Packets	Packets	Bytes	Mbit/s	End Packets	End Bytes	End Mbit/s
■ Frame	100.00 %	853	127932	0.017	0	0	0.000
⊟ Ethernet	100.00 %	853	127932	0.017	0	0	0.000
⊟ Internet Protocol	99.06 %	845	127506	0.017	0	0	0.000
⊟ Transmission Control Protocol	94.84 %	809	123218	0.017	74	4374	0.001
⊟ NetBIOS Session Service	86.17 %	735	118844	0.016	17	1536	0.000
⊟ SMB (Server Message Block Protocol)	84.17 %	718	117308	0.016	607	92285	0.012
DCE RPC	4.92 %	42	7980	0.001	42	7980	0.001
⊟ SMB Pipe Protocol	7.97 %	68	16713	0.002	0	0	0.000
⊟ DCE RPC	5.63 %	48	13220	0.002	0	0	0.000
Server Service	3.52 %	30	9456	0.001	30	9456	0.001
Workstation Service	0.94 %	8	1776	0.000	8	1776	0.000
Microsoft Spool Subsystem	0.47 %	4	852	0.000	4	852	0.000
Remote Registry Service	0.70 %	6	1136	0.000	6	1136	0.000
Microsoft Windows Lanman Remote API Protocol	2.34 %	20	3493	0.000	20	3493	0.000
⊟ NetBIOS Session Service	0.12 %	1	330	0.000	0	0	0.000
SMB (Server Message Block Protocol)	0.12 %	1	330	0.000	1	330	0.000
⊟ User Datagram Protocol	3.52 %	30	3844	0.001	0	0	0.000
⊟ NetBIOS Datagram Service	0.94 %	8	1760	0.000	0	0	0.000
⊟ SMB (Server Message Block Protocol)	0.94 %	8	1760	0.000	0	0	0.000
⊟ SMB MailSlot Protocol	0.94 %	8	1760	0.000	0	0	0.000
Microsoft Windows Browser Protocol	0.94 %	8	1760	0.000	8	1760	0.000
NetBIOS Name Service	2.58 %	22	2084	0.000	22	2084	0.000
Internet Control Message Protocol	0.70 %	6	444	0.000	6	444	0.000
Address Resolution Protocol	0.94 %	8	426	0.000	8	426	0.000
Help							Close

The **Wireshark: Protocol Hierarchy Statistics** dialog box provides you with a detailed list of statistics about each protocol captured and identified. Look over the list of protocols and notice that the dark blue bar in each of the **% Packets** column indicates the direct proportion of the protocol to the total amount of protocols captured. For example, Ethernet made up 100% of the frames captured, IP made up 99.06%, and TCP made up 94.84%, and so on.

20. _____ Close the **Wireshark: Protocol Hierarchy Statistics** dialog box.

21. _____ Now for some practice so you will become more familiar with using the Wireshark protocol analyzer. Answer the following questions about the Wireshark Sample 1 file capture.

■ What protocol(s) are used to encapsulate TCP? _____

■ What protocol(s) are used to encapsulate ARP? _____

■ What protocol(s) are used to encapsulate SMB? _____

_____

■ What does the acronym SMB represent? _____

■ What two port numbers are associated with TCP in frame 4? _____

■ How many seconds elapsed between the first and second frame captured? _____

■ How many frames total were captured? _____

■ How many minutes did the protocol analyzer run to capture all of the frames?

_____

22. _____ Close the Wireshark Sample 1 file by selecting **File I Close**.

23. _____ Start the protocol analyzer and capture your own sample of network activity. To generate network activity, access a shared folder on the network. After approximately one minute, stop the capture and view the contents. If you are not able to capture any contents, call your instructor for assistance.

24. _____ Save the contents of your first capture to the USB storage device. Use your name as the name of the captured file. Call your instructor to check your lab activity and look at the saved capture file.

25. _____ Select **Help | Contents** and familiarize yourself with the help file contents. The Help file will provide you with a lot of valuable information about the operation of Wireshark.

26. _____ Answer review questions and then return all materials to their proper storage area.

Review Questions

Choose answers based on the following protocols. Ethernet, IP, TCP, SMB.

1. Which protocol provides a field for the MAC address? _____

2. Which protocol provides a field for the IP address? _____

3. Which protocol provides a field for the port number? _____

4. Which protocol provided no address information or port number? _____

5. How does SMB know where to deliver a packet of data? _____

_____

Laboratory Activity

22

Name _____ Date _____

Class/Instructor _____

Using the ARP Command

After completing this laboratory activity, you will be able to:

- Recall the function of the Address Resolution Protocol (ARP).
- Use the **arp** command to identify contents of the ARP cache.
- Explain how to refresh and modify the contents of the ARP cache.
- Identify several utilities that cause the ARP cache to refresh.

Introduction

This laboratory activity will familiarize you with ARP as a protocol and as a command. ARP is used to resolve an assigned IP address to a MAC address on a local area network. The ARP cache is used in conjunction with the TCP/IP protocol to resolve IP addresses to MAC addresses. TCP/IP communications is only based on IP addresses, not MAC addresses or local computer names.

Look at the following illustration. It lists the typical sequence of ARP activity during the address resolution process. Notice the sequence of events that take place during an ARP request. Note that the ARP cache is updated at the computer sending the ARP request and at the computer receiving the ARP request.

Station1   Station2

1. ARP cache checked at Station1.
2. ARP request is sent to Station2.
3. ARP entry is added to Station2 ARP cache.
4. ARP reply is sent to Station1.
5. ARP entry is added to Station1 ARP cache.

The ARP cache is used to speed up the process of resolving IP addresses to MAC addresses. The ARP cache in the Windows operating system typically lasts for approximately 2 minutes unless it is requested again during the 2 minutes. If the ARP request is sent again during the 2-minute period, then the ARP cache will stay intact for 10 minutes. After 10 minutes, it must be refreshed by a complete series of ARP request steps.

Note
Exact time may vary according to the operating system and version being used.

Several switches can be used with the **arp** command. The most common switch is **-a**, which reveals the contents of the ARP cache. Another common switch is **/?** or **/help** which reveals all switches associated with the **arp** command.

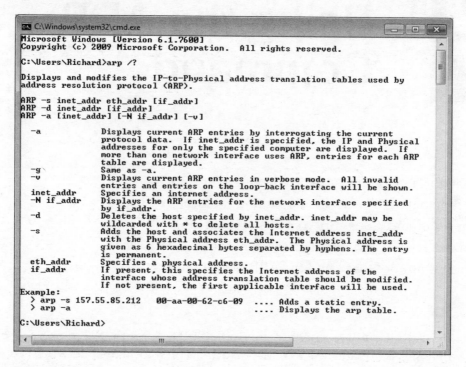

To add entries to the ARP cache, a function which requires generating an ARP request needs to be performed. Such requests are generated by the **ping** command or using the utilities that rely on the ARP request, such as viewing the network through Windows Explorer or looking at the **View Full Map** option in the Network and Sharing Center. Since the ARP cache can be refreshed by these various utilities, it is obvious that the utilities use ARP to identify local computers and equipment on the LAN.

Note

IPv6 does not use the ARP protocol to identify a workstation. The IPv6 protocol directly assigns an interface identifier to the network adapter. The interface identifier serves the same purpose as the MAC address. In the distant future, ARP will no longer be required to match an IP address to a MAC address. However, ARP will still exist for many years because Microsoft has always maintained backward compatibility with legacy operating systems.

When using Windows Vista or Windows 7, you must use an elevated permission to use all the various ARP switches. Simply open the command prompt from the **Start** menu by right-clicking **Command Prompt** and selecting **Run as Administrator** from the shortcut menu.

Equipment and Materials

❑ Two networked computers running Windows XP, Windows Vista, or Windows 7.

Note

This may be a partner lab.

Procedure

1. _____ Gather the required materials and report to your assigned workstation(s).

2. _____ Boot the computers and verify they are in working order.

3. _____ Identify the assigned IP address and MAC address for each computer in the lab activity. Use the **ipconfig/all** command as appropriate for the operating system. Record in the space provided the following information. You will need this information to verify the ARP request.

Station1 name: _____

MAC address: _____

IPv4 address: _____

_____

Station2 name: _____

MAC address: _____

IPv4 address: _____

4. _____ Open the command prompt and type and enter the **arp -a** command. The ARP cache should be empty and reveal no data. If not, wait approximately two minutes and then reissue the **arp -a** command. The ARP cache should clear after two minutes of no activity.

Note

If the computers are connected to a peer-to-peer network and if there is a gateway or router connected to it for Internet access, there will be a lot of background activity and the ARP cache will not clear. To clear the ARP cache, use the **-d** switch.

---

5. _____ Issue the **ping** command from Station1 to Station2 by typing and entering **ping Station2**. You need only send the command from one station, not both.

6. _____ Use the **arp -a** command at each of the two computers to see if the ARP cache has been updated. It should contain the IP address and MAC address of the other computer. If not, call your instructor for assistance.

7. _____ Wait two minutes to see if the ARP cache clears. Issue the **arp -a** command again to see if the cache is empty.

8. _____ After the ARP cache is empty, try using Network Neighborhood, My Network Places, or Computers Near Me to refresh the ARP cache. After using the appropriate utility, check the ARP cache at each computer using the **arp -a** command. The ARP cache should contain the IP address and MAC address of the opposite computer.

9. _____ Use the appropriate switch to view all the ARP command switches. In the spaces provided, and record their function.

10. _____ Practice using the **arp** command until you feel comfortable using it and know the expected results.

11. _____ Answer the review questions and then return the computers to their pre-lab activity condition.

Review Questions

1. What is the purpose of ARP? _____
   _____

2. How long does the initial ARP cache hold the resolved MAC and IP address? _____
   _____

3. What is the maximum amount of time the ARP cache remains before it requires to be refreshed?
   _____

4. Name several utilities that cause the ARP cache to refresh? _____
   _____
   _____

5. Which ARP switch produces the same result as **arp -a**? _____

Name_____ Date _____

Class/Instructor _____

Observing ARP, LLMNR, and NBNS with Wireshark

After completing this laboratory activity, you will be able to:

■ Explain the sequence of activities that occur when a workstation connects to a peer-to-peer network.

■ Explain the sequence of activities that occur when a workstation disconnects from a peer-to-peer network.

■ Interpret the contents of an ARP packet.

■ Recall the purpose of ARP.

■ Recall the purpose of NBNS.

■ Interpret the contents of an NBNS packet.

■ Recall the purpose of LLMNR.

■ Interpret the contents of an LLMNR packet.

■ Identify a broadcast packet by the destination IP address.

■ Recall the purpose of multicast.

■ Identify the address of IPv4 and IPv6 multicast.

Introduction

In this laboratory activity, you will use the Wireshark protocol analyzer to observe the sequence of activities that occur when a workstation connects to and disconnects from a peer-to-peer network. You will specifically examine three protocols: Address Resolution Protocol (ARP), Link-Local Multicast Name Resolution (LLMNR), and NetBIOS Name Server (NBNS). When a workstation with a static IP address is booted, it will perform two tasks: check if the workstation's IPv4 address is duplicated on the LAN and announce to the network browser that it has joined the workgroup. The workstation uses ARP to verify that the workstation's IPv4 address is not assigned to another workstation on the LAN. This verification is known as "gratuitous ARP request" or simply "ARP." ARP uses the Ethernet MAC address ff:ff:ff:ff:ff:ff to broadcast to all workstations when performing the verification.

The workstation then announces to the network browser that it has joined the workgroup. The Microsoft network browser is a software utility that maintains a central list of information about network devices and enables users to view the network devices. The NetBIOS Name Server (NBNS) protocol is used to carry the information about the workstation name. It is also used to match IP addresses to NetBIOS names. NBNS is designed to support the Windows Internet Naming Service (WINS). When the network browser receives this information, it adds the workstation's NetBIOS name to the browser list of workstations.

When you use Wireshark to observe the connectionless process, you will see the name of the workstation listed multiple times. This occurs for two reasons. First, the protocol used to broadcast the information is connectionless; hence, it does not guarantee packet delivery. The packet is sent repeatedly to ensure that the information is delivered. Second, the workstation performs more than one role and is identified by using a NetBIOS suffix attached to the name of the workstation. For example, a workstation called *Station1* may appear in the listing as Station 1 <00> and Station1 <20>. The <00> designates the workstation as a workstation. The <20> designates the workstation as a file server if it contains at least one file for sharing on the network. Some other common NetBIOS suffixes are listed below.

00 = workstation

01 = master browser

20 = file server

21 = Remote Access client

1B = domain master browser

Note

There are over 30 possible NetBIOS suffixes.

A Class C network is identified by the first three octets: 192.168.000. The last octet is used to identify the individual device on the Class C network. For example, *Workstation A* is 192.168.000.00**1**, and *Workstation B* is 192.168.000.00**2**. When a packet is broadcast to all devices in the 192.168.000 network, 255 is used in the last octet: 192.168.000.**255**.

Note

While performing the lab activity, the assigned network browser may attempt to update the browser listings. This can cause the sequence of displayed generated frames to be deceiving when viewed. Look at the source IP address to check if the first set of Ethernet frames captured are from *Workstation B* and not from *Workstation A* updating the browser lists. If the first frame captured is not ARP captured from *Workstation B*, you should run the experiment again.

The results for this lab activity will vary greatly during a live capture if you are using Windows XP. Windows Vista and Windows 7 use both the IPv4 and IPv6 protocol suites. As a result, there will be quite a difference in contents when a Windows XP capture is compared with a Windows Vista or Windows 7 capture.

The Wireshark Sample 2 file and Wireshark Sample 3 file are taken from a Windows XP capture containing only IPv4 packets. They will be used to provide a much simpler capture for example purposes.

Wireshark Sample 4 file was created using two Windows 7 computers connected directly together using a crossover cable to form a small peer-to-peer network. One computer ran the Wireshark protocol analyzer while the other computer was booted. Look at the three protocols (ARP, LLMNR, NBNS) that first appear during the boot process of Windows 7.

ARP is used to match the IPv4 address to the MAC address. LLMNR is a Microsoft protocol used for name resolution for IPv6. NBNS is another Microsoft protocol and is used for name resolution for legacy operating systems using IPv4.

A live Wireshark capture from a real peer-to-peer network will produce many more protocols because there will be much more protocol activity. You will most likely see protocol activity such as DHCP, SMB, Browser, HTTP, and LANMAN. Do not be overwhelmed by the number of frames and all the mysterious protocol acronyms. You will cover many protocols throughout this course. For now, we will concentrate on the three protocols directly associated with network device identification: ARP, NBNS, and LLMNR.

Duplicate IP Addresses

You cannot have duplicate IP addresses on a network even if you create the IP address manually. In Windows XP and Windows Vista, an error message will be displayed informing you of the duplicate IP address.

When Windows 7 detects a duplicate IPv4 address, it automatically configures the network adapter using a special IPv4 address that starts with 169.254. The 169.254.xxx.xxx address is known as an Automatic Private IP Address (APIPA). Windows 7 uses IPv6 for local link communications and does not require a valid IPv4 address.

Multicast Addresses

Multicast addresses are used for topology discovery, gateway discovery, and group membership. A computer or network device uses the multicast address to notify other devices on the local link when they join a network. You will see the IPv4 multicast address of 224.0.0.252 and the IPv6 multicast prefix address of ff02::1:3. These are standard multicast addresses. When these addresses are used, the broadcast is confined to the local link and will not pass through a network router.

Equipment and Materials

❑   Two Windows XP, Windows Vista, or Windows 7 workstations connected as a peer-to-peer. One workstation should have Wireshark installed. Workstations must be configured with a static IP address.

❑   Wireshark Sample 2 file.

   Wireshark Sample 2 file location: _____

❑   Wireshark Sample 3 file.

   Wireshark Sample 3 file location: _____

❑   Wireshark Sample 4 file.

   Wireshark Sample 4 file location: _____

Procedure

1. _____ Gather the required materials and report to your assigned workstation(s).

2. _____ Boot the computers and verify they are in working order and that Wireshark is installed on one of the workstations.

3. _____ Start the Wireshark protocol analyzer and then open the Wireshark Sample 2 file. This is a sample of a Windows XP computer starting up. Windows XP is using only IPv4 addresses. You will see ARP and NBNS.

4. _____ Look at the Ethernet II broadcast destination address and the ARP addresses. Use the screen capture below to assist you in finding the locations.

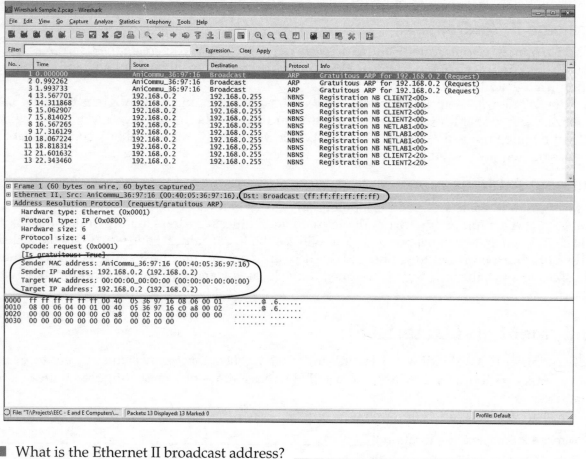

■ What is the Ethernet II broadcast address? _____

■ What is the ARP target MAC address? _____

■ What is the total number of ARP request? _____

■ What protocol is used to encapsulate ARP? _____

5. _____ Look at the third frame with the NBNS protocol.

■ What is the destination address of NBNS frame number 4? _____

6. _____ Select an NBNS frame with the mouse so that you can see the contents of the packet displayed in the middle section of the Wireshark screen.

■ Is NBNS carried inside a TCP or UDP packet? _____

■ Is NBNS considered connection-oriented or connectionless? _____

■ Which protocol or protocols are used to encapsulate the NBNS protocol? _____

_____

7. _____ Close the Wireshark Sample 2 file.

8. _____ Open the Wireshark Sample 3 file. This file contains an example of a workstation shutting down. As you can see in the example, the browser protocol and the NBNS protocol is used to announce the shutdown of the workstation.

■ What is the destination IPv4 address used by both Browser and NBNS. _____

_____

■ Which protocols are used in frame 2? _____

_____

9. _____ Close the Wireshark Sample 3 file.

10. _____ Open the Wireshark Sample 4 file.

11. _____ Expand frame four so you can see the contents of the Link-Local Multicast Name Resolution (LLMNR) protocol and the name of the computer workstation.

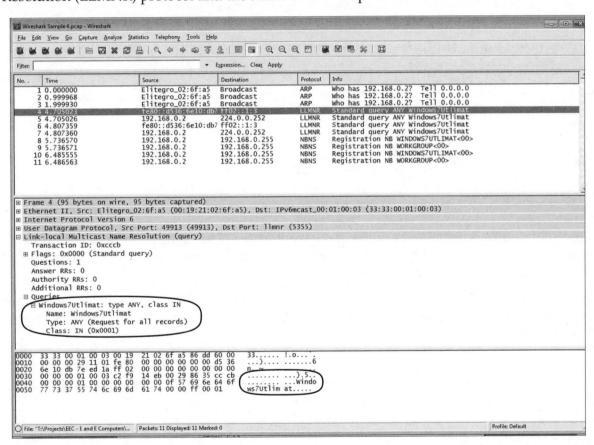

Notice the name of the workstation "Windows7Ultimate" is located in the center pane and in the bottom pane. The bottom pane shows the raw data that is transferred using the LLMNR protocol. The middle pane shows the converted raw data, which provides viewable information about the LLMNR packet contents.

12. _____ Select frame eight to view the contents of an NBNS packet.

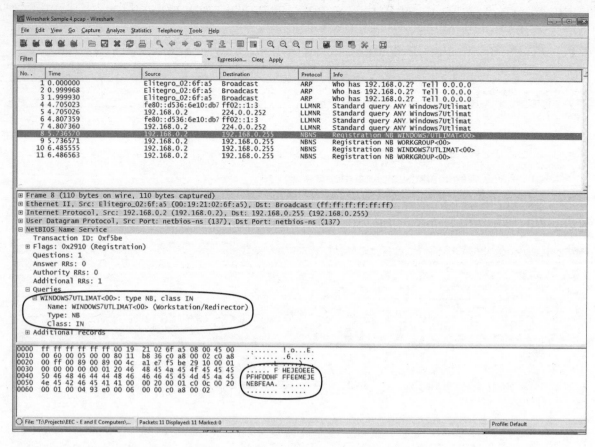

The NBNS packet identifies the name of the workstation "Windows7Ultimate." The bottom pane with raw data is encrypted. The workstation name does not appear in plain text as it did in the LLMNR raw data content.

As you can see, when both IPv4 and IPv6 are configured for a network adapter, three different protocols are used to identify the workstation: ARP, LLMNR, and NBNS. Only NBNS encrypts the contents of the packet.

Look closely at the destination IPv6 address for the LLMNR protocol. It will always be ff02::1:3.

Look at the destination IPv4 address for the LLMNR protocol. It will always be 224.0.0.252.

Now you will proceed to make your own capture and view the contents.

13. _____ Use the **ipconfig/all** command at each workstation and record the MAC address matching each workstation IP address.

Workstation A

MAC: _____

IP address: 192.168.000.1

Workstation B

MAC: _____

IP address: 192.168.000.2

14. _____ Shut down *Workstation B*.

15. _____ Start the Wireshark protocol analyzer on *Workstation A*. Be sure to select the proper interface card.

16. _____ Boot *Workstation B*. The Wireshark protocol analyzer will capture frames generated during the boot process of *Workstation B*.

17. _____ Wait approximately 1 minute and then stop the Wireshark protocol analyzer. The captured set of Ethernet frames will automatically display in the Wireshark GUI. The first frame captured must display the ARP protocol. If not, repeat the capture process.

18. _____ Answer review question 1 based on this capture.

19. _____ Unplug *Workstation B* from the network and then reboot the workstation.

20. _____ Attempt to change *Workstation B* IP address to match *Workstation A* creating a duplicate IP address. An error message will be presented when using Windows XP or Windows Vista. There will be no error message for Windows 7.

21. _____ Answer the remaining review questions and then restore the computers to their original configurations. You may save the Wireshark capture for later study and review.

Review Questions

1. What are the first two tasks carried out by a peer-to-peer workstation as it completes the boot process? _____

   _____

2. What would be the broadcast IP address for the last octet of a Class C network address identified as 192.168.000? _____

3. What is the destination Ethernet MAC address of a broadcast to all devices on a local network?

   _____

4. What does the acronym NBNS represent? _____

5. What is the purpose of NBNS? _____

   _____

   _____

6. What does the NetBIOS name suffix <20> indicate? _____

   _____

7. What is the purpose of LLMNR? _____

   _____

8. What does the acronym LLMNR represent? _____

   _____

9. What is the multicast destination address for IPv4? _____

10. What is the multicast destination address IPv6? _____

11. What is the purpose of multicast? _____

   _____

Laboratory Activity

24

Name_____ Date _____

Class/Instructor _____

Observing Background Communication with Wireshark

After completing this laboratory activity, you will be able to:

■ Identify common protocols used to support network background communication.

■ Summarize what generates network background activity.

Introduction

In this laboratory activity, you will become familiar with the various activities that take place in the background in a peer-to-peer network. These background activities occur without user intervention. The general purpose of the background communication is to identify users and equipment connected to the network to keep the browser information up-to-date. Other causes of background activity are the following:

■ Equipment such as routers sending out information about routes, which are constantly updated.

■ Mail client software automatically checking for e-mail.

■ The operating system continually looking for existing and newly-configured Plug and Play devices connected to local area network.

■ The workstation periodically checking for software and hardware updates. (The amount of activity generated by checking for updates varies according to the hardware devices and the software programs in the computer system.)

■ Servers periodically updating information about users and devices and storing the information in their database.

This normal background activity can be confusing when studying protocol activity. Most of the background activity can be eliminated by filtering the capture.

You will see references to computers in the Wireshark Sample 5 capture for this lab that are not turned on. For example, if a computer shares a printer with other computers, the name of the computer will show up in broadcast even when it is not connected to the network (turned off). This is because the computers connected to the network constantly check the status of other computers and devices on the network. If the computer is configured to access another computer's printer, you will see frames soliciting information about the status of the other computer and printer.

The Wireshark Sample 5 file used with this lab activity was created from a network containing a workstation with Internet access, several other workstations, and a printer. This sample capture will be very different from the sample capture you take during this lab activity.

Equipment and Materials

❑ Two computers running Windows 7 and configured as a peer-to-peer network with no Internet access.

❑   Wireshark Sample 5 file.

Wireshark Sample 5 file location:_____

Note
Be sure the firewall is not enabled on either workstation.

Procedure

1. _____ Report to your assigned workstation(s).

2. _____ Boot both computers. Wait two to three minutes for network activity to settle down, and then open the Wireshark network analyzer.

3. _____ Open the **Wireshark: Capture Options** dialog box and check that **Update list of packets in real time** and **Automatic scrolling in live capture** options are enabled. See the following screen capture.

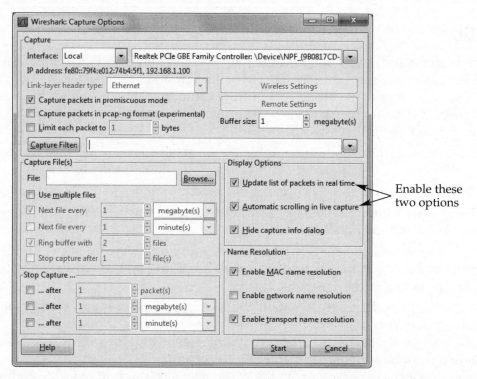

The **Update list of packets in real time** option allows you to see the packets being captured in "real time." The **Automatic scrolling in live capture** option causes the display window to scroll down as it fills with frames. This way, you will always see the very last frame captured as it occurs.

4. _____ Click **Start** to start the capture.

5. _____ Observe the packets being captured and wait approximately 20 minutes before stopping the capture.

6. _____ After you have stopped the capture, open the **Wireshark: Protocol Hierarchy Statistics** dialog box by accessing **Statistics | Protocol Hierarchy** as shown in the following screen capture.

A dialog box similar to the following will appear. Notice that the protocols are listed in their encapsulation order in the **Protocol** column. The percent of packets per protocol is indicated as a percentage and as a blue bar in the **Percentage** column.

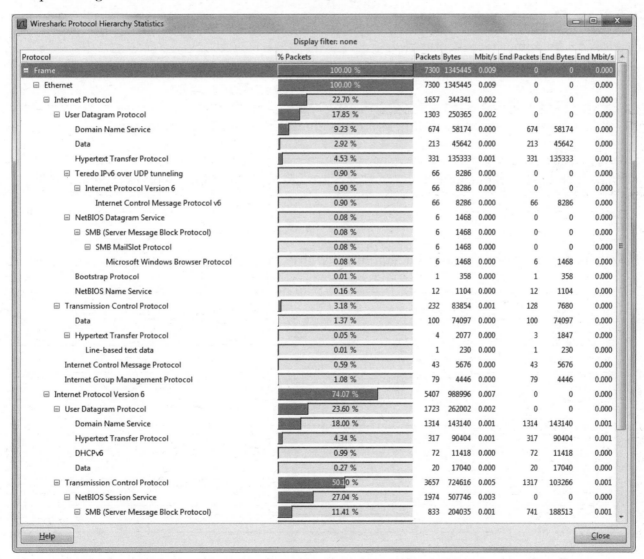

Use the information in the **Wireshark: Protocol Hierarchy Statistics** dialog box to answer the following questions:

How many frames were captured? _____

What were the most common three protocols identified in the protocol column? _____

_____

What was the purpose of most of the background activity? _____

_____

8. _____ Save your capture on a flash drive, naming the file "*<your name>* P2P idle 20 min." Use your name in place of *<your name>*.

9. _____ Open the Wireshark Sample 5 file provided by your instructor. This capture should be somewhat similar to the one you just made. Use the Wireshark Sample 5 capture to answer the review questions.

10. _____ Return all materials to their proper storage area.

Review Questions

1. How many frames were captured? _____

2. What was the purpose of most of the background activity? _____

_____

3. What were the most common three protocols identified in the **Protocol** column? _____

_____

4. What is the general purpose of network background communication while a system is idle?

_____

_____

5. What are some other causes of background activity? _____

_____

_____

_____

_____

_____

_____

_____

_____

_____

_____

_____

_____

_____

_____

Laboratory Activity

25

Name _____ Date _____

Class/Instructor _____

Observing Ping with Wireshark

After completing this laboratory activity, you will be able to:

- Use Wireshark to identify the protocols used to transport ping packets.
- Use Wireshark to read the data contents of a ping packet.

Introduction

In this laboratory activity, you will use Wireshark to capture ping packets sent between a source computer and a destination computer. You can use two workstations connected through a hub, switch, or crossover cable. If the two workstations are connected to a network that contains other workstations running at the same time you are performing the capture, you will need to filter the capture using the workstation's IPv4 address. Filtering by using the workstation's IPv4 address will eliminate the other packet activity and make the capture contents easier to read.

The **ping** command uses the ICMP or ICMPv6 protocol to carry the echo request. The version of the ICMP protocol depends on which operating system you are using and the format of the **ping** command issued. The following summarizes what occurs when using various formats of the **ping** command on a Windows Vista or later computer:

- **Ping** with the destination computer's IPv4 address forces ICMP to be used.
- **Ping** with the destination computer name uses ICMPv6 by default.
- **Ping -4** forces ICMP to be used.
- **Ping** with the IPv6 destination address forces ICMPv6 to be used.

When the **ping** command is issued on a Windows XP or earlier computer, ICMP is used by default. This is because Windows XP and earlier operating systems use IPv4 for local area network communication. Windows Vista and later use IPv6.

Note
ICMP is understood to represent ICMPv4 and does not usually appear with the "v4" designation.

Equipment and Materials

- ❑ Two Windows Vista or later computers connected as a peer-to-peer network using a hub, switch, or crossover cable.

Note

If more than two workstations are connected together as a local area network, you will need to filter the Wireshark capture limiting the captures to only the two workstations identified as source and destination.

Procedure

1. _____ Report to your assigned workstation(s).

2. _____ Boot both computers and verify they are in working order.

3. _____ Designate one of the computers as the source and the other as the destination.

4. _____ Run **ipconfig** and record the IP address of the source and destination computers.

Source IPv4 address: _____

Source name: _____

Destination of IPv4 address: _____

Destination name: _____

5. _____ On the source computer, open Wireshark and start a capture.

6. _____ Open the command prompt on the source computer and issue the **ping** command using the destination computer's IPv4 address. Note the protocol (ICMP or ICMPv6) used to carry the ping echo request.

7. _____ Start another capture and then ping the destination workstation by name. Note the protocol (ICMP or ICMPv6) used to carry the echo request.

8. _____ Start another capture and then ping the destination computer using the destination computer's name and the **-4** switch. Note the protocol (ICMP or ICMPv6) used to carry the ping echo request.

9. _____ Repeat the observations until you are sure of the results of using the **ping** command and the destination computer's IPv4 address, the **ping** command and the destination computer's name, and the **ping -4** command and the destination computer's name.

10. _____ Answer the review questions and then return all materials to their proper storage area.

Review Questions

1. Which protocol is used to carry a ping request using the **-4** switch? _____

2. What protocol is used to carry the ping request when identifying the destination by workstation name? _____

3. What is the total number of bytes contained in the Ethernet frame that utilizes the ICMP protocol? _____

4. What is the total number of bytes contained in the Ethernet frame that utilizes the ICMPv6 protocol? _____

5. What is the total number of bytes contained in the data field of ICMP?_____

6. What is the total number of bytes contained in the data field of ICMPv6? _____

7. Describe the contents of the ICMP data field that is readable. _____

_____

8. Describe the contents of the ICMPv6 data field that is readable._____

_____

9. What other identification of the source and destination besides the IP address is present in the Ethernet frame of the ping echo request and reply for both the ICMP and ICMPv6? (Hint: Look in the Ethernet frame.) _____

_____

Laboratory Activity

26

Name_____ Date _____

Class/Instructor _____

Installing Windows Server 2008

After completing this laboratory activity, you will be able to:

■ Summarize the overall installation process for Windows Server 2008 Standard.

■ Differentiate between a system upgrade and a custom (clean) installation.

■ Identify the minimum hardware requirements for Windows Server 2008 Standard.

■ Recall the guidelines used to create a secure server password.

■ Carry out proper procedures to install Windows Server 2008.

Introduction

In this laboratory activity, you will perform a custom installation of Windows Server 2008 Standard edition. This lab activity can be used as a guide for installing other Microsoft Server editions because they have very similar installation procedures.

If you have experience installing Windows Vista or Windows 7, you will find the procedure for installing Windows Server 2008 Standard very similar. If the hardware you are using is compatible, the installation will be very easy. Basically, all you do is follow a series of screen presentations that ask some very basic questions. The following table lists the hardware requirements for Windows Server 2008 Standard.

Hardware Component	Specifications
Processor	Minimum: 1 GHz for x86 or 1.4 GHz for x64 Recommended: 2 GHz
Memory	Minimum: 512 MB RAM Maximum (32-bit systems): 4 GB Maximum (64-bit systems): 32 GB Recommended: 2 GB or greater
Disk Space	Minimum (32-bit systems): 20 GB Minimum (64-bit systems): 32 GB Recommended: 40 GB or greater. *Computers containing more than 16 GB of RAM will require more disk space for hibernation, paging, and file dumps.
Display	Super VGA (800 × 600) or higher
Installation Drive	DVD-ROM

Note

Windows Server 2008 R2 is only available as 64-bit.

The minimum requirements will differ for a 32-bit and 64-bit system. The major difference is the speed of the CPU, the amount of RAM, and the required disk space. Most newly purchased computers will exceed the minimum requirements, but older systems that will be upgraded should be checked carefully to ensure they meet the minimal specifications.

Windows Server 2008 does not require activation and does not require a product key for evaluation purposes. Your instructor may request that you do not activate the copy of Windows Server 2008. You can operate Windows Server 2008 for 60 days without activation. This may be sufficient time for your course of study.

There are two types of server installation modes: upgrade and custom. The custom is also referred to as a *clean install*. When you perform a server upgrade, you replace the operating system but retain all user files such as documents and pictures. When you perform a custom installation, all user files are lost because the installation process automatically formats the partition using the default file format, NTFS.

During the installation process, one default user account, the Administrator account, is set up automatically. You will be prompted to create a password for the Administrator account. The password should consist of at least seven characters and be a combination of letters (both uppercase and lowercase); special characters such as $, %, !, and #; and numbers. For example, a password such as "baseball" is at least seven characters, but it is not acceptable because it is a common word easily found in the dictionary. A better password based on the word *baseball* would be *Ba$eBa11*. The dollar sign is used to represent the letter *S* and the number *1* is used to represent the letter *L*. Also notice that the letter *B* is in uppercase. All these factors help create a more secure password than just a plain word. Your instructor will recommend a password for this lab activity.

At the end of the lab activity, you will see a screen used to configure the server. You will not actually configure the server in this lab activity. You will configure the server in a later lab activity.

Earlier Microsoft server systems required that you pick the server role and other specifics during the installation process. This is now done after the server operating system has been installed. During a later lab activity, you will select the server role such as a domain controller, stand-alone server, DHCP server, print server, and DNS server.

Note

Screen captures for this lab activity were created using Windows Virtual PC and Windows Server 2008. Most screen captures will closely match but will not be an exact match to your screen images.

Equipment and Materials

❑ Computer that meets the minimum hardware requirements for Windows Server 2008 Standard.
❑ Windows Server 2008 installation DVD. (You can usually download a trial version from the Microsoft Web site. Use key words "Windows Server 2008 download" or the following URL address to locate the trial software: www.microsoft.com/windowsserver2008/en/us/trial-software.aspx.)
❑ The following information provided by your instructor:

Administrator password: _____

Instructor requires product activation and product key? Yes _____ No _____

Install 32-bit or 64-bit version? _____

Create a custom sized partition for the installation? Yes _____ No _____
  If yes, what size? _____ (20 GB Minimum).

Note

Problems can arise in a networking lab environment that is not normally encountered in the field. Often, the hard disk drive used for the computer may have been used by a previous class and may need to be formatted or even low level formatted to remove any existing partitions. This is especially true if the hard disk drive had a Linux partition. Linux partitions are not always detected by Microsoft operating systems. You can perform a complete clean install, and then the server fails to successfully boot. If the system meets the hardware requirements and the workstation was used by a previous class, you may need to perform a low-level format. You can also go to the hard disk drive manufacturer's Web site and download a diagnostic utility to inspect the hard disk drive for undetected partitions. The hard disk drive manufacturer will have all information needed to run the diagnostic software.

Procedure

1. _____ Report to your assigned workstation.

2. _____ Boot the server and verify it is in working order.

3. _____ Insert the Windows Server 2008 installation DVD into the DVD drive. You must reboot the server after the installation DVD has been inserted into the drive. If the system fails to start the installation from the DVD and instead loads the contents of the hard disk drive, you will need to change the boot order in the BIOS setup.

After the workstation reboots, you should see a black screen similar to the one in the following screen capture. This means that the installation media is running and files are being copied to RAM to begin the installation process.

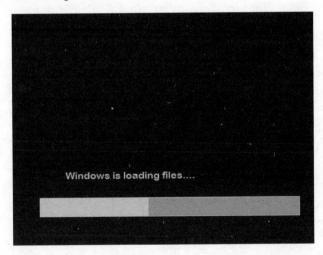

Windows is loading files....

Next, a screen will appear similar to the one in the screen capture below. You are prompted to select the appropriate language, time and currency format, and keyboard or input method.

4. _____ Accept the defaults and click **Next**. The next screen to appear will present you with several options: **Install now, What to know before installing Windows,** and **Repair your computer**.

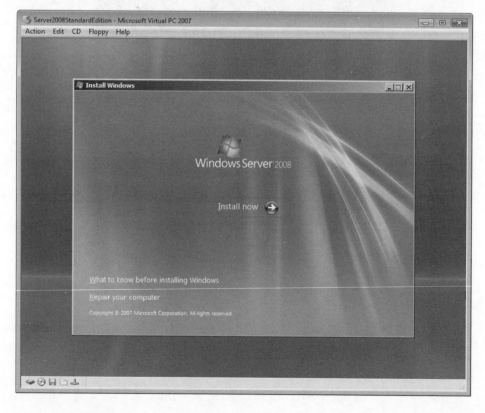

5. _____ Select the **Install now** option. The next screen to appear is the product key and activation screen similar to that in the following screen capture.

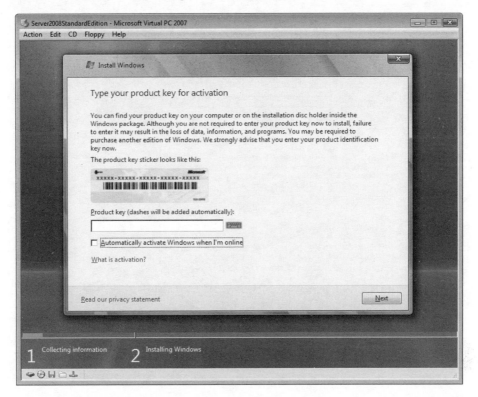

Unless your instructor specifically told you to activate and enter a product key, do *not* enter the product key and be sure the **Automatically activate Windows when I'm online** option is *unchecked*. You will have 60 days to activate the software.

6. _____ Click **Next**. A message warning you about not entering a product key will appear on the screen similar to the following.

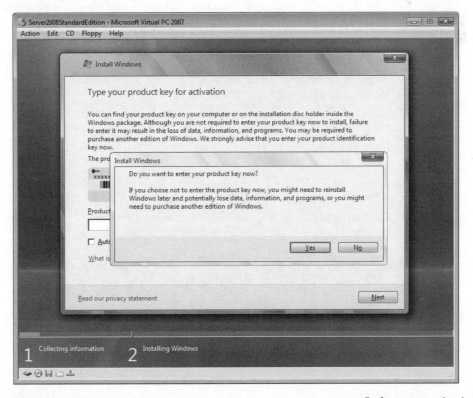

7. _____ Ignore the message and click **No**. Now you will be prompted to select the server edition.

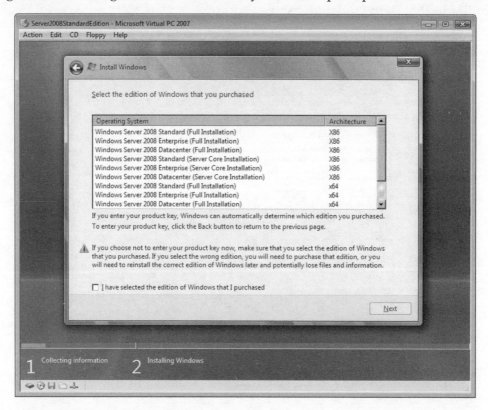

8. _____ For this lab activity, select the Windows Server 2008 Standard edition that matches your hardware (x86 or x64). Next, the license terms will appear on the screen.

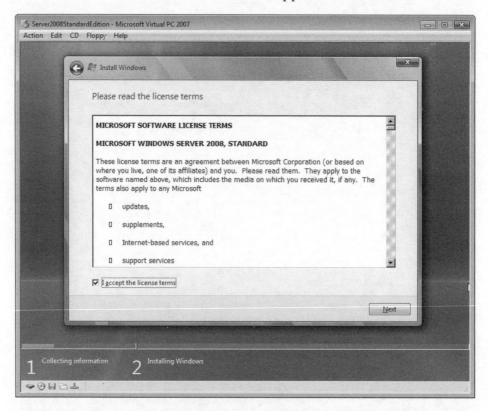

9. _____ Accept the terms to continue with the installation by selecting **I accept the license terms** and clicking **Next**. You will be presented with two choices of installation: **Upgrade** or **Custom (advanced)**.

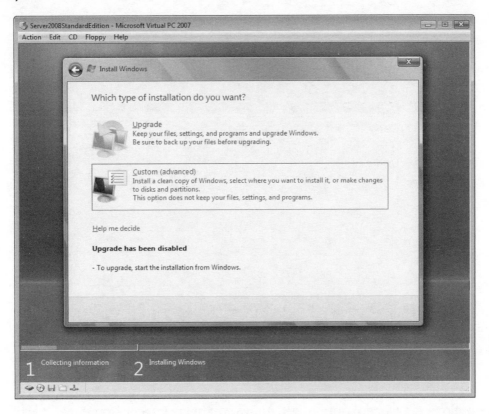

The **Upgrade** option will not be available if a previous version of Windows Server was not installed on the computer. Your only option should be **Custom (advanced)**, which is also referred to as a *clean install*. When performing a custom installation, you will be presented with options to create a partition automatically or to select existing partitions. The **Custom (advanced)** option will overwrite any existing files in the partition it is installed on. The **Upgrade** option will preserve any existing files that may already exist on the partition.

10. _____ Select the **Custom (advanced)** option. The next screen to appear will present any available partitions that exist on the disk drive.

The **Drive options (advanced)** option will allow you to create a custom-sized partition for the server. In the screen capture, the default drive is identified as "Disk 0" which means the first physical or only hard disk drive. If a second physical disk drive is installed, it would be identified as "Disk 1". Remember that physical disk numbering starts at zero (0). There is also the **Load Driver** option, which you can use to load software for a hard drive connected to the SCSI interface. You would insert the installation media provided by the SCSI manufacturer at this point.

11. _____ Accept the default by clicking **Next**, unless your instructor has requested that you perform a custom setup and create a small partition. Small partitions take less time for the installation process than large partitions.

After clicking **Next**, the installation program will perform several routine steps and identify the progress on the screen. This may take 20 minutes or more. Look at the following screen capture.

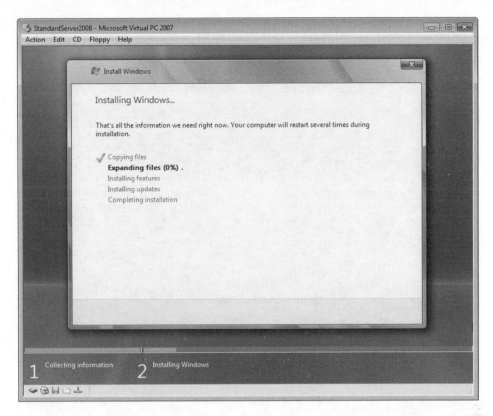

The installation software will expand files and install features and updates. These steps are typically automatic with little or no user intervention. The workstation will reboot several times during this portion of the installation. The next screen image to appear is a message telling you that the password must be changed. This is a little strange since you have not tried to enter a password yet.

12. _____ Simply click **OK**. You will be prompted for the new password for the Administrator account. The Administrator is the only account installed by default during the clean installation. For this exercise, use the password as provided by your instructor.

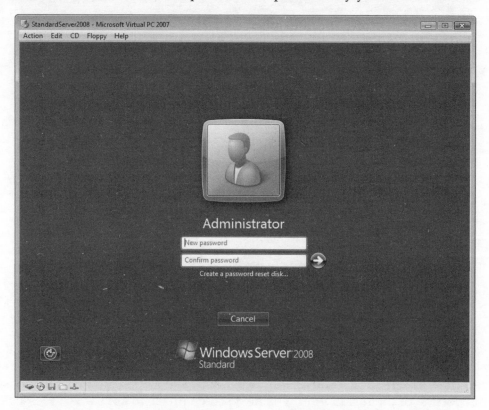

Passwords are recommended to be composed of at least seven characters. The characters should be composed of letters, symbol(s), and number(s). For example, Pa$$word123. Check the beginning of the lab activity for the Administrator password suggested by your instructor. You will need to type the password and then retype it to confirm it. Then, you will see a notice telling you that the new password has been accepted.

The last screen to appear is **Initial Configuration Tasks** similar to the one in the following screen capture.

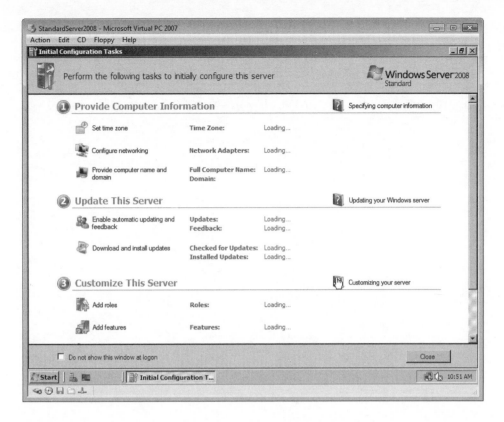

The installation is now complete. You will be presented with a screen similar to this one each time the server is started unless you select **Do not show this window at logon**.

The server operating system is installed but not configured. You will configure the server in the next laboratory activity.

13. _____ Call your instructor to inspect your project at this time. After your instructor inspects your project, you can shut down the server.

14. _____ Answer the review questions and then return all materials to their proper storage area.

Review Questions

1. What is the minimum amount of RAM for a Windows Server 2008 Standard 32-bit installation? _____

_____

2. What is the recommended amount of RAM for a Windows Server 2008 Standard installation?

_____

3. What are the two Windows Server 2008 installation options? _____

_____

4. What is the difference between an upgrade and a custom installation? _____

_____

_____

5. What is another name used for *custom installation*? _____

6. What is the name of the default user account? _____

7. What are the general guidelines for creating a secure server password? _____

_____

_____

8. What file format is used by default for Windows Server 2008? _____

Name_____ Date _____

Class/Instructor _____

Configuring Windows Server 2008 Roles

After completing this laboratory activity, you will be able to:

- Identify the most commonly selected roles and recall their purpose.
- Carry out proper procedures for adding the Active Directory Domain Services role.

Introduction

In this laboratory activity, you will first view the various server roles available for configuration. A Windows Server 2008 role is a specific function for the server to perform, such as DNS server, DHCP server, and file server. The following screen capture shows the various roles available in Windows Server 2008.

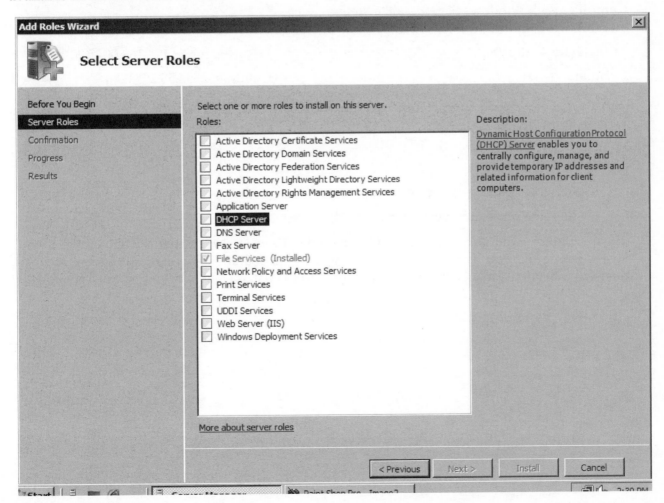

After viewing the roles, you will select only Active Directory Domain Services (AD DS). You cannot add other roles such as DNS Server or File Services until after Active Directory Domain Services has been configured. After AD DS is configured, you will run **dcpromo.exe**, from the **Search** box off of the **Start** menu. After **dcpromo.exe** runs, it will automatically start the domain controller promotion wizard.

Note

When Windows Server 2008 Standard is installed, it is automatically configured as a member of a workgroup. This fact is also true for Windows XP and Windows Vista.

In this lab, you will also assign a DNS namespace for the server. A DNS namespace is a unique name that can consist of the top level domain name, domain name, subdomain name, and computer name each separated by a period. For example, Workstation1.corp.netclass.private consists of the computer name *Workstation1*, the domain name *corp*, the subdomain *netclass*, and the nonexistent top-level domain *private*. Some examples of real top-level domains are .com, .org, and .edu.

Note

Before performing this lab activity, be sure you have configured a static IPv4 address for the server.

Equipment and Materials

❏ Computer with Windows Server 2008 installed.
❏ The following information provided by your instructor:

Static IPv4 address: _____ (Example, 192.168.001.200)

Subnet mask: _____ (Example, 255.255.255.000)

FQDN: _____ (Example, corp.netclass.private)

Forest function level: _____ (Example, Windows Server 2008)

Procedure

1. _____ Report to your assigned workstation.

2. _____ Boot the server and verify it is in working order.

3. _____ Open Server Manager (**Start | Administrative Tools | Server Manager**). You can also access Server Manager by typing **Server Manager** in the **Search** box located off of the **Start** menu. The Server Manager program will appear in the list as soon as you type the letter *S*.

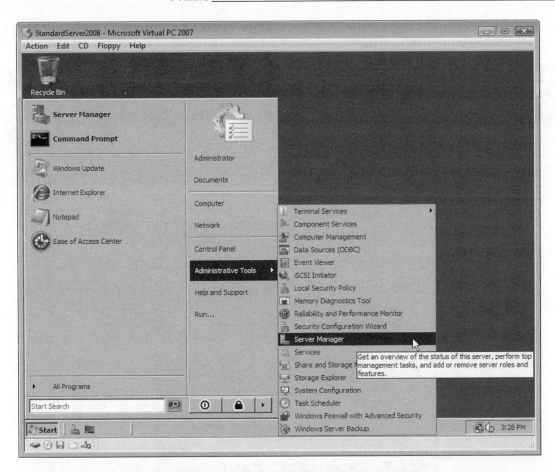

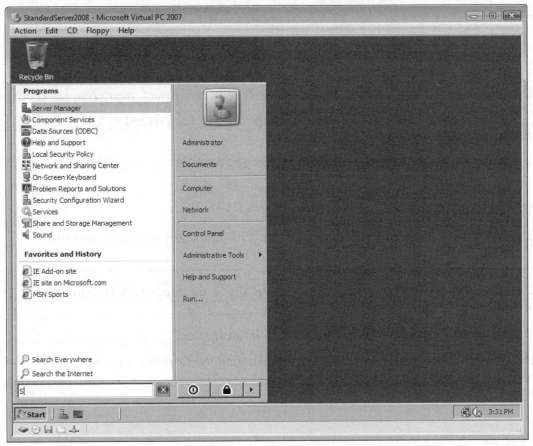

4. _____ After Server Manager opens, scroll down to **Roles Summary**. There should be no roles assigned to the server at this time.

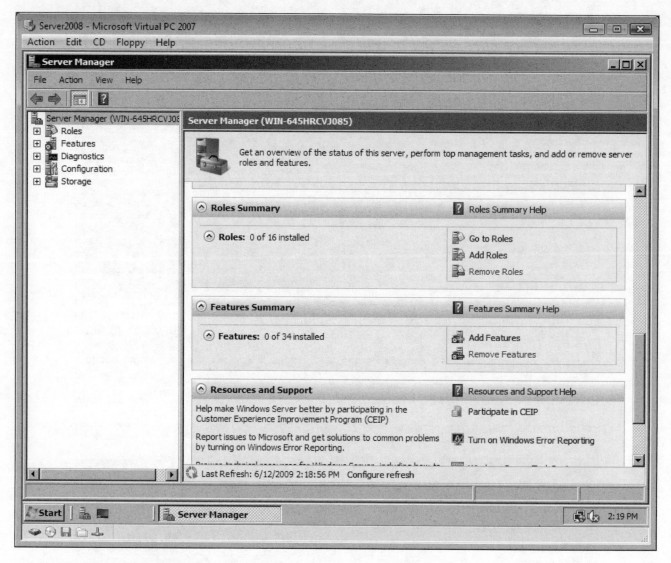

5. _____ Select **Add Roles**. You should see a screen with a notice concerning three very important items:

■ Administrator password should have a strong password.

■ Network setting should be configured for a static IP address.

■ The latest security updates should be installed.

For this lab activity, your only real concern is that a static IP address should be configured before assigning the server roles. Security updates and a strong password are not necessary for this lab.

6. _____ If you have already configured a static IP address, click **Next**. If not, abort the installation and configure a static IP address and then return to this step.

7. _____ Select **Active Directory Domain Services** from the list of server roles and then click **Next**.

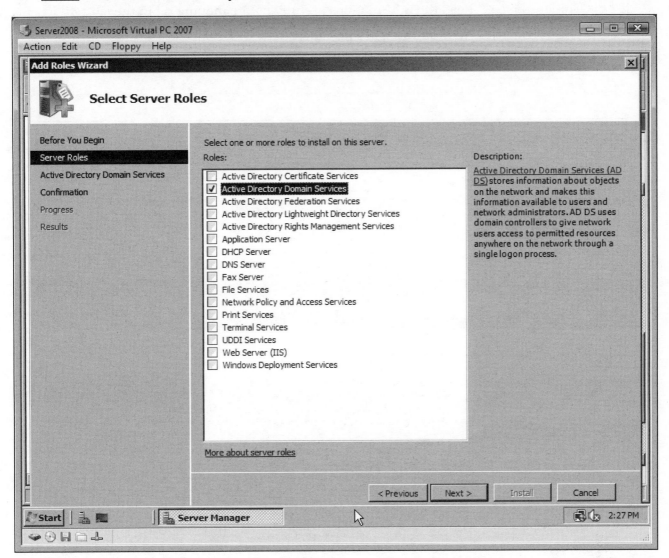

8. _____ The next screen to appear is an introduction to Active Directory Domain Services and a list of "Things to Note." Read the information carefully before moving on in the lab activity.

List the four "Things to Note" in the space provided.

_____

_____

_____

_____

_____

_____

_____

_____

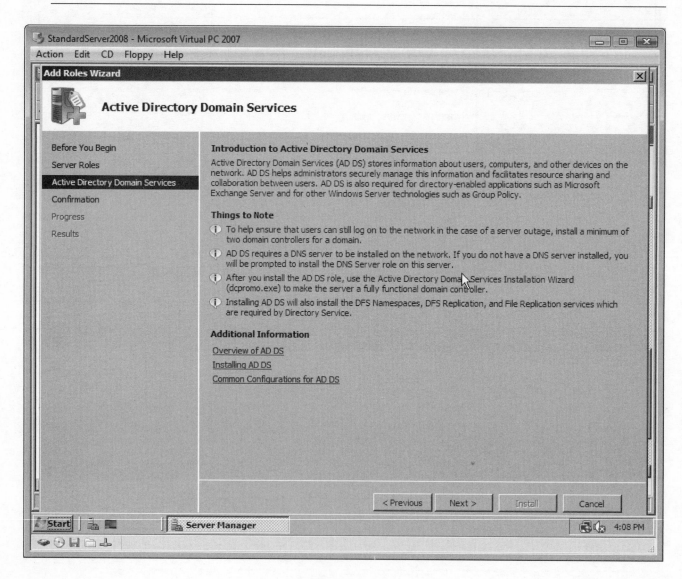

9. _____ Click **Next** to continue. A screen will appear confirming the installation selection of roles. You will be reminded about running **dcpromo.exe**.

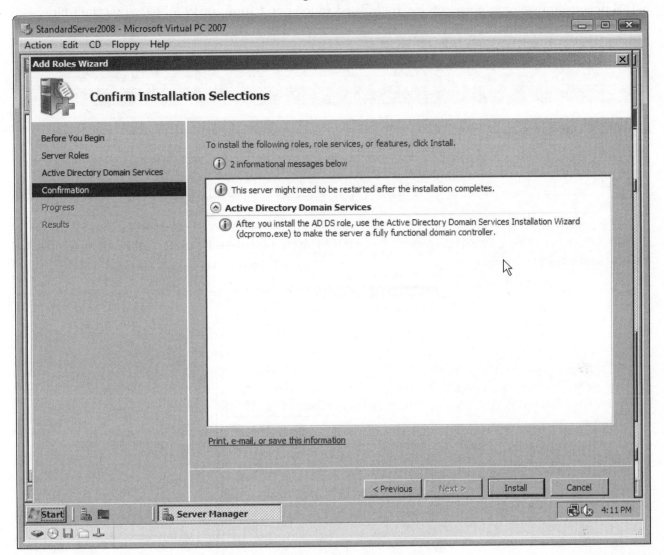

10. _____ Click **Install**. The wizard will run for a few minutes to complete the installation and initialization of the chosen role. Be patient. The server may also reboot during this time. You will see a message stating that the installation succeeded, and you will again be reminded to run **dcpromo.exe**.

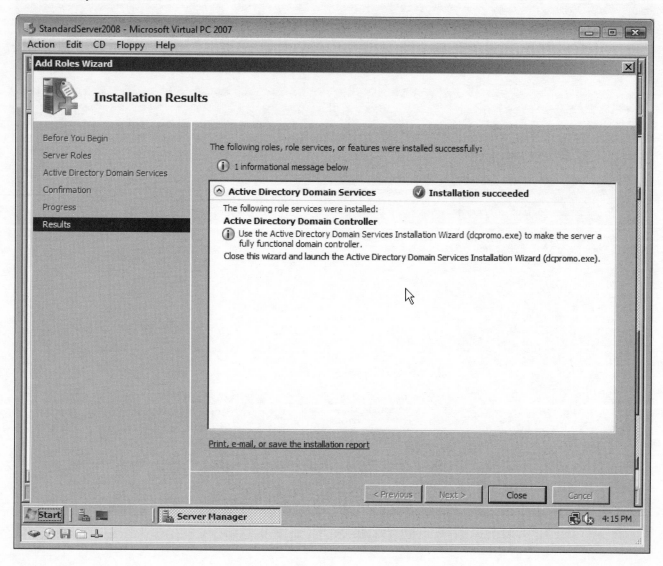

11. _____ In the **Search** box, enter **dcpromo.exe**. You will see **dcpromo** appear at the top of the list under **Programs**. Select **dcpromo**. The Active Directory Domain Services Installation Wizard will appear.

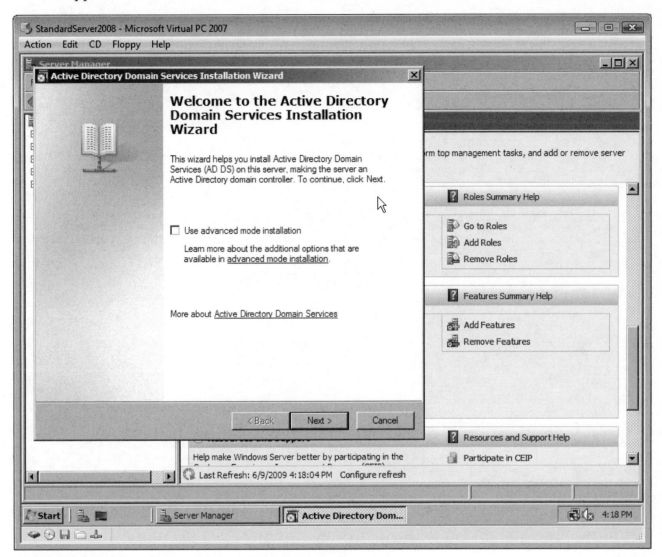

12. _____ Click **Next**. Do *not* select the **Use advanced mode installation** option. The advanced mode is only for experienced technicians. The next screen will present information about operating system compatibility. Take a few minutes to read it, and then click **Next**.

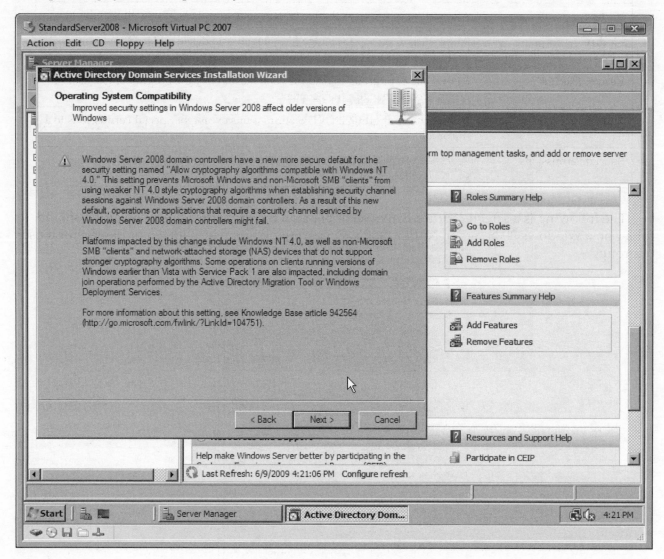

13. _____ Select the **Create a new domain in a new forest** option and then click **Next**.

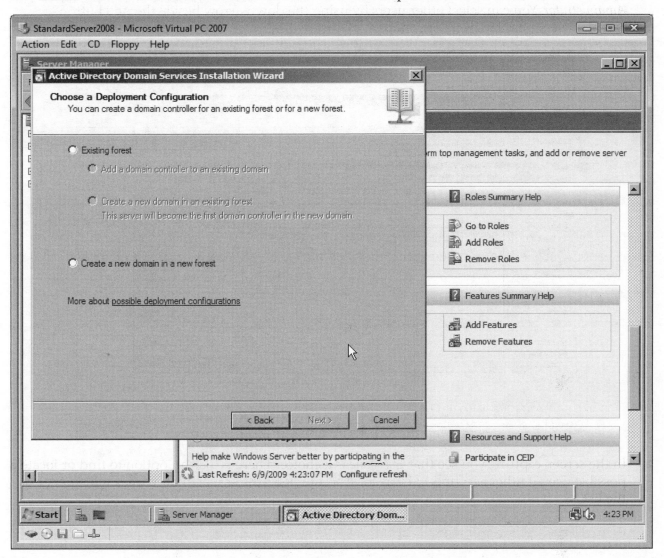

14. _____ Enter the FDQN of the forest root domain provided by your instructor and then click
Next.

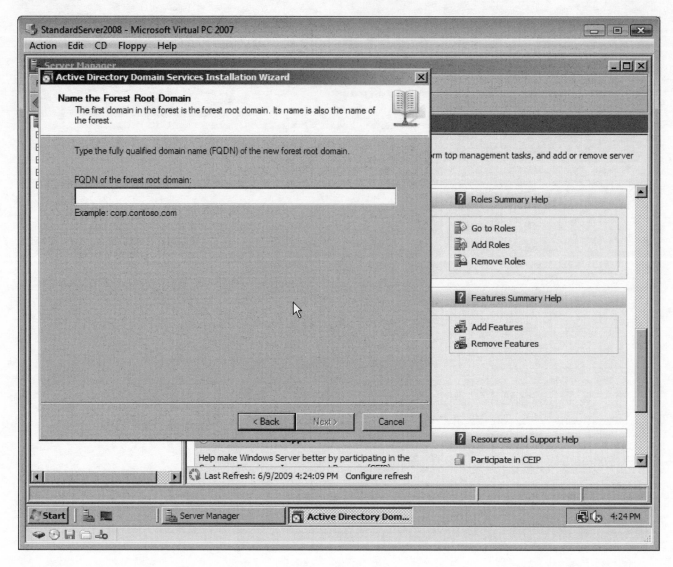

15. _____ You will be prompted to select the forest function level. Select the network operating system that matches the forest function level supplied by your instructor. Click **Next**.

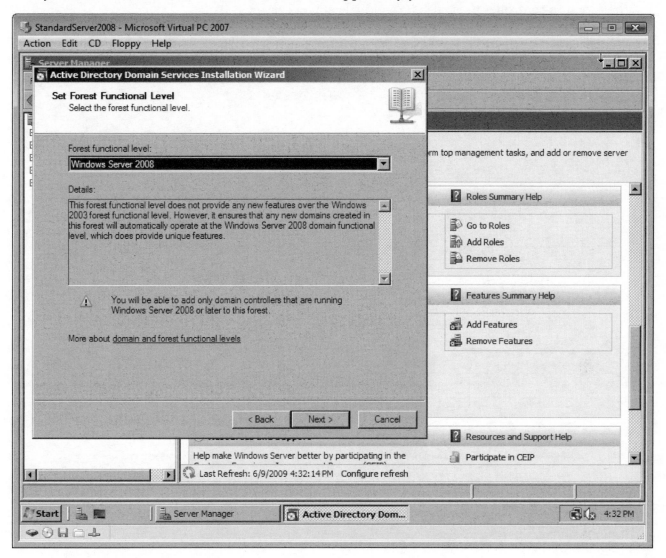

The **Additional Domain Controller Options** screen will appear. The **DNS server** and the **Global catalog** option should be selected by default. Some information will appear explaining that the first domain controller must also be a global catalog server.

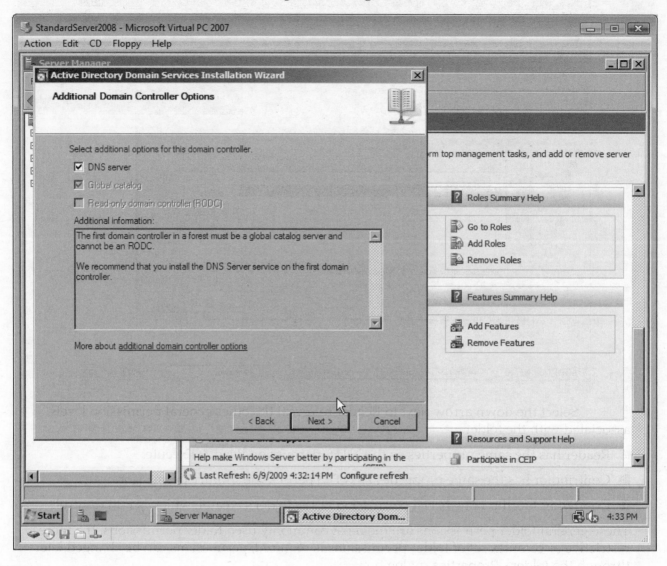

16. _____ Click **Next**. A screen will appear with the default locations suggested for storing the database and log files. Accept the defaults and click **Next**.

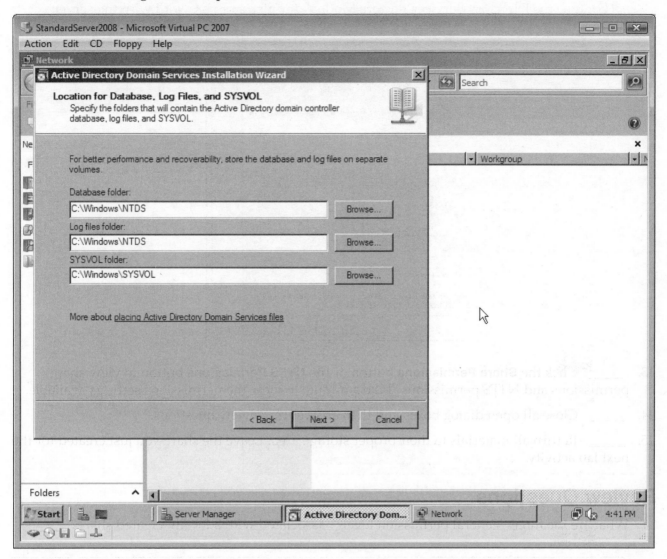

17. _____ You will be prompted to create a Directory Services Restore Mode Administrator password. Use the one provided by your instructor or use the following: Pa$$word12345. Do *not* confuse the Directory Services Restore Mode Administrator password with the server administrator password.

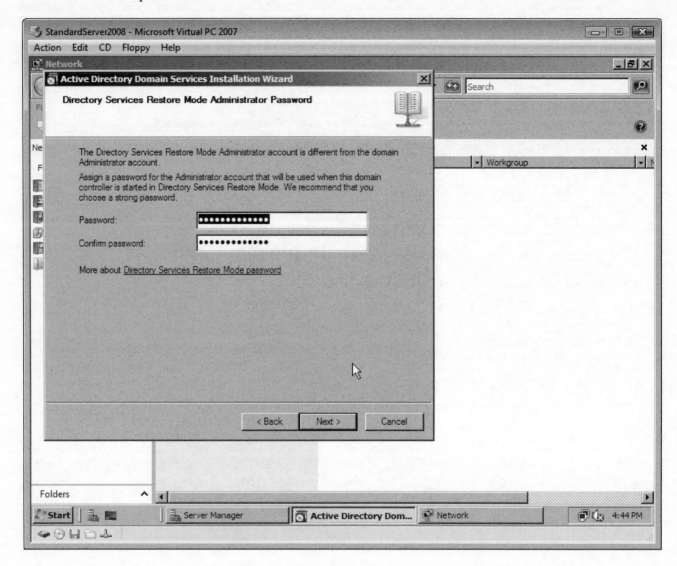

Networking Fundamentals Laboratory Manual   Copyright by Goodheart-Willcox Co., Inc.

The summary will appear on the screen similar to the one in the following screen capture.

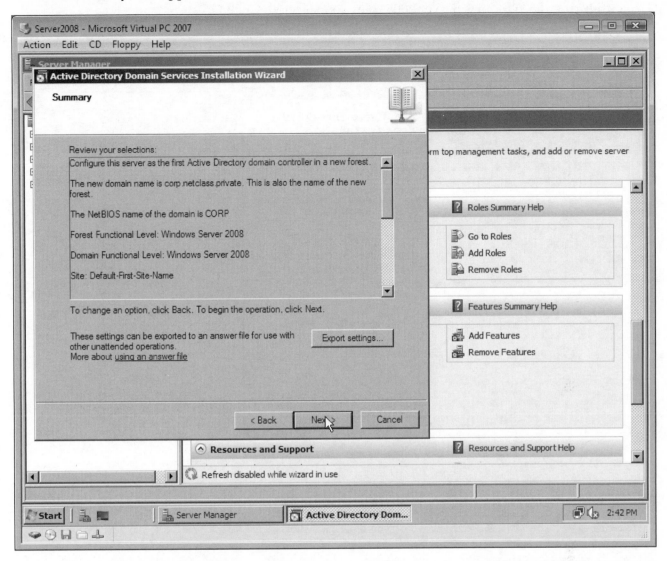

18. _____ Click **Next** to continue or **Back** to make changes. After clicking **Next**, the wizard will run for a few minutes making final configurations for the Domain Controller and the DNS Server roles.

19. _____ The last screen to appear verifies that the wizard has completed all tasks related to configuring the Windows Server 2008 roles you selected. Click **Finish**.

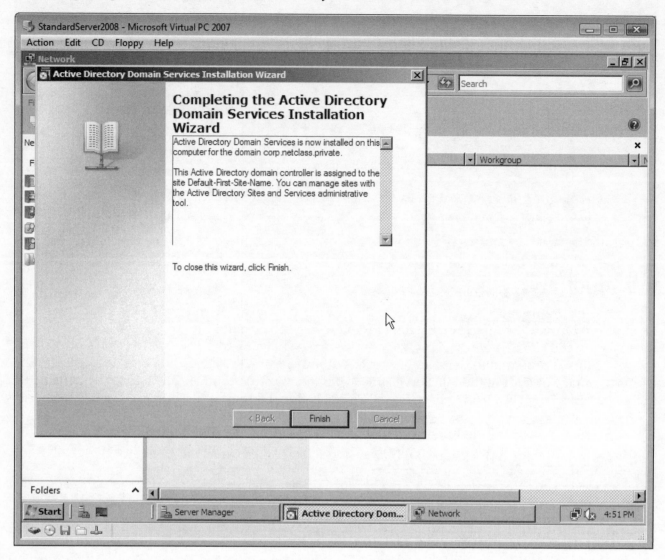

20. _____ When prompted to restart the computer to finalize the Active Directory Domain Services installation, click **Restart Now**.

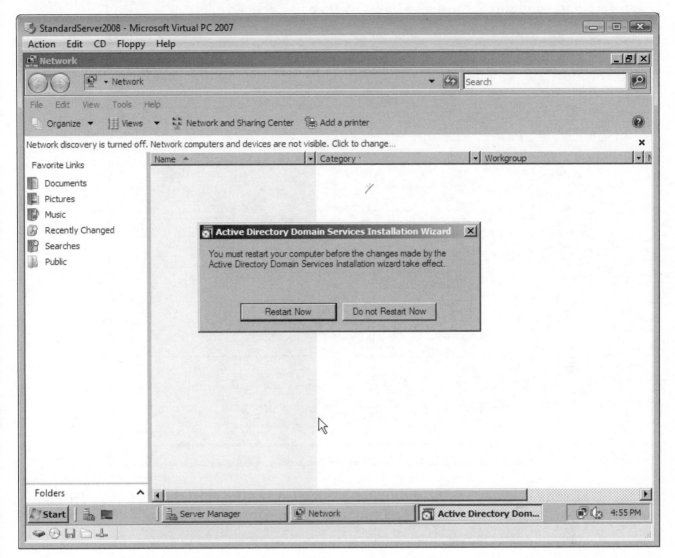

21. _____ When the server is restarted, look at the **Start | Administrative Tools** menu and notice that there are administrative utilities related to Active Directory that were not present in the menu before configuring the **Active Directory Domain Services** role.

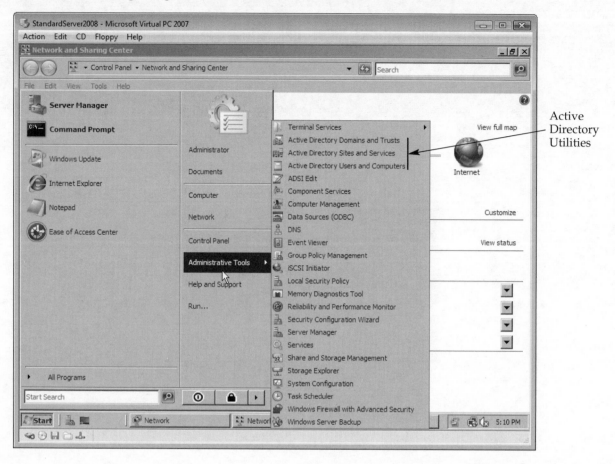

22. _____ You have now successfully completed configuring a domain controller role referred to as *Active Directory Domain Services*. Call your instructor to inspect your completed lab.

23. _____ Use the **Select Server Roles** screen in the Add Roles Wizard to answer the review questions.

24. _____ Return all materials to their proper storage area.

Review Questions

1. What server role is configured by default when Windows Server 2008 is installed? _____

   _____

2. Which server role would you select to automatically issue temporary IP addresses to computers on the local network? _____

3. Which server role provides name resolution to IP addresses? _____

4. Which server role provides centralized printer management tasks such as sharing a printer on a network? _____

5. Which server role provides support for Web application infrastructure? _____

_____

6. What is the executable program that starts the domain controller promotion wizard? _____

_____

Laboratory Activity

28

Name_____ Date _____

Class/Instructor _____

Creating a Shared Folder in Windows Server 2008

After completing this laboratory activity, you will be able to:
- Use the File Sharing wizard to create a shared resource.
- Select the proper NTFS permissions for a share.
- Identify shared folders in Windows Explorer.
- Differentiate between share permissions and NTFS permission.

Introduction

This laboratory activity is the first in a series of three that explore folder and file sharing in relation to a file server share. You will first create a folder and then configure it as a share on the local computer/server. In the next lab activity, you will add the File Server role to the server. In the last lab, you will share the folder using the server administration tool Share and Storage Management.

Creating a shared folder on a Windows 2008 server is very similar to creating a shared folder for any Windows operating system such as Windows XP, Windows Vista, or Windows 7. You simply create or select a folder, right-click the folder, and then select **Share with**, **Sharing**, or **Properties** from the shortcut menu to start the sharing process. After the folder is shared, you will be able to modify the share at any time.

Share and NTFS Permissions

There are two systems used to control access to files and folders: share permissions and NTFS permissions. NTFS permissions are also referred to as *security access controls*, *security access permissions*, or simply *access controls*. Share permissions are based on the FAT and FAT32 file system while NTFS permissions are based on the NTFS enhanced security of the NTFS file system. The mixture of the two systems can be very confusing because both are often referred to as *share permissions*. Technically speaking, share permissions are assigned to network shares. NTFS permissions are really security access controls used to control access to files and folders even when they are not network shares. As you work through this lab activity, many of the differences will become apparent. For example, when a device such as a CD or DVD drive is shared, only share permissions apply. When a file or folder is shared, both share permissions and NTFS permissions apply if the file system where the file or folder resides is formatted as NTFS.

Share Permissions

Share permissions are much simpler in design and have fewer options when compared to NTFS permissions. Share permissions are limited to Read, Change, and Full Control. The following table describes each share permission.

Share Permission	Description
Read	Allows user or group to view file names and subfolders, view data in files, and run programs.
Change	Allows user or group to add files and subfolders, change data in files, and delete subfolders and files.
Full Control	Allows user or group to read and change permissions and to assign permissions to files and folders

The following is a screen capture of the **Share Permissions** tab in the **Properties** dialog box for a shared folder on a Windows 2008 server. Notice that share permissions can be allowed or denied for a user or group.

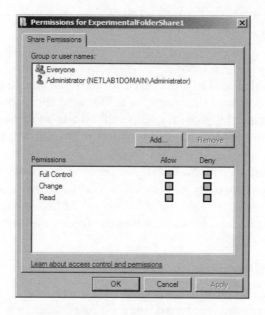

NTFS Permissions

NTFS permissions are Full Control, Modify, Read & Execute, List Folder Contents, Read, Write, and Special Permissions. The following table describes each NTFS permission. Notice that there are more NTFS permissions than share permissions.

NTFS Permission	Description
Read	Allows user or group to view file and folder contents.
Write	Allows user or group to change folder contents and create new files and folders.
Modify	Allows user or group to change file contents and delete folders. Provides the same privileges as the Read and Change share permissions.
Read & Execute	Allows a user or group to read file contents and execute programs. The user or group cannot change a file's contents.
Full Control	Allows a user or group all NTFS permissions except for Special Permissions to a file or folder.
Special Permissions	Special Permissions are additional enhanced security permissions used with the NTFS file system.

The following is a screen capture of the **Security** tab in the **Properties** dialog box for a shared folder on a Windows 2008 server. Notice that NTFS permissions can be allowed or denied for a user or group.

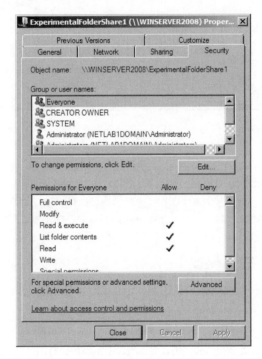

General Permission Levels

NTFS permissions are located under the **Security** tab of the **Properties** dialog box for a shared folder. Starting with Windows Vista, Microsoft introduced a new set of names for share permissions known as Reader, Contributor, and Co-Owner. This was Microsoft's attempt to make the permission selection more user friendly for novice users. This lab activity will refer to these three new permissions as *general permission levels*. The general permission levels are typically encountered when using the File Sharing wizard.

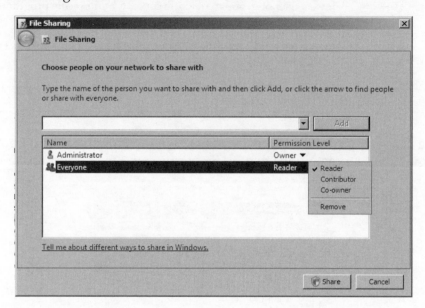

Inheritance

When a folder has a set of permissions assigned, that same set of permissions is applied to all of its subfolders. The assignment of the original folder permissions to subfolders is referred to as *inheritance*. Inheritance is typically indicated in permission dialog boxes with shaded check boxes. An inherited permission can be overridden in most cases by deselecting the inherited permission (clicking the shaded check box).

Important Facts about Shares

■ In Windows Server, the *Everyone* group is assigned the Read permission automatically.

■ The Read permission is the most restrictive permission because users can only read the contents of the share. The only thing more restrictive is no access at all.

■ The Administrator group is assigned Full Control by default.

■ When sharing a device such as a DVD drive, only share permissions apply.

■ Share permissions only apply when a folder is accessed across a network.

■ Share permissions are lost if a folder is moved or renamed.

■ NTFS permissions apply if a folder is accessed across a network or accessed locally (on the computer).

■ NTFS permissions are retained when the folder is moved or renamed.

■ A file or folder can have NTFS permissions without having share permissions.

You can access more information about shares and permissions using Help and Support located off the **Start** menu of Windows Vista, Windows 7, or Windows Server.

Equipment and Materials

❑ Computer with Windows Server 2008 installed.

❑ The following information provided by your instructor:

Shared folder location: _____ (For example, C:/)

Shared folder name: _____ (Use your student first initial and last name and "SharedFolder." For example, RRobertsSharedFolder.)

Note

If a server is not available, you could use a Windows Vista or Windows 7 workstation.

Note

The lab activity screen captures are based on Windows Server 2008. If you are using a different operating system, there will be some variation, but most of the instructions and screen captures will be very similar.

Procedure

1. _____ Report to your assigned workstation.

2. _____ Boot the server and verify it is in working order.

3. _____ Create a folder using the name and location indicated by your instructor.

4. _____ Right-click the folder and then select **Share with** from the shortcut menu. You should see a dialog box similar to following.

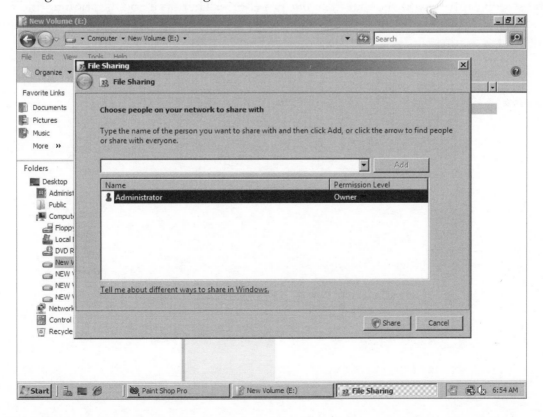

By default, the folder is automatically shared with its creator. In the example, the creator is the *Administrator*. You can select other users by using the down arrow beside the **Add** button to reveal a list of possible users or groups.

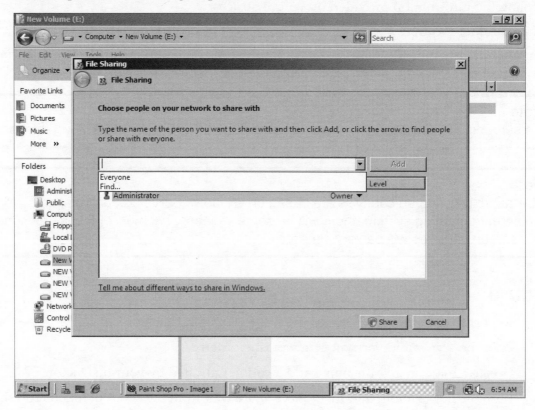

In the screen capture, you see that *Everyone* is a choice. There is also an option to find or locate a possible user. If other accounts exist as local accounts on the server, their names will appear on the list.

5. _____ Select **Everyone**. Notice that the default permission for *Everyone* is Reader. This a general permission level.

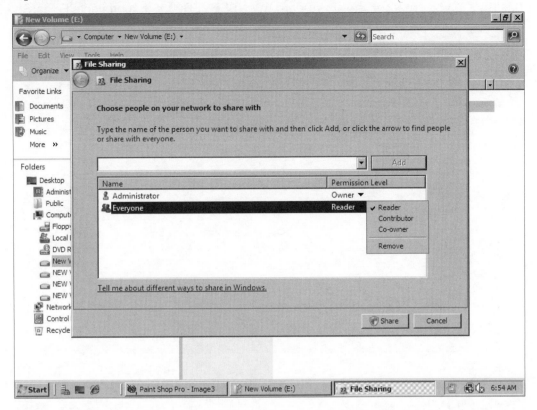

6. _____ Select the down arrow next to Reader to reveal the other general permission levels associated with the folder.

■ Reader has the same properties as the NTFS permission Read & Execute.

■ Contributor has the same properties as NTFS permission Modify permission.

■ Co-Owner has the same NTFS permission as the folder's creator, which is Full Control.

These general folder permissions are the most commonly used folder permissions. If a more restrictive or complex set of folder permissions is required, permissions can be changed later through the folder's **Properties** dialog box.

7. _____ Leave the Reader permission assigned to *Everyone* and click **Share**.

8. _____ The next dialog box to automatically appear will confirm the creation of the folder share. It will appear similar to the one in the following screen capture. Notice that the shared folder has the UNC format for the share path \\WINSERVER2008\ExperimentalFolderShare1.

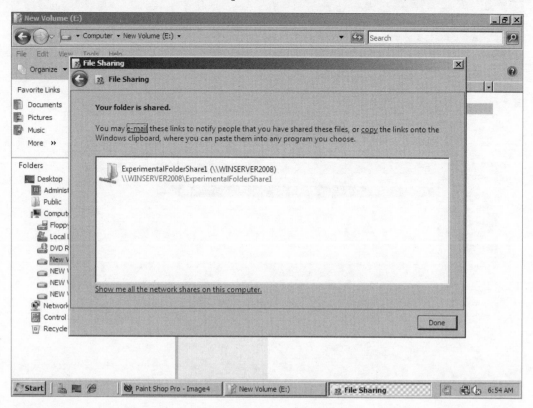

Selecting the **Show me all the network shares on this computer** link will reveal all shares on the computer/server similar to the following screen capture.

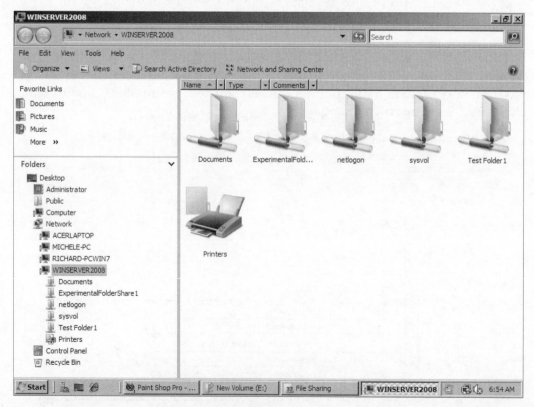

Each share is displayed using the network share icon—a folder connected to a cable. Shares are identified in the navigation pane with an icon of two users side by side as in the following screen capture.

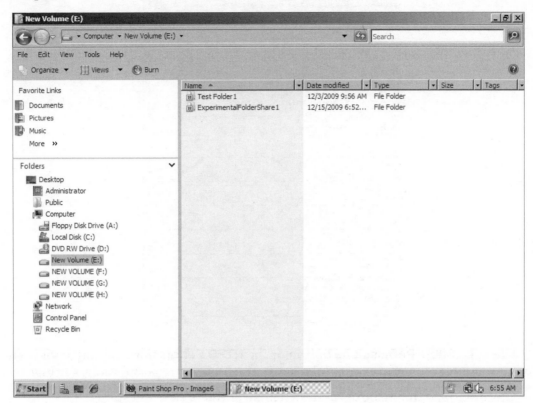

9. _____ Add files to the folder. The files will be automatically shared with all user accounts or groups you have selected.

10. _____ Open Share and Storage Management (**Start | Administrative Tools | Share and Storage Management**).

11. _____ Locate the shared folder you just created.

12. _____ Double-click the shared folder and select the **Permissions** tab. A dialog box similar to the following will appear.

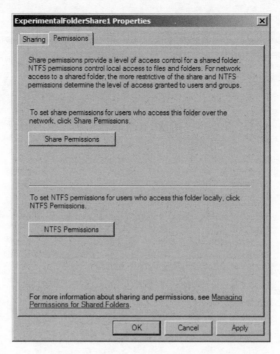

13. _____ Click the **Share Permissions** button or the **NTFS Permissions** button to view share permissions and NTFS permissions. Take a minute to view the permissions settings available.

14. _____ Close all open dialog boxes and then answer the review questions.

15. _____ Return all materials to their proper storage area. Leave the share you just created for the next lab activity.

Review Questions

1. What are the three "general permission levels" associated with a locally-created share? _____
   _____

2. What are the three available share permissions? _____

3. What share permissions are available for a DVD? _____

4. Under which folder **Properties** tab (**Share** or **Security**) are the NTFS permissions located? _____
   _____

5. What NTFS permission is similar to Reader? _____

6. Which general permission level will allow you to delete the folder share? _____

7. Which general permission level will allow a group to make changes to the share folder contents but not allow it to delete the share folder? _____

8. Which NTFS permission only allows a user or group to view the contents of a file or folder? ___
   _____

9. Which NTFS permission would you assign to a user to read, write, execute, and modify file and folder contents?_____

Laboratory Activity

29

Name_____ Date _____

Class/Instructor _____

Adding the File Server Role to Windows Server 2008

After completing this laboratory activity, you will be able to:

- Carry out proper procedures to add the File Server role to Windows Server 2008.
- Recall the various features provided when a server is configured as a file server.

Introduction

In this laboratory activity, you will add the File Server role to a Windows 2008 server. In Laboratory Activity 27, you configured the Active Directory Domain Controller and DNS Server roles. To add the File Server role, you will open Server Manager and select the **Add Roles** option.

You can create shared folders on the server without adding the File Server role. However, the main advantage of adding the File Server role is that the wizard automatically adds special features to the file server such as DFS Namespace, DFS Replication, File Server Resource Manager, and Services for Network File System.

DFS stands for Distributed File System. It provides support for distributing files across the entire network and provides folder replication services. The File Services Resource Manager provides a suite of tools for monitoring file system resources such as disk space and generating reports. Services for Network File System supports sharing files with UNIX- and Linux-based computers.

Equipment and Materials

☐ Computer with Windows Server 2008 installed.

Procedure

1. _____ Report to your assigned workstation.

2. _____ Boot the server and verify it is in working order.

3. _____ Open Server Manager and select the **Add Roles** option. The **Select Server Roles** screen will display.

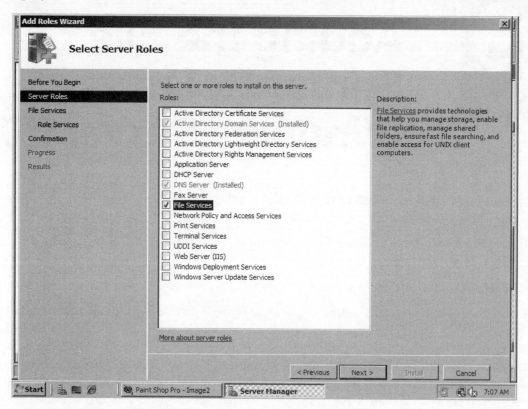

4. _____ Select **File Services** from the list of server roles.

5. _____ Click the **File Services** link to read more about the file server features.

6. _____ After briefly scanning the information, close the Files Services help window. You will be returned to the Add Roles Wizard screen. Click **Next** to continue.

7. _____ The next dialog box to appear will prompt you to select additional roles for the file server. Select only **Distributed File System**, **File Server Resource Manager**, and **Services for Network File System**. As you select each role, information about the role will be provided on the right. Take a few minutes to read the information about each role, even the ones not selected for this exercise.

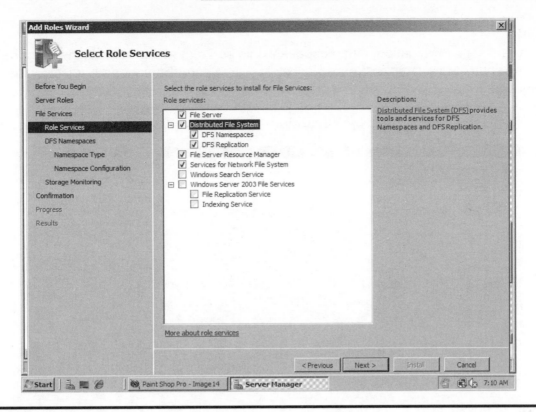

Note

Services for Network File System will be needed for a later lab activity when you install a Linux operating system computer and use it to access files on the Microsoft 2008 server.

---

8. _____ Click Next. A dialog box similar to the following will appear, prompting you to choose a Distributed File Service (DFS) namespace. The default name is *Namespace1*. Use the default for this exercise and click **Next**.

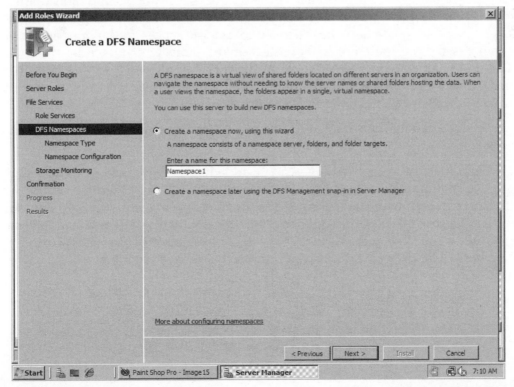

Note

In a real network situation, a namespace would be created that reflects the purpose of the share. For example, "SharedSalesFiles" or "SharedEngineeringProjects" could be used.

You will be prompted to select the namespace type as shown in the following dialog box.

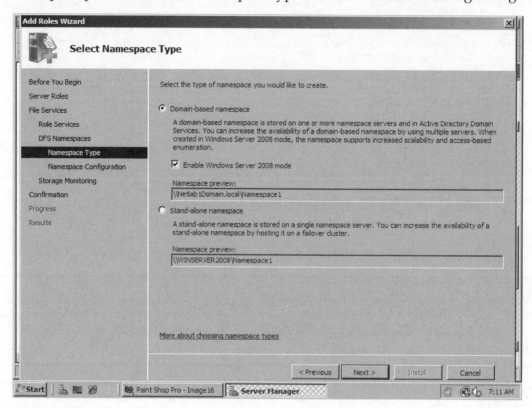

The two types of namespace are "domain-based namespace" and "stand-alone namespace." The domain-based namespace can be stored in multiple locations spread across the entire Active Directory. A stand-alone namespace is limited to a single server. In the previous screen capture, the domain-based namespace is based on the domain name, which includes the URL extension .local. The stand-alone namespace is based on the server name *WINSERVER2008*. In both examples, the names conform to the Universal Naming Convention (UNC) in which the server name follows the share name: \\Server_Name\Share_name.

9. _____ Leave the default namespace type and click **Next**. The namespace will be automatically configured.

After the namespace is configured, files can be added to the namespace by clicking the **Add** button in the **Configure Namespace** screen, shown in the following screen capture. The administrator can then navigate to a file location anywhere in the network or domain system and then simply select the file. It would be automatically configured as a "virtual" share in the namespace folder. When referred to as a *virtual share*, it means that the file can be located anywhere but will appear as if it is directly under the namespace folder.

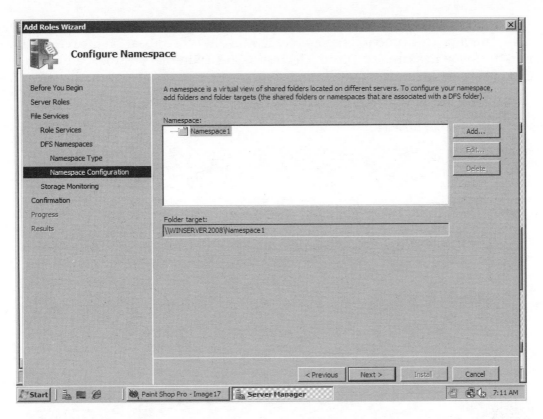

10. _____ Click **Next**. Now you will be prompted to select which drives to use for storage monitoring. In the following screen capture, notice that two drives are indicated. When a drive is selected, you will see additional prompts for capacity and threshold limits. Do *not* select a drive. Click **Next** to continue.

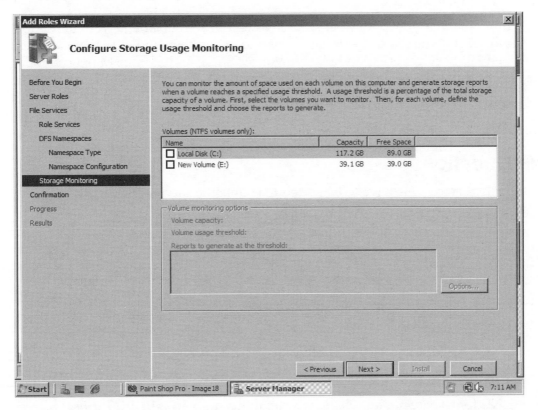

11. _____ Confirm the roles and features you selected and click **Next**. The installation begins. After a few minutes, the process is complete. The results will appear on the screen similar to that in the following screen capture. The results are a summary of the features and roles configured for the file server.

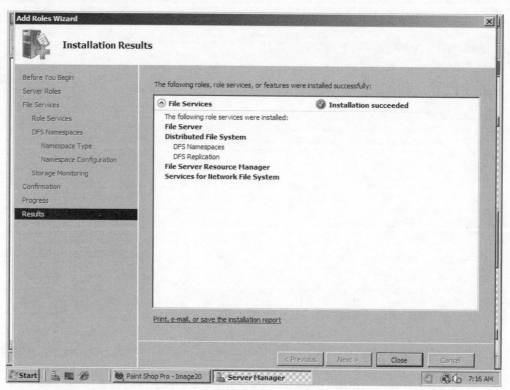

12. _____ Click **Close**.

13. _____ From the **Start** menu, right-click **Computer** and select **Manage** from the shortcut menu. You should see that the file server role (File Services) has been added to the list of server roles. When File Services is expanded, you will see Share and Storage Management and DFS Management listed. These are the same options you selected earlier in the lab activity.

14. _____ Call your instructor to check your lab.

15. _____ Answer the review questions.

Review Questions

1. Does the File Services role have to be added to enable the server to share files? _____

2. Name four features added with the File Services role. _____

   _____

   _____

   _____

3. What is contained in a UNC path? _____

4. Write a UNC path for a share named *MyShare* located on a server called *Server1*. _____

   _____

5. Write a UNC for a share named *MyShare* located in a domain called *USF.edu*. _____

   _____

Name_____ Date _____

Class/Instructor _____

Provisioning a Network Share in Windows Server 2008

After completing this laboratory activity, you will be able to:

- Summarize the advantages of provisioning a share.
- Use the Share and Storage Management tool to provision a network folder share.
- Use the Provision a Shared Folder Wizard to configure the share for SMB and NFS.
- Use the Provision a Shared Folder Wizard to assign NTFS and NFS permissions to a share.

Introduction

In this laboratory activity, you will use the Share and Storage Management tool to provision a network share. Shares can be easily made by right-clicking the desired folder and then selecting **Share with** or **Properties** from the shortcut menu to create a share. You can assign user accounts and groups to the share and set NTFS permissions or share permissions. These are all basic shared configuration options.

Using the Share and Storage Management **Provision Share** option runs a wizard which enables you to select enhancements to basic sharing. For example, you can select the file sharing protocol, SMB or NFS. You can also create a Distributed File System (DFS) namespace for the share. If the Server Resource Management role has been installed on the server, you can filter the type of files that are permitted to be stored in the share. As you can see, there are many advantages to provisioning a share.

Note

At the time of this writing, a share must be created first before you provision it. There is no tool available in the Windows 2008 Server Share and Storage Management tool for creating a shared folder.

Equipment and Materials

❏ Computer with Windows Server 2008 installed.

Procedure

1. _____ Report to your assigned workstation.

2. _____ Boot the server and verify it is in working order.

3. _____ Open the Share and Storage Management tool by accessing **Start | Administrative Tools | Share and Storage Management**.

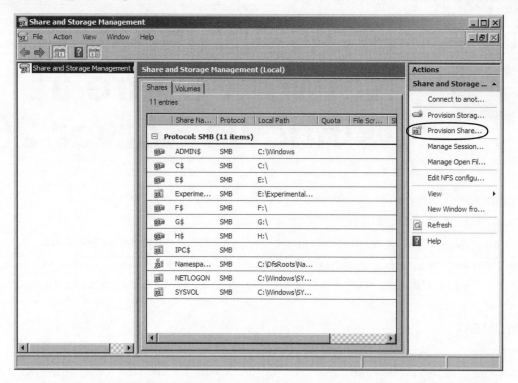

4. _____ Select the **Provision Share** option located in the right-hand pane under **Actions**. The Provision a Shared Folder Wizard will open as shown in the following screen capture.

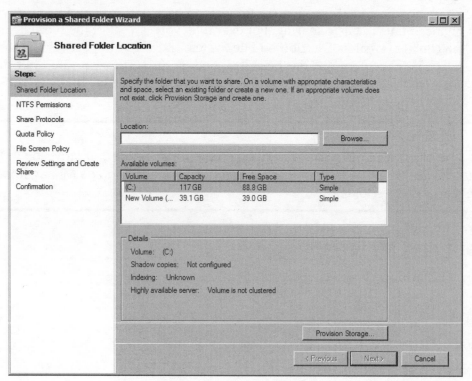

5. _____ Use the **Browse** button to locate the desired folder to share. This will be the folder you created earlier. You will see the directory structure of all shared file locations, similar to that in the following screen capture.

6. _____ Select the desired folder by highlighting it and clicking **OK**. You will be returned to the Provision a Shared Folder Wizard with the selected file location displayed similar to that in the following screen capture.

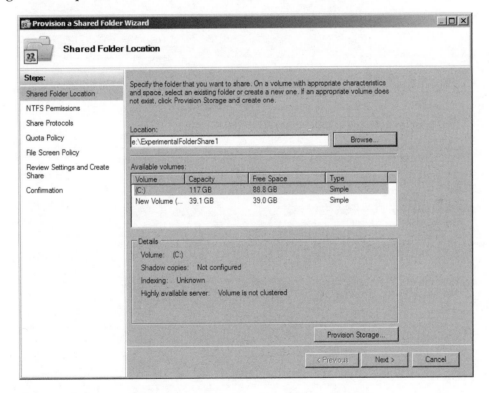

7. _____ Click **Next**. You will be prompted to change or not change the NTFS permission.

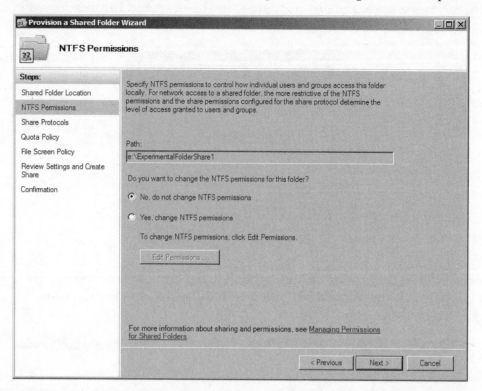

8. _____ Click **Next** to accept the default. Now you will be prompted to select the protocol to use to support access to the shared folder. Your choices are SMB and NFS. Select both SMB and NFS. You will need NFS for later lab activities.

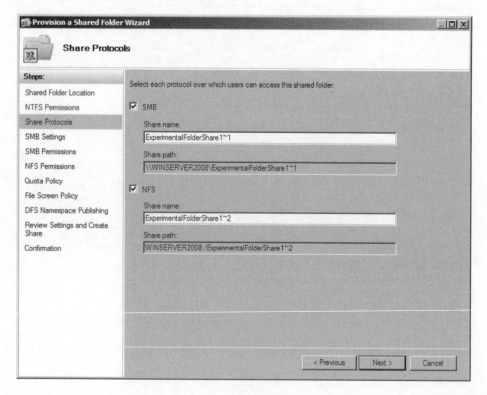

9. _____ Click **Next**. You will be prompted to select SMB settings.

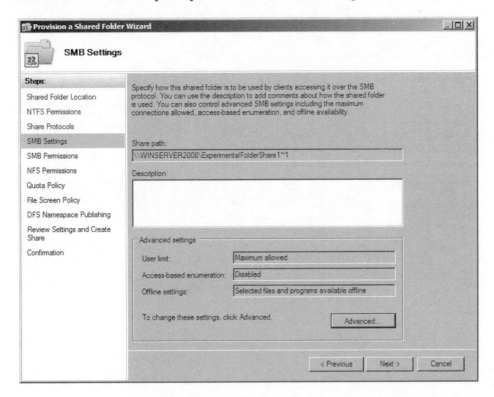

10. _____ Accept the default by clicking **Next**. You will be prompted to select the NFS permissions. You will learn about the NFS permissions in the next chapter and in later lab activities. NFS permissions are very different from NTFS permissions.

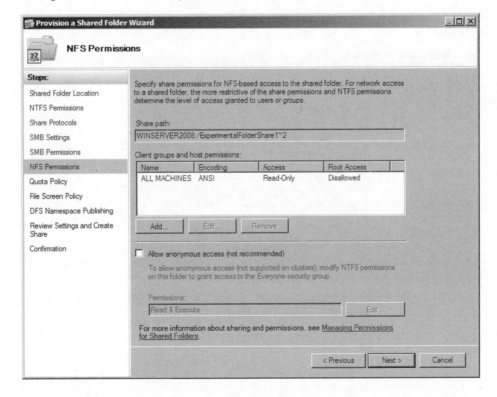

11. _____ Accept the default by clicking **Next**. Now you will be prompted to set the quota policy.

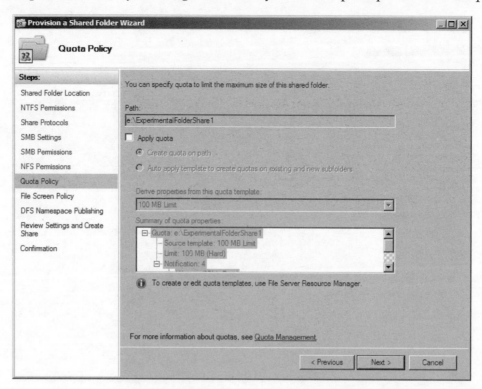

You can configure quotas to control the amount of storage space used by users and groups. When a user or group nears the limit, an e-mail is automatically generated and distributed notifying them they are going to exceed the limit.

12. _____ Accept the default settings by clicking **Next**. You will be prompted for input concerning the file screen policy.

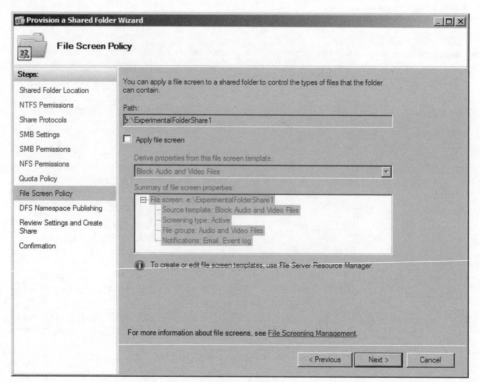

The file screen policy allows the administrator to configure a policy for the type of files that can be stored. For example, you can create a policy to not allow music or video files to be stored in the folder. Music and video files are typically not appropriate in the workplace and consume large volumes of storage space.

13. _____ For this lab activity, accept the default settings and click **Next**. Now you are prompted for a name for the folder share that will be located in the DFS namespace.

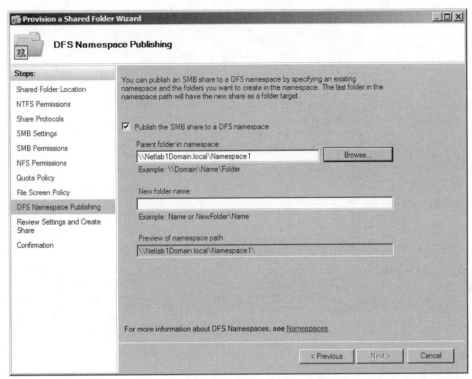

14. _____ Provide a name for the shared folder such as ExperimentalShare and then click **Next**. A preview of the shared folder configuration information will be presented.

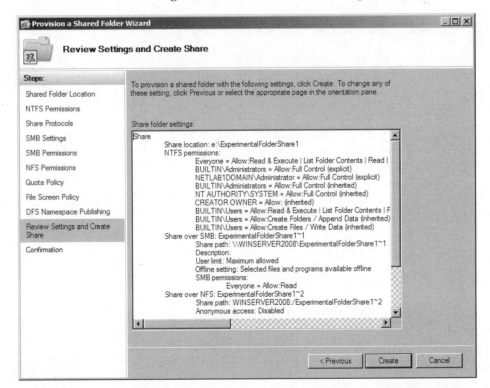

15. _____ Take a minute to look at the configuration details in the **Share folder settings** box. If everything is acceptable, click the **Create** button. If it is not acceptable, you have an opportunity to go back and make appropriate changes. If you clicked **Create**, the **Confirmation** screen appears similar to that shown in the following screen capture.

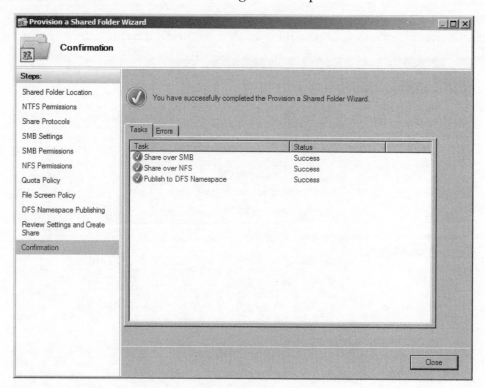

16. _____ Call your instructor to inspect your lab.

17. _____ After you instructor inspects your lab, click **Close**. You will be returned to the Share and Management tool. Notice that SMB shares and NFS shares are located separately even though they are the same folder.

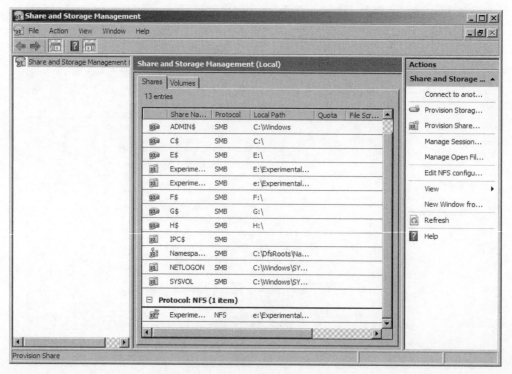

The share you provisioned should appear at the bottom and be identified as an NFS protocol share. Above it, you should see the same share located with the other entries that are SMB shares. Take a minute to verify both locations.

18. _____ Double-click the SMB shared folder and then select the **Permissions** tab. A dialog box similar to the following will appear.

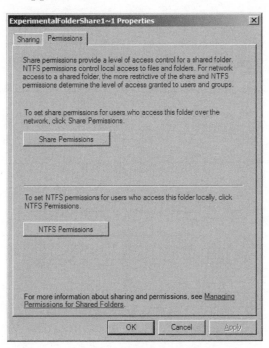

Selecting the **Share Permissions** button will allow you to view the three share permissions: Full Control, Change, and Read. Selecting the **NTFS Permissions** button will allow you to view and configure the NTFS permissions. Take a minute and view both sets of permissions for the SMB share.

19. _____ Close the dialog boxes to return to the Share and Storage Management tool.

20. _____ Double-click the NFS shared folder and then select the **Permissions** tab. Click the **NFS Permissions** button to see the permissions for the NFS shared folder.

21. _____ Close all dialog boxes and the Share and Storage Management tool and then answer the review questions

Review Questions

1. What are the two protocols used to support file sharing? _____

2. What does the file screen policy provide? _____

_____

_____

3. Which provides the most detailed configuration possibilities for a share: NTFS permissions or share permissions? _____

_____

Laboratory Activity

31

Name _____ Date _____

Class/Instructor _____

Adding Users to Windows Server 2008

After completing this laboratory activity, you will be able to:

■ Recall the purpose of a user account.

■ Recall the basic requirements of a user account.

■ Identify the various password options available.

■ Use Active Directory Users and Computers to create a new user account.

Introduction

In this laboratory activity, you will add a new user to a Windows 2008 Server domain. One of the most common jobs a network technician performs is adding new users and giving users new passwords when the user forgets his or her password. Adding new users to a network system is also known as *creating a user account*. A user cannot access system resources on a network without a user account. At minimum, the user account requires a user name and a password.

There are two types of user and group accounts that can be created: domain and local. A local account is created for accessing the local computer or server. A local account is typically used on a peer-to-peer network. The domain user account is created on a server that is a domain controller. With the proper permission, this domain account is good for the entire domain. Once the domain user account is created, a user can log on to the network from any workstation. (The user must have permissions to log on from any workstation.) A local account only allows a user to log on to the computer the user is at, not the entire network.

A domain user account serves two main purposes: authentication and authorization. Authorization is the process of verifying a user's rights to access specific network services, such as printers and shares. Authentication is the process of verifying a user's identity. The user name and password is used for this purpose. This is why it is so important to keep the password secret. Anyone who knows the user password can authenticate as the real user. Active Directory requires user passwords to be more than simple passwords. If you attempt to use a simple password, you will generate an error message similar to that in the following screen capture.

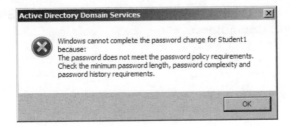

As you can see, the password failed to meet one or more of the following requirements: length, history, and complexity. The requirements are a minimum password length of six characters; a history of 24 passwords; and a complex password, which includes uppercase and lowercase letters, numbers, and at least one special character. You can learn more about user accounts by accessing **Help and Support** located off the **Start** menu. The following list includes a few basic rules for setting up user accounts:

- Passwords can contain a maximum of 127 characters.
- User names must be unique.
- User names should not contain the characters / \ [ ] ; : | = , + * ? < > because they have special meaning to the computer system and can cause an unexpected problem. You are free to use any remaining special characters, such as ! $ # % and &.

Companies generally have a naming convention in place for user names. Typically, they use a last name followed by the initial of the first name. The last name is placed first so that the user will be listed alphabetically in the Active Directory Users and Computers window. It makes it easy to locate a user when all names are listed alphabetically by last name.

For this laboratory activity, the naming scheme you will use for entering user names and group names will be a combination of your name and the name of the object you are creating followed by a decimal number: 1, 2, or 3. For example, a student named *Karen* will create the following users: *KarenUser1*, *KarenUser2*, and so on. This naming scheme will make it easy for your instructor to check your project.

Read the entire laboratory activity before you begin. The laboratory activity contains many examples. Familiarizing yourself with the examples and reading the laboratory activity will give you a clear understanding of what is to be accomplished. After reading the entire laboratory activity, you may begin.

Equipment and Materials

❑   A computer with Windows Server 2008.
❑   Record any additional instructor notes that will be needed to complete the laboratory activity:

_____

_____

_____

_____

Procedure

1. _____ Report to your assigned workstation.

2. _____ Boot the server and verify it is in working order.

3. _____ Access the Active Directory Users and Computers utility (**Start | Administrative Tools | Active Directory Users and Computers**).

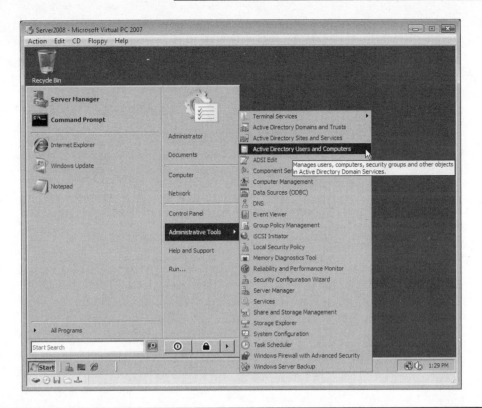

Note

If Active Directory is not installed, there will be no option for **Active Directory Users and Computers**. Select **Computer Management** instead. Creating a new user in the Computer Management utility is similar to creating a new user in Active Directory Users and Computers.

Look at the following screen capture of the Active Directory Users and Computers utility. Notice how the right pane of the window lists users and groups currently in the domain. The left pane is displayed in a typical, Windows directory format. At the top of the directory is the name of the Active Directory that contains all the listed users, groups, domain controllers, and more.

4. _____ From the **Action** menu, select **New | User**. Take note that you can also select **Computer**, **Contact**, **Group**, or **Printer**.

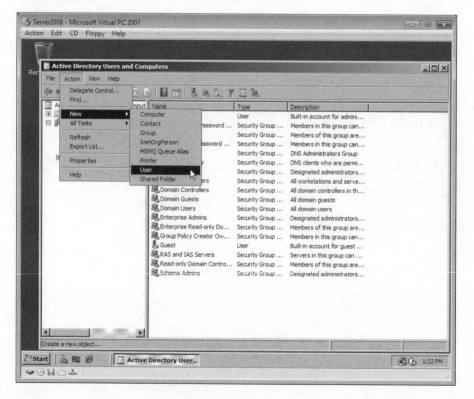

5. _____ The **New Object—User** dialog box will display. You will be required to fill in a series of dialog boxes. The first dialog box should look similar to that in the following screen capture. Fill in the required information and then click **Next**. Remember to create a new user based on your name, such as *BillUser1*.

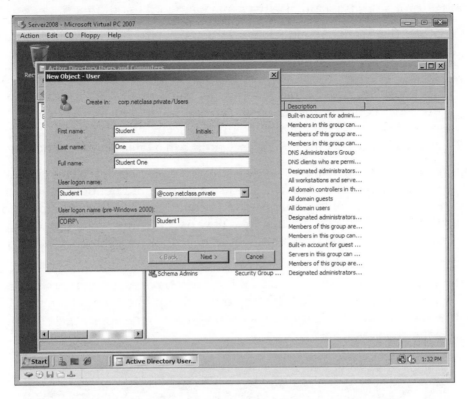

6. _____ In the next dialog box, enter a user password. For this laboratory activity, you will use *PwD123#* for the password, unless otherwise instructed by your teacher. This password meets the complexity required by Active Directory.

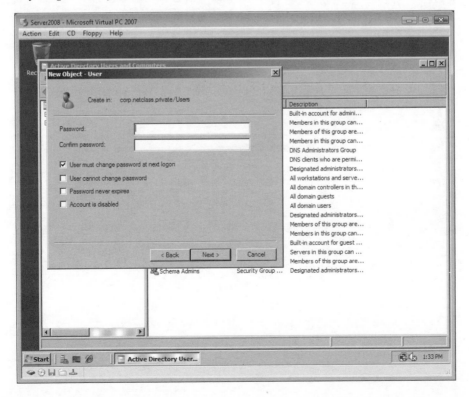

Take special note of the password options available. The first option, **User must change password at next logon**, means the administrator will assign a password. Then, the first time the user logs on to the system, the user will be prompted to change the password. This option allows users to choose their own password so that only they know what it is, not the administrator. Companies typically use the same password for all first time users.

The second option, **User cannot change password**, means the network administrator will assign a password to the user, and the user must use the assigned password each time he or she logs on to the system. The user cannot change the password, only the Administrator can.

The next option, **Password never expires**, means as stated that the assigned password will never expire. Typically, a network administrator sets an expiration date for passwords, forcing the user to change the password periodically to enhance security. This is a common practice. You will learn to set the expiration date and other features in a later laboratory activity.

The last option, **Account is disabled**, is used to disable a user account. This option is used when personnel go on vacation or take an extended leave. You would not delete the user account because the user would lose all permissions and privileges. The associated permissions and privileges would not be regained by creating a new user account using the previous user name and password. Permissions and privileges would have to be reassigned. It is much easier, therefore, to disable and re-enable an account.

7. _____ After entering the password information, click **Next**. A summary of the user information you entered will display. You can either accept the information by clicking **Finish**, or modify the information by clicking **Back** until you reach the appropriate dialog box to which you want to make changes.

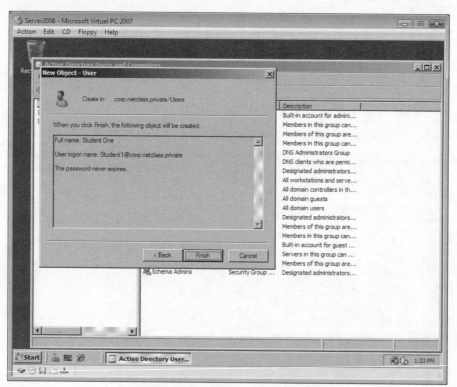

8. _____ After clicking **Finish**, the new user you just created will be automatically added to the list of users. Check the **Users** folder in the Active Directory Users and Computers utility for this user. If you have successfully created a new account, repeat the steps five through seven until you have created two more users. Remember to create user names based on your name, such as *BillUser2* and *BillUser3*. If you do *not* see the user account you have just created, call your instructor.

9. _____ Answer the review questions.

10. _____ If required by your instructor, return the server to its original condition.

Review Questions

1. What are the minimum requirements for a user account? List two items. _____

_____

2. What are the two main types of user accounts? _____

_____

3. What are the two main reasons for a user account? _____

_____

4. What options are available for the user password? _____

_____

5. What must a password contain to meet the complexity requirement? _____

_____

_____

Name _____ Date _____

Class/Instructor _____

32 Adding a Group in Windows Server 2008

After completing this laboratory activity, you will be able to:

- Use **Active Directory Users and Computers** to create a group on a Windows 2008 server.
- Summarize the administrative advantage of groups.
- Differentiate between domain local, global, and universal group scopes.
- Differentiate between distributive group types and security group types.

Introduction

In this laboratory activity, you will create a group. A group is a collection of user accounts that can be managed as a single unit. In a school setting, there are typically several logical groups of people, such as administrators, teachers, and students. A group can be created on the server for each of these logical groups. For example, a teachers' group can be created for all teacher user accounts. Permissions to resources, such as directory shares containing grades, financial data, school policy manuals, school forms, and software programs, can be assigned to groups instead of user accounts. Any user account added to the group automatically inherits the group's rights. This method of assigning permissions greatly reduces administrative time.

Groups can be either directory-based (part of the Active Directory) or local. Local groups exist only on the individual (local) computer. Directory-based groups belong to the Active Directory and are therefore part of a domain. In this laboratory activity, you will create a directory-based group.

Directory-based groups are associated with a group scope and group type. A group scope defines what domains can be accessed and how many domains the group can be a member of. A group type refers to how the group is used—as a security group for access to shared resources or as a distribution group for e-mail distribution. You will be creating a global security-type group. The following lists group scopes and group types with a description of each.

Group Scope

- **Domain local:** Includes users from a single domain and permissions to access resources in only that domain.
- **Global:** Includes users from the domain in which it is created, but can be granted permissions to resources in other domains.
- **Universal:** Includes users from any domain and can be granted permissions to access resources in any domain.

Group Type

- **Security:** Used to assign permissions to shares.
- **Distribution:** Used only to create e-mail distribution lists.

Note

Do not confuse the term *local group* used in reference to a group created on a local computer with the term *domain local group* used in reference to an Active Directory group.

Equipment and Materials

❑ Computer with Windows Server 2008 installed.
❑ The following information provided by your instructor:

Group name: _____ (Example, *Group1*)

Procedure

1. _____ Report to your assigned workstation.

2. _____ Boot the Windows 2008 server and verify it is in working order.

3. _____ Open Active Directory Users and Computers (**Start | Administrative Tools | Active Directory Users and Computers**). A dialog box similar to the following will display.

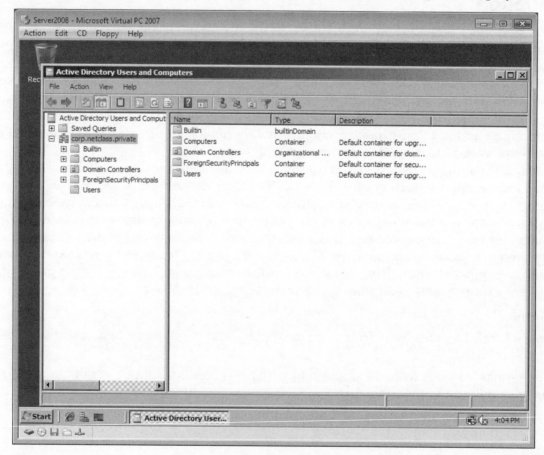

4. _____ In the right pane, select the domain and the Users folder.

5. _____ From the **Action** menu, select **New | Group**.

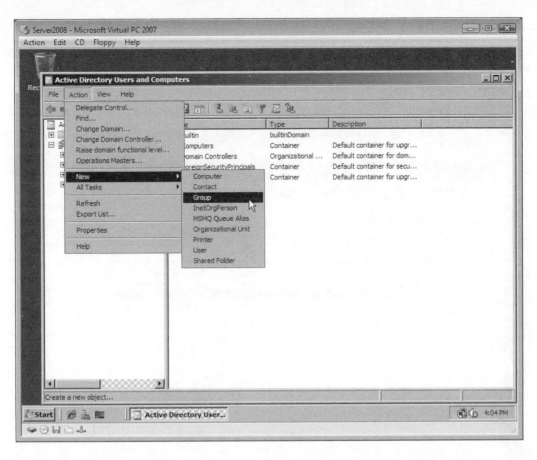

6. _____ The **New Object-Group** dialog box will display. Look at the **Group scope** and **Group type** areas and their options. The default options are **Global** and **Security**. Keep the default settings.

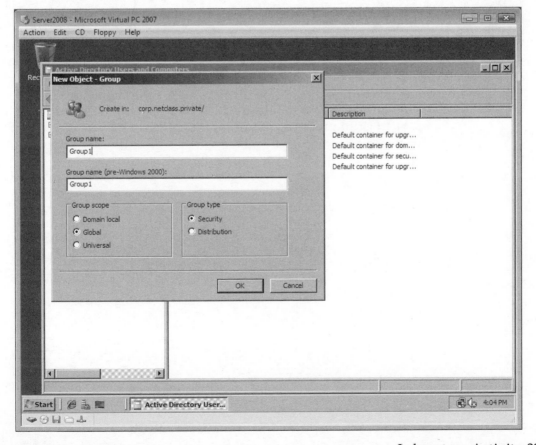

7. _____ Enter the group name and then click **OK**. The new group will be created.

8. _____ Look at the **Active Directory Users and Computers** window to verify the new group has been created. If the new group was not created, call your instructor for assistance.

9. _____ Now, you will assign the user you created in the last laboratory activity to the group. To assign a user to a group, right-click the group and select **Properties** from the shortcut menu.

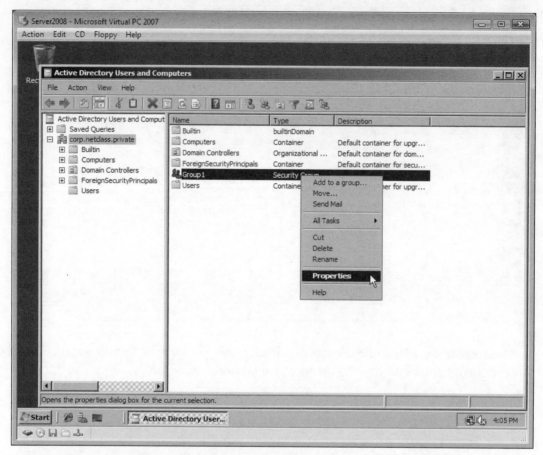

10. _____ When the group's **Properties** dialog box displays, select the **Members** tab.

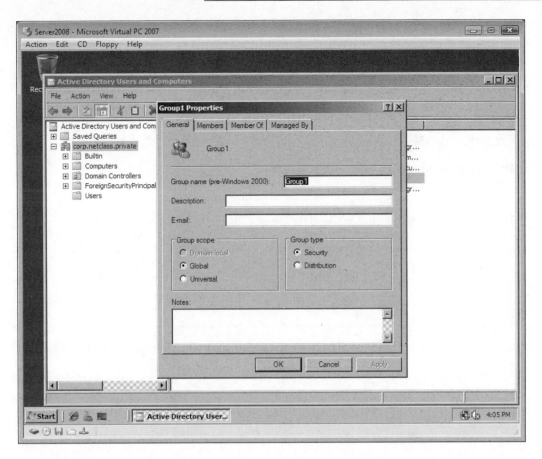

11. _____ A dialog box similar to the following will display. Notice that the new group has no members. Click **Add** to add a member to the group.

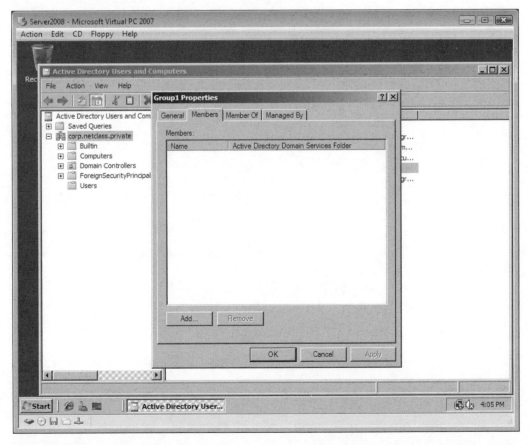

12. _____ Add members by entering the names of users in the text box or click **Advanced** to search for users.

13. _____ After you feel comfortable with creating a group and adding members to the group, answer the review questions.

Review Questions

1. What is the main purpose for creating groups? _____

   _____

2. What is the difference between a security group and a distributive group? _____

   _____

   _____

   _____

   _____

3. Which group scope is limited to a single domain and has access rights to that domain? _____

   _____

Laboratory Activity

33

Name_____ Date _____

Class/Instructor _____

Joining a Domain

After completing this laboratory activity, you will be able to:

- Carry out proper procedures to join a computer to a network domain.
- Give examples of common problems associated with joining a domain.
- Summarize the Microsoft "best practice" for joining a workstation to a domain.

Introduction

In this laboratory activity, you will configure a computer to join a network domain. By default, a Windows-based computer is configured as part of a workgroup. The typical name for the workgroup is *Workgroup*. There is an exception for the home version of Windows. This version, which cannot join a domain, uses the workgroup name *MSHOME*.

The following is the **Computer Name/Domain Changes** dialog box as it looks in Microsoft Vista. If you do not see the option **Domain** in this dialog box, then the version of the operating system does not allow the computer to join a domain.

The appearance of the Windows Vista **Computer Name/Domain Changes** dialog box is similar in Windows 7 and Windows XP. To join a domain you simply select the radio button labeled **Domain** and then enter the name of the domain. The domain name can be either the domain name or the complete DNS name. The computer typically requires a reboot to complete the process of joining a domain.

Every computer that joins a domain has a security account similar to a user account. The computer must also authenticate before successfully joining the domain. Authentication is done without the user being aware that the computer is being authenticated.

The following screen capture from a Windows 2008 server reveals the properties of a computer named *VIRTUALWIN7* that has become a member of the corp.netclass.private domain. Each computer in the domain must have a unique DNS name. The DNS name is a combination of the server domain name and the computer name. In the screen capture, you can see that the complete DNS name is VIRTUALWIN7.corp.netclass.private.

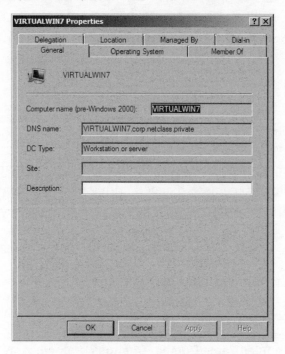

After you join a computer to a domain, it will appear in the Active Directory Users and Computers structure. Look at the following screen capture, which shows two computers listed in the Computers folder under the corp.netclass.private domain tree.

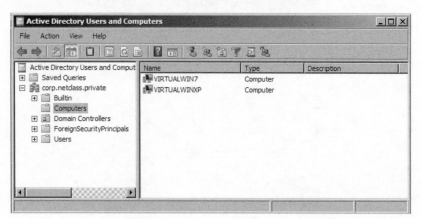

The computers were added automatically when the properties of the computers were changed from a member of a workgroup called *Workgroup* to a member of a domain called *corp*. It is not always necessary to enter the complete DNS name when joining a network domain. If the DNS server is not working correctly or is unavailable, then you will need to supply the Fully Qualified Domain Name (FQDN). Joining a computer to a network in this manner is very common in a small local area network, but it is not the recommended best practice according to Microsoft. The best practice is to add the computer object to the directory structure prior to joining the computer to the domain. Adding an object to the Active Directory structure before the object is actually joined to the active directory domain is referred to as *pre-stage*.

One common reason that you may not be able to join the domain is the network adapter properties may need to be reconfigured by changing the preferred DNS to the IP address of the domain controller. Another reason is making a simple typo when entering the desired domain name. Also, each workstation must have a unique name; otherwise, it will not be able to join the domain.

Equipment and Materials

❑ Computer with Windows Server 2008 installed and set up as a domain controller.
❑ Computer running Windows XP or later connected to a network containing the domain controller.
❑ A user account on the domain controller.
❑ The following information provided by your instructor:

User account name: _____

User account password: _____

Domain name: _____

Note
This lab activity can be completed without a network, but you will not be able to connect to a network or verify the connection to a domain controller.

Procedure

1. _____ Report to your assigned workstation.

2. _____ Boot the computer running Windows XP or later and verify it is in working order.

3. _____ If using Windows Vista or Windows 7, open the **System Properties** dialog box by right-clicking **Computer** and selecting **Properties** from the shortcut menu. Select **Advanced System Settings** and then the **Computer Name** tab. Click the **Change** button.

   If using Windows XP, open the **System Properties** dialog box by right-clicking **Computer** and selecting **Manage** from the shortcut menu. Select the **Computer Name** tab and click the **Change** button.

4. _____ Enter the domain name.

Note
You will be prompted to supply an account name and password to make changes to the domain logon.

5. _____ The computer typically requires a reboot before joining a domain. You will also see a [Ctrl] [Alt] [Del] prompt to produce the typical logon screen.

6. _____ After logging on, call your instructor to inspect your lab.

7. _____ Answer the review questions and then log off of the computer.

Review Questions

1. What is typically required before joining a domain? _____

   _____

2. To which folder of Active Directory Users and Computers is the computer name added? _____

   _____

3. What is the Microsoft best practice method for joining a computer to a domain? _____

   _____

   _____

4. Is pre-staging the computer object absolutely essential to join a domain? _____

   _____

   _____

5. What network adapter configuration IP address might need to be changed if you encounter difficulty successfully joining a domain? _____

   _____

   _____

Name_____ Date _____

Class/Instructor _____

Adding the Print Services Role in Windows Server 2008

After completing this laboratory activity, you will be able to:

- Use the Add Roles Wizard to install the Print Services role.
- Recall the printer configuration tasks available in Print Management.

Introduction

In this laboratory activity, you will run the Add Roles Wizard to install the Print Services role. If an actual printer is available, you may go on to install a printer to the print server. At the end of this lab activity, you will start to see how easy it is to configure the most common server roles.

Equipment and Materials

❑ Computer with Windows Server 2008 installed.

Note
Although it is desired, no printer is necessary for this lab activity. You can still run the lab activity and complete the review questions.

Procedure

1. _____ Report to your assigned workstation.

2. _____ Boot the server and verify it is in working order.

3. _____ Open Server Manager (**Start | Administrative Tools | Server Manager**).

4. _____ After Server Manager opens, scroll down to **Roles Summary** and select **Add Roles**.

5. _____ Select **Print Services** from the list of roles.

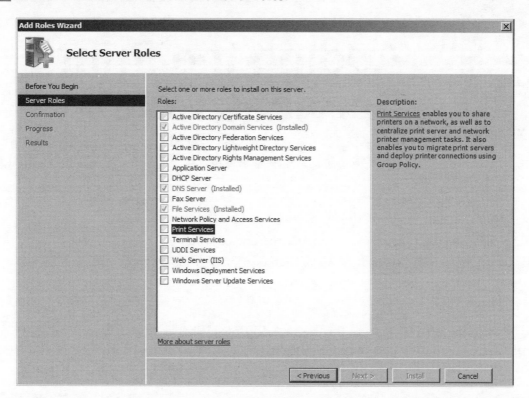

You can find out more about Print Services by clicking the **Print Services** link located on the right of the screen under **Description**. Do this now and scan the information before continuing with the lab.

6. _____ Close the Print Services information window and then click **Next**. A dialog box similar to the following will appear providing important information concerning this role.

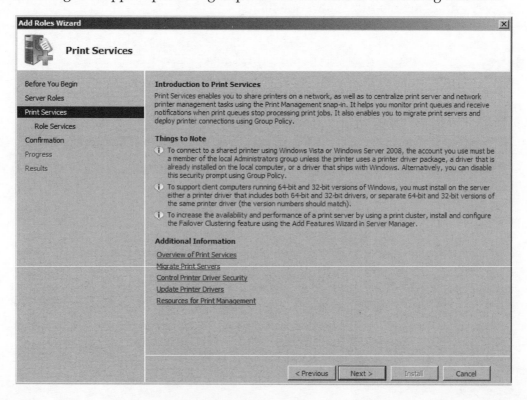

Note that you must install a 64-bit or 32-bit driver to match the Windows operating systems that will access the printer. Also, a failover cluster configuration is recommended to ensure printer availability. Additional information is also available through a list of links displayed in the dialog box. You may review any of the items before continuing.

7. _____ Click **Next**. A dialog box appears presenting three Print Services roles: Print Server, LPD Service, and Internet Printing.

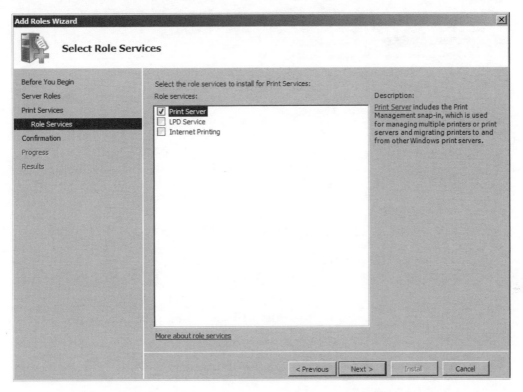

To view information about any of these services, highlight the service. Information will appear on the right under **Description**.

Look at the description for LPD Service and Internet Printing. The review questions are based on the information listed here. Answer the review questions before proceeding.

8. _____ Select only the **Print Server** option. Do *not* select the other two options at this time.

9. _____ Click **Next**. A dialog box confirming your choice of printer role(s) will appear.

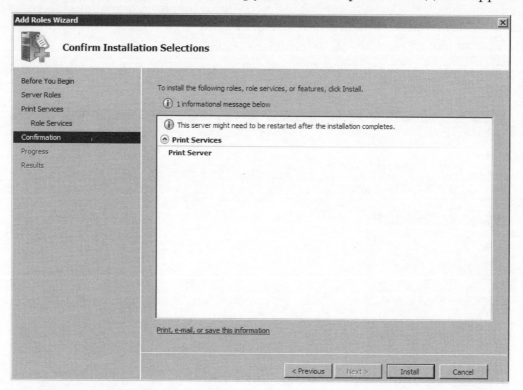

10. _____ Click **Install**. After a few minutes, you will see a dialog box confirming the successful installation of the Printer Services role.

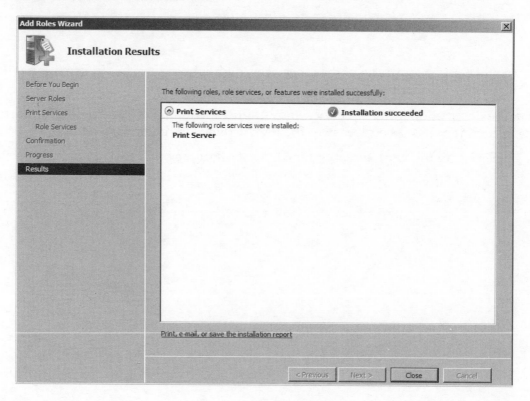

11. _____ Click **Close**. If you have a printer available to connect directly to the server, do so now. The printer will be automatically detected and configured for the server.

12. _____ Open Print Management (**Start | Administrative Tools | Print Management**). The Print Management utility becomes available when the Print Services role is installed. Print Management provides a centralized location to manage all aspects of the printer configuration, such as installing drivers and checking the status of print jobs.

13. _____ Open the **Help** menu item and take a minute to look at the information provided concerning the Print Management utility.

14. _____ Close Print Management and return all materials to their proper storage area.

Review Questions

1. What the acronym LPD represent? _____

2. What is the LPD service used for? _____

_____

3. What does Internet Printing provide? _____

_____

4. What does the acronym IPP represent? _____

Laboratory Activity

35

Name_____ Date _____

Class/Instructor _____

Observing Share Transactions with Wireshark

After completing this laboratory activity, you will be able to:

- Use Wireshark to capture a share transaction between two nodes on a network.
- Compare SMB, SMB2, and other related protocols to the OSI model.
- Summarize why actual bandwidth exceeds the calculated bandwidth for transferring a file based on file contents.
- Summarize why segmentation is necessary.

Introduction

In this laboratory activity, you will share a file and then transfer the file while running Wireshark. You will also open and view the contents of sample capture files to learn the general concepts of what happens during a file transfer.

There are two versions of Server Message Protocol (SMB): SMB and the revised version, SMB2. You will not necessarily see the original version identified as SMB 1.0 because when expressed as SMB it is implied that it is version one. SMB2 was first released with Windows Vista and then later incorporated into Windows 7 and Windows Server 2008. You may see both SMB and SMB2 during the capture because Microsoft still maintains backward compatibility with Windows XP and earlier operating systems.

You probably think that a simple file transfer would not be very complex. In reality, a lot of information is transferred before and after the exchange of one simple file. In the first SMB capture, Wireshark Sample 6, there are 252 frames. Over 200 frames are encountered before the actual file contained in the share is transferred to the client. Only one frame contains the actual contents of the small file being accessed and transferred.

Later, you will perform a file transfer based on SMB2. You will see a significant reduction in the number of frames required for a file transfer. SMB2 has combined many of the commands and now relies on newer security features incorporated into the operating system. This results in fewer required frames. On a local area network, SMB2 uses the IPv6 protocol for encapsulating the SMB2 packets.

Microsoft uses SMB to support file and print sharing activities. SMB is an upper-level protocol which handles the OSI model application and presentation level responsibilities. SMB relies on other protocols to establish a session and to transport commands and data over the network. NetBIOS is used to set up the session and is found at the session level of the OSI model. SMB also relies on the TCP, UDP, IP, and Ethernet protocols to carry it. Look at the following illustration to see the relationship of the protocols.

Application Presentation	SMB & SMB2
Session	NetBIOS
Transport	TCP & UDP
Network	IPv4 & IPv6
Data link	Ethernet
Physical	

Notice how SMB/SMB2 is identified at the application and presentation layers. The encapsulation process of SMB/SMB2 also uses NetBIOS, TCP, UDP, IPv4, IPv6, and Ethernet.

You may see both SMB and SMB2 appear in a capture series. The SMB protocol will appear when there are Windows XP or older operating systems in the network. Windows Vista and later will typically only contain SMB2 packets.

Your Wireshark capture will not match the example exactly. Reasons for this include but are not limited to the following:

- Which updates or service pack have been installed.
- How you access the file.
- Background activity such as time synchronization of the network by the Network Time Protocol (NTP).
- Browser update activity.
- Other workstations connected to the network.
- Antivirus software activity.
- Other software programs that use network capabilities.

Equipment and Materials

- Windows Vista or later workstation with Wireshark installed.
- Windows Server 2008 with a folder ready to share.
- Wireshark Sample 6 file.
  Wireshark Sample 6 file location: _____
- Wireshark Sample 7 file.
  Wireshark Sample 7 file location: _____
- Wireshark Sample 8 file.
  Wireshark Sample 8 file location: _____

Procedure

1. _____ Gather required materials and report to your assigned workstation.

2. _____ Boot the server and the workstation and verify they are in working order.

3. _____ On the workstation, open the Wireshark program and the Wireshark Sample 6 file.

4. _____ Look at frame 7. Notice that in the middle pane under NetBIOS Session Service the terms *called* and *calling* are used to identify the two nodes.

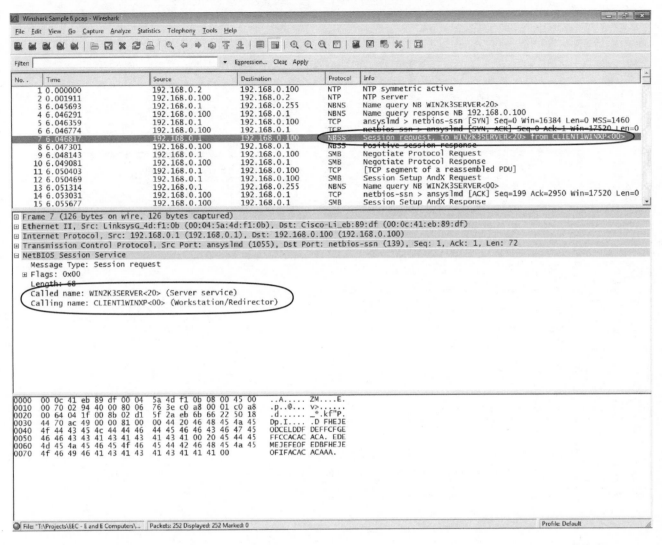

In the example, the server is identified as the "called name" and the workstation is identified as the "calling name." The called and calling names are NetBIOS names.

5. _____ Highlight frame 9. Notice in the middle pane under SMB (Server Message Block Protocol) that the particular "dialect" of SMB is negotiated.

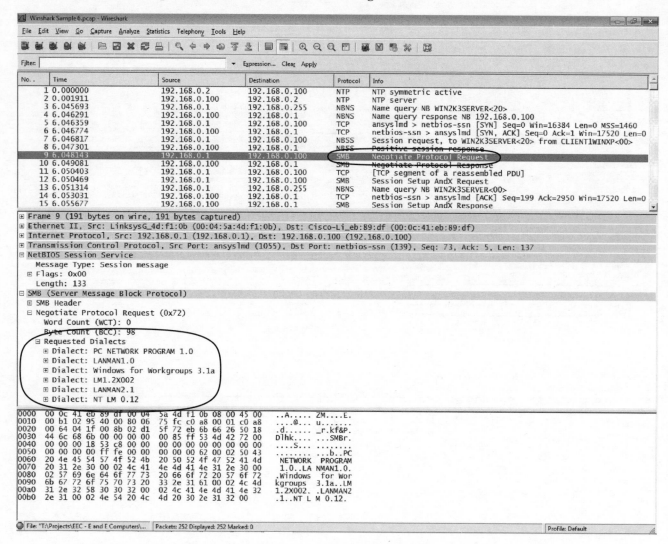

SMB has been developed over many years and several "dialects" exist. A specific dialect must be agreed on to ensure the most compatible communications. An early version may not contain all the various enhancements and thus could generate errors while attempting to transfer data or while attempting to access a share.

6. _____ Highlight frame 19. Notice that the client is requesting a connection to the shares located on the server.

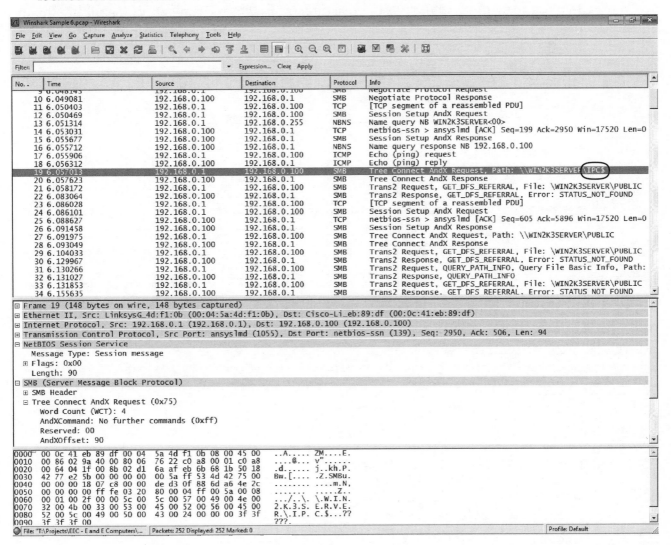

Take note of the IPC$ share designation. This is a general share rather than a specific share. It is used to initiate a temporary connection between a client and server.

In the following frames, more messages are exchanged concerning mostly security issues. Each step in the path to the network share is negotiated, such as the hard disk drive access, the share directory structure, and the file. On reaching frame 238, the contents of the file are finally accessed.

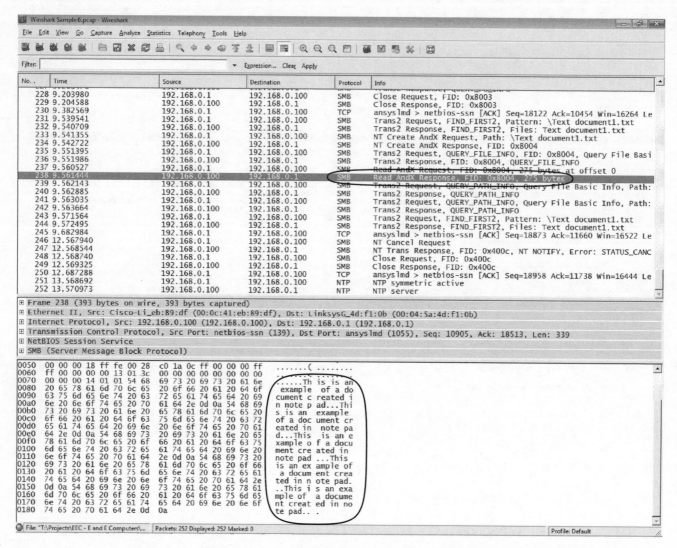

You can see the actual file contents at the bottom of the screen. The words "This is an example of a document created in note pad" are displayed several times as they are in the actual contents of the file. You will create a similar file for viewing later in this lab activity. Take note of the "Read AndX Response" located on frame 238 of the **Info** column. This is an abbreviation for the SMB command used to display the contents of the file. This can only be issued after all the other command steps have been responded to correctly.

As you can see, there is a lot of network activity that takes place whenever you access a share on a client /server network. The amount of frames is significantly reduced on a peer-to-peer network system, but accessing a share still requires approximately 50 frames. This overhead should be taken into account when calculating bandwidth requirements for a network file transfer. In the Wireshark Sample 6 file containing a few lines of text, the ratio of overhead to actual file transfer bandwidth is very high. As the size of the file contents increases, the ratio is reduced.

Note

Calculated bandwidth or how long it takes to download a file is typically based on file size divided by device bandwidth. As you can see in the screen capture, many frames are required to negotiate the connection to the file before it is downloaded or transferred. This is why calculations are not accurate at all.

7. _____ Open the Wireshark Sample 7 file. Examine frames 168 to 189.

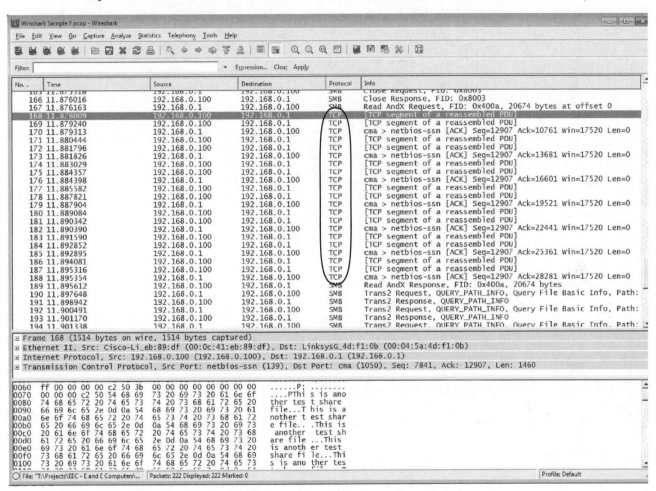

Notice the series of frames using the TCP protocol. The TCP protocol is used to transfer the remaining segments of the file contents after the first segment was transferred using SMB. When a file is too large to fit inside one frame, the file must be divided into smaller sections or packets. Dividing the large collection of data into smaller packages is called *segmenting the data* or *segmentation*. The entire Ethernet frame and payload is a maximum of 1514 bytes.

8. _____ Open the Wireshark Sample 8 file. This sample capture was created using Windows 7 and Windows Server 2008. Notice that the entire SMB2 transaction takes less than 100 frames. That's significantly a lesser amount of frames when compared to SMB.

9. _____ Highlight and examine frame 71. You will be able to view the contents of the shared file.

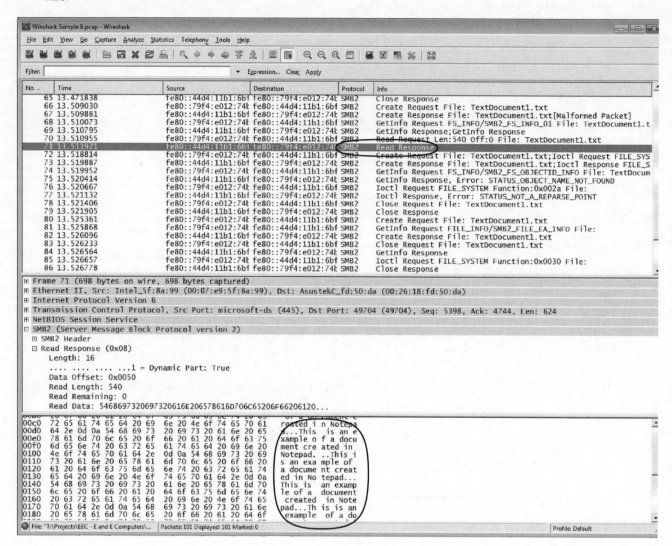

10. _____ Highlight and examine frame 66. Notice that the share permission settings for the TextDocument1.txt file are shown. The permissions are read and write, but not delete.

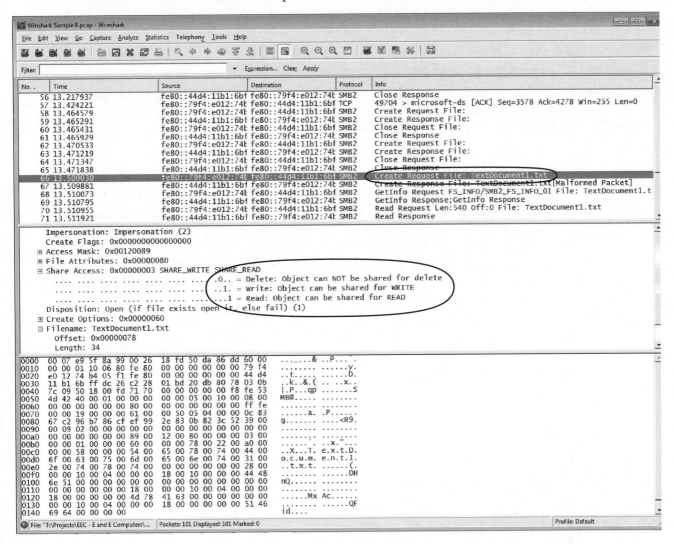

11. _____ Open any frame that contains the SMB2 and the NetBIOS protocol and expand the NetBIOS Session Service entry in the middle pane. You will see that it is practically void of any critical information. SMB2 does not rely on NetBIOS name resolution when using IPv6. As you can see, all the frames identified as SMB2 use IPv6 to support packet exchanges. SMB relies solely on IPv4.

12. _____ Now you will create a document for viewing on the server. At the server, access the Notepad program. Create a document containing the sentence, "This is an example of a document created in Notepad" without the quotation marks. Copy and paste the line nine more times. You will have a total of ten lines. Save the file using the name TextDocument1. Create a shared folder on the server and place the document in the shared folder.

13. _____ At the workstation, start a Wireshark capture.

14. _____ From the workstation, access the text document you just created.

15. _____ After you have successfully accessed the shared document, stop the protocol analyzer capture and view its contents. Look for the captured frame that contains the contents of the document. Look for "Read Response" in the **Info** column to help locate the frame. You should be able to read the contents of the document.

16. _____ Create a document of much greater length. Copy the contents of the Notepad document to a new file called TextDocument2. Copy and paste the 10 lines approximately 20 to 30 more times to create a much larger document. Place the new file in the shared folder, and then access the new document from the client while Wireshark is capturing frames.

17. _____ Stop the capture and then view the contents of the capture to see if you can locate the series of TCP segments used to carry the contents of the larger document.

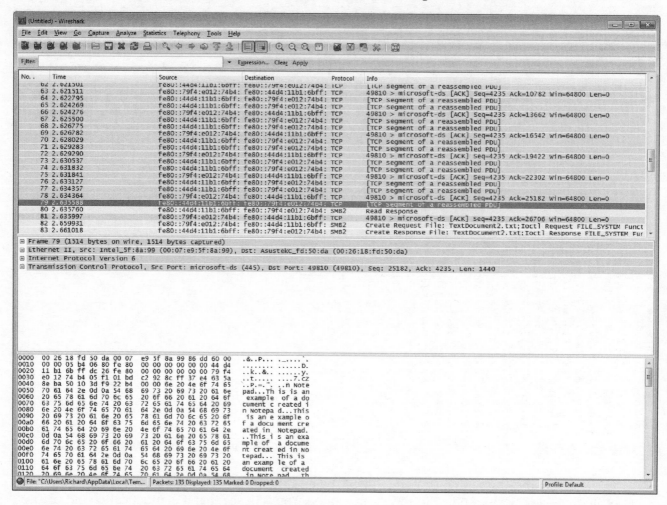

The series of TCP protocol packets contain sections of the entire file. The last section delivered will be a SMB2 Read Response. Look for the series of segmentations in your capture. If you cannot locate this series, call your instructor for assistance.

Note

Large files must be segmented because TCP/IP limits the maximum size of a frame. In general, the maximum TCP segment size is 1514 bytes.

---

18. _____ Return the server and the workstation to their original condition.

19. _____ Answer the review questions.

Review Questions

1. At what OSI layer(s) does the SMB/SMB2 protocol align? _____
   _____

2. What other protocols does SMB/SMB2 require to communicate with another node?_____
   _____

3. What is the purpose of the IPC$ share? _____
   _____
   _____

4. Why are there so many frames for a file transfer? _____
   _____
   _____
   _____

5. What is the maximum size of the Ethernet frame? _____

6. What is segmentation? _____
   _____

7. After the file contents transfer begins, which high-level protocol is used to continue transferring data to support segmentation? _____

8. Which protocol version, IPv4 or IPv6, is used for SMB2? _____

9. Why would the original SMB protocol show up in a capture series? _____
   _____
   _____
   _____

10. Why is calculated bandwidth much lower than actual bandwidth? _____
    _____
    _____

openSUSE 11 LINUX

Name_____ Date _____

Class/Instructor _____

Installing openSUSE 11 Linux

After completing this laboratory activity, you will be able to:

- Carry out a default installation of openSUSE Linux.
- Recall the three default partitions created during the openSUSE installation process.
- Summarize the purpose of various installation options.
- Summarize the role of YaST when used as part of the installation process.
- Use the YaST installation program to modify the default configuration settings.

Introduction

In this laboratory activity, you will install openSUSE Linux, an open source version of the Novell SUSE Linux operating system. You can download a copy from the openSUSE organization located at http://software.opensuse.org/112/en. If this Web address is no longer valid, conduct an Internet search using the key words "openSUSE Linux download."

The two main problems typically encountered during a Linux installation are hardware compatibility and understanding terminology unique to UNIX/Linux operating systems. While the terminology problem still exists, hardware compatibility issues have become less of a problem. However, there is no need to fully understand Linux terminology to complete a successful installation process. This does not mean you do not need to understand the terminology, but rather how easy it has become to install Linux.

YaST is the default installer program for openSUSE 11. The YaST program automatically conducts a series of hardware probes to determine the best default configuration to use. In general, if you accept the defaults, you should not encounter any difficulties with the installation.

You can start the installation process in similar fashion to performing a Windows operating system installation. Place the openSUSE installation DVD into the DVD drive. The disk will be autodetected and the installation program started. You can also place the installation DVD into the drive and then reboot the computer. If the installation does not start from the DVD after the reboot, you may need to configure the boot device sequence so that the DVD drive is listed as the first boot device. You will need to configure the boot options in the BIOS setup.

After the installation DVD boots, you will be presented with several menu options such as those in the following table.

Menu Option	Description
Boot from Hard Disk	Boot directly from the hard disk drive. Only applicable after the operating system has been installed.
Installation	Normal installation of openSUSE Linux on the hard disk drive.
Repair Installed System	Boots to the graphic repair system.
Rescue System	Starts as a minimal, command-line only Linux operating system.
Firmware Test	Determines if the system BIOS or firmware is compatible.
Memory Test	Performs RAM memory tests to detect memory problems.
Boot Options	Allows for additional modified options entered as command syntax. For advanced users only.

Normally, you would select the **Installation** option to begin the installation process. The installation process typically starts the GRUB boot loader and then performs a quick system check to verify that the minimum required hardware exists. Next, the Linux kernel is loaded into RAM. After the kernel loads, the YaST program is loaded into RAM and continues the installation process using a graphical user interface. YaST is also the main system configuration tool used by SUSE Linux.

Note
YaST is an acronym for Yet Another Setup Program. As you will see in the study of UNIX/Linux, programmers have a strange sense of humor and reflect it in their choice of program names and acronyms.

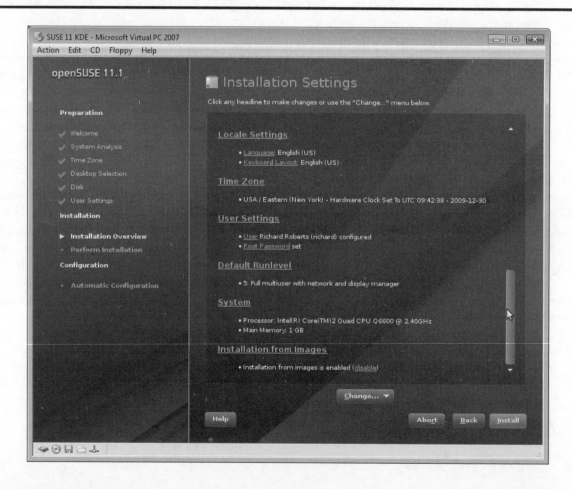

YaST performs the installation in two stages: the base installation stage and the system configuration stage. Base installation includes language selection, major hardware component detection, and hardware profile creation. It also installs the required files and drivers.

The second part of the installation is the system configuration. It includes setting up the root password and network settings, the online update, removing temporary installation files, and the final device configuration. The exact configuration will vary according to the version being installed. As the installation process moves through the various stages, you can interact with each stage to accept or modify the default recommendations. You can abort the installation at any time by clicking the **Abort** button at the bottom of the screen. You can access help at any time during the installation by clicking the **Help** button.

One problem that is commonly encountered in the classroom lab environment is the use of hard drives that contain previously-installed operating systems. This laboratory is intended for a clean installation. All previously-installed operating systems and all partitions should be removed prior to the openSUSE installation unless told otherwise by your instructor. The existence of an operating system on the hard drive could cause Linux to install as a dual-boot system.

During the openSUSE installation, the hard drive will be automatically partitioned into three partitions and formatted. The three partitions are /swap, /home, and / (root). The /swap partition is used in similar fashion as the Windows swap partition. The /swap partition supplements the available RAM. The /home partition is used for user home directories. The Linux operating system is installed in the root partition symbolized by the backslash (/) symbol. This partition is also called the *system partition* and is where all the required operating system files are installed. It is not used for user storage.

Novell has chosen ext3 as the default file system for formatting the partitions. Other possible file systems are ReiserFS, ext, ext2, ext3, ext4 and JFS. Again, the default file system is dictated by the Linux operating system version.

During the installation process, you will create a password for the "superuser." *Superuser* is another name for *root user*. The password should consist of a combination of uppercase and lowercase letters as well as numbers and special keyboard symbols. You can even use spaces in a password. If the password does not meet the complexity recommendations, you will generate a warning message. The complexity of the password is not mandatory, just strongly recommended.

To find out more information about openSUSE Linux, go to the Novell Web page located at http://en.opensuse.org/Welcome_to_openSUSE.org. openSUSE documentation is also available at www.novell.com/documentation/opensuse110. To learn more about other Linux versions, look at the Linux organization Web site located at www.linux.org. You can access a selection of open source PDF booklets for openSUSE Linux at my Web site at www.RMRoberts.com/FTP_files/ OpenSUSE11Documentation.

Note

When performing this lab, do *not* make changes to the recommended default configuration unless told to do so by your instructor.

Equipment and Materials

❑ openSuSE 11.1 or later set of DVD discs.
❑ Computer meeting the following requirements:
    ❑ 512 MB RAM.
    ❑ 5 GB or more available hard disk space.
    ❑ CPU: Intel Pentium 1 to 4 or Xeon; AMD Duron, Athlon, Athlon XP, Athlon MP, Athlon 64, or Sempron.

❑ The following information, provided by your instructor:

   ❑ Root password: _____

   ❑ User name: _____

   ❑ User password: _____

   ❑ Additional user names: _____

Procedure

1. _____ Gather all required materials and report to your assigned workstation.

2. _____ Boot the computer and then place the first installation DVD in the DVD boot device.

Note

You may need to access the BIOS setup program to reconfigure the computer to boot from the DVD device first rather than from the hard disk drive.

---

3. _____ With the openSUSE installation DVD in the DVD drive, reboot the system to start the installation. In a few seconds, you will be presented with several options similar to those in the following screen capture. The exact appearance and options will vary according to the version of Linux you are installing.

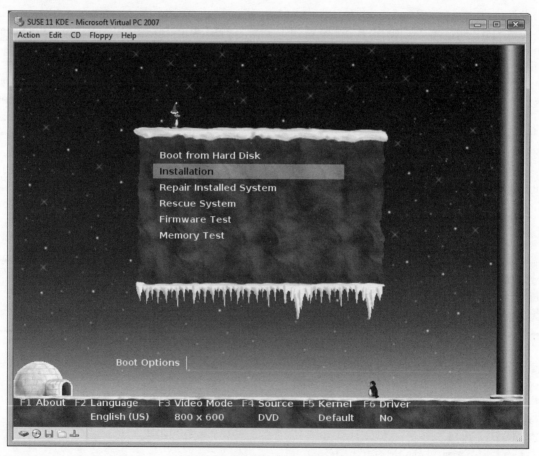

4. _____ Select **Installation**. A progress bar located under the word *openSUSE* will indicate the progress of loading the required minimal installation programs.

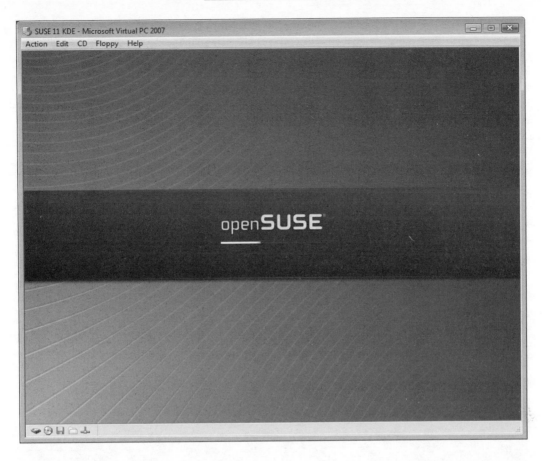

After about a few minutes to 20 minutes, a minimal SUSE Linux operating system will load and take control of the installation operation.

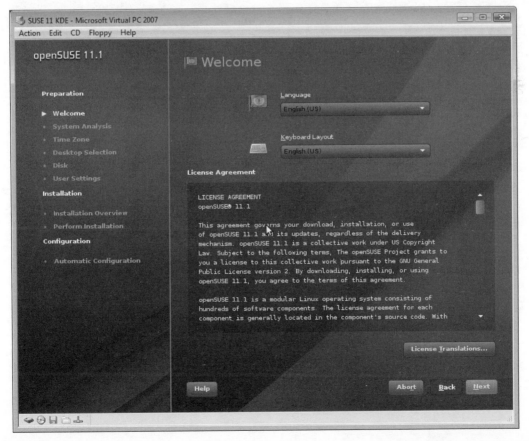

You are prompted to select the language and keyboard layout for the installation. You are also presented with the license agreement. Notice the list of preparation activities located in the left pane. It allows you to track the progress of the installation process. Completed steps are identified with a check mark.

5. _____ Click **Next** to continue. The installation program will probe the system to identify hardware and determine if any partitions are already created and if an operating system is already installed. This will take a few minutes.

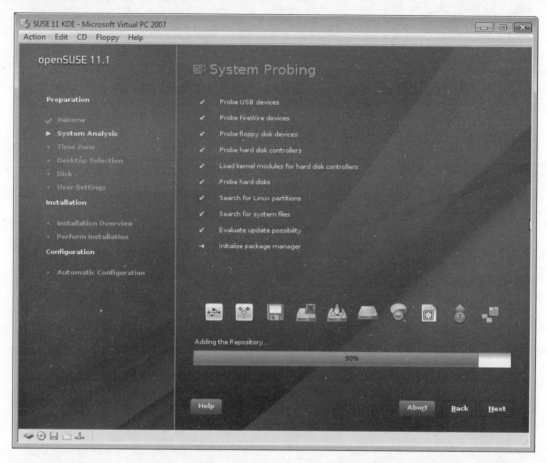

Note
You have the option to abort the installation at any time by clicking the **Abort** button or by pressing the key combination [Ctrl] [Alt] [Del].

---

6. _____ You are now prompted to select an installation mode. The three choices are **New Installation**, **Update**, and **Repair Installed System**. Select **New Installation** and then click **Next** to continue.

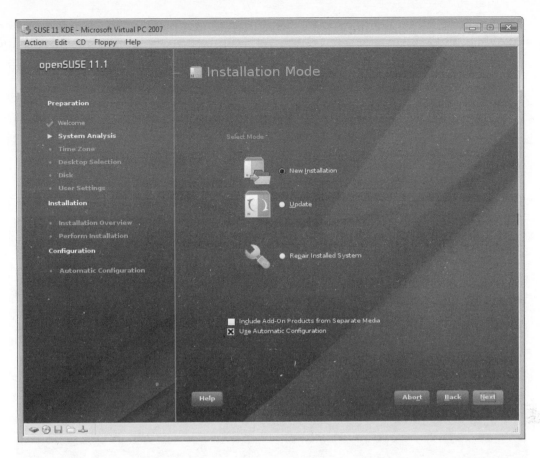

7. _____ You are prompted to set the clock and select the time zone. You can adjust the time by clicking the **Change** button or clicking **Next** to continue.

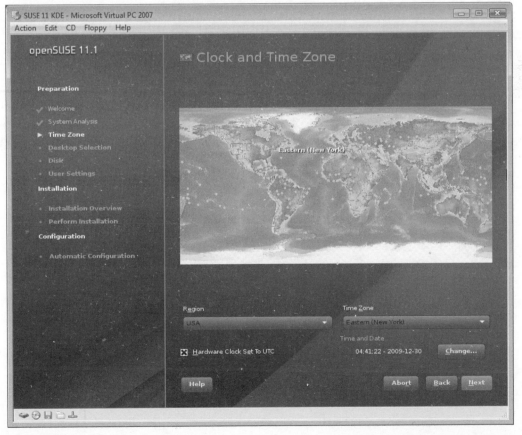

8. _____ You will be prompted to choose between Gnome or KDE for the user interface. Select **KDE 4.1** so that your system will match the screen captures in the upcoming lab activities.

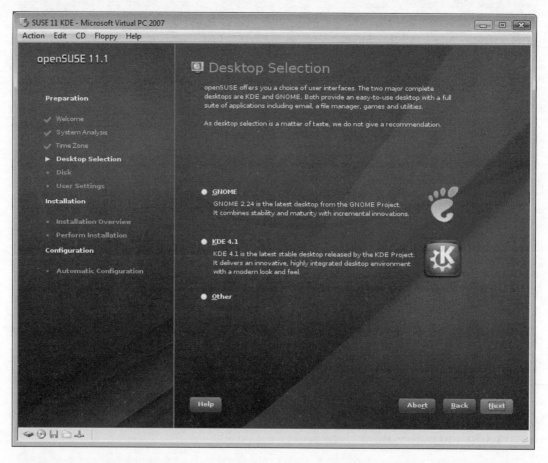

Note

You will not always be presented with two choices. Some versions of Linux only offer one user interface, especially if the Linux version is a beta release.

9. _____ Click **Next**. You are now prompted to choose a partition style. The **Partition Based** option will create a set of three typical Linux partitions using ext3. The **LVM Based** option represents the Logical Volume Manager (LVM). LVM is used to manage large disk volumes, such as a disk farm. It also has a feature to adjust the size of Microsoft partitions and volumes.

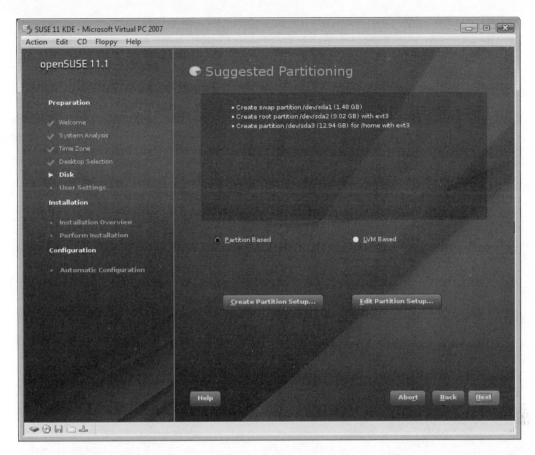

10. _____ Select the **Partition Based** option. You will be prompted to create the default user account and password.

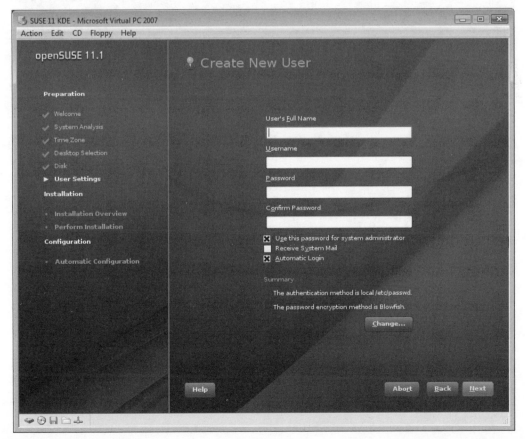

You must supply the user's full name. The user account name will be automatically created based on the user name. For example, the full user name "Richard M. Roberts" will automatically generate the user account name "richard." Notice that the automatically-generated user name is in lowercase letters. You may change the user name to match an established naming scheme.

You will need to create a user account password. If the password does not meet sufficient complexity, a message will appear informing you that the password can be easily guessed. Click **Yes** to accept your password choice and to close this message box.

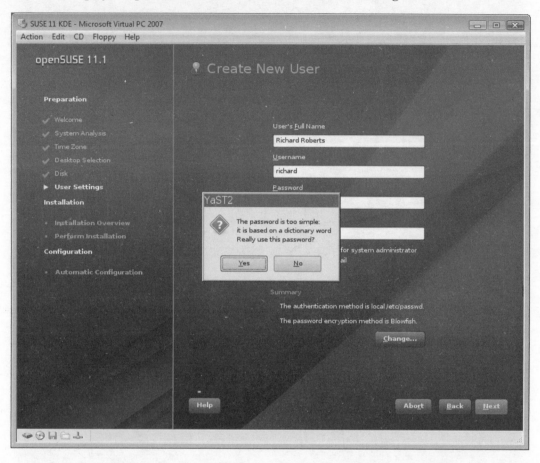

Notice the "Summary" information provided about the location of the password and the type of encryption used.

11. _____ Click **Next**. You will be presented with a list of installation settings. You can review the settings if you like before moving on. At this point in the installation, you can still make changes to the configuration selections. If the configuration selections are to your liking, click **Install**.

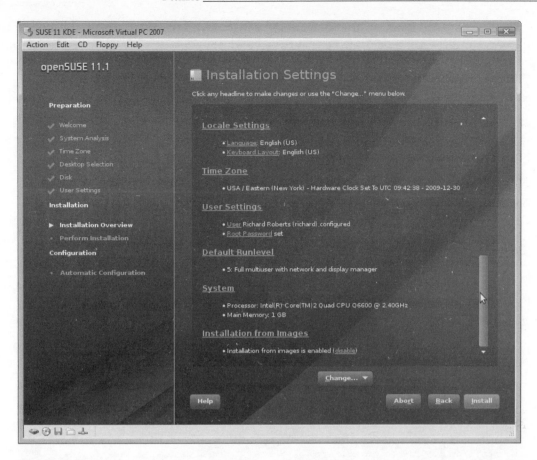

After accepting the settings in the last step, you will be prompted once more to confirm the selection.

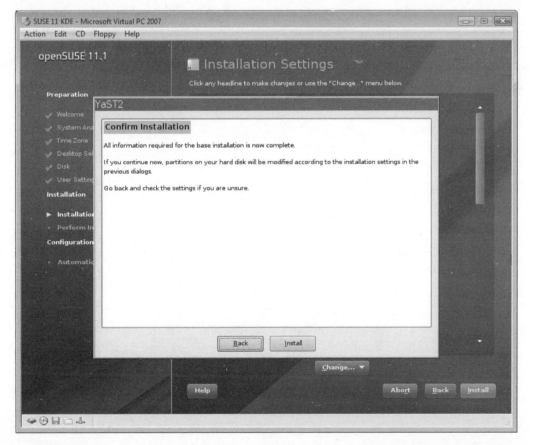

12. _____ Click **Install** to confirm the installation settings. A screen similar to the following will appear, showing the installation progress. It can take a long time (30 minutes or more) to complete the configuration.

When the installation is complete, the desktop will load and a message box will appear similar to that in the following screen capture.

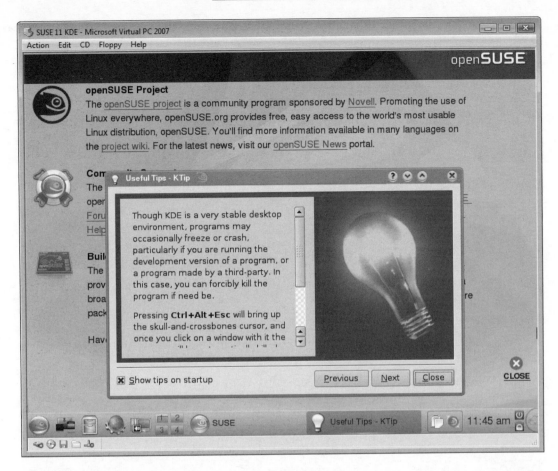

Typically, a **Useful Tips** message box will be displayed. Again, this type of screen display will vary according to the version of Linux you are installing. There may not be a message box at all. You can deselect the **Show tips at startup** option if you wish.

13. _____ Close the message box to see the **openSUSE** screen with links to information about openSUSE.

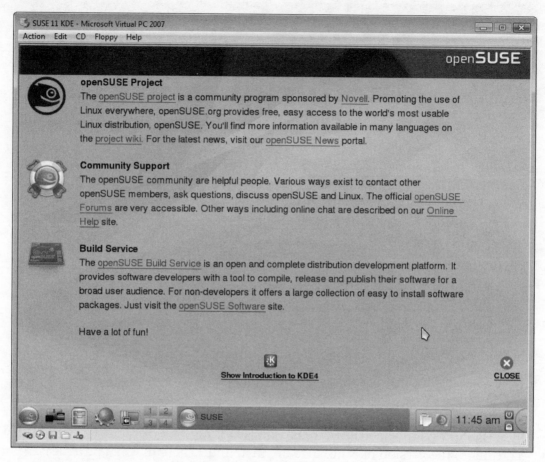

14. _____ Close the **openSUSE** screen. You will see a typical SUSE Linux desktop similar to the following.

The exact appearance of the desktop will vary according to the version of Linux as well as which desktop package you selected. The desktop shown in the screen capture is based on openSUSE 11.1 KDE.

15. _____ Call your instructor to inspect your lab activity.

16. _____ Go on to answer the review questions. Return all materials to their proper storage area.

Review Questions

1. What is the name assigned to the Linux administrator by default? _____

2. What is another name for the root user? _____

3. What other user is equal to the root? _____

4. What elements should be incorporated into a secure Linux password? _____

_____

5. Can spaces be used in the password? _____

6. What is the purpose of the /swap partition? _____

_____

7. What is the purpose of the boot partition? _____

_____

8. What are the two common Linux desktop user interfaces for openSUSE Linux? _____
   _____

9. What three partitions are created by default? _____
   _____

10. Which partition is used for user home directories? _____

Name_____ Date _____

Class/Instructor _____

Adding a New User in openSUSE

After completing this laboratory activity, you will be able to:

- Differentiate between the two general types of Linux user accounts.
- Use the YaST User and Group Management module to create new user accounts.
- Summarize the purpose of the password configuration settings.
- Use the YaST User and Group Management module to modify user accounts.
- Use the YaST User and Group Management module to delete user accounts.

Introduction

In this laboratory activity, you will create and edit a new user account on a SUSE Linux system with the YaST User and Group Management module. YaST is similar in function as Windows Control Panel. YaST is used to make system configuration changes. The following is a screen capture of the YaST display.

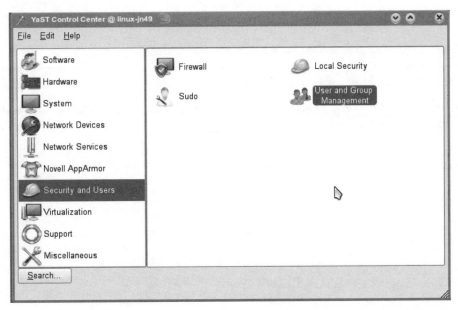

In the left pane, notice the major categories, such as **Software**, **Hardware**, **System**, and **Network Devices**. For this lab activity, you will select the **Security and Users** category and then the **User and Group Management** option, which will be located in the right-hand pane.

Only the root user has permission to create a new user account. If you are already logged on to the system and are not the root, you will be prompted for the root password when attempting to change the system configuration. When you are prompted for the root user password, you are automatically granted permission to make system changes such as creating a new account.

There are two general types of user accounts: local user and domain user. In this lab activity, you will create a local user account which is a user account on the Linux computer. A domain user account is associated with a client/server network.

Equipment and Materials

❏ Computer with openSUSE 11 or later installed.
❏ The following information provided by your instructor:

Root password: _____

LDAP server password: _____ (If required)

First new user account name: _____ (Example, *Student1*)

Second new user account name: _____ (Example, *Student2*)

First new user password: _____ (Example, *pa$$word*)

Second new user password: _____ (Example, *pa$$word*)

Note
The user account password can be the same for both user accounts.

Procedure

1. _____ Report to your assigned workstation.

2. _____ Boot the computer and log on to the KDE system using your assigned user account or as root.

Note
You will need the root password to add users and groups.

---

3. _____ At the KDE desktop, open YaST located in **Application Launcher | Computer** tab.

4. _____ Select the **Security and Users** category in the left pane and then select the **User and Group Management** option in the right pane. The **User and Group Administration** dialog box will display.

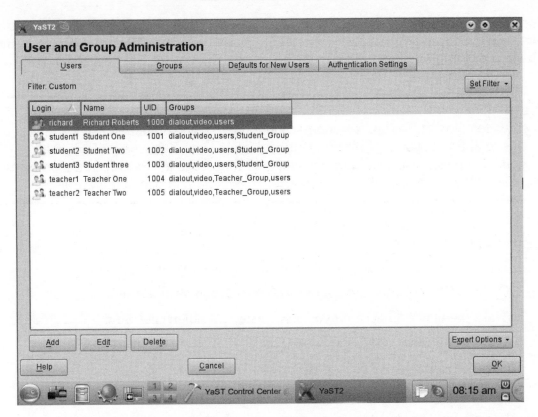

Notice how existing user accounts are displayed and that each user has a User ID (UID). The UID is a unique number associated with a user account. Any groups the user is assigned to are also displayed. The three buttons that you will use to manage user accounts are **Add**, **Edit**, and **Delete**.

5. _____ Click **Add** to create a new user account. The **New Local User** dialog box will display.

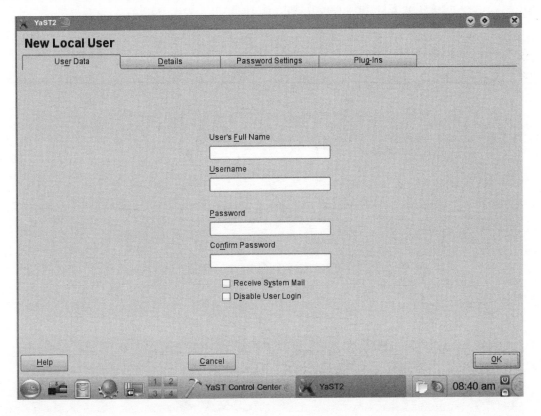

6. _____ Enter the user's full name (first name and last name), the user name (the account logon name), and the password, and then confirm the password. Click **OK**. You will be returned to the **User and Group Administration** dialog box. The new account will be listed. If not, call your instructor for assistance.

Note

If you attempt to create a user logon account name using an uppercase letter, you will be warned but you can still create the account. Linux systems prefer that all accounts and files use only lowercase letters. Uppercase letters can create problems for some Linux e-mail application software. That is the purpose of the warning.

---

7. _____ Close YaST.

8. _____ Log off the system.

9. _____ Log back on to the system using the new account you just created.

10. _____ Open **YaST | Security and Users | User and Group Management**.

11. _____ Select the new user account you just created and then click **Edit**.

12. _____ Change the password to Pa$$word123.

13. _____ Change the password back to the original password.

14. _____ Create another new user account.

15. _____ Log off and then back on using the second newly created user account.

16. _____ Log off and then back on using the first account you created in this lab activity.

17. _____ While logged on using the first account you created, delete the second account. To delete the second account, select the account user name and then click **Delete**.

18. _____ In the **User and Group Administration** dialog box, double-click the name of the first account you created. The **Existing Local User** dialog box will display.

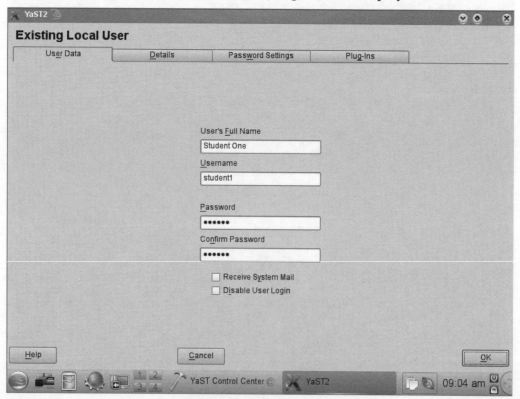

The **Existing Local User** dialog box provides a quick and easy way to change the user account password and provide more information about the account through the tabs at the top of the box.

19. _____ Select the **Details** tab and view the information provided. Information such as the user ID, home directory, and group membership is displayed.

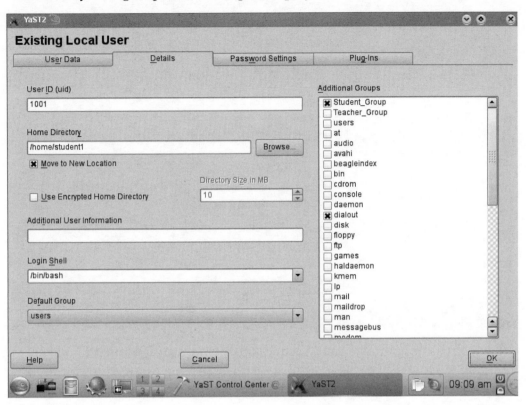

You can also reconfigure such items as the location of the home directory, encrypt the home directory, and add additional group memberships to the user account.

Do *not* make any changes. Simply view the information.

20. _____ Select the **Password Settings** tab. A dialog box similar to the following will display.

In this dialog box, you can make changes to the password configuration to make it expire after a specific number of days or by indicating an expiration date. Many of the SUSE Linux account features are similar to the ones in Windows operating systems.

21. _____ Click **Cancel** and then close YaST.

22. _____ Answer the review questions.

Review Questions

1. What are the two general types of user accounts? _____

   _____

2. Who is authorized to create a new user account? _____

3. If you create a new user account and are not the root, what will happen? _____

   _____

4. What YaST module is used to create a new user account? _____

   _____

5. What is the UID? _____

   _____

6. Which button is used to delete an account? _____

7. Which button is used to modify a user account? _____

8. What is the default maximum number of days for a new user password? _____

9. What is the default number of days before the password warning is issued? _____

Name_____ Date _____

Class/Instructor _____

openSUSE Application Launcher

After completing this laboratory activity, you will be able to:

- Identify the various program categories associated with Application Launcher.
- Identify several applications that are similar in function when compared to Windows operating systems.
- Use Application Launcher to load programs.

Introduction

In this laboratory activity, you will become familiar with SUSE Application Launcher. SUSE Linux is similar in many ways to the Windows operating systems and provides many of the same features. The biggest difference is the terminology and the software application names. Look at the following screen capture of the SUSE Linux 11.1 KDE desktop.

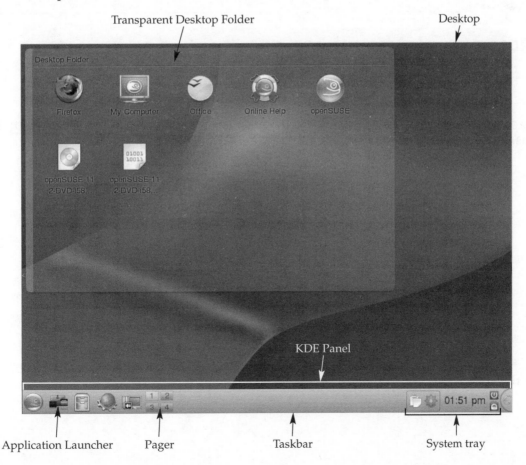

The following table compares some SUSE Linux terminology and software application names with those in Microsoft Windows.

SUSE Linux	Microsoft Windows
Launch Application button	Start menu button
Task Manager Panel	taskbar
YaST Control Center	Control Panel
Firefox	Internet Explorer
Konqueror	Windows Explorer
openOffice	Microsoft Office

Note
In Linux operating systems, there are many different Web browser and explorer programs, not just the ones mentioned here.

Equipment and Materials

❑ Computer with openSUSE 11 or later installed.
❑ The following information:

Logon user name: _____

Password: _____

Procedure

1. _____ Report to your assigned workstation.

2. _____ Boot the computer and log on using your assigned user account or as root.

3. _____ Select each icon in the KDE Panel, but do *not* click any of the items. Simply hover the mouse pointer over each item to see the information provided.

4. _____ Hover the mouse over the **Application Launcher** to present a message box with information about the function of the application.

5. _____ Click the **Application Launcher** to reveal the five major application groupings or menus: **Favorites, Applications, Computer, Recently Used**, and **Leave**.

Name _____

The **Favorites** menu is listed when the star icon is selected. Notice the **Search** text box located at the top of the **Favorites** menu. Also notice that the user account name and the computer name is displayed at the top. In the example, the user account is *richard* and the computer name is *linux-jn49*. The **Search** text box, user name, and computer name are displayed in each of the five menus.

6. _____ Select the **Applications** tab to reveal its menu or list of application categories. The categories listed are **Games**, **Graphics**, **Internet**, **Multimedia**, **Office**, **System**, **Utilities**, **Configure Desktop**, and **Find Files/Folders**.

You can expand each subcategory by double-clicking its name or by clicking the arrow at the right.

Click the arrow to reveal a list of
programs contained in Office

Click the left side to return
to the original menu

Notice how after **Office** is selected, you will see all the available office-type applications listed in the sub-menu. Take a minute to explore some of the items listed, but do not run the applications.

7. _____ Select the **Computer** tab.

Some of the most common applications required by a technician are revealed, such as YaST and Network. You will learn more about these items in later lab activities.

8. _____ Select the **Recently Used** tab. Any recently used application or recently accessed documents will appear.

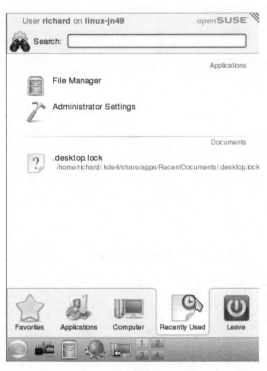

9. _____ Select the **Leave** tab.

The selections available are similar in function as the Windows **Shut down** options.

- ■ **Logout** disconnects the current user.
- ■ **Lock** will lock the desktop until the password is used to unlock it.
- ■ **Switch User** switches to another user account.
- ■ **Hibernate** puts the system to sleep and saves the present condition to the hard disk drive.
- ■ **Shutdown** turns off the system.
- ■ **Restart** reboots the system.

Take a minute or two to practice using the various **Leave** options.

10. _____ Answer the review questions before shutting down the workstation. You will need the system running to answer various questions.

11. _____ Shut down the system and return all materials to their proper storage area.

Review Questions

1. What are the default five major application groupings? _____

_____

2. What options are available from the **Leave** tab? _____

_____

3. What SUSE application is similar to the Microsoft Windows Control Panel? _____

4. What SUSE application is similar to Microsoft Windows Internet Explorer? _____

5. What SUSE application is similar to Microsoft Windows Explorer? _____

Name_____ Date _____

Class/Instructor _____

Introduction to KDE Terminal Konsole

After completing this laboratory activity, you will be able to:

■ Use the KDE Terminal Konsole to enter basic commands.
■ Use the commands **ls**, **ls -al**, **dir**, **mkdir**, and **whoami**.
■ Recall the functions of the commands **ls**, **ls -al**, **dir**, **mkdir**, and **whoami**.
■ Identify three common troubleshooting commands.

Introduction

This laboratory activity introduces you to one of the many command line interfaces available in UNIX/Linux operating systems and to a few of the most basic commands. The command line interface you will be using for this lab activity is the console called *Konsole*. It is also referred to as a *terminal*.

Note
In the KDE system, many features are written with the capital letter *K* in place of the first letter to reflect the fact it was modified for the KDE system.

The original UNIX system did not use a graphical user interface (GUI) but rather was a command line interface (CLI) similar to the command prompt in Windows operating systems. The CLI is referred to as a *shell*. Even today, the CLI is used to issue commands on a Linux server to minimize system resources. For example, there is no need to start the GUI on the server to add a new user to an existing system. Starting the GUI reduces system performance because the GUI requires RAM to run. A GUI affects the overall performance of the server when it is supporting many users (clients). Using the command line interface will have minimal effect on server performance.

Another reason for learning to use the CLI is when the GUI fails to load. When the GUI fails to load, the CLI may be the only way to repair the server.

There are many different command line interfaces used in UNIX/Linux. Two very well-known CLI shells are Bourne Again Shell (bash) and Korn Shell (ksh). When the shell is incorporated into a desktop system, it is referred to as a *shell console* or *terminal emulator*.

An important difference between commands issued in UNIX/Linux is that they are case-sensitive. This means that commands designed to be issued in lowercase letters will not be recognized if issued in uppercase letters. Microsoft Windows systems recognize commands in uppercase or lowercase.

In UNIX/Linux, certain commands are restricted to use by the superuser or root and cannot be issued by ordinary users. For example, the **fdisk** command will not be recognized by the Linux system except when issued by the superuser. The following table contains a list of the most common UNIX/Linux commands. Notice that many of them are similar to those found in Microsoft Windows.

cd	Change the current directory.
clear	Clear the display area.
dir	Display the current directory.
finger	Display information about the current user.
halt	Shut down the system.
ifconfig	Show IP configuration information. Similar to Microsoft **ipconfig**.
l	List files in the current directory.
ls	List files in the current directory.
ls -a	List both hidden and system files.
ls -l	List files in long fashion.
man	Access the manual pages.
mkdir	Make or create a new directory.
ping	Similar to Microsoft **ping** command.
pwd	Print or display the current working directory path.
reboot	Reboot the system.
rm	Remove or delete a file.
rmdir	Remove or delete a directory.
su	Switch from the current user.
touch	Create a file.
traceroute	Similar to Microsoft **tracert**.
who	Display all users currently logged on.
whoami	Display who the current user is.

To leave or close the KDE Konsole issue the **quit** command at the prompt or select **Close session** or **Quit** from the **Session** menu located at the top-left corner of the Konsole screen.

Note

Previous versions of KDE Konsole used the **Quit** menu item to end a session.

Check the openSUSE Web site for basic information about CLI: http://en.opensuse.org/Some_CLI_Basics#Introduction.

Equipment and Materials

❑ Computer with openSUSE 11 or later installed.

Note

You can perform this lab activity on most versions of SUSE Linux as well as some other Linux operating systems.

Procedure

1. _____ Report to your assigned workstation.

2. _____ Boot the computer and log on using your assigned user account, *not* as root.

3. _____ Open the KDE Konsole (**Application Launcher | Favorites** tab | **Terminal**).

4. _____ Issue the **ls** command and note what appears on the screen. The **ls** command consists of lowercase letters *L* and *S*. You should see a display of directories and files similar to the ones in the following screen capture.

5. _____ Issue the **ls** command using uppercase letters (**LS**). What is the result?

_____

6. _____ The **ls** command has switches that will modify the command. Two switches often used are **-a** and **-l**. The **-a** switch modifies the **ls** command to list <u>all</u> files. This means to show hidden and system files also. The **-l** switch modifies the **ls** command to list the files in long list fashion. Issue the command **ls -al** and observe the results. You should see a screen display similar to the following.

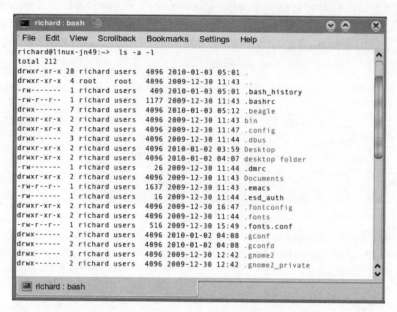

All the information about the files and directories are displayed across the screen. Information about the file is read from left to right. The name of the file is displayed at the far right. The other information about the file will be explained in detail in a later lab activity. For now, you are just becoming familiar with how to use Konsole.

7. _____ Enter the **l** (lowercase *L*) command and observe the results.

8. _____ Now issue the **dir** command. The directories should be listed.

9. _____ Create an empty file by using the **touch** command. Issue the command **touch zfile** and then view the current directory contents using the **l** or **ls** command to verify the creation of the new file called zfile. The file should appear at the bottom of the list.

10. _____ Now create another file called zzfile and verify its creation using the **l** or **ls** command.

11. _____ Create a directory called zdir using the **mkdir** command. For example, **mkdir zdir**. Verify the creation of the zdir directory using the **l** or **ls** command.

12. _____ You can remove or delete the directory by using the **rmdir** command. Files can be removed or deleted using the **rm** command. To remove the directory, simply issue the command **rmdir** followed by the name of the directory. For example, **rmdir zdir**. To remove a file, simply issue the **rm** command followed by the file name. For example, **rm zfile**. Remove the zdir directory and the zfile and zzfile files using the appropriate commands. Verify they have all been removed using the **l** or **ls** command.

13. _____ Issue the **whoami** command to display the current user. The current user account name should be displayed.

14. _____ Issue the **who** command to display current information about the user.

15. _____ Another useful command that will allow you to view current information about the user is **finger**. Issue the command **finger** and view the results.

16. _____ Log on as a different user using the **Switch user** option (**Application Launcher | Leave** tab **| Switch user**). A message dialog box will ask if you would like to create a new session using desktop 2. You will also see an option asking if you would like to lock the current screen or desktop. Do *not* select the option to lock the screen.

17. _____ After the new user session loads, open Konsole and issue the **whoami**, **who**, and **finger** commands. Observe the results of each command and write a brief summary of the observation.

    whoami: _____

    who: _____

    finger: _____

18. _____ Log off the current user and return to your own logon session.

Note

Do *not* shut down the system. Select the **Logoff** option.

---

19. _____ Some commands require the root password or you must be logged on as the root. You need not log off and back on as the root. A quick way to change to the root is to issue the **su** command. You will be prompted for the root password. After providing the root password, you will be issuing commands as the root user. You will remain the root user until you exit the CLI or switch to another user.

20. _____ Enter **exit** and then the **su root** command followed with the root password.

21. _____ You can shut down or reboot the Linux computer from the Konsole using the commands **halt** and **reboot**. The **halt** command will shut down the computer, and the **reboot** command will reboot the computer. Try each command now. Notice that a message will be broadcast to all users that the system will halt or reboot as applicable. You must be the root to perform these commands.

22. _____ Standard in all versions of UNIX/Linux is the user manual referred to as the *man pages* or *manual pages*. The manual pages are written in text-only format. To access the manual pages, enter the **man** command at the prompt followed by the command you want information about. For example, **man finger** will display information in the man pages about the **finger** command, including options and arguments. Issue the **man finger** command now and observe the results. You can use the [Enter] key or [Spacebar] to view additional lines of text. The [Spacebar] key displays an additional page and the [Enter] key displays one additional line of text. After you finish viewing the information, you can use the lowercase [q] key to quit or close the man pages. You can also use the mouse to close the manual pages.

23. _____ Close the manual pages.

24. _____ Display information about the **ls** command using the man pages by entering **man ls**.

25. _____ Display information about the **su**, **finger**, and **who** commands.

26. _____ Another handy command is **pwd**. The **pwd** command displays the current working directory (the directory structure you are presently in when you issue the command). For example, when the user "richard" issues the **pwd** command, his exact location in the directory structure will be displayed as related to his home directory. The results will be similar to /home/richard. Issue the **pwd** command now and observe the results.

27. _____ Three very important troubleshooting commands are **ping**, **traceroute**, and **ifconfig**. The **ping** command is issued in a similar fashion as **ping** when using the Windows command

prompt. The one big difference is that when you issue the **ping** command in Linux, it will continually repeat until you use the keyboard combination [Ctrl] [C]. Enter **ping 127.0.0.1**. Wait for the results and then use the [Ctrl] [C] key combination to stop the ping.

28. _____ Issue the **ping** command again, but this time use the **ping 127.0.0.1 -c** command followed by a number. The **-c** represents count, which is the number of times to issue the **ping** command. For example, **ping 127.0.0.1 -c4** will result in only four pings being issued. Try the command now: **ping 127.0.0.1 -c4**.

29. _____ The Linux **traceroute** command is similar to Microsoft's **tracert** command and produces similar results. If your Linux workstation is connected to the Internet, try issuing the **traceroute** command now to a known Internet location such as www.rmroberts.com. For example, **traceroute www.rmroberts.com** or some other known URL. Observe the results.

Note

Any user can issue a **ping** command but only the root can issue the **traceroute** command.

---

30. _____ The **ifconfig** command is similar to the **ipconfig** command used in Windows. Issue the **ifconfig** command at the command prompt and observe the results. You should see the assigned IP address for the network adapter.

31. _____ Access the man pages to learn more about the **ping**, **traceroute**, and **ifconfig** commands.

32. _____ Review the commands used in this lab activity.

33. _____ Answer the review questions.

Review Questions

1. What is the name of the KDE terminal emulator? _____

2. What does the acronym CLI represent? _____

3. Why would a system administrator use the command line interface rather than a graphical user interface? _____
   _____

4. What command ends the Konsole session? _____

5. What command can be used to list all the files in a directory including the hidden files? _____
   _____

6. What command is used to display the current logged on user? _____

7. What command is used to display all currently logged on to the system? _____

8. What command can be used to display more detailed information about the user other than **whoami**? _____

9. What command is used to create an empty file? _____

10. What command is used to stop or shut down the system? _____

11. What command is used to remove or delete a file? _____

12. What command is used to delete or remove a directory? _____

13. Who can use the **halt** command? _____

14. What are the results of the following command **ping 127.0.0.1 -c8**? _____

_____

15. What keyboard combination is used to stop the **ping** command? _____

16. What command would you use to find more information about the **finger** command? _____

_____

17. What are the two most common reasons for a student to fail to properly issue a command from the Konsole command prompt? _____

_____

_____

Name_____ Date _____

Class/Instructor _____

Exploring the Linux File System

After completing this laboratory activity, you will be able to:

■ Differentiate between the Linux and Microsoft directory and file structure.

■ Recall UNIX/Linux file and directory permissions.

■ Use the GUI to modify file and directory permissions.

■ Identify the services used to share directories and files between UNIX/Linux and Microsoft operating system users.

Introduction

In this laboratory activity, you will explore the SUSE Linux directory structure. You will explore and modify directory and file permissions using the graphical user interface (GUI). The SUSE Linux directory structure is similar to the directory structure of other Linux operating systems. The Linux directory structure is hierarchical. The top of the directory is the root directory represented by the forward slash (/) symbol. The Linux system does not use letters in the directory structure to represent the top of the directory structure or partitions as in NTFS and FAT systems. There is no C drive in the directory structure, only /.

Note
Do *not* confuse the / directory with the /root directory. The /root directory is the root user's home directory.

When a new user account is created, a home directory is automatically created for the new user account. Look at the /root directory contents in the following screen capture. The Linux application used in the screen capture is Dolphin. Dolphin is a KDE file manager application. It is similar to Windows Explorer. Look at the following screen capture to become familiar with the Dolphin interface.

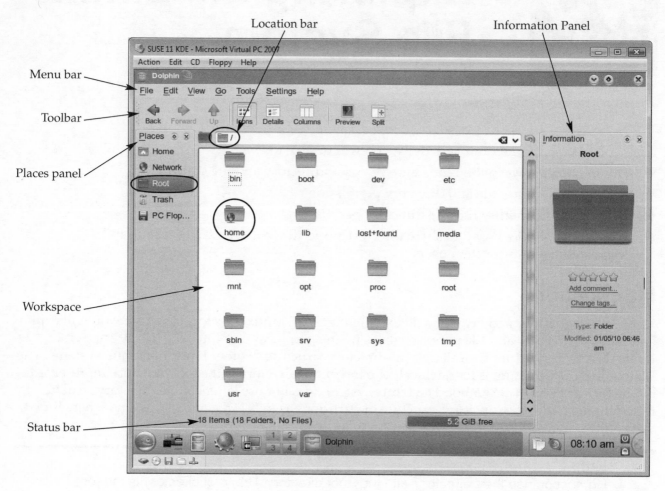

The location bar, at the top, allows you to enter a path to a folder such as /home/student1/ documents. This will result in opening the documents folder belonging to the student1 account. When **Network** is selected from the Places Panel, various network locations are revealed. When **Root** is selected, the top-level directories in / are displayed as they are in the previous screen capture. Notice that the forward slash (/) symbol is in the location bar. This indicates the root of the directory structure. Notice that the default directory names shown in the workspace are in lowercase letters. Also notice that one of the folders shown is called *home*. The following screen capture shows the contents of the /home directory.

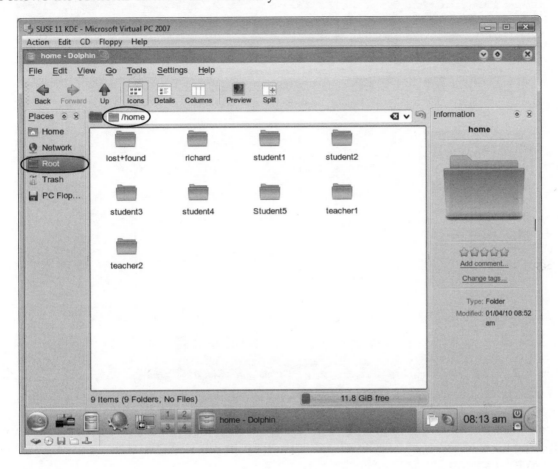

You can see that there are many different user accounts in the /home directory such as *richard*, *student1*, *student2*, *teacher1*, and more. When a user account is created, a corresponding directory with the user name is created. The directory with the user account name is where that particular user will store his or her files and applications by default. The next screen capture shows the contents of the user directory for user account *richard*.

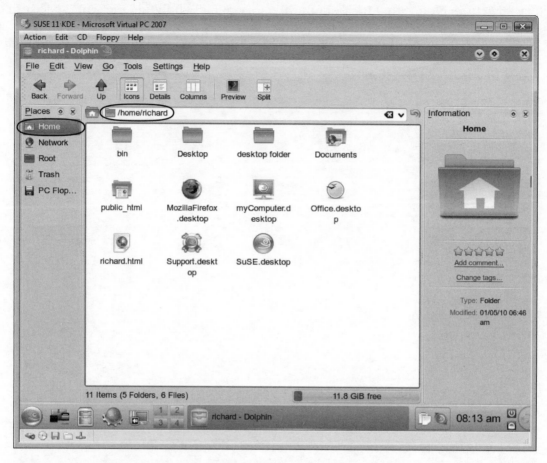

In the screen capture, **Home** has been selected from the Places Panel, which has automatically redirected the view to the default user's home directory. In this case, the default user is *richard* as indicated in the location bar as /home/richard.

There are two large arrows in the Dolphin menu bar: the **Up** arrow and the **Back** arrow. The **Up** arrow automatically takes you up one level in the directory structure. The **Back** arrow takes you back to the last displayed view of the directory.

There are three main differences between Microsoft NTFS and FAT directory structures and the UNIX/Linux directory structure. File and directory names are case-sensitive in UNIX/Linux operating systems; they are not case-sensitive in Microsoft Windows operating systems. Microsoft Windows uses the backslash (\) character in the directory structure. UNIX/Linux operating systems use the forward slash (/). Look at the following screen capture that compares a Linux file path with a Windows file path.

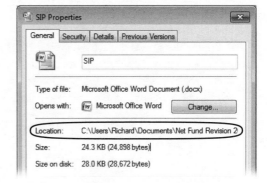

Linux User Path　　　　　　　　　**Windows User Path**

Windows operating systems use letters such as C, D, and E to identify partitions and storage devices. UNIX/Linux uses mount points identified by the forward slash (no letter) followed by the partition or directory name. Devices such as DVD drives and USB drives are located in the directory structure typically under the /media directory in SUSE and the /mnt directory in many other Linux systems such as Red Hat.

openSUSE 11 offers two applications for managing files: Dolphin and Konqueror. Dolphin is the default openSUSE KDE file manager. Konqueror functions as both a Web browser and a file manager.

Equipment and Materials

❑　Computer with openSUSE 11 or later installed.
❑　The following information:

　　　User account name: _____

　　　User account password: _____

　　　Root password: _____

Procedure

1. _____　Report to your assigned workstation.

2. _____　Boot the computer and log on using your assigned user account, *not* as root. Later, you may need the root password to access certain configuration options.

3. _____　After you log on, open Dolphin by selecting the icon in the KDE Panel that resembles a file cabinet.

Dolphin file manager

4. _____　You should now see the Dolphin file manager similar to the one presented in the lab introduction.

5. _____　Select **Home** located from the Places Panel to reveal the home directory contents associated with your user account.

6. _____ Right-click one of the folders to reveal a shortcut menu with various options similar to that in the following screen capture. These same options are available in the menu bar, but the right-click method is more convenient.

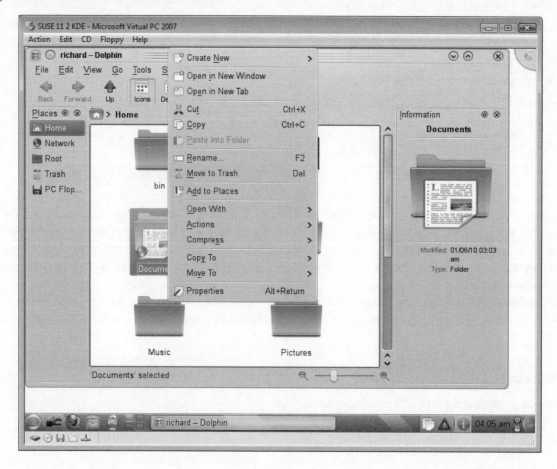

7. _____ Select **Properties** from the shortcut menu. The **General** tab should be displayed by default and will appear similar to that in the following screen capture. The **General** tab provides information such as the folder's location.

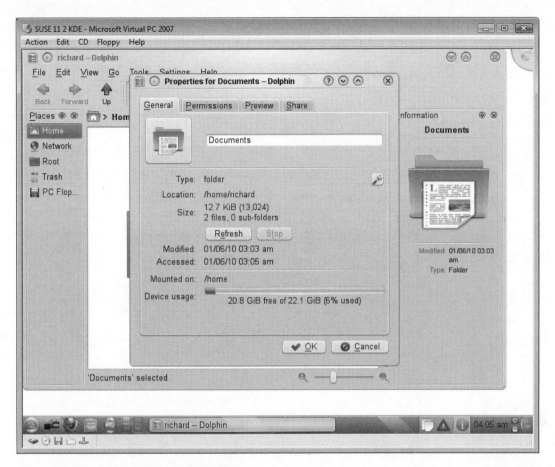

8. _____ Now select the **Permissions** tab.

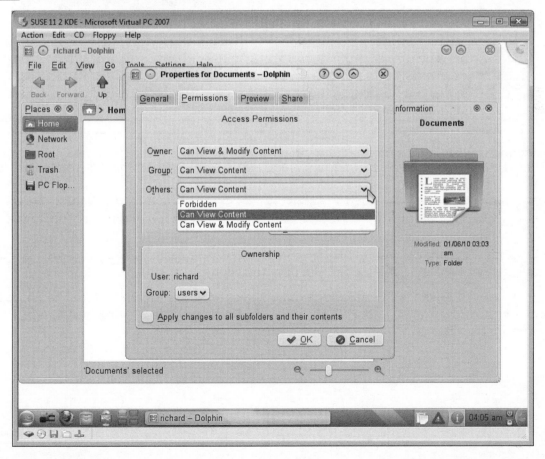

The three general access permissions are the following:

- Forbidden
- Can View Content
- Can View & Modify Content

The **Advanced** button will allow you to configure the typical Linux set of permissions.

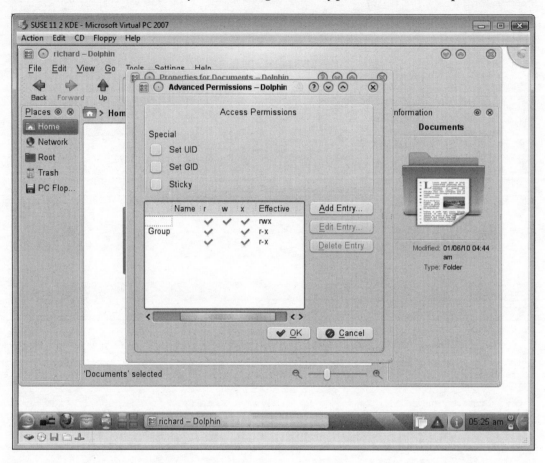

The advanced permissions are the following:

- Read (r)
- Write (w)
- Execute (x)

The Dolphin file manager refers to these as "advanced permissions," but read, write, and execute are the standard UNIX/Linux set of permissions.

9. _____ Close the **Advanced Permissions** dialog box and select the **Share** tab. The **Share** tab allows you to configure the folder for sharing. The **Configure File Sharing** button will allow you to configure the selected folder or file for sharing.

Name _____

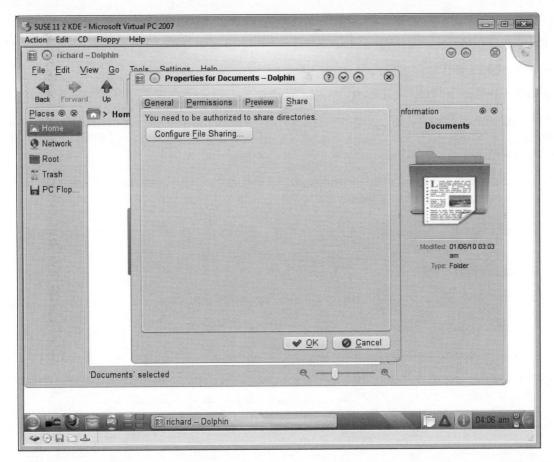

10. _____ Click the **Configure File Sharing** button. The configuration options for the share will display.

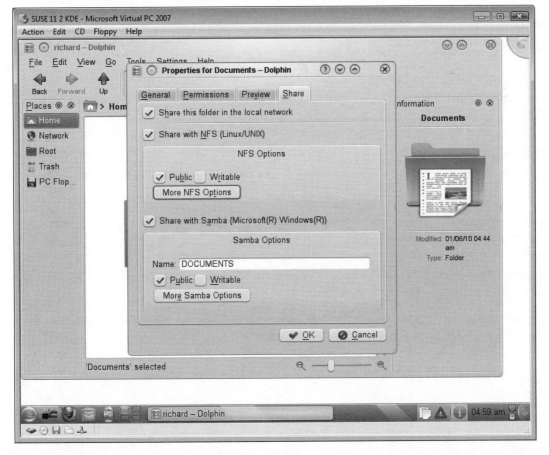

The three main options listed are the following:

- **Share this folder in the local network**
- **Share with NFS (Linux/UNIX)**
- **Share with Samba (Microsoft (R) Windows(R))**

Notice that two of the sharing options are Samba and NFS. In a previous lab activity, you configured a Windows Server share for NFS so that the share could be accessed by UNIX/Linux systems.

11. _____ Take a few minutes to explore the various directory and folder options. Also, practice accessing and navigating Dolphin.

12. _____ Answer the review questions.

Review Questions

1. What are the three general Linux file and directory permissions? _____
   _____
   _____

2. What are the three major differences between the Microsoft file and directory structure and the Linux file and directory structure? _____
   _____
   _____
   _____
   _____
   _____
   _____
   _____

3. What does UNIX/Linux use in place of a partition identified by the colon and letter symbol?
   _____

4. What general file permission would you apply to allow users to modify the contents of a memo? _____
   _____

5. What file permission would you apply to allow a user to only view the contents of a memo?
   _____

6. Which service is used to allow Windows operating system users to access files on a UNIX/Linux computer over a network connection? _____

7. Which service is used to allow UNIX/Linux operating system users to access files on a Windows computer over a network connection? _____

Name_____ Date _____

Class/Instructor _____

Introduction to Samba

After completing this laboratory activity, you will be able to:

- Carry out proper procedures to install and configure the Samba service.
- Use the Dolphin file manager to browse the local area network.
- Identify Samba shares on the network.
- Differentiate between Samba shares and NTFS shares.
- Use the **net view** command to view all available computers on the local network.

Introduction

In this laboratory activity, you will explore how to configure the Samba service on a SUSE Linux computer. Samba allows Microsoft computers to access files on a UNIX/Linux system. NFS is used to support sharing between UNIX/Linux computers and to allow UNIX/Linux computers to access Windows shares. Windows Server 2008 can be configured for NFS so that UNIX/Linux operating system users can access shares on the Windows Server.

Note

When viewed with a protocol analyzer at a Windows computer, you will see SMB, SMB2, or CIFS identified as the application level protocol used to support share transfers for both Samba and NFS.

Samba is generally referred to as a *service* and includes a software package that allows a computer to serve as a Samba server or as a Samba client. Samba is generally not configured automatically in UNIX/Linux. It generally needs to be configured and started as a service on the host computer. Today, many versions of Linux operating systems automatically configure Samba and NFS when a directory or file is configured for sharing.

When a peer-to-peer network is configured to share files and printers, all computers must be members of the same workgroup. This means all computers in the same peer-to-peer should have the same workgroup name.

All computers including the Samba server should have an identical user account configured with identical passwords. For example, a user account with a user name such as *student1* and password *Pa$$word123* must be created on each computer. The identical accounts may already exist from previous labs.

Computers in the local area network will have the same IPv4 subnet mask and the same network address. For example, all computers should have 255.255.255.0 for a subnet mask and 192.168.0.xxx for an IPv4 address. The "192.168.0" indicates the network address and the "xxx" indicates the computer or host address. The host address is unique for each computer on the network. Be aware that each computer typically generates a random IPv6 address. All local network traffic uses an IPv6 address to exchange frames and packets.

Before you install the Samba service, you should exchange pings between a Windows computer and the Linux computers. This will verify that TCP/IP is configured on each computer and is working correctly.

A handy tool is the **net view** command. When issued from the command prompt of a Windows computer, all locally-connected computers are identified, even Linux computers. Look at the sample screen capture of the command prompt after issuing the **net view** command.

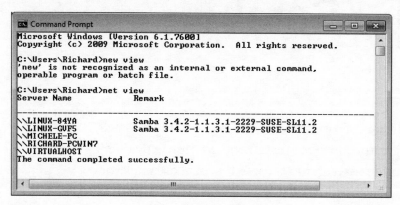

Notice that the names of two Linux computers are listed as well as their Samba versions and their Linux operating system versions. Be aware that a firewall can prevent seeing other computers in the peer-to-peer network. You should disable the firewall on each computer for this lab activity. Be aware that you typically must enable sharing on each computer before it can be viewed by other members of the peer-to-peer network.

When using Samba, packet exchanges are somewhat slow and you may experience slight delays before changes to the configuration take effect. Some versions of Linux require a reboot before the new configuration takes effect. Typically, there will be a message to inform you if a reboot is necessary. Be sure to read all messages as they appear on the screen when performing the configuration.

You can view more in-depth information about openSUSE network configurations and sharing at the www.openSUSE.org Web site. There is also extensive SUSE documentation in PDF and HTML format at the Novel Web site www.novell.com/documentation/opensuse112. You can also download a copy of all open source documentation from my Web site at the following link: www.rmroberts.com/FTP_files/OpenSUSE11Documentation. The Microsoft support Web site has an article about configuring NFS on a Windows server: http://support.microsoft.com/kb/324089.

Equipment and Materials

❑ Two computers with openSUSE 11 or later installed.
❑ Computer with Windows Vista or Windows 7 installed.
❑ The following information provided by your instructor:

Linux root password: _____

Matching user account name and password: _____

Workgroup name: _____

Domain name: _____

Note

At the time of this writing, Windows 7 could view and access shares on a Linux machine but not support access by Linux. This will most likely be fixed through a patch in the near future and may be corrected by the time you are performing this lab activity.

Procedure

1. _____ Report to your assigned workstation.

2. _____ Boot and log on to the Linux computers and the Windows computer and verify they are in working order.

3. _____ Write down the computer name and IPv4 address assigned to each computer. Use the **ipconfig/all** command on the Windows computer and use the **ifconfig** command on the Linux computers to view the assigned addresses.

Note

At the Linux computer, you need to be the root to use the **ifconfig** command. The command prompt will provide the name of the Linux workstation.

Linux computer 1 name: _____

Linux computer 1 IPv4 address: _____

Linux computer 2 name: _____

Linux computer 2 IPv4 address: _____

Windows computer name: _____

Windows computer 1 IPv4 address: _____

4. _____ Exchange pings between the computers to ensure they are in the same network and that the TCP/IP stack is configured correctly. You can use one computer, such as the Windows computer, to ping the others. This will generally confirm the TCP/IP connections. Do this before progressing in the lab activity. If you cannot exchange pings, call your instructor for assistance.

5. _____ On one of the Linux computers, open YAST and then select **Network Services | Windows Domain Membership** as indicated in the following screen capture.

This is a new feature in SUSE that allows for a much easier configuration as a member of a Windows domain or workgroup.

6. _____ In the **Windows Domain Membership** dialog box, type in the name of the Windows workgroup the Linux computers will be joining. For example, enter "Workgroup," which is the default Windows Vista and Windows 7 workgroup name. Your instructor may be using a different workgroup name for this project. Also, select the **Allow Users to Share Their Directories** option. Click **OK** when finished to close the dialog box and return to the YaST Control Center.

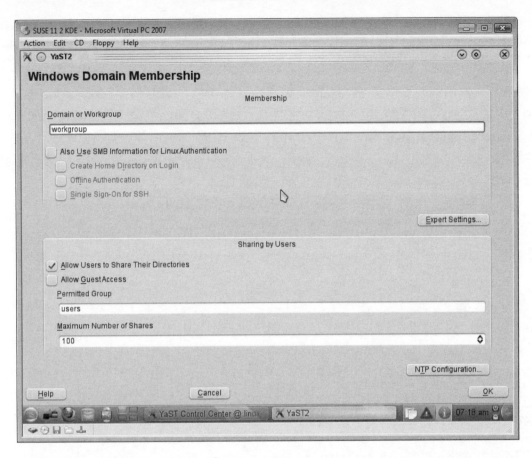

7. _____ From the YaST Control Center, access **Network Services | Samba Server**. This option is used to configure a Samba server.

The **Samba Configuration** dialog box should open to the **Shares** tab. If not, select the **Shares** tab now. All available shares should be listed. If the desired share is not listed, add it by clicking the **Add** button and entering the share name, share description, and share path. Click **OK**.

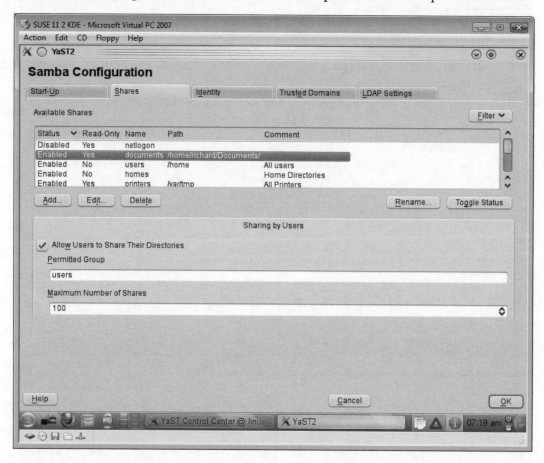

8. _____ Select the **Start-Up** tab and then select the **During Boot** option. This will allow the Samba service to start automatically each time the Linux computer is started. If not selected, the service must be manually started after the computer is booted. Click **OK**. The computer should be configured as a Samba server allowing Windows computers to access its shares.

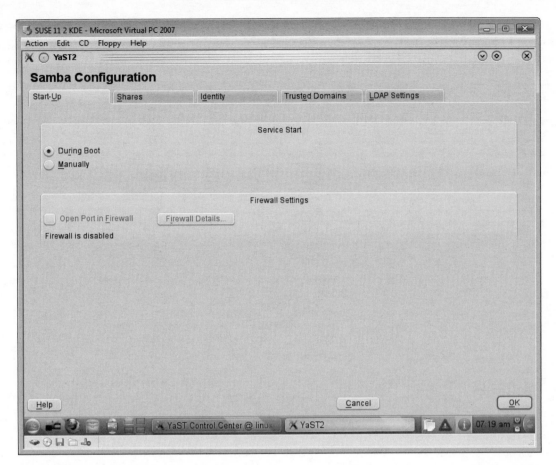

9. _____ Repeat steps 5 through 8 on the other Linux computer.

10. _____ At the Windows computer, type "Network" in the **Search** box and then click **Network** from the **Programs** list. Network will open and look similar to that in the following screen capture.

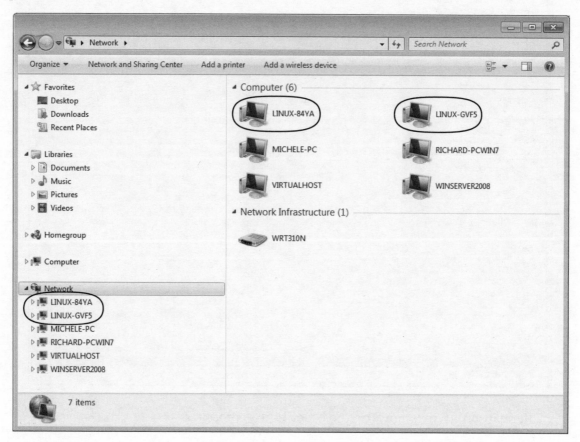

In the screen capture, you will see that the two Linux computers have identical icons as the Windows computers. Only the assigned names are different. If the Linux computers are not viewable on your Windows computer, restart the Linux computers.

11. _____ At the Windows computer, open the command prompt and issue the **net view** command. You should see all local computers listed, including the Linux computers. If not, call your instructor for assistance.

12. _____ At either Linux computer open Dolphin.

13. _____ Select the **Network** option from the **Places Panel**. You should see results similar to that in the following screen capture such as the **Network**, **Network Services**, **Samba Shares**, and **Add Network Folder** icons. Your view may be different, especially if your workstation is shared by other students.

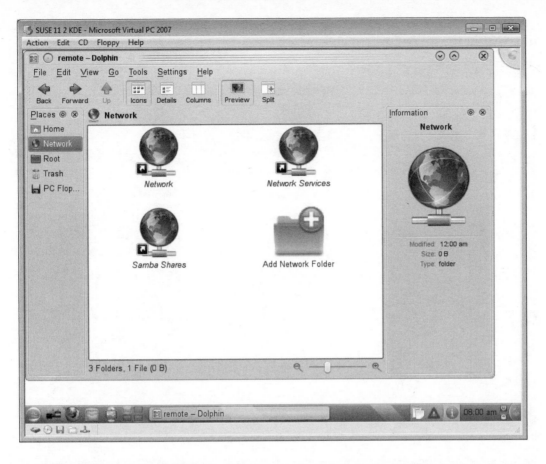

14. _____ Click the **Samba Shares** icon. The **Globe** icon labeled with the workgroup name you selected will display.

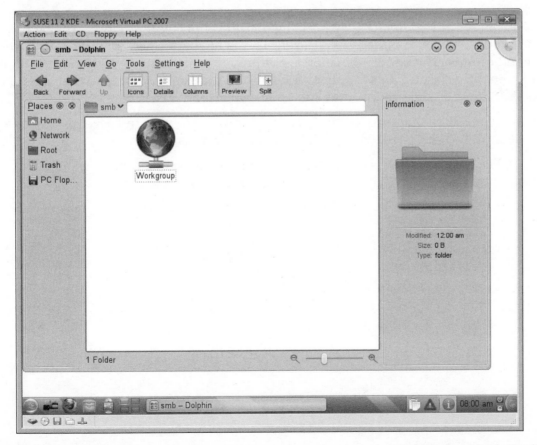

15. _____ Click the **Globe** icon. You should see the computers that are members of the workgroup similar to that in the following screen capture.

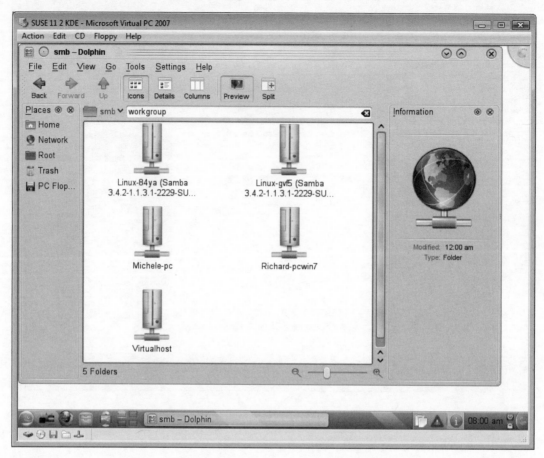

If you do not see any computers, try pressing [Alt] [F2] which will produce a dialog box. Enter **smb:///** in the text box and then press [Enter]. This is not performed from the terminal or command prompt. The key combination is performed while Dolphin is opened. Be sure to include the three slashes. This is not a typo. This is a Linux text command that should produce the **Globe** icon and workgroup. If not, call your instructor for assistance.

In the previous screen capture, you can see two Linux computers and several Windows computers. Your display will be similar, but not an exact match.

16. _____ Click one of the Linux computer icons. Wait a few seconds and you should see the available shares similar to that in the following screen capture.

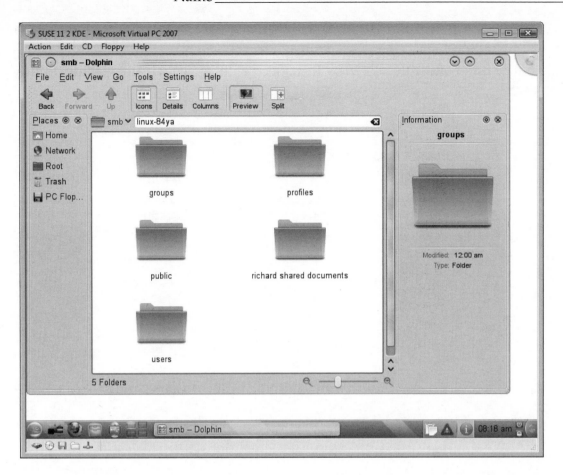

The shared folder labeled "richard shared documents" was created especially for this screen capture. It is not a default Linux share. The other shares are typical Linux SUSE shares.

17. _____ Use the **Back** arrow to go back or simply select the **Network** from the **Places Panel**.

18. _____ Click the **Globe** icon. This time, access a Windows share.

19. _____ Return all computers to the configuration specified by your instructor.

20. _____ Answer the review questions.

Review Questions

1. What is the purpose of Samba? _____

_____

2. What is the purpose of NFS? _____

_____

3. What does a successful ping exchange between a Microsoft computer and a Linux computer indicate? _____

_____

4. What service is available in Linux SUSE 11.2 that supports access to a Windows Domain? _____

_____

5. What command can be entered from a Windows command prompt that will display all local area network computers? _____

6. What will be listed under the Net View **Remark** column, which will help identify Linux computers? _____

42

Name_____ Date _____

Class/Instructor _____

Inspecting and Defragmenting Partitions

After completing this laboratory activity, you will be able to:
- Use the Disk Management utility to inspect hard disk drive partitions.
- Use the Disk Defragmenter utility to defragment hard disk drive partitions.

Introduction

In this laboratory activity, you will inspect and defragment the hard disk drives on a Windows 2008 server using the Disk Management and Disk Defragmenter utilities.

The Disk Management utility allows you to inspect the condition of the server's hard disk drives. The Disk Management utility can be accessed through **Start | Administrative Tools**. It can also be accessed through Server Manager or Computer Management by right-clicking **Computer** and selecting **Manage** from the shortcut menu.

Information such as the drive's storage capacity, unused disk space, file system type (FAT, NTFS), and disk type (basic, dynamic) will display. Look at the following figure. Notice that the bottom pane reveals a graphical view of the server's hard disk drive configuration. It also displays details about the drive and its partitions. The first physical drive is named *Disk 0*. One partition of Disk 0 is labeled *C:*. The first drive also contains a partition labeled *E:* and an unallocated area. The unallocated area contains no partitions and is unformatted at this time. The term *unallocated* indicates an unformatted and unpartitioned area on a primary partition. Both Disk 0 and Disk 1 are basic disks. Disk 1 contains NTFS as well as FAT32 partitions and an area labeled *Free space*. The term *free space* refers to an area on an extended partition that can be used to create logical drives.

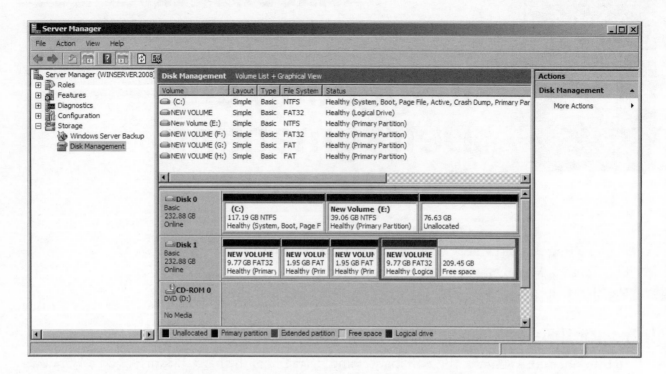

Right-clicking the disk identification area in the bottom pane reveals a shortcut menu with the option to convert the drive to dynamic disk. A different shortcut menu displays when you right-click the partition. This shortcut menu allows you to change the volume label and to view the partition's properties.

Information about the system's drives is also revealed in the top pane. Notice the information presented about partition C, which states it is a simple (layout), basic (type), NTFS (file system) partition that is healthy (status). It also indicates that it is a system and boot partition as well as an active partition with a page file and other attributes.

The Disk Defragmenter utility is used to enhance disk access performance by organizing files into contiguous sectors. Files are stored in small areas on the disk drive called *sectors*. The smallest sector size is 512 bytes. If a file is larger than the sector size, it is stored in two or more sectors. As files are added, deleted, and modified on the hard disk drive, files become fragmented. Fragmented means that a file is no longer stored in contiguous sectors.

Note

The size of a sector depends on the storage capacity of the hard disk drive and the type of file system used, such as FAT32 and NTFS.

The Disk Defragmenter utility can be accessed from the **Tools** tab of the disk **Properties** dialog box as shown in the following screen capture.

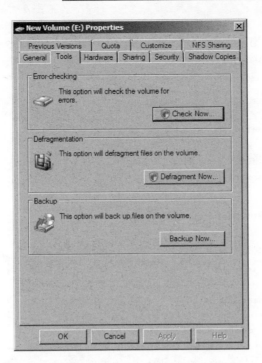

Disk Defragmenter can also be run from the command prompt using the **defrag** command. For example, you would enter **defrag e: -a** to analyze drive C. A window similar to the following will display information about the size of the drive, amount of free space, and how much of the drive is fragmented. If the disk is severely fragmented, a message will appear telling you to defragment the drive.

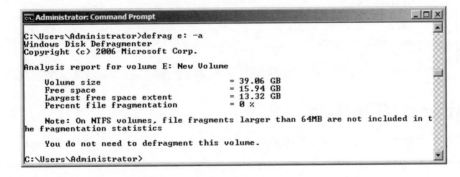

The Disk Defragmenter utility is similar in Windows XP, Windows Vista, Windows 7, and Windows Server 2008. The following is a screen capture of the **defrag help** command results. This command reveals a list of command switches, also known as *parameters*, and several examples of the command.

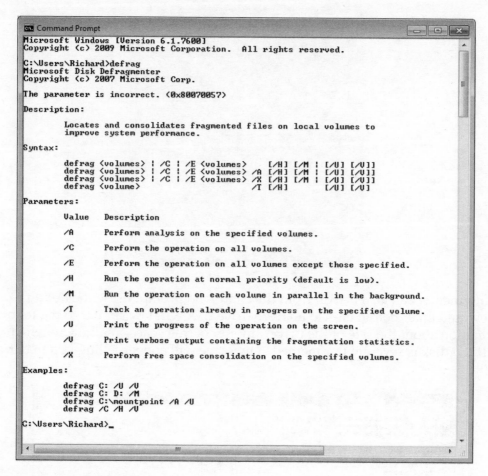

Equipment and Materials

❑ Computer with Windows Server 2008, Windows Vista, or Windows 7 installed.

Note

The Disk Defragmenter utility is so similar in the various Microsoft operating systems you can use any of them to perform this lab activity. The procedure and screen captures for this lab activity were created on a Windows 7 computer.

Procedure

1. _____ Report to your assigned workstation.

2. _____ Boot the computer and verify that it is in working order.

3. _____ After logging on to the computer, open Server Manager (Windows Server 2008) or Computer Management (Windows Vista and Windows 7) by right-clicking **Computer** and selecting **Manage** from the shortcut menu.

4. _____ Select **Disk Management** from the right-hand pane as shown in the following screen capture. Information similar to the following about the disk drives and partitions should display.

Name _____

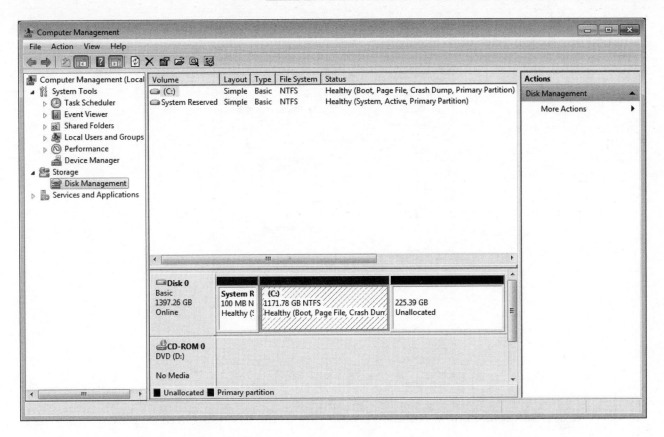

5. _____ Answer the following questions about the hard disk drive you are inspecting.

Physical size: _____

First partition size: _____

First partition file type: _____

Type of partition (basic disk or dynamic): _____

6. _____ Right-click the C partition and select **Properties** from the shortcut menu. The **Properties** dialog box for the drive will display.

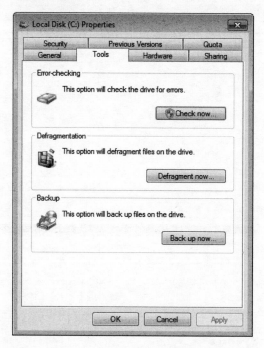

7. _____ Click **Defragment now**. A dialog box similar to the following will display.

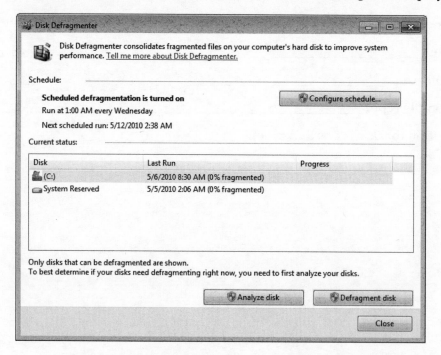

The dialog box will vary somewhat according to the operating system you are using for this laboratory activity. For example, Windows Server 2008 will not provide the **Analyze disk** option. The disk will be automatically analyzed when the dialog box opens.

Note

You may be informed that the disk does not need to be defragmented.

Look at the **Configure schedule** button. The option allows you to choose a day of the week and the hour to perform a routine defragmentation of the disk drive, if necessary. Also, notice that the time of the last defragmentation appears in the **Current status** text box.

8. _____ Close Disk Defragmenter, the disk **Properties** dialog box, and Server Manager or Computer Management.

9. _____ Access the command prompt and enter the following command: **defrag c: -a**. The Disk Defragmenter utility should automatically start analyzing the disk. The results should display after a few minutes. Write down the analysis results in the space provided.

_____

_____

_____

_____

_____

_____

10. _____ Answer the review questions and then return all materials to their proper storage area.

Review Questions

1. What information is revealed by the Disk Management utility? _____

_____

_____

2. What is the purpose of deframenting a hard disk drive? _____

_____

_____

3. What command is issued at the command prompt to defragment drive C? _____

_____

4. In general, what is the smallest sector size? _____

Laboratory Activity

43

Name_____ Date _____

Class/Instructor _____

Using the DiskPart Command Interpreter

After completing this laboratory activity, you will be able to:

■ Use the DiskPart command interpreter.

■ Use common DiskPart commands to retrieve information about the number of disks installed in a system and about disk partitions or volumes.

■ Use the DiskPart **help** command to reveal a list of DiskPart commands.

Introduction

Disk management is usually performed in the Disk Management utility. The DiskPart command interpreter is an alternative way to manage disks and partitions. At times, the DiskPart command interpreter may be the only alternative for inspecting and manipulating the master boot record (MBR) and partition table should the GUI fail. Also, certain tasks can be performed using the DiskPart command interpreter that cannot be performed using the Disk Management utility. For example, you must use the DiskPart command interpreter to convert a dynamic disk to a basic disk and to delete or replace the MBR in the active partition. The Disk Management utility does not allow the performance of these tasks because it is designed to protect the integrity of the disk structure from accidental deletion.

You can think of the DiskPart command interpreter as an updated version of the **fdisk** command. Starting with Windows XP, the **fdisk** command is no longer supported. The DiskPart utility is used in place of **fdisk** to inspect, create, and delete partitions or volumes on a disk drive.

The DiskPart command interpreter will not make changes to removable media such as a USB drive and an IEEE-1394 drive. These types of media are identified as a "super floppy" by the DiskPart utility rather than as a hard disk drive.

In this laboratory activity, you will perform some basic DiskPart operations to become familiar with this utility. While you most likely will never need to use the full capability of this utility, more information can be obtained at the Microsoft Tech Support Web site.

Look at the following screen capture. Notice that the **detail disk** command has been entered at the DiskPart command line. The **detail disk** command reveals details about the selected disk, such as the hard disk drive manufacturer and type. It also shows that the hard disk drive has two partitions or volumes. Volume 1 is assigned letter *C* and volume 2 is assigned letter *D*. Notice that both volumes are indicated as healthy.

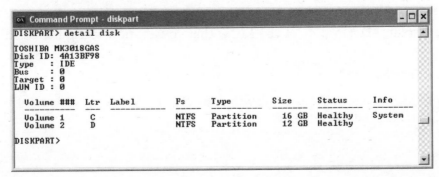

The **list** command can be used with the disk, volume, and partition object. When using the DiskPart command interpreter, disks, partitions, and volumes are referred to as *objects*. Look at the following screen capture. It shows the **list disk**, **list partition**, and **list volume** commands. The **list disk** command lists the disk(s) installed starting with disk 0. The **list volume** command lists the volumes contained in the system. The **list partition** command lists the partitions located on a selected disk. Notice how the DVD-ROM drive is identified after issuing the **list volume** command. Also, notice how the removable drive is identified even though it is no longer present.

```
Command Prompt - diskpart                                          _ □ ×

DISKPART> list disk

  Disk ###  Status       Size     Free    Dyn  Gpt
  --------  ----------   -------  -------  ---  ---
* Disk 0    Online       28 GB     0 B

DISKPART> list partition

  Partition ###  Type          Size      Offset
  -------------  ----------   --------   --------
  Partition 1    Primary       16 GB     32 KB
  Partition 2    Extended      12 GB     16 GB
  Partition 3    Logical       12 GB     16 GB

DISKPART> list volume

  Volume ###  Ltr  Label     Fs     Type        Size    Status     Info
  ----------  ---  --------  -----  ----------  ------  --------   ------
  Volume 0    E              DUD-ROM              0 B
  Volume 1    C              NTFS   Partition    16 GB  Healthy    System
  Volume 2    D              NTFS   Partition    12 GB  Healthy
  Volume 3    F                     Removeable    0 B

DISKPART>
```

Before issuing the **list partition** command, you must select the disk you wish to view. For example, to view the partition information for a single hard disk drive, you would issue the **select disk** command. Then you would issue the **list partition** command. Otherwise, you will generate an error message stating, "There is no disk selected to list partitions."

Selecting the disk is also known as *setting focus*. When you set focus, you focus the **list partition** command on a selected disk. You must also set the focus on the partition you wish to list. If you do not, the default partition you are presently running the DiskPart command interpreter from is automatically selected.

For more information on the DiskPart command interpreter, read the following Microsoft Support article: 300415—A Description of the DiskPart Command Line Utility.

Equipment and Materials

❑   Computer with Windows XP, Windows Vista, or Windows 7 installed.

Procedure

1. _____ Report to your assigned workstation.

2. _____ Boot the computer and verify it is in working order.

3. _____ Open the command prompt (**Start | All Programs | Accessories | Command Prompt**, or **Start | Run** and enter **cmd** in the **Run** dialog box).

4. _____ At the command line, type and enter the **DiskPart** command. If successful, the prompt will display > DiskPart to let you know that you are now using the DiskPart command interpreter.

5. _____ Enter the **Help** or **/?** command to reveal a list of commands.

6. _____ Enter the **list** command to display the objects that can be specified with the **list** command. Disk, partition, and volume are listed.

7. _____ Try each of the following commands to reveal information about the disk drive(s): **list disk, list partition, list volume**. Remember, the **list partition** command requires focus. You must use the **select** command to select the disk drive you wish to list partition information about. For example, you would enter **select disk 0** to set the focus on the first disk in the system. The **select** command is only required for the **list partition** command. After running each command, record on a separate sheet of paper the information revealed.

8. _____ The **detail** command reveals similar content but with more detailed information about an object. Enter each of the following commands and then record the information revealed in the space provided.

detail disk: _____

_____

detail volume: _____

_____

detail partition: _____

_____

9. _____ Practice using the commands covered thus far until you are very familiar with them. They are difficult to learn at first because some involve setting focus and using two words for a valid command.

10. _____ Use the **help** command to reveal what the following commands are used for. Do *not* attempt to use any of the following commands without explicit permission from the instructor.

Command	Purpose
add	
active	
assign	
break	
clean	
create	
delete	
detail	
exit	
extend	
help	
import	
inactive	
list	

Command	Purpose
online	
rem	
remove	
repair	
rescan	
retain	
select	

11. _____ Enter the **exit** command to return to the command prompt and then again to return to the Windows desktop. Leave your computer in the condition as specified by your instructor.

12. _____ Answer the review questions.

Review Questions

1. What are objects when using the DiskPart command interpreter? _____

   _____

2. What command is used to reveal information about a particular partition? _____

3. Which command is used to set focus on a particular drive? _____

4. What does the command prompt look like when you are running the DiskPart command interpreter? _____

5. How can you see a list of the various DiskPart commands? _____

   _____

6. A particular computer has only one hard disk drive. What command is used to set focus on that one hard disk drive? _____

7. What command will stop the DiskPart command interpreter and return you to the default prompt? _____

Laboratory Activity

44

Name_____ Date _____

Class/Instructor _____

Using the Disk Management Utility

After completing this laboratory activity, you will be able to:

■ Differentiate between a partition and volume.

■ Use the Disk Management utility to create, format, and remove a partition or volume.

■ Use the Disk Management utility to extend or shrink a volume.

Introduction

In this laboratory activity, you will create and format a volume. You will then remove the newly created volume. A volume is a section of one or more hard disk drives treated as a single disk space. It is identified with either a drive letter or a mount point. A mount point is a location inside an existing empty folder formatted as NTFS. A mounted drive functions the same as any other volume, but it is identified by a name rather than a drive letter.

A partition is a section of one hard disk drive treated as a single disk space. Partitions and volumes identified by drive letters have a maximum of 26 possible letters. A mount point uses a name rather than a letter, which means there is no limit to the number of volumes that can be created on one or more hard disk drives.

Note
The terms *partition* and *volume* are used interchangeably today. Originally, the term *partition* was used to describe a section of a physical disk. The term *volume* was introduced with the concept of dynamic disk and the NTFS file system. A volume is a section of a physical disk, but it can also span across two or more physical disks.

In the following screen capture, the shortcut menu is shown as it appears for the unallocated portion of the hard disk drive.

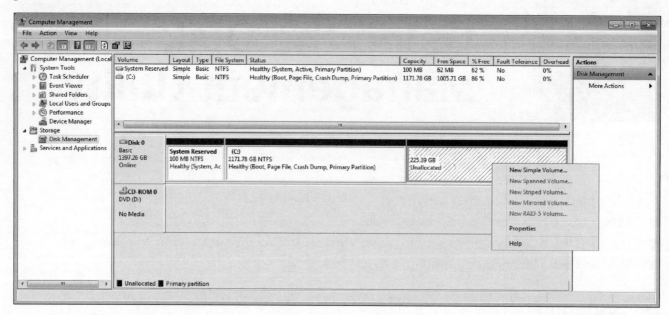

The only options available are **New Simple Volume**, **Properties**, and **Help**. The other options, **New Spanned Volume**, **New Striped Volume**, **New Mirrored Volume**, and **New RAID-5 Volume**, are not available because they require a second physical disk drive, which is not installed on this particular computer. Right-clicking drive C will reveal several options that are different from the unallocated drive portion as shown in the following screen capture. The available options are **Open**, **Explore**, **Mark Partition as Active**, **Change Drive Letter and Paths**, **Extend Volume**, **Shrink Volume**, **Properties**, and **Help**.

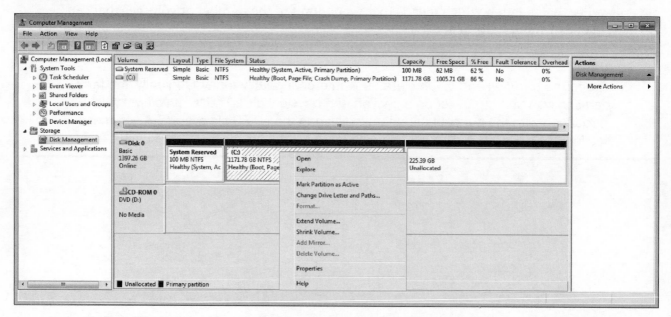

Notice in the previous screen capture the System Reserved partition, which is also known as the *Microsoft Reserved Partition*. The existence of the System Reserved partition will depend on the computer firmware. There are two types of firmware: Basic Input Output System (BIOS) and Extensible Firmware Interface (EFI). The EFI is an enhanced version of the BIOS found on modern computers.

In addition, the type of partition table used, master boot record (MBR) or globally unique identifier (GUID), will depend on the firmware. MBR is the original and most common partition table used. It is supported by all current Microsoft operating systems. The globally unique identifier partition table (GPT) is an updated version of the MBR partition table. There are many advantages to the GPT, but the two most important advantages are the capability of larger partitions than MBR and exceeding the MBR limitation of four primary partitions. GPT can support disks larger than 2 TB; MBR cannot. MBR partition table supports only 4 partitions or 3 partitions and 1 extended partition. GPT can support up to 128 partitions.

Note
All disks with a GPT also contain an MBR partition table. The reason is to protect the GPT from older software utilities that may think that the MBR partition table is missing and try to repair or recreate it, thus damaging the GPT.

NTFS has two classifications of disks: dynamic and basic. Basic disk refers to the original Microsoft Disk Operating system (MS-DOS) style of partitioning and formatting a disk. Dynamic disk was first introduced with the Windows 2000 operating system. Basic disk is created by default. It can then be converted to dynamic disk. Dynamic disk overcomes many limitations of basic disk.

Basic Disk	Dynamic Disk
Can be accessed by MS-DOS programs, such as Fdisk.	Cannot be viewed or modified by Fdisk. Uses the DiskPart utility instead to view and modify volumes/partitions.
Does not support RAID configurations.	Required for RAID configurations on Microsoft computers.
Cannot span multiple physical disks.	Can span multiple physical disks.
Cannot use mount points.	Uses mount points.

Equipment and Materials

❏ Windows Vista or Windows 7 computer. The hard disk drive should have unallocated space available. (A server is not required for this laboratory activity.)
❏ Simple volume size: _____ MB (5 GB recommended)

Note
Because of limited class time, you may wish to create and format a small partition. The amount of time for the lab will be directly related to the size of the partition you format.

Note
Do *not* alter the partitions on the computer without explicit permission of your instructor.

Procedure

1. _____ Report to your assigned workstation.
2. _____ Boot the computer and verify that it is in working order.

3. _____ Open Computer Management and then select Disk Management.

4. _____ Right-click the unallocated disk space area and then select **New Simple Volume** from the shortcut menu. The **New Simple Volume Wizard** dialog box will automatically appear similar to the one in the following screen capture.

Note

The exact appearance of the New Simple Volume Wizard will vary somewhat according to the operating system you are using.

5. _____ Click **Next** to continue. A dialog box similar to the following will display prompting you for the simple volume size in megabytes.

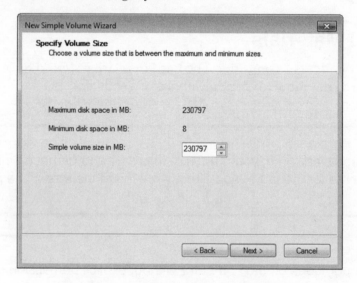

For this laboratory activity, enter the value of the new simple volume as indicated by your instructor at the beginning of this lab activity. The recommended value is 5 GB.

6. _____ Click **Next**. A dialog box similar to the following will prompt you to assign a drive letter for the partition. Notice that you also have the option to mount the volume in an empty NTFS folder. This allows you to use a folder rather than a drive letter.

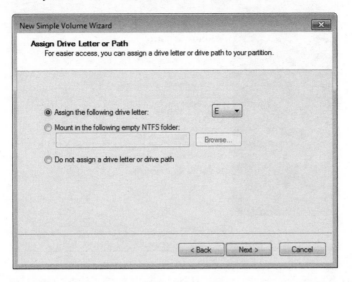

7. _____ Click **Next**. You will be prompted for the file system type and allocation unit size. The default file system is NTFS, but you may also choose FAT32. The default allocation unit size is automatically selected by the New Simple Volume Wizard, but the minimum size is 512 bytes.

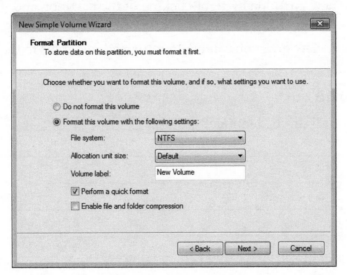

There may also be an option for a volume label, which is a name for the partition. The default name is "New Volume," but you could name it anything you like. The volume label cannot exceed 32 characters for NTFS and 11 characters for FAT. Similar to file naming restrictions, it cannot contain spaces or any of the following characters:

*? | . , ; + = [ ] < >

8. _____ Click **Next**. A summary of the settings you selected will be displayed for your review. You can accept the settings, go back and make appropriate changes, or cancel the operation.

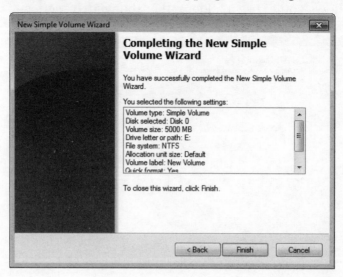

9. _____ Click **Finish**. The new partition will be created and formatted as specified. The format operation should take a few minutes. The larger the partition, the longer it will take.

10. _____ After the partition has been formatted, have your instructor inspect your new partition.

11. _____ Remove the new partition by right-clicking of the partition and then selecting the **Delete Volume** from the shortcut menu.

12. _____ Answer the review questions and then return all materials to their proper storage area.

Review Questions

1. How is the first physical drive identified?_____

   A. Disk 0 _____

   B. Disk 1_____

   C. Disk A: _____

   D. Drive 1 _____

2. What is the difference between a partition and a volume? _____

   _____

   _____

   _____

   _____

   _____

3. What is the maximum number of primary partitions that can be created using MBR?_____

4. What is the maximum number of partitions that can be created using GPT?_____

Name_____ Date _____

Class/Instructor _____

Installing a RAID System

After completing this laboratory activity, you will be able to:
- Use the Disk Management utility to install a RAID 1 system.
- Summarize how fault tolerance is achieved using a RAID 1 and RAID 5 system.

Introduction

In this laboratory activity, you will install and configure a RAID 1 system, also known as a *mirror* or *duplex* configuration. RAID 1 uses two disk drives. Each hard disk drive contains a volume that is a duplicate of the other. RAID 1 is one way of providing fault tolerance. RAID 5 is another. It requires three hard disk drives. The data is striped across all three drives. If one of the three drives fails, it can be replaced by a new hard disk drive. After the failed drive is replaced, the stripe of data is automatically rebuilt based on data and information stored on the other two drives.

Microsoft operating systems require that dynamic disk be used for RAID configurations. So, when creating a RAID configuration on a basic disk, a dialog box with a warning similar to the following will appear.

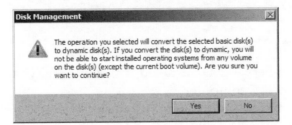

The warning states that if you convert a basic disk to a dynamic disk, any operating systems contained on the volume, except the boot volume, will not start. This warning is especially important for multiboot operating systems. If your workstation contains a multiboot operating system, you may not be able to boot any other operating system other than the default.

The following screen capture shows how a mirror configuration will appear in the Disk Management utility. Notice that both physical disks have been converted to dynamic disk and that both physical disks share a mirrored partition (F). Also, notice that the mirrored partitions are the same size. Every time data is saved to partition F, the data is saved to both partitions labeled as F:. The mirror ensures redundancy and prevents data loss caused by a failed drive. The only disadvantage is that it takes longer to save data because the data is written twice, once to each drive.

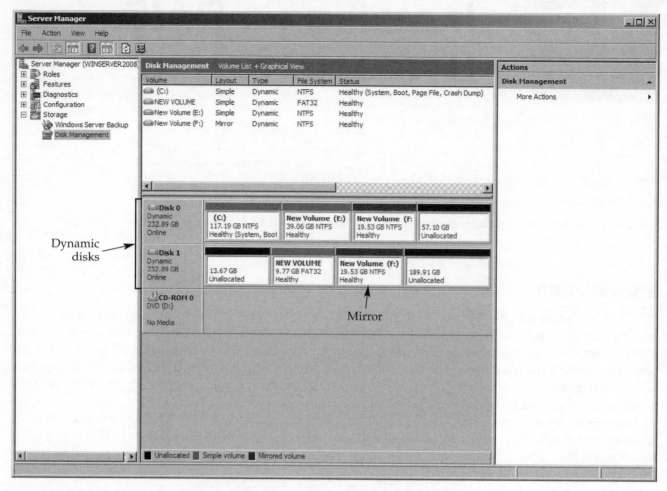

Equipment and Materials

❑ Computer with Windows Server 2008 installed. This lab activity can also be performed on a Windows Vista or Windows 7 computer.
❑ ATA or SATA hard disk drive to match existing hard disk drive.
❑ A set of tweezers if using an ATA drive. (You will need this to remove jumpers when configuring the drives as slave and master.)
❑ Antistatic wrist strap.
❑ Flat-tip or Philips screwdriver.

Note

This lab activity is based in part on knowledge acquired in the previous lab activity.

Note

The instructor may wish you to remove the mirror configuration and the newly-added hard disk drive so that the computer can be used by other students. Check with your instructor to verify if the computer should be returned to its original condition.

Procedure

1. _____ Gather all required materials and report to your assigned workstation.

2. _____ Boot the computer and verify it is in working order.

3. _____ Check if there is unallocated disk space on the first hard disk drive (Disk 0) that can serve as part of the mirrored disk set.

4. _____ Shut down the computer and unplug the power cord before installing the second hard disk drive (Disk 1). Be sure to follow the manufacturer's installation recommendations and procedures. Remember to use an antistatic wrist strap during this procedure.

5. _____ After the second drive (Disk 1) has been installed, reboot the computer. The second hard disk drive should be automatically detected and initialized. If the drive is not automatically detected, access the Disk Management utility and select **Action | Rescan Disks** from the menu. If the drive is still not detected, call your instructor for assistance.

Note

Because you are in a school laboratory environment, the exact procedure could vary because the disk could have been mirrored in a previous class. If it has, check with your instructor before proceeding.

6. _____ Create a small partition (approximately 20 GB) on Disk 0. Format the partition as NTFS.

7. _____ To start the RAID configuration, right-click the 20-GB partition on Disk 0 then select the **Add Mirror** option from the shortcut menu. You will be prompted to select the location of the mirror drive. It will be Disk 1.

8. _____ Disk Management will automatically mirror the drives. When finished, you should be able to view two identical partitions on Disk 0 and Disk 1. They should have the same drive letter and be the same size.

9. _____ Call your instructor to verify your lab. After inspecting your lab activity, your instructor may want you to restore the computer to its original state (remove the mirror, the newly created partition, and the additional drive). Check with your instructor before continuing this lab activity. If your instructor wants you to return the computer to its original state, go on to step 10. If not, answer the review questions.

10. _____ To remove the mirror, right-click the Disk 1 mirror and select **Remove Mirror** from the shortcut menu. The mirror will be automatically removed, leaving only the 20-GB partition on Disk 0. You can remove the 20-GB partition from Disk 0 by right-clicking the partition and selecting **Delete Volume** from the shortcut menu. When you are finished, call your instructor to view the Disk Management configuration.

11. _____ Power off the computer and remove the second hard disk drive (Disk 1).

12. _____ Power on the computer to verify it is in working order.

13. _____ Return all materials to their proper storage area and then answer the review questions.

Review Questions

1. Which RAID configuration (RAID 0, RAID 1 or RAID 5) requires at least three physical drives?

   _____

2. Which RAID configuration provides no fault tolerance? _____

   _____

3. Which type of disk is required for Windows Server 2008 RAID systems: basic or dynamic? _____

   _____

4. Which RAID type provides the fastest data access? _____

   _____

5. You have just configured Disk 0, partition F as RAID 1 with the mirror located on Disk 1. What letter is used to identify the mirrored partition on Disk 1? _____

Laboratory Activity

46

Name_____ Date _____

Class/Instructor _____

Configuring a Static IPv6 Address

After completing this laboratory activity, you will be able to:

■ Use the **Internet Protocol Version 6 (TCP/IP) Properties** dialog box to configure a static IPv6 address.

■ Use the **Network Connection Details** dialog box to view details about a network adapter card's settings.

Introduction

In this laboratory activity, you will configure a static IPv6 address and then view the change in the **Network Connection Details** dialog box. In general, you most likely will not need to configure a static IPv6 address for a workstation, but you may need to configure a static IPv6 address for a server or a router.

Two values you will need to enter are the IPv6 address and the subnet prefix length. The IPv6 address includes a subnet prefix. The *subnet prefix* determines how a router should handle the IPv6 packets. The *subnet prefix length* indicates which portion of the IPv6 address is the network portion. The following screen capture shows the static IPv6 address fe80::1234 with a subnet prefix length of 64 bits. The default subnet prefix length is 64 bits, but the length can be changed to any value within the range of the IPv6 address 128-bit length.

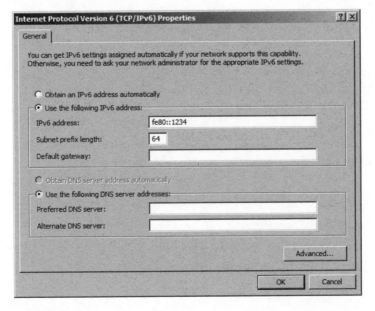

The DNS server address and the default gateway are optional. These device addresses are located automatically by Network Discovery and the exchange of protocols.

Equipment and Materials

❑ Computer with Windows Vista or Windows 7.

Note

Do *not* attempt this lab activity using Windows XP.

Procedure

1. _____ Report to your assigned workstation.

2. _____ Boot the computer and verify it is in working order.

3. _____ Access the **Local Area Connection Properties** dialog box either through the Network and Sharing Center or Control Panel. Select **Internet Protocol Version 6 (TCP/IPv6)** as shown in the following screen capture and then click the **Properties** button.

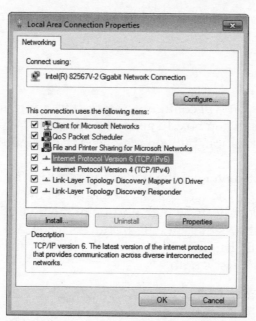

4. _____ You should see the **Internet Protocol Version 6 (TCP/IPv6) Properties** dialog box similar to the one in the following screen capture. Select the **Use the following IPv6 address** option. Then, enter the following information:

IPv6 address: fe08::1234

Subnet prefix length: 64

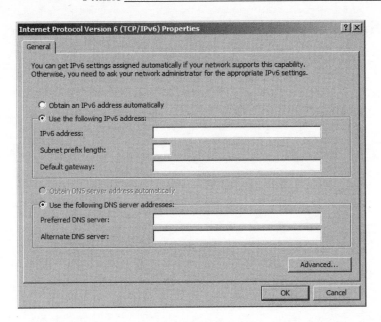

5. _____ Click **OK** to close the **Internet Protocol Version 6 (TCP/IPv6) Properties** dialog box. Then, close the **Local Area Connection Properties** dialog box by clicking **OK** again.

6. _____ Access the **Network Connection Details** dialog box (**Network and Sharing Center | Local Area Connection | Details** button) to view the status of the IPv6 address. You should see two IPv6 addresses assigned to the network adapter. The original link-local IPv6 address and the static IPv6 address you just configured.

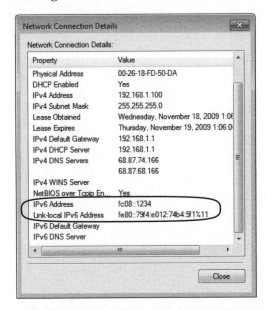

7. _____ Call your instructor to inspect your **Network Connection Details** dialog box.

8. _____ Reconfigure the network adapter to obtain an IPv6 automatically by accessing the **Internet Protocol Version 6 (TCP/IPv6) Properties** dialog box and selecting the **Obtain an IPv6 address automatically** option.

9. _____ Open the **Network Connection Details** dialog box to verify that the "fc08::1234" static address has been removed. You should only see the original IPv6 link-local address.

10. _____ Answer the review questions.

Review Questions

1. What two items must be provided to configure a static IPv6 address? _____

   _____

2. What items are optional for an IPv6 static address configuration? _____

   _____

Name_____ Date _____

Class/Instructor _____

Configuring a DHCP Server

After completing this laboratory activity, you will be able to:

■ Summarize how IP addresses are assigned from an address pool.

■ Recall the purpose of reserved addresses.

■ Recall the purpose of a lease period.

■ Use the Add Roles Wizard to configure a scope on a DHCP server.

Introduction

In this laboratory activity, you will configure the DHCP Server role on a Windows 2008 server. A DHCP server is responsible for automatically issuing IP addresses to DHCP clients. The DHCP server draws IP addresses from a pool of addresses indicated in the "scope." The scope is an administrative grouping of DHCP clients. A Windows workstation is configured by default to receive an IP address, called a *dynamic address*, from a DHCP server. A workstation that is configured to receive a dynamic address is called a *DHCP client*.

An IP address dynamically assigned to a DHCP client has a maximum lease period. The default lease period for Windows Server 2008 is six days. In previous versions of Windows Server operating systems, the default lease period is eight days. After the lease period expires, the IP address is released and is made available to the IP address pool. Before the lease expires, the client will attempt to contact the DHCP server and renew the lease. The lease period prevents a DHCP client from using an IP address from the pool when it is no longer needed. Some network administrators set the lease period quite short, such as to an hour or less. This is especially true when there are an insufficient number of IP addresses for the number of DHCP clients on the network.

Not all network devices receive dynamic addresses. Certain devices, such as servers and printers, must use static addresses so that clients who require their services can locate them. When included in a DHCP scope, these types of static addresses are considered reserved addresses. Reserved addresses are matched to the MAC address of the network device requiring a constant IP address.

You will use the Add Role Wizard to configure and add the DHCP Server role. The major stages (**Add Role Wizard** screens) of the DHCP Server role configuration are as follows.

1. Network Connection Bindings.

2. IPv4 DNS Settings.

3. IPv4 WINS Settings.

4. DHCP Scopes.

5. DHCPv6 Stateless Mode.

6. IPv6 DNS Settings.

7. DHCP Server Authorization.

8. Confirmation.

At each of these stages, you will either enter information required to configure the DHCP server or accept the default settings.

Note

Be aware that the new DHCP Server role you create will automatically send a new IPv4 address to other workstations that connect to the same local area network. This may cause a problem for other student workstations, and may prevent them from accessing the Internet.

Equipment and Materials

❑ Windows 2008 server.
❑ Windows 7 computer for verifying the DHCP operation (optional).
❑ The following information provided by your instructor:

Parent domain name: _____ (Server domain name)

Preferred DNS address: _____ (Can be the same as the DHCP server.)

Scope name: _____

DHCP address pool: _____ to _____

Reserved address block: _____ to _____

MAC addresses of reserved address devices: _____

_____

Lease duration: _____ days

_____ hours

_____ minutes

Note

The DHCP server must be configured with a static IP address. Use static IPv4 address 10.0.0.100 and subnet mask 255.0.0.0 for the DHCP server.

Procedure

1. _____ Report to your assigned workstation.

2. _____ Boot the server and verify it is in working order.

3. _____ Open Server Manager (**Start | Administrative Tools | Server Manager**) and then select **Roles** to view which roles are configured on the server. You should see a screen similar to the following.

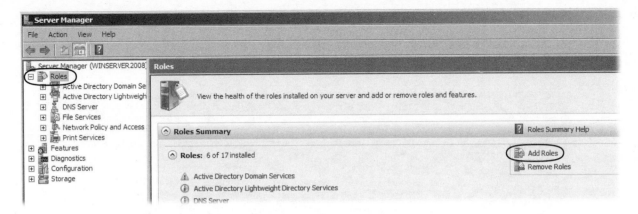

4. _____ Select **Add Roles**, which is located on the right side of the screen. You should see a dialog box similar to that in the following screen capture.

Note

The server may already be configured for the DHCP Server role. If it is, call your instructor for assistance. You will need to remove the DHCP Server role before proceeding in the lab activity.

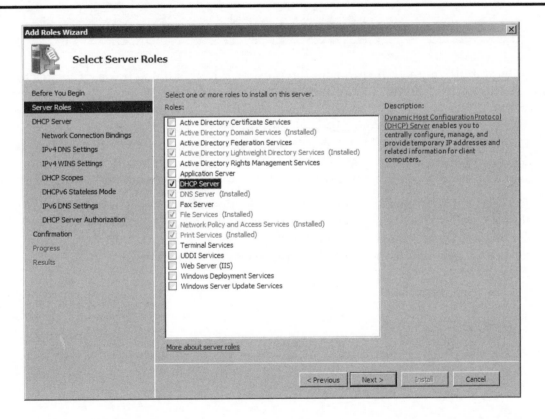

5. _____ Select the DHCP Server role. Then, look at the description on the right as related to Dynamic Host Configuration Protocol (DHCP) Server before moving on to the next step.

6. _____ Click **Next**. A dialog box similar to the following will appear.

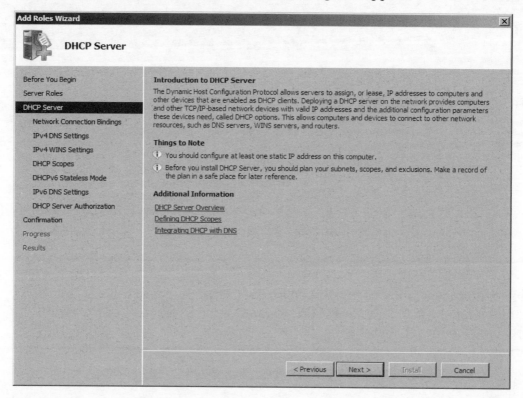

Take a few minutes to read the information presented in the dialog box as it relates to DHCP. Notice in the section "Things to Note" that the computer acting as the DHCP server should be configured with a static IP address. Also notice that it is recommended to make a plan for the subnets, scopes, and exclusions before configuring the DHCP server. It is also suggested that you make a record of the DHCP configuration and store it in a safe place. This will not be necessary for this lab activity as you have already received this information from your instructor. Open the "Additional Information" links and skim through the information provided.

7. _____ When you are finished reading the information, click **Next**. The dialog box similar to the following will display listing network connection bindings. Network connection bindings are a list of static IP addresses associated with the DHCP server network connection. It is possible to have more than one static IP address on a DHCP server.

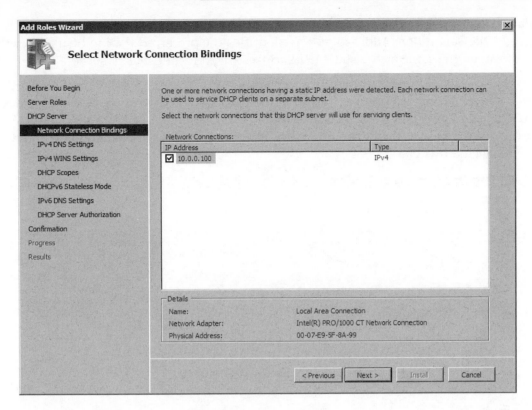

In this dialog box, the static IPv4 address configured for the computer will be automatically detected and then presented. The IPv4 address in the screen capture is 10.0.0.100. This address may not necessarily match your assigned IPv4 address.

8. _____ Accept the default settings and click **Next**. The next dialog box to appear will prompt you for IPv4 DNS settings and will look similar to that in the following screen capture.

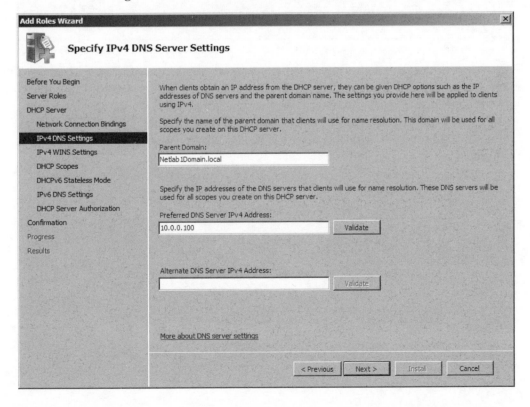

The **Parent Domain** option specifies the name used to identify the network domain. The **Preferred DNS Server IPv4 Address** option identifies the preferred IPv4 to be used for the DNS server. It can be the same as the static IPv4 address used for the DHCP server.

9. _____ The next dialog box to appear prompts you for WINS server setting. These settings ensure backward compatibility with older Windows operating systems. A WINS server is not required for networks that only contain Windows 2000 and later operating systems. As you can see in the following screen capture, the **WINS is not required for applications on this network** option is selected by default.

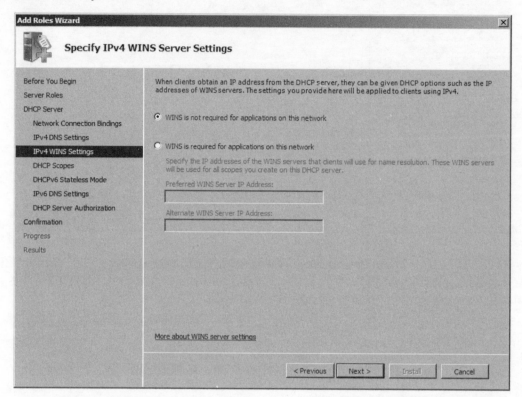

10. _____ The next dialog box to appear prompts you for the scope of IPv4 addresses. The scope is also referred to as the *DHCP address pool*. The DHCP server issues network clients IP addresses from the scope. Notice in the screen capture that the scope is given a name, a starting IP address, an ending IP address, and a subnet mask. The default lease period for the address is six days. The default gateway is optional because the operating system will automatically identify the default gateway.

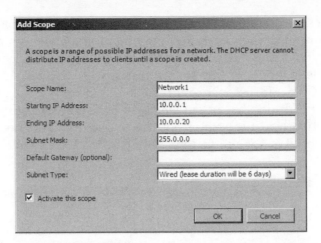

11. _____ The next dialog box is a summary of the scopes. This option allows you to add additional scopes for another part of the network.

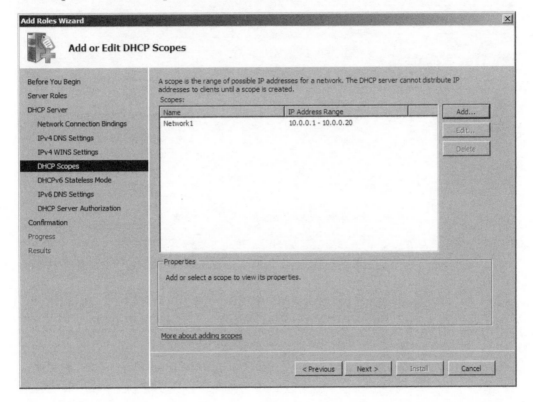

12. _____ The next dialog box to appear prompts you to enable or disable the stateless mode for the IPv6 address assignment. Each workstation will automatically assign its own IPv6 address when the **Enable DHCPv6 stateless mode for this server** option is selected. The other option, **Disable DHCPv6 stateless mode for this server**, configures the DHCP server to assign IPv6 addresses. Assigning IPv6 addresses through a DHCP server is not a preferred method at the time of this writing. This option has obviously been included for future use when IPv4 becomes obsolete or when a network administrator decides to use IPv6 assigned addresses from a DHCP server pool of addresses. It is not a requirement of this lab activity to configure an IPv6 DHCP server pool.

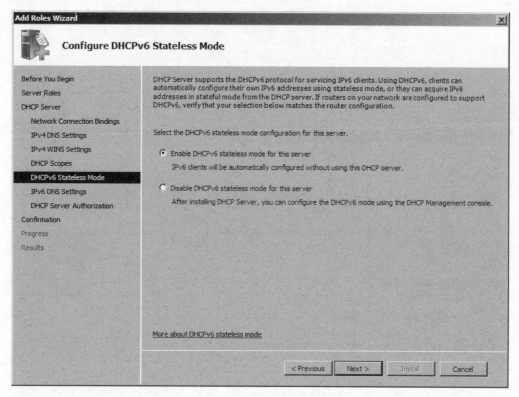

13. _____ The next dialog box prompts you to configure the IPv6 DNS server settings. The operating system will automatically detect and suggest the parent domain and the preferred DNS server IPv6 address. Simply accept the default settings.

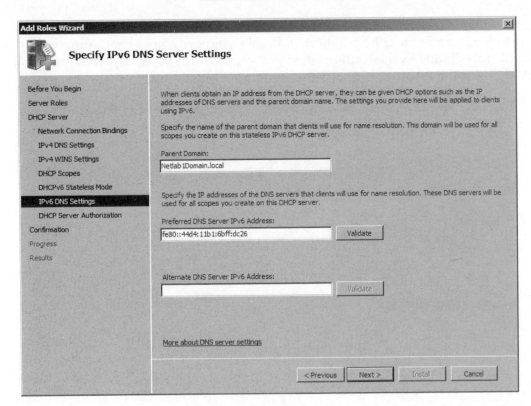

14. _____ The next dialog box prompts you to select or configure the credentials that allow for authorizing the DHCP server as part of the Active Directory Domain Services (AD DS). Again, the operating system will automatically detect the default credentials. Simply accept them.

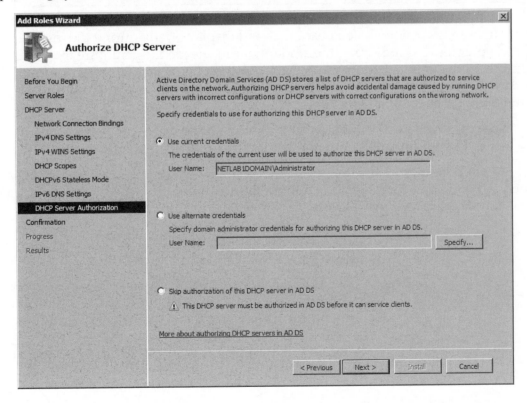

15. _____ The next dialog box to appear confirms the DHCP configuration. You have an opportunity to review the configuration and make changes before continuing with the DHCP Server role installation. If the configuration is acceptable click **Install**. If the configuration is not acceptable, click the **Previous** button as needed and make the appropriate changes.

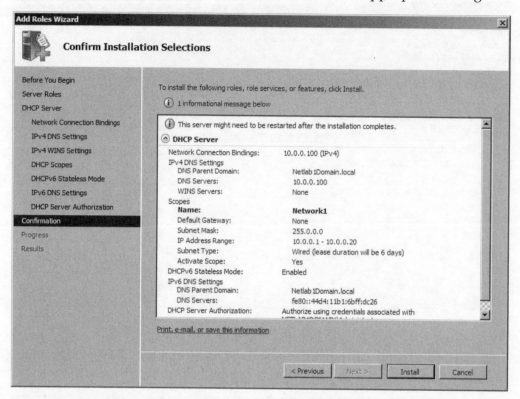

16. _____ There are two more dialog boxes that will display briefly during the installation. One is simply a progress bar indicating the amount of time needed to configure the DHCP server and the other is a summary confirming the completion of the DHCP server configuration. Once the installation is completed, the DHCP server will be ready to issue IPv4 addresses to any workstation connected to the same network as the DHCP server.

17. _____ Boot the Windows 7 computer, which should be connected to the same network as the DHCP server. Use the **ipconfig** command to view the IPv4 address issued.

18. _____ At the Windows 2008 server, open Server Manager and then view the address lease assigned to Windows 7 computer. You will be able to see the computer name and domain location and the assigned IPv4 address.

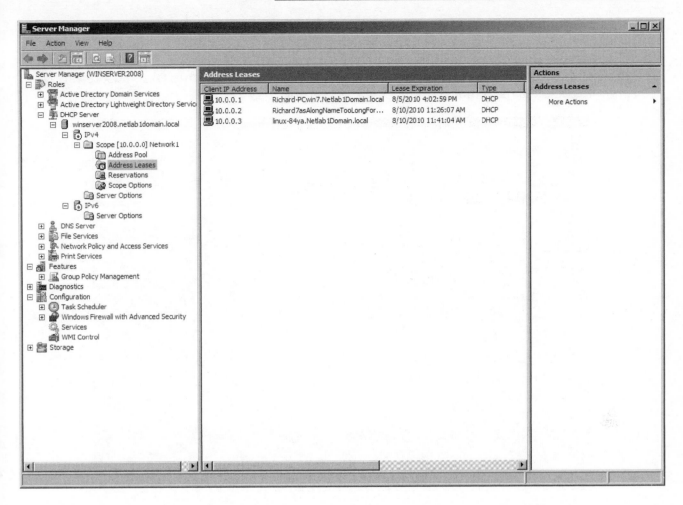

19. _____ Call your instructor to inspect your laboratory activity at this time. With your instructor's permission, you may practice configuring additional DHCP server scopes.

20. _____ After completing the DHCP configuration, you can remove the DHCP Server role by selecting **Start | All Programs | Administrative Tools | Server Manager**. In Server Manager, select **Remove Roles** from the **Roles Summary** section. The Remove Roles Wizard will display. Deselect the DHCP Server role as shown in the following screen capture. You must restart the server to complete the removal of the DHCP Server role.

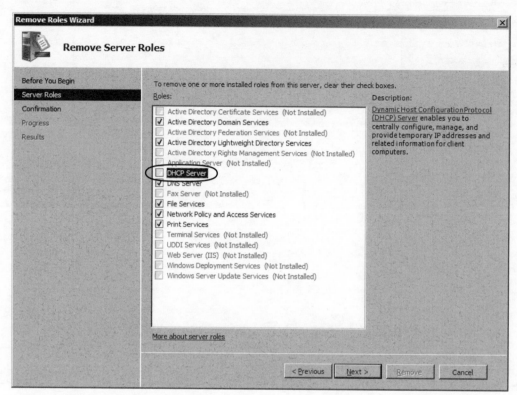

21. _____ Call your instructor to verify the DHCP Server role has been removed.

22. _____ Answer the review questions.

Review Questions

1. What does the acronym DHCP represent? _____

   _____

2. What is the default IP configuration (static or dynamic) of a Windows workstation?_____

   _____

3. What is the purpose of a reserved address? _____

   _____

4. What is a lease period?_____

   _____

5. In what order does a DHCP server assign IP addresses?_____

   _____

6. What happens when the DHCP server is configured for IPv6 stateless mode? _____

   _____

WINDOWS XP OR LATER

Name_____ Date _____

Class/Instructor _____

Observing APIPA

After completing this laboratory activity, you will be able to:

■ Recall the purpose of Automatic Private IP Addressing (APIPA).

■ Identify the APIPA address range.

Introduction

In this laboratory activity, you will observe the Automatic Private IP Addressing (APIPA) feature. APIPA was first introduced in Windows 98 second edition. The purpose of APIPA is to automatically assign an IP address to a workstation to allow it and the other workstations to communicate in the local area network when the DHCP server cannot be contacted. APIPA generates a Class B IP address when a workstation is configured to obtain a dynamic IP address. This means that a local area peer-to-peer network is automatically created to support communication between workstations. All the workstations will have an APIPA-generated IP address within the range of 169.254.0.1 to 169.254.255.254 and a subnet mask of 255.255.0.0.

You can check if the computer is using an APIPA address by issuing the **ipconfig** command from the command prompt. A response of an IP address within the APIPA range means that the workstation is running the APIPA service. An APIPA assigned IP address is a good way to identify a problem between the workstation and a DHCP server when troubleshooting a network problem. The following table describes the **ipconfig** command used with various switches.

Command	Description
ipconfig	Reveals the IP address configured for the network adapter(s).
ipconfig/all	Reveals detailed information about the network adapter(s).
ipconfig/renew	Renews the IP address of the network adapter(s).
ipconfig/release	Releases the IP address resulting in 0.0.0.0 as the IP address of the network adapter(s), unless a DHCP server is connected to the local network.

Equipment and Materials

❑ Microsoft Windows XP or later computer connected to a network with a DHCP server.

Procedure

1. _____ Report to your assigned workstation.

2. _____ Boot the computer and verify it is in working order.

3. _____ Run **ipconfig** from the command prompt to identify the assigned IP address. Write the IP address in the space provided.

4. _____ Disconnect the network cable at the hub that is connected to the DHCP server. This will simulate a DHCP server failure.

5. _____ At the computer, open the command prompt and issue the command **ipconfig/release** to release the assigned IP address.

6. _____ Issue the command **ipconfig** and observe the new IP address assignment. Write this IP address in the space provided.

_____

7. _____ Issue the **ipconfig/renew** command. Be patient. The command will appear to lock up the workstation. It will take a short period of time to activate the APIPA address as a result of the failure to locate the DHCP server. Write the error that appears on the screen in the space provided.

_____

_____

_____

8. _____ Issue the **ipconfig** command and observe the APIPA address that is assigned to the computer. Write the APIPA address in the space provided.

_____

9. _____ Reconnect the DHCP server and then use the **ipconfig/renew** command to generate a new IP address from the DHCP server.

10. _____ Use the **ipconfig** command to observe the new IP address assigned by the DHCP server. Write this address in the space provided.

_____

11. _____ Repeat the procedure until you understand the concept of APIPA and the **ipconfig/renew** and **ipconfig/release** commands and their effect on the IP address assignment of the workstation.

12. _____ Answer the review questions.

Review Questions

1. What does the acronym APIPA represent? _____

_____

2. What subnet mask is used for APIPA? _____

3. What class (Class A, Class B, or Class C) of network is APIPA? _____

4. What are the first two octets of an APIPA IP address? _____

5. What is the purpose of APIPA? _____

_____

_____

6. What would an APIPA address assigned to a workstation indicate while troubleshooting an Internet connection problem? _____

_____

Name_____ Date _____

Class/Instructor _____

Configuring an Alternate IPv4 Address

After completing this laboratory activity, you will be able to:

■ Use the **Internet Protocol Version 4 (TCP/IPv4) Properties** dialog box to configure an alternative IPv4 address.

■ Give examples of when an alternate IPv4 address might be required.

Introduction

In this laboratory activity, you will configure a workstation for an alternate IPv4 address. Laptop computers often require more than one IPv4 address when they are used at home and at work. The laptop may be configured with a dynamic address to connect to a network at home and require a static IPv4 address to connect to the network at work.

Alternate IPv4 configuration options are only available when a workstation has been configured for DHCP. If a static address is assigned to the workstation, you will not be able to configure an alternate address. A workstation configured with an alternate IPv4 address will automatically attempt to connect to the network when a DHCP server cannot be located.

Windows operating systems are automatically configured for DHCP by default when first installed. The Automatic Private IP Address (APIPA) feature is also enabled by default. If a workstation cannot establish a connection with a DHCP server, it will automatically assign an IPv4 address to itself in the range from 169.254.0.1 to 169.254.255.254 with a subnet mask of 255.255.0.0. The APIPA feature allows a workstation to communicate with other workstations on a network in the event of a DHCP server failure.

The APIPA feature is disabled when a computer is configured with an alternate IPv4 address. Windows Vista and later computers use IPv6 to communicate in the local area network. With IPv6 enabled, APIPA is not needed to communicate on the local area network should the DHCP server fail; however, the computer will not be able to access remote locations on the Internet that require an IPv4 address.

Equipment and Materials

❑ Windows 7 computer connected to a network.
❑ The following information provided by your instructor:

Static IPv4 assignment: _____

Procedure

1. _____ Report to your assigned workstation.

2. _____ Boot the computer and verify it is in working order.

3. _____ Use the **ipconfig/all** command to verify the network adapter settings. Record the information in spaces provided.

IPv4 address: _____

Subnet mask: _____

Default gateway: _____

DNS server: _____

4. _____ If the computer is configured to obtain an IPv4 address automatically, proceed to step 5. If the computer is not configured to obtain an IPv4 address automatically, configure it now by opening the **Local Area Connection Status** dialog box. Click the **Properties** button.

The **Local Area Connection Properties** dialog box will display. Highlight **Internet Protocol Version 4 (TCP/IPv4)** and then click **Properties**. A dialog box similar to the following will appear. Select the **Obtain an IP address automatically** option and then click **OK**. Then, click **Close** to close the dialog boxes.

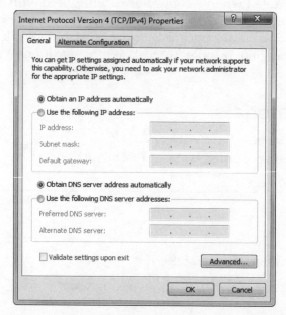

5. _____ Open the **Local Area Connection Properties** dialog box.

6. _____ Select the **Alternate Configuration** tab. A dialog box similar the following will appear.

Note

The **Alternate Configuration** tab is only available when the workstation is configured to obtain an IP address automatically. If the computer is configured for a static IPv4 address, the **Alternate Configuration** tab will not be available.

7. _____ Select the **User configured** option, which allows you to configure a static IPv4 address for the network adapter. Pay particular attention to the **Preferred DNS server** and the **Preferred WINS server** options. These two options do *not* need to be configured, but when they are, connections are established quicker on the network. Also, notice that **Automatic private IP address** and the **User configured** options use radio buttons. The use of radio buttons means you can only use one option or the other, not both. Therefore, when selecting the **User configured** option, APIPA is disabled.

8. _____ Click **OK**. The computer has now successfully been configured for an alternate IPv4 address. Call your instructor to inspect your lab activity.

9. _____ Restore the workstation to its original TCP/IP settings and then answer the review questions.

Review Questions

1. When might you use an alternate IPv4 address? _____

_____

2. You attempt to configure an alternate IPv4 address for your computer and you find the feature is not available. What might be the cause for the feature not to be available? _____

_____

3. When configuring an alternate IPv4 address, what other two optional addresses may be configured that will provide a faster network connection? _____

_____

4. How is the APIPA feature affected by a static IPv4 address configuration? _____

_____

Name_____ Date _____

Class/Instructor _____

Configuring ICS

After completing this laboratory activity, you will be able to:

■ Recall the purpose of NAT.

■ Identify the three groups of private IP addresses associated with NAT.

■ Differentiate between a public and a private IP address.

■ Use the **Local Area Connection Properties** dialog box to configure a workstation as an ICS host.

■ Use the **Local Area Network (LAN) Settings** dialog box to configure a workstation as an ICS client.

Introduction

In this laboratory activity, you will configure Microsoft's Internet Connection Sharing (ICS) feature, which allows multiple workstations to share a single Internet connection. ICS is Microsoft's implementation of Network Address Translation (NAT). NAT is a standard developed by the Internet Engineering Task Force (IETF), which allows one public IPv4 address to translate into multiple private IPv4 addresses. The following private IPv4 addresses are associated with NAT:

■ 10.0.0.0–10.255.255.255

■ 172.16.0.0–172.32.255.255

■ 192.168.0.0–192.168.255.255

Note
ICS is only designed to support private IPv4 addresses in the range of 192.168.0.0 to 192.168.255.255.

Private IPv4 addresses are also referred to as *non-routable IPv4 addresses*. This is because they are blocked by default by a router and cannot be used to directly communicate across the Internet.

A workstation or server configured to share an Internet connection using Microsoft ICS is called an *ICS host*. A workstation configured to access the Internet through an ICS host is called an *ICS client*. The ICS host must be running for the ICS host to be able to connect to the Internet. The ICS host not only provides a connection to the Internet, but also acts as a DHCP server, automatically issuing a private IPv4 address to each ICS client.

An additional network adapter card may be needed to be installed in the ICS host if the Internet connection is being provided directly through a DSL or Cable modem. An additional network adapter installed in the ICS host is not required if the ICS host connects to the Internet directly by a dial-up telephone modem.

Note
You normally do not configure ICS if the Internet connection is provided through a router or gateway device.

Look at the following figure. Notice that two network interface cards are located in the ICS host. One network interface card is configured with the public address and connects directly to the ISP provider. The other network interface card is configured with a private IPv4 address and is used to share the connection with one or more other clients.

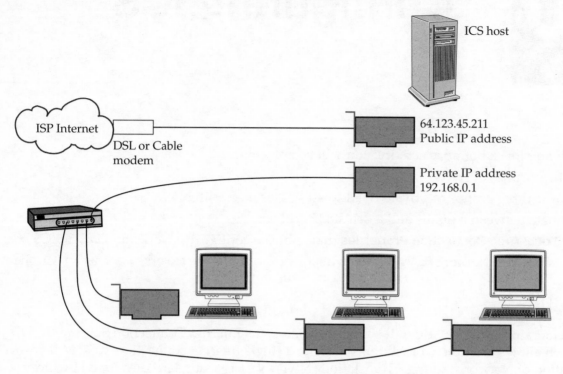

ICS clients 192.168.0.10–192.168.0.XXX

The ICS configuration can be set up during the initial network configuration or at a later time manually. ICS is very easy to configure. At the workstation designated as the ICS host, you must first configure two network interface cards. The Internet connection is configured with the public IPv4 address provided through the ISP. The LAN connection is assigned the IPv4 private address of 192.168.0.1 and subnet mask 255.255.255.0. The ICS clients in the LAN should be configured for DHCP.

IPv4 addresses in the range of 129.168.0.1 to 192.168.0.255 are automatically assigned to ICS clients using the DHCP feature of the ICS host.

Keep in mind that a router or gateway device can provide NAT and share Internet access with all clients in the LAN. A router typically supports a full range of private IPv4 addresses. The router connects directly to the Internet provider via a DSL or Cable modem connection. The network cable from the client workstations can be plugged into the router's RJ-45 ports. Typical ICS devices also provide wireless connection service to wireless devices such as laptops. If more wired connections are needed than the number provided by the ICS device, a hub or switch can be connected to the ICS device.

Equipment and Materials

❑ Two Windows 7 computers. (One must have either two LAN connections built into the motherboard or an additional network adapter.)
❑ DSL, Cable modem, or a dial-up telephone modem. (Required to access the Internet.)
❑ A hub or a switch. (Needed to share the connection to the ICS client. You can use a crossover cable instead to connect the ICS host to the ICS client.)

Name _____

❑ The following information provided by your instructor:

Static IPv4 address: _____

Subnet mask: _____

DNS server 1: _____

DNS server 2: _____

Internet access user name: _____

Internet access password: _____

Procedure

1. _____ Gather the required materials and then report to your assigned workstation.

2. _____ Boot the Windows computers and verify they are in working order.

3. _____ If necessary, shut down the computer designated to be the ICS host and install the additional network adapter. If the additional adapter is installed, go on to step 4.

4. _____ On the ICS host, the default name of the installed network adapter is Local Area Connection. Each additional network adapter will have the same name followed by a sequential number, for example, Local Area Connection 2. For this lab activity, you will need to rename the Local Area Connection name that connects the ISP to the ISP connection. To do this, open the Network and Sharing Center and then select **Change adapter settings**.

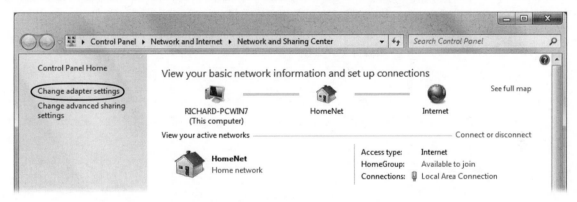

5. _____ Right-click the **Local Area Connection** icon and select **Rename** from the shortcut menu.

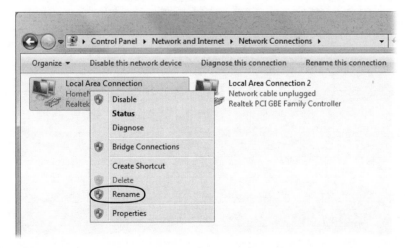

6. _____ Right-click the **Local Area Connection** icon again and then select **Properties** from the shortcut menu.

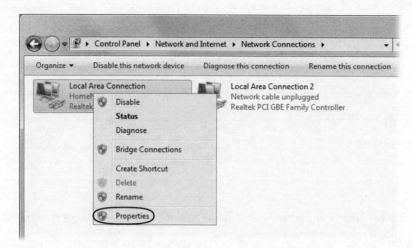

7. _____ When the **Local Area Connection Properties** dialog box appears, select the **Sharing** tab. Notice there are two options that allow the network adapter to be configured for ICS. Select both options.

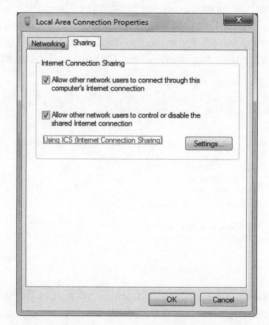

8. _____ Click the Using ICS (Internet Connection Sharing) link and you will see information about Internet Connection Sharing similar to that in the following screen capture. Take a few minutes to review this information. You may also locate the information using Help and Support located off the **Start** menu. You can also access Help and Support information by entering "Using ICS" in the **Start** menu **Search** box.

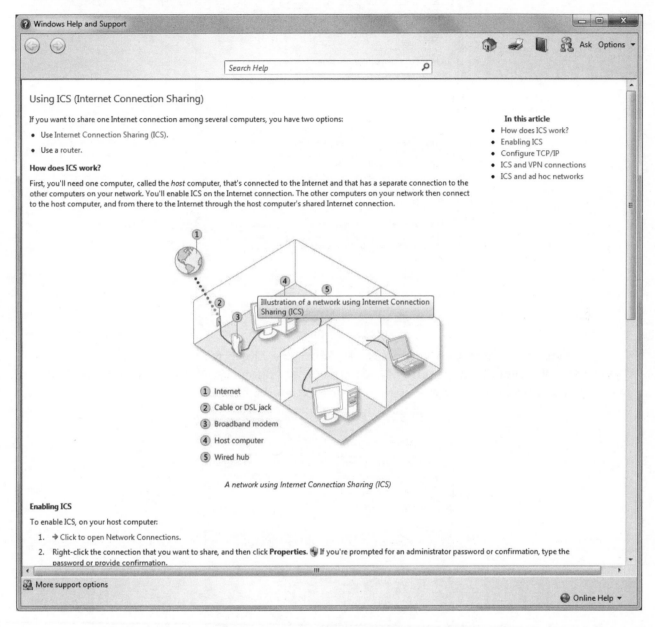

9. _____ When you are finished reviewing the information, close the information screen by clicking the X in the top right-hand corner. Click **OK** to close the **Local Area Connection Properties** dialog box.

10. _____ At the ICS client, open the **Internet Properties** dialog box (**Start | Control Panel | Network and Internet | Internet Options**). Select the **Connections** tab and then click the **LAN settings** button.

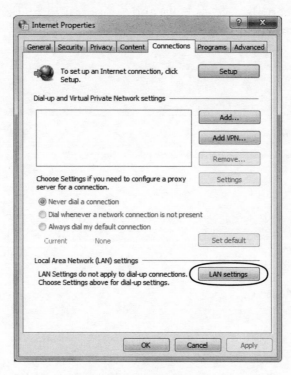

11. _____ When the **Local Area Network (LAN) Settings** dialog box appears, select the **Automatically detect settings** option. Leave the other options unselected. The ICS client network adapter will now accept the private IPv4 address from the ICS host.

12. _____ Close all open dialog boxes and then test the Internet connection from the ICS client. Remember that the ICS host must be running in order for the ICS client to connect to the Internet through the ICS host.

13. _____ Use the **ipconfig** command to verify the assigned IPv4 address of the ICS host and ICS client.

14. _____ Have your instructor inspect your laboratory activity.

15. _____ Return the computers to their original configuration. You can use System Restore to quickly return the computers to their original configurations.

16. _____ Return all materials to their proper storage area and then complete the review questions.

Review Questions

1. What does the acronym ICS represent? _____

2. What does the acronym NAT represent? _____

3. What is the purpose of NAT? _____
_____

4. What are the three private IPv4 address ranges? _____
_____

5. What is the difference between a public and a private IPv4 address? _____
_____
_____

Laboratory Activity

51

Name_____ Date _____

Class/Instructor _____

Observing DHCP Commands with Wireshark

After completing this laboratory activity, you will be able to:

- Recall the purpose of the Bootstrap Protocol.
- Explain what happens when the **ipconfig/release** command is issued.
- Explain what happens when the **ipconfig/renew** command is issued.
- Use the **Local Area Connection Properties** dialog box to disable and enable the IPv6 protocol.

Introduction

In this laboratory activity, you will use Wireshark to observe the protocol actions that occur when the **ipconfig/release** and **ipconfig/renew** commands are issued. The **ipconfig/release** command causes the assigned IPv4 address to be released from the network adapter configuration. When the IPv4 address is released, the workstation has no assigned IPv4 address. The **ipconfig/renew** command causes the workstation network adapter to request a new IPv4 address from the DHCP server.

For this lab activity, you will need two computers connected to a network with a DHCP server: one configured for DHCP and the other with Wireshark installed. If Wireshark is installed on the workstation using the **ipconfig/release** command, Wireshark may quit working. Wireshark must maintain a connection to the network to work properly. This may not be possible when the IPv4 address is released.

The two IPv4 addresses used for communication between the DHCP client and server are 0.0.0.0 and 255.255.255.255. The IPv4 address 0.0.0.0 is reserved for use by the client when requesting an IPv4 assigned address from the DHCP server. The 255.255.255.255 IPv4 address is also reserved and is known as the *IPv4 broadcast address*. The workstation requesting the IPv4 address does not yet know the assigned IPv4 address of the DHCP server, so it sends out the DHCP request to destination location 255.255.255.255. The DHCP server accepts all broadcasts to 255.255.255.255. The DHCP server then selects the next available IPv4 address from the pool of IPv4 addresses and sends it to the requesting workstation with the 0.0.0.0 IPv4 address. After the requesting workstation accepts the new IPv4 address, it will no longer use the 0.0.0.0 address. As you can see, the automatic assignment of the IPv4 address is quite simple.

You will see the Bootstrap Protocol (BOOTP) identified by Wireshark at the start of the IPv4 address request. BOOTP facilitates IP request when the network adapter is configured for DHCP. If you look closely at the BOOTP packet contents, you will see it contains the same last IPv4 address used by the workstation. This is normal. The just released IPv4 address will be the first new IPv4 to be issued from the pool of IPv4 addresses.

To identify in the Wireshark capture the workstation making the DHCP request, record the workstations' MAC address before performing the capture. The MAC address can be used to identify the workstation originating the DHCP request. Looking at all of the frame captures can be quite confusing. The MAC address will help you to more easily identify the proper frame.

Equipment and Materials

❑ Two Windows 7 computers connected to a network with a DHCP server. One computer should be configured for DHCP and the other should have Wireshark installed.

❑ Wireshark Sample 9 file.

Wireshark Sample 9 file location: _____

Procedure

1. _____ Report to your assigned workstation(s).

2. _____ Boot the Windows 7 workstations and verify they are in working order.

3. _____ On the workstation configured for DHCP, check the current IPv4 configuration by issuing the **ipconfig/all** command from the command prompt. Record the information in the spaces provided.

IPv4 address: _____

Subnet mask: _____

Default gateway: _____

Preferred DNS server: _____

DHCP enabled: _____ (Yes or No)

MAC address: _____

4. _____ On the workstation with Wireshark installed, open the Wireshark Sample 9 file and look at frames 105 through 111. Notice that in frame 105, the IPv4 address is released. In the next frame, the workstation is requesting an IPv4 address from the DHCP server. The source IPv4 address of the requesting workstation is 0.0.0.0. It uses the broadcast IPv4 address 255.255.255.255 to contact the DHCP server. The protocol used to send the request for a DHCP IPv4 address is BOOTP.

In the next few frames, the IPv4 address 192.168.1.104 is issued to the workstation. The workstation then sends out an ARP request to verify no other device has been assigned the 192.168.1.104 IPv4 address. This precaution ensures that each IPv4 address in the local network is unique.

You cannot duplicate IP addresses in the same local area network. When a duplicate address is found, the workstation sending the ARP request will disable its own network adapter. This might occur when one of the IPv4 addresses found in the DHCP pool of addresses has been manually assigned as a static IPv4 address to some device such as a printer. Static IPv4 addresses used on the local area network with a DHCP server should be reserved by registering them with the DHCP server.

5. _____ Open frame 110 and closely look at the contents of BOOTP. If you expand the contents, you will see that the workstation is requesting its original IPv4 address of 192.168.1.104 from the DHCP server. Do not automatically think that a brand new IPv4 address is assigned. The old IPv4 address is typically available and will be assigned to workstation. This is the reason that you see workstations with a consistent IPv4 address even when configured for DHCP.

6. _____ Close the Wireshark Sample 9 file.

7. _____ Before starting your own capture, you may wish to disable the IPv6 protocol to make it easier to observe the IPv4 DHCP function. To disable the IPv6 protocol, open the **Local Area Connection Properties** dialog box. Deselect **Internet Protocol Version 6 (TCP/IPv6)** and then click **OK**.

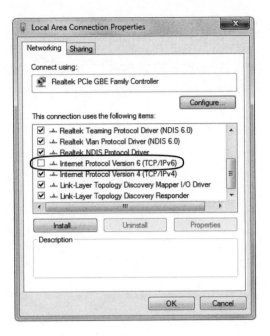

8. _____ Start a Wireshark capture.

9. _____ On the workstation configured for DHCP, open a command prompt and issue the **ipconfig/release** command followed by the **ipconfig/renew** command.

10. _____ Stop the Wireshark capture and then inspect the contents of the frames. You can quickly locate the start of the DHCP renewal process by looking for the frame containing the first 0.0.0.0 source IPv4 address.

11. _____ Using the captured contents as a reference, answer the review questions.

12. _____ After completing the review questions, return the workstations to their original configuration. Do not forget to enable the IPv6 protocol on the Wireshark computer.

13. _____ Return the workstation to its original configuration.

Review Questions

1. What protocol is used to issue the DHCP request? _____

2. DHCP requests are carried by which type of packet: TCP or UDP?_____

3. Which two IPv4 addresses are used to communicate between a workstation and a DHCP server? _____

_____

4. What IPv4 address is used by a workstation when requesting an IPv4 address from the DHCP server? _____

5. To what IPv4 address does the workstation send the DHCP request? _____

_____

6. What protocols are used to encapsulate BOOTP?_____

7. What is the purpose of BOOTP? _____

8. What port numbers are associated with BOOTP?_____

9. What command issued from the command prompt will generate a new IPv4 address from the DHCP server? _____

10. What command issued from the command prompt will release the assigned IPv4 from the network adapter? _____

Name_____ Date _____

Class/Instructor _____

Observing ICS Activity with Wireshark

After completing this laboratory activity, you will be able to:

■ Explain the boot process of an ICS client.

Introduction

In this laboratory activity, you will set up a simple experiment and then observe the results. You will use the results to answer the review questions.

Look at the following screen capture. In it are two arrangements that can be used when observing ICS activity with Wireshark. In the first arrangement, Wireshark is run from the ICS host. In the second arrangement, Wireshark is run from a workstation that is not part of the ICS configuration. The experiment will not produce the desired results if you run Wireshark from the ICS client. Also, Wireshark must be running before you turn on the ICS host.

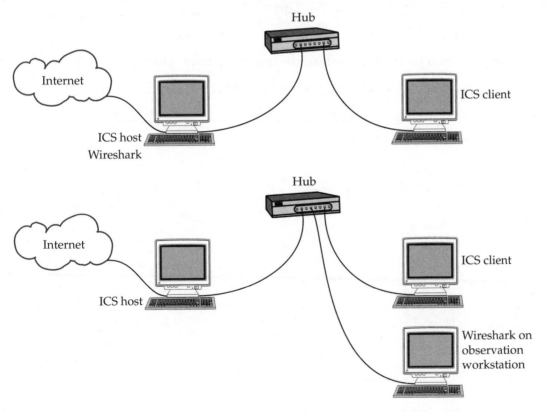

In either of the two network arrangements, Wireshark will capture all of the network traffic between the workstations. After performing a Wireshark capture, you will view the contents and then answer the review questions.

Equipment and Materials

❑ Two Windows 7 computers (if using the first configuration), one with Wireshark installed on the ICS host.

❑ Three Windows 7 computers (if using the second configuration), one with Wireshark installed on the computer that will not be part of the ICS configuration.

Procedure

1. _____ Report to your assigned workstation(s).

2. _____ Boot the Windows 7 computers and verify they are in working order.

3. _____ Shut down the ICS client.

4. _____ Verify the ICS host has an Internet connection.

5. _____ Start a Wireshark capture.

6. _____ Boot the ICS client and then connect to the Internet from this workstation.

7. _____ After successfully connecting to the Internet, stop the Wireshark capture.

8. _____ Examine the captured series of frames/packets.

9. _____ Answer the review questions.

Review Questions

1. From where did the ICS client receive its IPv4 address? _____

2. What IPv4 address did the ICS client use when making the request? _____

3. What IPv4 address is used by the ICS host for the local area network? _____

4. What IPv4 address is used by the ICS host for the Internet connection? _____

_____

5. Which computer acted like a DHCP server? _____

Laboratory Activity

53

Name_____ Date _____

Class/Instructor _____

Using Microsoft Calculator for Binary Conversion

After completing this laboratory activity, you will be able to:

■ Use the Microsoft Calculator menu to change the view from standard to scientific.

■ Use the Microsoft Calculator to convert binary numbers to decimal.

■ Use the Microsoft Calculator to convert decimal numbers to binary.

Introduction

Calculator is a program that comes with most Microsoft Windows operating systems. Knowing how to use the Calculator program for binary conversion will prove valuable when studying subnet masks.

The Calculator program is located at **Start | All Programs | Accessories**. In Windows versions earlier than Windows 7, two views are available: standard and scientific. To switch views, select the **Standard** or **Scientific** option from the **View** menu, as shown in the following screen capture.

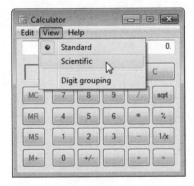

In Windows 7, many views are available, as shown in the following screen capture. To switch views, select the view type from the **View** menu.

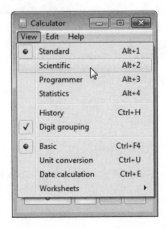

For this lab activity, you will select the **Scientific** view if using a version of Windows earlier than Windows 7, and you will select the **Programmer** view if using Windows 7. The Scientific or Programmer view is handy for converting binary numbers to decimal and decimal numbers to binary. When Calculator is in the Scientific or Programmer view, the options **Hex**, **Dec**, **Oct**, and **Bin** are listed. Selecting one of these options configures the calculator to accept numeric values of the type chosen or changes the value in the display window to that type. For example, if you want to enter a binary value, you would first select the binary option before entering the binary value. To convert the binary value to a decimal value, you would select the **Dec** option. The binary value will automatically convert to decimal. In versions of Windows earlier than Windows 7, the **Hex**, **Dec**, **Oct**, and **Bin** options are listed beneath the display window.

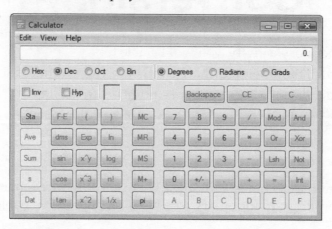

The following screen capture shows the Windows 7 Calculator Programmer view. Notice that the options **Hex**, **Dec**, **Oct**, and **Bin** are listed in a box on the left side of the calculator.

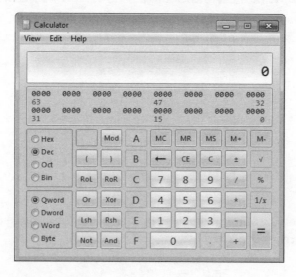

Equipment and Materials

❑   Windows XP or later computer.

Procedure

1. _____ Report to your assigned workstation.

2. _____ Boot the computer and verify it is in working order.

3. _____ Open the Calculator program.

4. _____ Select **Scientific** option from the **View** menu if using a version of Windows earlier than Windows 7. Select the **Programmer** option from the **View** menu if using Windows 7.

5. _____ Convert the following binary numbers to decimal. Before entering the binary number, be sure to set the calculator to binary by selecting the **Bin** option. After you have entered the binary number, select the **Dec** option to convert it to decimal. Record the decimal number in the space provided. To clear a value from the display window, click the **C** button. Do not forget to select the **Bin** option before entering the next binary number.

1101 = _____

1111 = _____

0001 = _____

0010 = _____

6. _____ Convert the following decimal numbers to binary. Before entering the decimal number, be sure to select the **Dec** option. After you have entered the decimal number, select the **Bin** option to convert it to binary. Record the binary number in the spaces provided.

25 = _____

30 = _____

124 = _____

8 = _____

16 = _____

Review Questions

1. Use Calculator to convert the following binary numbers to decimal.

   a. 0011 = _____

   b. 0100 = _____

   c. 0101 = _____

   d. 11 = _____

   e. 111 = _____

   f. 1111 = _____

   g. 11111 = _____

   h. 111111 = _____

   i. 1111111 = _____

   j. 11111111 = _____

k. 10000000 = _____

l. 11000000 = _____

m. 11100000 = _____

n. 11110000 = _____

o. 11111000 = _____

2. Use Calculator to convert the decimal number to binary.

a. 32 = _____

b. 64 = _____

c. 128 = _____

d. 256 = _____

e. 512 = _____

f. 1024 = _____

g. 2048 = _____

h. 4096 = _____

i. 111 = _____

j. 15 = _____

Name_____ Date _____

Class/Instructor _____

Subnet Mask Calculator

After completing this laboratory activity, you will be able to:

■ Carry out download and installation procedures for the WildPackets IP Subnet Calculator.

■ Use the WildPackets IP Subnet Calculator to determine the number of hosts and subnetworks associated with a given subnet mask.

■ Identify the binary pattern associated with a given subnet mask or IP address.

Introduction

In this laboratory activity, you will download the WildPackets IP Subnet Calculator from the WildPackets Web site. The WildPackets IP Subnet Calculator is a very handy utility, and it is free. If the WildPackets IP Subnet Calculator is not available, you can conduct an Internet search to locate another subnet calculator.

Note

While the Network+ Certification exam does not require network subnet mask calculations at this time, some other network certifications do require subnet mask calculations by hand. You cannot use a calculator during these exams. Always check for the latest test specifications concerning this area.

The calculations for subnets can be very difficult for students and also for many technicians. It is one of the most difficult aspects of networking. The concept of creating a subnet out of an assigned IP address is very simple. The subnet mask is divided into two portions: the network portion and the host portion. For example, the subnet mask of a typical Class C network is 255.255.255.0. Each of the first three octets has the number *255* representing the network portion of the subnet mask and the number *0* representing the host portion of the subnet mask. The value 255 is equal to eight binary ones, or an entire octet filled with ones, such as 11111111. The series of ones represents the network portion of the subnet mask.

To create a subnet from a Class C network assignment, the host assignment of 0 is changed to some other value, such as 160, 192, or 224. The new value extends the network portion into the host portion of an assigned address. Remember, when subnetting, bits are borrowed from the host portion of an IP address. The borrowed bits are the extended portion of the network address. In a Class C subnet mask, this means that the fourth octet will begin (starting at the left of the octet) with a series of ones.

To calculate the decimal number that represents the series of binary ones is very difficult for most people, especially if they do not have a background in digital electronics. This is where the WildPackets IP Subnet Calculator comes in handy. The calculator allows you to choose a class of network, such as Class A, Class B, or Class C, and select the number of subnets you desire. The WildPackets IP Subnet Calculator instantly gives you all the information you need. Let's see how this is done.

When provided with an IP address, the calculator immediately displays the network class, the bit-map pattern of the host and network, and the hexadecimal equivalent of the address. The following screen capture shows the information given for the IP address 128.15.10.5.

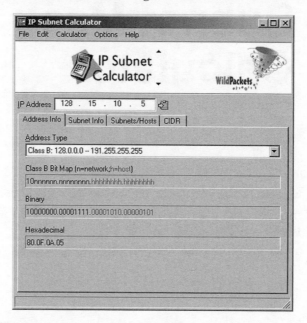

Now look at the next screen capture. Notice the tabs beneath the IP Address text box. The **Subnet Info** tab allows you to enter values for the calculation based on the number of subnets required or the number of hosts required for each subnet. These two values are the main values you will typically work with.

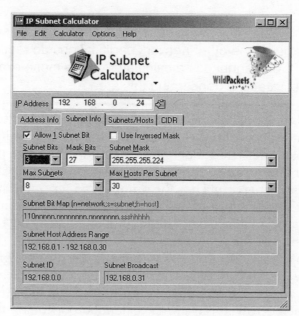

Notice the **Allow 1 Subnet Bit** option. This option allows all zeros and all ones to be used in the extended portion of a network address. Look at the following table. Notice the first two binary positions of the host portion of the address.

Network	Network	Network	Host	
NA	NA	NA	0000000000	**All zeros**
NA	NA	NA	0100000000	
NA	NA	NA	1000000000	
NA	NA	NA	1100000000	**All ones**

Note: NA = Not Applicable

Originally, all zeros and all ones were not allowed in the lead position of the host address used for subnetting. The binary pattern containing all zeros and all ones were reserved values. A bit pattern of all zeros is typically used for special functions, such as a temporary address of a network card when it is configured for an automatic IP address assignment from a DHCP server. Some routers recognize the use of the binary one in the first part network address as reserved for broadcasts. The generally accepted convention today, however, is to allow all zeros and ones. Notice that in the previous table, when all zeros and ones are allowed, four subnets can be created.

Note

While running the laboratory activity, select and unselect the **Allow 1 Subnet Bit** option to see the effect on the number of hosts and subnetworks.

Now look at the following screen capture. Notice that a complete list of all possible host IP addresses is automatically listed under the **Subnets/Hosts** tab. As you can see, the WildPackets IP Subnet Calculator is a handy tool. The best way to learn how to use this calculator is by downloading it and experimenting with different scenarios.

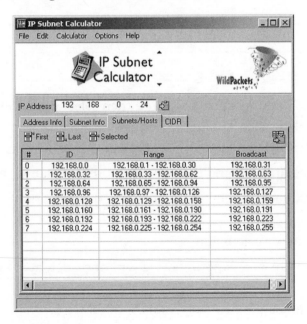

Equipment and Materials

❑ Windows XP or later computer with Internet access.
❑ E-mail address. (An e-mail address is typically required by WildPackets. The e-mail address is used to supply a user name and password for completing the download and the installation of the software package.)

Procedure

1. _____ Report to your assigned workstation.

2. _____ Boot the computer and verify it is in working order.

3. _____ Use the following URL to locate the WildPackets IP Subnet Calculator: www.wildpackets. com. The WildPackets IP Subnet Calculator is found under the Resources | Free Utilities link.

4. _____ Download and install the WildPackets IP Subnet Calculator.

5. _____ Open the WildPackets IP Subnet Calculator program.

6. _____ In the IP Address textbox, enter the following IP addresses and identify the class of network for each. Record your answers in the following table.

IP Address	Network Class
192.168.0.0	
202.111.0.0	
68.0.0.0	
234.0.0.0	
254.0.0.0	
127.1.1.1	
126.0.0.0	
128.0.0.0	
192.0.0.0	
191.0.0.0	

7. _____ Now, enter the IP address 192.168.0.0 and then select the **Subnet Info** tab. Check if the **Allow 1 Subnet Bit** option is selected. If it is, unselect it.

8. _____ Select the **Subnets/Hosts** tab to reveal the number of subnets and hosts generated.

9. _____ Select the **Subnet Info** tab and then select the **Allow 1 Subnet Bit** option.

10. _____ Return to the **Subnets/Hosts** tab and observe the effect on the total number of hosts and subnets.

11. _____ Experiment with the calculator.

12. _____ When you have finished experimenting with the calculator, answer the review questions.

13. _____ Return your workstation to its original condition.

Review Questions

1. What is the generally accepted convention of having all zeros and ones in the extended portion of a network address? _____

   _____

   _____

2. What is the number of hosts for any Class C network? _____

3. What is the maximum number of hosts for one subnet on a Class C network that has been divided into two subnets? _____

4. What is the maximum number of hosts for one subnet on a Class C network that has been divided into six subnets? _____

5. What is the maximum number of hosts for a Class C network that has been divided into 14 subnets? _____

6. A Class C network is divided into six equal subnets. What is the range of IP addresses of host IP assignments for the first subnet when the **Allow 1 Subnet Bit** option is selected? _____

   _____

7. A Class C network is divided into six equal subnets. What is the range of IP addresses of host IP assignments for the first subnet when the **Allow 1 Subnet Bit** option is not selected? _____

   _____

8. What is the broadcast IP address of the first IP range for a Class C network that is divided into six equal subnets with the **Allow 1 Subnet Bit** option selected? _____

   _____

9. What decimal number is represented by 11110000? _____

10. What decimal number is represented by 01000000? _____

Laboratory Activity

55

Name _____ Date _____

Class/Instructor _____

Observing the Effects of an IPv4 Subnet Mask

After completing this laboratory activity, you will be able to:

■ Explain the effects subnetting has on viewing computers in a physical network.

■ Identify the network address associated with an IPv4 subnet mask.

■ Identify the broadcast address associated with an IPv4 subnet mask.

Introduction

In this laboratory activity, you will experiment with a subnetwork configuration. Two or more logical networks can be created from a single physical network by assigning an IPv4 subnet mask such as 255.255.255.192. The following table lists four subnets that have been created by using the subnet mask 255.255.255.192.

Subnet	Subnet ID	Subnet Range	Broadcast
0	192.168.0.0	192.168.0.1–192.168.0.62	192.168.0.63
1	192.168.0.64	192.168.0.65–192.168.9.126	192.168.0.127
2	192.168.0.128	192.168.0.129–192.168.0.190	192.168.0.191
3	192.168.0.192	192.168.0.193–192.168.0.254	192.168.0.255

The four subnets are identified as subnets 0 through 3. The subnet ID is the IPv4 address. For example, subnet 0 uses 192.168.0.0 as the network address. The range of IPv4 addresses available for subnet 0 are 192.168.0.1 through 192.168.0.62. The IPv4 address 192.168.0.63 is reserved as the broadcast address. The broadcast address is used to send a broadcast packet to only members of subnet 0.

Subnets are typically created for security reasons. Workstations in different networks cannot see each other in the Network folder; although, they can still communicate. Keeping a department's workstations out of sight from users in other departments can add to security. Users will be less likely to seek out and browse a workstation that is not in their assigned department. For example, you may want all of a company's financial workstations on a separate network so users in other departments will be less likely to explore them.

During the laboratory activity, you will use the network map feature in the Network and Sharing Center and the Network folder to view the computers in the local area network and how they are affected by changing the assigned subnet.

The network map feature maps Windows 7 and Windows Vista computers located in the local area network using IPv6 and the Network Discovery protocols. Any device that does not support the Network Discovery feature or is only configured for IPv4 may not show up correctly in the map. The Link-Layer Discovery Protocol (LLDP) uses the Ethernet address to locate devices on the local area network.

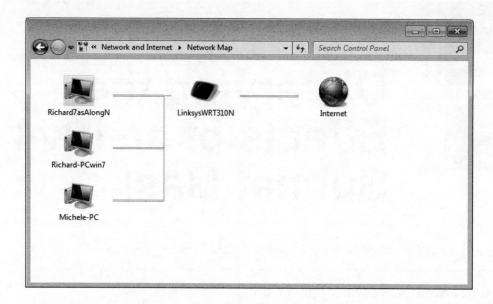

The Network folder also relies on the Network Discovery protocols. To provide backward compatibility with previous versions of Windows operating systems, the Network folder relies on protocols such as NetBIOS Name Server (NBNS), Link-Local Multicast Name Resolution (LLMNR), LANMAN, and SMB. Whether a workstation appears depends on the operating system and the method used to view the other computers in the local area network.

Both of the previous screen captures were made using the same device. Notice the different results displayed in the network map and the Network folder. As you can see, they produce very different results. Changes in the Network folder may take several minutes to appear correctly. Each time the Network Discovery protocols send packets out to explore the local area network, the results are cached and will display the cache contents for a period of time depending on the operating system and structure of the network. Be patient.

Note

For this lab activity, you should disable the IPv6 protocol in the **Local Area Network Properties** dialog box. This will ensure that the results you view are based on the IPv4 protocol, not the IPv6 protocol.

Equipment and Materials

❑ Two Windows 7 computers configured as a peer-to-peer network.

Procedure

1. _____ Report to your assigned workstation(s).

2. _____ Boot the computers and verify they are in working order.

3. _____ Configure the computers to be in the same subnet by assigning IP address 192.168.0.5 to one and 192.168.0.6 to the other. Both should have the same subnet mask of 255.255.255.192.

4. _____ Test the connection between the two computers using the **ping** command.

   Was the ping successful? _____ (Yes or No)

5. _____ Create a map of the network by opening the Network and Sharing Center and then selecting **See full map**. Can you see the other computer in the map? _____ (Yes or No)

6. _____ Open the Network folder. Can you see both computers? _____ (Yes or No)

7. _____ Change the assigned IP address of 192.168.0.6 to 192.168.0.70. The two workstations are now in different subnets.

8. _____ Test the connection between the two computers using the **ping** command. Was the ping successful? _____ (Yes or No)

9. _____ View the two workstations by opening the Network and Sharing Center and selecting **See full map**. Can you see both computers? _____ (Yes or No)

10. _____ Open the Network folder. Can you see both computers? _____ (Yes or No)

11. _____ Call your instructor to inspect your lab activity.

12. _____ Assign a new IPv4 address to both computers based on the same subnet mask. Run both previous tests and observe the results.

13. _____ Now, assign the IP address 192.168.0.63 to one of the computers. The 192.168.0.63 is the broadcast address that corresponds with subnet 0. An error message should be generated and appear on the screen. Record the error message in the space provided.

_____

_____

_____

_____

_____

_____

14. _____ Try assigning the subnet ID 192.168.0.64. The network address is used to identify the network and should not be assigned. Write the error message in the space provided.

_____

_____

_____

_____

_____

15. _____ Experiment by assigning other similar subnet mask IP addresses.

16. _____ Return all materials to their proper storage area and return both computers to their original configurations. Be sure to enable the IPv6 protocol on each computer.

17. _____ Answer the review questions.

Review Questions

1. Can you successfully see workstations on a different subnet mask that are in the same physical local area network? _____

2. Can you create a map of computers on different subnets within the same physical local area network? _____

3. Can you successfully ping workstations assigned to different subnets on the same physical local area network? _____

4. Can you successfully ping workstations on the same subnet? _____

5. Why can't the IPv4 address 192.168.0.64 be assigned to a workstation in this lab activity?_____

_____

6. Why can't IPv4 address 192.168.0.191 be assigned to a workstation? _____

_____

7. Convert the last octet (host) of the subnet 0 broadcast IP address to binary. You may use the Windows Calculator program (**Start | All Programs |Accessories | Calculator**).

192.168.0.63 = _____

8. What binary pattern represents a broadcast? _____

9. What binary pattern would represent a network? _____

WINDOWS VISTA

Name_____ Date _____

Class/Instructor _____

Windows Meeting Space

After completing this laboratory activity, you will be able to:

■ Use the Windows Meeting Space set up dialog boxes to configure Meeting Space.
■ Use Windows Meeting Space to set up an online collaboration activity.
■ Use Windows Meeting Space to join an online collaboration activity.

Introduction

In this laboratory activity, you will become familiar with Windows Meeting Space. Microsoft has developed many different online collaboration tools, such as NetMeeting (Windows XP), Windows Meeting Space (Windows Vista), and People Near Me (Windows 7).

NetMeeting allows for conferencing and collaboration and provides a white board feature and live video and audio support. Windows Meeting Space does not include these features. People Near Me requires an e-mail account for configuration.

Windows Meeting Space allows you to share your documents, programs, and your desktop with selected individuals or a group on the local area network or across the Internet. You can also connect to a network-enabled projector and make a presentation using Windows Meeting Space. Invitations to join the meeting can be sent directly to individuals by Instant Messenger or by e-mail.

All data exchanged is encrypted, and all users can be authenticated by password to join the meeting. Data encryption for Microsoft collaboration is new starting in Windows Vista.

NetMeeting allows microphone support for online sound exchange and video support for Web cams. These two options are not included in Windows Meeting Space.

Equipment and Materials

❑ Two Windows Vista computers set up as part of a peer-to-peer network.
❑ The following information provided by your instructor:

Display name: _____

Allow invitations from: _____

Procedure

1. _____ Report to your assigned workstation(s).

2. _____ Boot the computers and verify they are in working order.

3. _____ On one of the computers, open Windows Meeting Space from the **Start** menu (**Start | All Programs | Windows Meeting Space**).

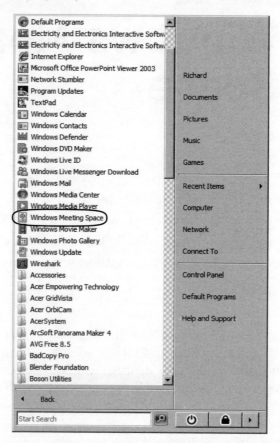

The first time Windows Meeting Space is opened, the program will automatically run in configuration mode. The next two screen captures show what you will see if Windows Meeting Space has not been configured.

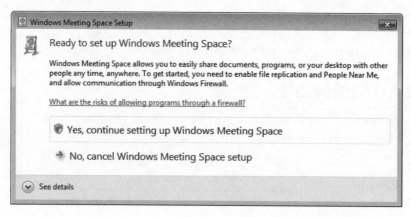

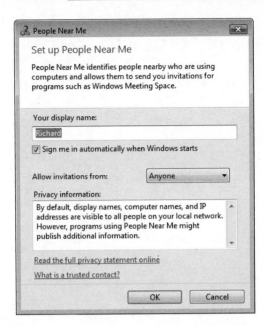

4. _____ If Windows Meeting Space has not been previously configured, configure it now by filling in the display name and selecting from whom to allow invitations. Refer to the information that was provided by your instructor.

5. _____ Open Windows Meeting Space. A dialog box similar to that in the following screen capture will appear.

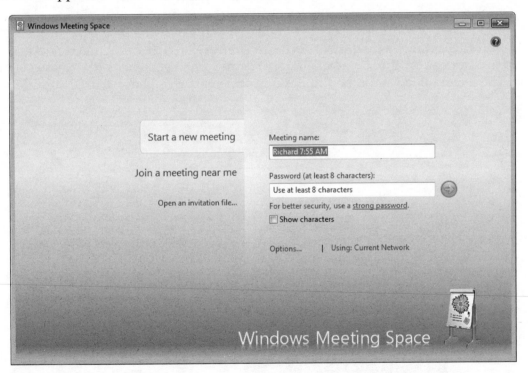

The meeting name has a default title of the account user name and time. You can change the meeting title if you want it to be more meaningful such as "Budget Meeting."

You are also presented with an option to create a password. Users joining the meeting must supply the matching password. You may use the default meeting title and then use "Pa$$word" for the meeting password.

6. _____ The invitations are automatically sent out to all Windows Vista computers in the peer-to-peer network. Invitees will see a dialog box similar to the one in the following screen capture.

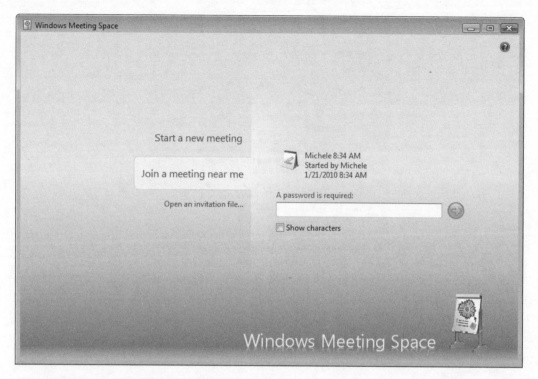

7. _____ Input the password to accept the invitation to the meeting. The next images show how Windows Meeting Space might appear on your desktop. The first image shows how your desktop will appear to other members in the meeting when you enable the **Share your desktop** option. The second image is of the full desktop screen after you have shared your desktop.

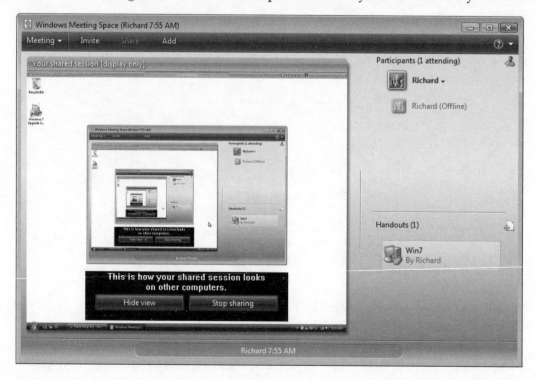

The meeting participants will appear as a list on the right side. You have an option to share your desktop and another option to provide handouts for the meeting. The handout, such as a document, will be automatically sent to the other participants as a shared folder.

8. _____ Click the **Invite** option.

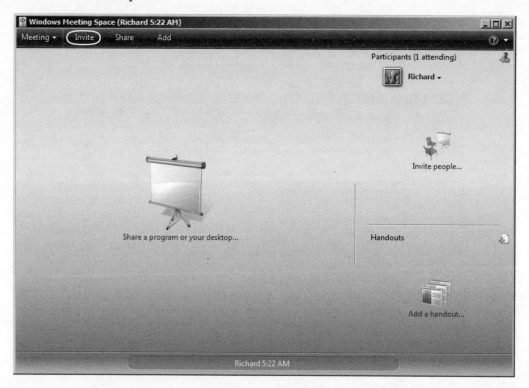

A list of peer-to-peer members will appear. Select individuals to send a meeting invitation to.

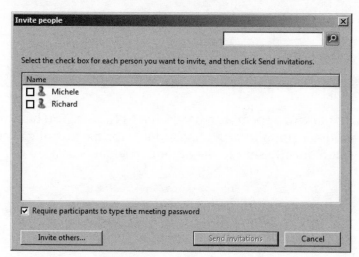

You also are presented with an **Invite others** button, which will allow you to send an e-mail to persons who do not appear in the list. After you have selected people to join the meeting, you can send them text messages. To text a member of the meeting, simply double-click the participants name.

9. _____ Take a few minutes to explore the features of Windows Meeting Space by trying the following tasks:

■ Sharing a file as a handout

■ Sending a text message to the other participants

■ Sharing your desktop with the other participants

10. _____ Close Windows Meeting Space and then answer the review questions.

Review Questions

1. Which version of Microsoft Windows uses Meeting Space? _____

2. Can you share your desktop in Windows Meeting Space? _____

3. In which two ways can invitations be sent in Windows Meeting Space? _____

_____

_____

_____

4. Which two featured options that were available in Windows NetMeeting are no longer available in Windows Meeting Space? _____

_____

Laboratory Activity

57

Name_____ Date _____

Class/Instructor _____

Inspecting Protocols Associated with NetMeeting

After completing this laboratory activity, you will be able to:

- Identify various protocols used to support NetMeeting communication.
- Recall the roll of H.323, H.255, H.245, and RTCP protocols.

Introduction

In this laboratory activity, you will inspect a series of frames captured during a NetMeeting session running on the Windows XP operating system. You will view the various roles of protocols used to support Microsoft NetMeeting. Several of these protocols were developed by the International Telecommunications Union (ITU).

Note

Microsoft NetMeeting is not compatible with later versions of meeting software developed by Microsoft. Also, later versions depend on TCP/IP to support communications, not the H.xxx series of protocols.

The ITU was originally organized to create standards for the telegraph and telephone industries. Today, telephone systems are integrated with network systems, especially WANs. The protocols developed by ITU are recognized and adopted by IEEE. The ITU standards are used by equipment and software manufacturers. This ensures the equipment and software they develop will be compatible with a variety of equipment, operating systems, and software applications.

Look at the following Wireshark capture. It shows the protocols used to establish a NetMeeting connection. Notice that the protocols use the TCP/IP protocol for network communications.

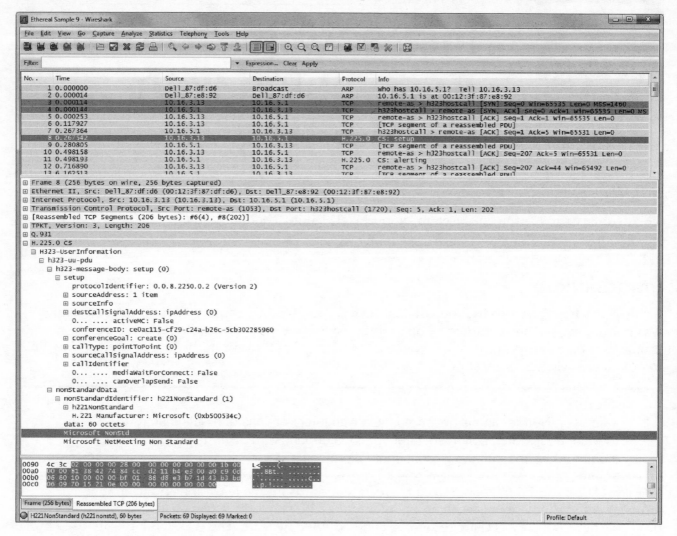

NetMeeting can communicate over long distances using various media, such as telephone lines, satellite links, and the Internet. As such, there are many ITU protocols integrated into the NetMeeting system. Several new protocols are introduced during the capture inspection of frame content such as H.323, H.225, and H.245.

H.323 is generally referred to as a *suite of ITU protocols* much the same way TCP/IP is referred to as a *suite of protocols*. The various protocols are selected automatically depending on the type of network media, such as ISDN, DSL, ATM, and Ethernet; the type of data being exchanged, such as audio, full-motion live video, illustrations, and text; security information; codec; error detection; and more. For example, the H.225 standard defines multiplexing transmitting formats for media stream packets, while H.245 defines the control procedures associated with audio, video, and Voice over IP (VoIP).

Real Time Transport Control Protocol (RTCP) supports real time transmission of audio and visual data and provides quality by prioritizing time-sensitive data. These protocols work together to set up the conference and ensure the best possible quality based on the available systems. These new protocols are all upper-level protocols that run on top of TCP/IP. Some of the protocols are listed in the following table. To learn more about each of these protocols, visit www.protocols.com or www.protocolbase.net.

Protocol	Description
H.323	Packet-based multimedia communications.
H.225	Call control.
H.235	Security.
H.245	Media control for non-telephone lines.
H.261	Video codec for > = 64 kbps.
H.263	Video codec for < 64 kbps.
Q.931	Establish and end call connections.
RTCP	Provide support for audio and video streaming.

Equipment and Materials

❑ Windows Vista or later computer with Wireshark installed.
❑ Wireshark Sample 10 file.
   Wireshark Sample 10 file location: _____
❑ Wireshark Sample 11 file.
   Wireshark Sample 11 file location: _____
❑ Wireshark Sample 12 file.
   Wireshark Sample 12 file location: _____

Procedure

1. _____ Report to your assigned workstation.

2. _____ Boot the computer and verify it is in working order.

3. _____ Start Wireshark and open the Wireshark Sample 10 file.

4. _____ Look at frames 8, 11, and 15. These frames contain the H.225 protocol. You can expand the frame contents to reveal the H.323 protocol as well as the Q.931. Together, these protocols establish the connection between the two computers. You will repeatedly see the H.245 protocol later in the frame sequence. The H.245 is used for media control or flow control between the two computers. As you scroll down the list of protocols, you will see the RTCP protocol starting in frame 63. RTCP is used to manage live video streaming.

5. _____ Close the Wireshark Sample 10 file and open the Wireshark Sample 11 file. Wireshark Sample 11 is an example of NetMeeting chat between two computers after a connection has been established without the use of a Web cam or other video streaming source. You will see that it consists of a series of UDP and TCP protocol packets. There is no requirement for any special ITU protocol formats.

6. _____ Close Wireshark Sample 11 and open Wireshark Sample 12. Wireshark Sample 12 is a sample capture of NetMeeting that uses a Web cam to display video to a computer. You will see the protocols displayed in the previous Wireshark captures as well as a new protocol, H.263. H.263 provides codec support for the streaming live video from the Web cam. When closely inspected, you will see that H.263 is encapsulated inside the RTCP protocol, which is in turn encapsulated inside UDP packets. UDP, rather than TCP, is used for live streaming video. UDP does not require confirmation that the data sent from the source has reached the destination. TCP does require confirmation, which would require packets to be sent back to the source

from the destination. UDP is the only logical choice for streaming video. Take a few minutes to inspect the sample capture.

7. _____ Use the Wireshark sample files to assist you in answering the review questions.

8. _____ Return all materials to their proper storage area.

Review Questions

1. Who developed the H.xxx protocols? _____

2. Which upper-level protocols are used to support the NetMeeting conference?_____

_____

3. Which sample contained the largest volume of traffic and what type of data was being streamed? _____

4. Which protocol (TCP or UDP) is the most appropriate for streaming video content?_____

_____

Name_____ Date _____

Class/Instructor _____

Installing Internet Information Services (IIS)

After completing this laboratory activity, you will be able to:

- Recall the limitations of Internet Information Services (IIS) on a Windows Vista and Windows 7 computer.
- Recall the purpose and characteristics of Internet Information Services (IIS).
- Use the **Windows Features** dialog box to install Internet Information Services (IIS).
- Use an Internet browser to access and display the default Internet Information Services (IIS) Web page.
- Use Computer Management to explore the IIS directory structure.

Introduction

In this laboratory activity, you will install Internet Information Services (IIS) on a Windows Vista or Windows 7 computer to provide Web site and FTP services to a maximum of ten simultaneous computer connections. IIS can be installed on a computer that is part of a peer-to-peer network to form an intranet. IIS can also be installed on a stand-alone computer to test Web page development before posting the Web pages to a company Web site.

IIS is not installed during a typical Windows installation. To install IIS, you must access **Start | Control Panel | Programs | Turn Windows features on or off**. The **Windows Features** dialog box will display. In the following screen capture, you can see Internet Information Services listed. You will select this component by clicking the checkbox.

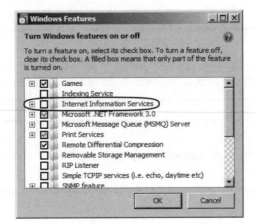

Setting up a computer as a Web server limited to LAN access is equal to an intranet. When compared with the Internet, an intranet is limited in scope. The Internet is a World Wide Web service while an intranet is limited to a single corporation, business, school, or such. The intranet is intended for a specific audience rather than for users on the World Wide Web. The intranet can be used as a means of accessing company information and providing a mechanism for downloading files. Many employees find it easier to navigate a Web site than a network environment. The Web site can be set up to provide to all employees a newsletter, a business calendar, company forms, a company policy book, employee benefits, and files for download. The use of the intranet is limited only to the designer's imagination.

After IIS has been installed, you can test the service by typing **http://localhost**, **http://127.0.0.1**, or the assigned IP address in the Internet Explorer address bar. The first part of the URL is the type of protocol used: typically, HTTP or FTP. The second part of the URL after the double slash (//) is the location of the Web server. The location will be the Web server's domain name or IP address. To resolve a domain name, a DNS server is required. A direct connection using the IP address does not require a DNS server.

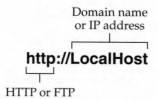

IIS can be used to provide Web services to users on the Internet; however, there are several requirements with which you need to be familiar. Your local Internet Service Provider (ISP) can provide you with the first three items on the following list.

- The Web server must have an assigned IP address.
- The Web server must have a legal domain name, such as MyCorporation.com.
- The Web server will need to stay connected to the Internet 24/7.
- A router is recommended so that the Web site and the Internet connection can be shared with users on the LAN.

Equipment and Materials

❏ Two Windows Vista or Windows 7 computers connected as peer-to-peer network. (You will install IIS on one computer and access the Web server from the other. If this is a two-student project, simply take turns, switching the responsibility for the Web server and the other computer.)

Warning
Do *not* install IIS on a computer connected to a client/server network. The IIS installation can create unexpected results, such as system lockups.

Note
Windows Home Basic will not support this laboratory activity, but Home Premium or better editions will.

Procedure

1. _____ Report to your assigned workstation(s).

2. _____ Boot the computers and verify they are in working order.

3. _____ Create a Restore Point on the computer on which you will install IIS. This will allow you to uninstall IIS if a problem arises.

4. _____ Access **Start | Control Panel | Programs | Turn Windows features on or off**. The **Turn Windows features on or off** option is similar in Windows Vista and Windows 7.

5. _____ After the **Windows Features** dialog box opens, select **Internet Information Services**.

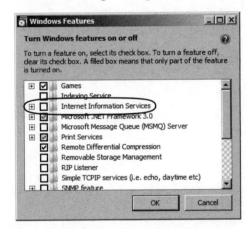

6. _____ Click **OK** to automatically install the most commonly required IIS components. After Internet Information Services (IIS) and its subcomponents have been installed, the wizard will display a window informing you the components have been successfully installed.

7. _____ Verify IIS has been installed by opening Computer Management (right-click **Computer** and select **Manage** from the shortcut menu). You should see the Internet Information Services (IIS) Manager folder listed under the Services and Applications folder. If you do not see this folder, call your instructor.

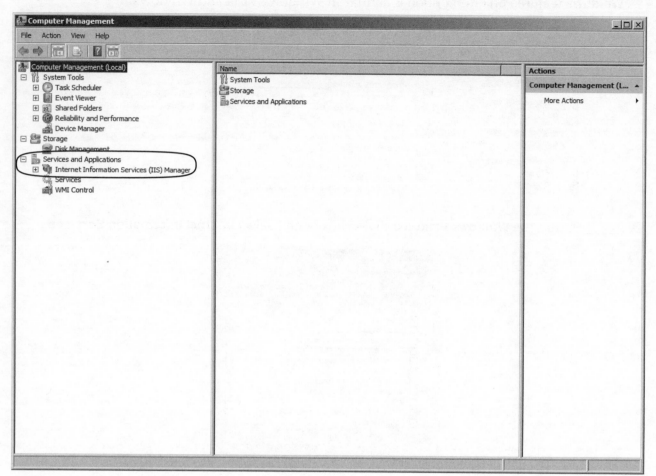

8. _____ Before you can access the default Web page, you may need to disable Windows Firewall on the Web server. After you turn off Windows Firewall, you can access the default Web page from any computer on the local area network. To turn off Windows Firewall, access **Control Panel | System and Security | Windows Firewall**. Enabling and disabling Windows Firewall is intuitive.

9. _____ From the computer without IIS, enter the IP address of the Web server or the default Web site folder, for example, http://192.168.000.075. A Web page should appear similar to the one in the following screen capture. If the Web page does not appear, call your instructor.

If you have an Internet connection on your computer, you can double-click the IIS 7 image, which will automatically redirect you to the Microsoft IIS Web site. The Web site contains extensive information about IIS.

10. _____ Enter the following URLs and observe the results. First, test the URL address from the Web server and then from the other computer. Use the IP address of the Web server in place of 192.168.0.75 used in the examples.

Web Server:

- Use http://localhost at the Web server to display the default Web page.
- Use http://192.168.0.75 at the Web server to display the default Web page.
- Use http://<hostname> at the Web server and use the computer name of the Web server in place of <hostname>, for example, http://station1.

Computer:

- Use http://192.168.0.75 at the computer to display the default Web page.
- Use http://<hostname> at the computer to display the default Web page.
- If you installed and configured the FTP Service, use ftp://<hostname> or ftp://192.168.0.75 from the computer to expose any files available for file transfer from the Web server. (The FTP Service is not installed by default in Windows Vista and Windows 7.)

Note

To view help and information, simply click the default Web page when it appears on the screen.

---

11. _____ If you have a Web page authoring utility, make a Web page to replace the default IIS Web page. Simply create a Web page and save it as default.htm in the C:\inetpub\wwwroot

directory. You could use Microsoft Word to create a Web page. To create a Web page using Microsoft Word, simply open Word and create a document. When you save the document, save it in the HTML format by using the **Save As** command from the **File** menu. Locate the C:\ inetpub\wwwroot directory in the **Save in** list box and then select **Web Page** from the **Save as type** list box. Enter the file name default in the **File name** text box and then click **Save**.

12. _____ Open Computer Management on the Web server (right-click **Computer** and select **Manage** from the shortcut menu). You should see the Internet Information Services (IIS) Manager folder located under the Service and Applications folder in the left pane.

You can expand the Internet Information Services (IIS) Manager folder by selecting it with the mouse. After selecting it, you will see related Web site functions such as Authentication, Default Document, and Error Pages similar to that in the following screen capture.

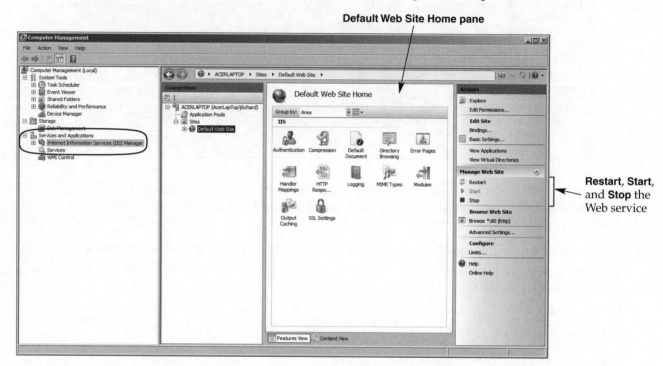

The **Default Web Site Home** pane contains an array of features that modify the default Web page. You may take a minute to view the options, but you will not understand most of the features presented. Web host configuration is an extensive topic, well beyond the scope of this lab activity. Do take note of the option in the right pane that allows you to stop and start the Web service.

13. _____ Close all open dialog boxes and then answer the review questions.

14. _____ Leave the computer and Web server in the condition specified by your instructor.

Review Questions

1. What does the acronym IIS represent? _____

2. On what version of Windows can IIS be installed? _____

3. What is the maximum number of simultaneous connections IIS allows when installed on Windows Vista or Windows 7? _____

4. True *or* False. IIS is installed by default when a typical installation of Windows is performed.

_____

5. What is the difference between the URL of a Web page and the URL of an FTP site? _____

_____

_____

6. What common Windows program will prevent network users from viewing the default home page?_____

Name_____ Date _____

Class/Instructor _____

Creating a Web Page Using HTML

After completing this laboratory activity, you will be able to:

■ Identify the four fundamental markup tags used for designing a simple Web page.

■ Recall the function of a Web browser.

■ Create a Web page.

■ Use a Web browser to view an HTML coded page.

Introduction

In this laboratory activity, you will create a Web page using the Hypertext Markup Language (HTML). In the next laboratory activity, you will post the page on your local area network for viewing by other workstations. This will simulate an office intranet.

Web browsers interpret and then display Web page content written in code such as HTML. HTML code allows Web page contents to be displayed identically regardless of the computer's hardware type or operating system. The four fundamental markup tags used for designing a simple Web page are listed in the following table. These tags are used to identify certain elements of a Web page, such as its code type and title.

Markup Tag	Description
<html>	Informs the Internet browser of the code type used.
<head>	Identifies the first part of the Web page, which contains the title.
<title>	This title is not to be confused with a title that will be displayed on the page itself. Search engines use the title to identify the Web page. This title is *not* displayed.
<body>	Contains the content of the Web page.

Note

HTML code is not case-sensitive.

HTML tags must precede the content they are to identify or format. End tags are used at the end of the contents to indicate to the Web browser where the identification or format should end. An end tag is similar to an HTML tag, but begins with a slash. For example, the end tag for the <B> HTML tag is </B>.

When writing HTML code, you should use a text editor such as Notepad. Do *not* use a full-blown word processor program such as Microsoft Word. Using a full-blown word processor program can cause a Web page to display incorrectly. The code interpreted by the Web browser must be written in a simple ASCII code. Most word processor programs use many different fonts and formatting code that cannot be interpreted correctly by a Web browser.

A Web page can be saved with the .htm or .html file extension. For this laboratory activity, you will save the Web page with the .htm file extension. Other HTML tags are used to format the Web page's contents. These tags are listed in the following table.

HTML Tag	Description
<P>	Format the contents as a paragraph.
<P ALIGN=CENTER>	Format as a paragraph and center align it.
<P ALIGN=LEFT>	Format as a paragraph and left align it.
<P ALIGN=RIGHT>	Format as a paragraph and right align it.
<B>	Format as bold.
<I>	Format as italicized.
<U>	Format as underlined.
<FONT COLOR = "blue">	Format font color as blue.
 	Insert a line break. Two breaks equal the effect of one <P>.
<H1> to <H6>	Indicate the font size. H1 is the largest and H6 is the smallest.

Microsoft Office Word is a word processor application used to create document-type files and is capable of also creating Web page files. For this lab activity, do *not* use Microsoft Office Word to create the Web page. Use the Microsoft Notepad application, instead. You may experiment with the Microsoft Word application after completing this lab activity, but only with your instructor's permission.

Equipment and Materials

❑   Windows Vista or later computer.

Procedure

1. _____ Report to your assigned workstation.

2. _____ Boot the computer and verify it is in working order.

3. _____ Create a directory on drive C using your name as the folder title. This is where you will store your Web page.

4. _____ Open a text editor such as Notepad.

5. _____ Type the following:

<html>

<head>

<title>This is the title.</title>

</head>

<body>

This is my first Web page written in HTML code.

</body>

</html>

6. _____ Save the Web page as a text file (with the .txt extension) in the directory you created. Then, save the Web page as an HTML file (with the .htm extension). A file saved as a text file is interpreted as a plain ASCII file. A file saved as an HTML file is interpreted as a Web page.

7. _____ To view the Web page, navigate to the .htm file and then right-click the file. From the shortcut menu, select **Open with | Internet Explorer**.

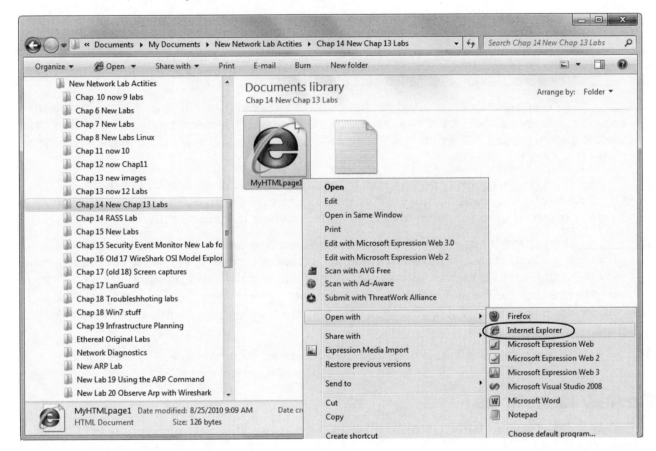

You can also simply click the file and it should open in Internet Explorer unless it is not the default viewer for HTML type documents. Notice that the HTML version of the file has the Internet Explorer letter "e" icon that is used to represent files that are in browser format.

When the browser opens the page, it should appear exactly as it would if viewed through an Internet connection. You should not see any tags, only the contents. If the Web page fails to display or if you receive an error message, ask your instructor for assistance. The most common problems are generally generated by typos when coding the page. Be sure to check your Web page code for typos.

8. _____ After successfully displaying your first Web page, modify the page so that it looks like the following:

<html>

<head>

```
<title>This is the title and cannot be seen in the displayed page.</title>

</head>

<body>

<H1>This is an H1 heading.</H1>

<H6>This is an H6 heading.</H6>

<H1>This is my first Web page written in HTML code.</H1>

</body>

</html>
```

9. _____ Save the file using first a (.txt) text extension and then as an HTML file.

10. _____ Open the Web page using Internet Explorer to view the page changes.

11. _____ You can view the code used to create an HTML Web page being displayed by Internet Explorer. Simply right-click the Web page while it is viewed in Internet Explorer and then select **View Source** from the shortcut menu. The HTML code will be revealed if the page was written using standard HTML code.

12. _____ Modify your code by using other HTML tags. For example, use <B> and <FONT COLOR> to create a headline in your Web page. Experiment with other tags and attributes. Retain your work from this laboratory activity for the next laboratory activity.

13. _____ If you have Internet access, you can perform a Google search to find much more information about HTML coding and Web page creation. One excellent source of information is W3schools located at www.w3schools.com. It even has a HTML coding simulator so that you can practice code online and instantly see the results. Information about many more Web page coding languages is also available. You might want to try inserting an image into your Web page.

14. _____ Answer the review questions and then return all materials to their proper storage area.

Review Questions

1. What are the four fundamental markup language tags used for creating a simple HTML Web page?_____

2. What file extensions are used to identify an HTML file? _____

3. What does the acronym HTML represent? _____

   _____

4. What is the function of a Web browser?_____

   _____

5. True *or* False. HTML tags are case-sensitive._____

6. What is the most common problem for an HTML coded page to fail to display properly?_____

   _____

7. What tag is used to indicate the end of a paragraph? _____

8. What tag is used to create the largest heading font? _____

Laboratory Activity

60

Name_____ Date _____

Class/Instructor _____

Setting Up an Intranet Web Page

After completing this laboratory activity, you will be able to:

- ■ Identify the default directory location for a Web page.
- ■ Identify the common file names for the default Web page.
- ■ Carry out simple diagnostics if a Web page fails to display.
- ■ Construct a simple intranet.

Introduction

In the last laboratory activity, you created a simple Web page using HTML coding. In this laboratory activity, you will configure your Web page as the home page for a simple intranet, similar to one that could be found in a small office.

When a Web browser is directed to a Web site, it looks for a default Web page on that site. A default Web page can be named default.htm, default.html, index.htm, index.html, or index.asp. For this laboratory activity, you will save your Web page as default.htm. After the Web page is saved, you will place it in the C:\inetpub\wwwroot directory, as shown in the following screen capture. The C:\inetpub\ wwwroot directory is created when Microsoft's Internet Information Service (IIS) is installed.

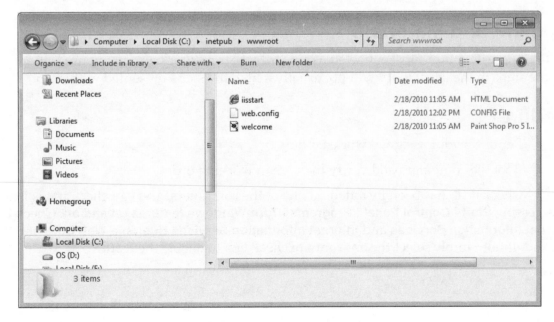

Notice that the complete path is C:\inetpub\wwroot. By default, when a Web page is placed in this directory, it will automatically be given file permissions that permit access to anonymous users. If the Web page were not given these permissions, anonymous users would receive a message saying that they do not have permission to access or to view the Web page.

To access the intranet Web site, enter **http://<computer_name>** or the IPv4 address of the workstation into the Internet Explorer address bar. You may also add the port number to the IP address. For example, you can enter 192.168.0.5:80, where "192.168.0.5" is the IP address of the computer hosting the Web page and ":80" is the port number for the Web page service. If you have problems accessing the Web page across the network, try the following:

■ Ping the localhost from the computer hosting the Web page to verify that the TCP/IP protocol is configured.

■ Ping the host from a different computer on the network to verify that there is a complete cable connection.

■ Check if Windows Firewall is turned off or is configured to allow access to HTTP port 80.

There is extensive information about IIS available at the Microsoft IIS Web site located at www.iis.net. If you visit the Web site during this lab activity, please be brief. The information is quite extensive, and you could use too much lab time reviewing the information and not be able to complete the lab activity.

The key steps for posting a Web page and viewing from another computer on the same local area network are as follows.

1. Enable IIS on the Web server.
2. Create a document and save it as an HTML file.
3. Rename the file to "default" and then place a copy on the Web server in the C:\inetpub\wwroot directory.
4. Access the default Web page from any computer on the local area network using the Web server IPv4 address, for example, http://192.168.0.5.

The Web page will not be viewable from a distant Internet location because you are using a private IPv4 type address. When a page is hosted by a web hosting service, a public IPv4 address is assigned to the default Web page location.

Equipment and Materials

❏ Two Windows 7 computers connected as a peer-to-peer network. (You may use Windows Vista, but the steps in the lab activity will not exactly match the steps presented in this lab.)

Procedure

1. _____ Report to your assigned workstation(s).

2. _____ Boot the computers and verify they are in working order.

3. _____ Check if IIS has been installed on one of the computers. You can check if it is installed by accessing **Start | Control Panel | Programs | Turn Windows features on and off**. Check if **Internet Information Services** and **Internet Information Services Hostable Web Core** have been enabled. If not, simply select the appropriate check box to enable the features.

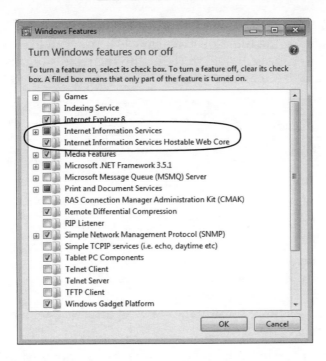

4. _____ After enabling the IIS service, you can check if the service is running by entering "localhost" into the address bar.

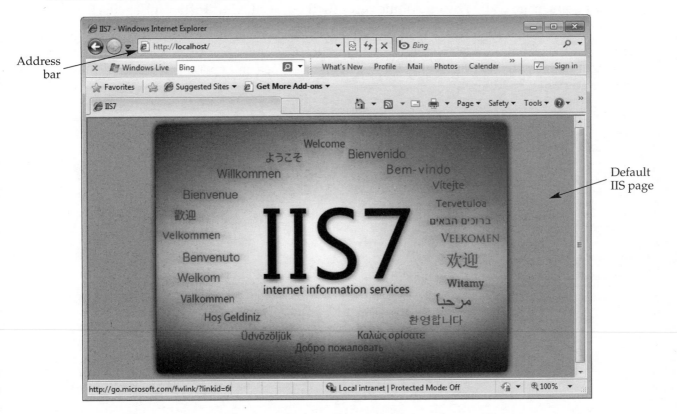

You will replace the function of the default IIS page with your own Web page. The two Web pages can coexist in the same directory. Your Web page will be renamed default.htm, making it the default Web page for the computer.

5. _____ Copy the Web page you created in the last laboratory activity to the C:\inetpub\wwwroot directory. You must include the file type extension .htm. You can leave the iisstart.htm page in the directory. The iisstart.htm page will not interfere with the results of this lab activity. Look at the following screen capture to see an example of a default page added to the wwwroot folder.

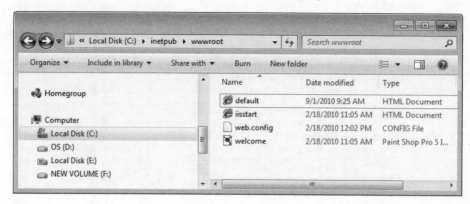

Notice the default.htm file is placed inside the wwwroot directory folder which in turn resides inside the inetpub directory folder.

6. _____ Access the default page from the other workstation, not the host. Use the following methods: IP address (http://192.168.0.5), IP address and the port number (http://192.168.0.5:80), and the name of the Web hosting computer (http://Station1). You should be able to view the default home page using any one of the three methods. Call your instructor to check your work.

7. _____ Now, you will view some of the IIS properties associated with the Web page you created. Open Computer Management. (Right-click **Computer** and then select **Manage** from the shortcut menu.) The IIS Manager is located under Services and Application folder located in the left-hand pane.

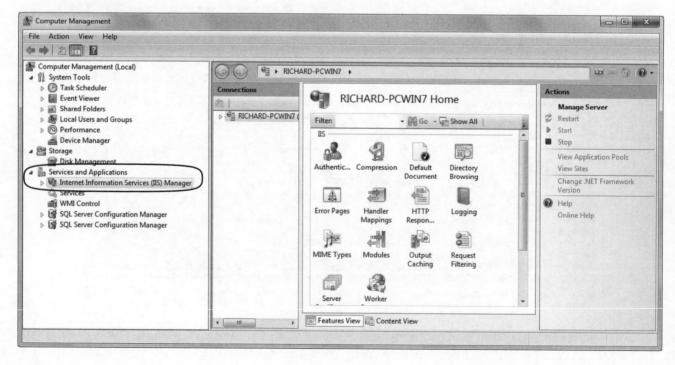

8. _____ Take a few minutes to explore the many configuration options available through the IIS Manager console. Do *not* make any changes at this time.

9. _____ Return the computers to their original configuration and then answer the review questions.

Review Questions

1. Where is the default directory location for the Web page? _____

2. What file names are used to identify the default Web page? _____
   _____

3. What will happen when you type "localhost" into the Internet Explorer address bar? _____
   _____

4. List three simple diagnostic steps to perform if a Web page does not display._____
   _____
   _____
   _____
   _____

5. Why is the default Web page not viewable across the Internet? _____
   _____

Laboratory Activity

61

Name_____ Date _____

Class/Instructor _____

Observing E-Mail Activity with Wireshark

After completing this laboratory activity, you will be able to:

- Explain the operation of SMTP, IMAP, and POP3 servers.
- Identify port numbers assigned to IMAP, POP3, and SMTP.
- Identify which protocols are used to encapsulate SMTP.

Introduction

In this laboratory activity, you will use Wireshark to capture e-mail packets as they travel to and from your computer. You will examine the capture and identify the port numbers assigned to IMAP, POP3, and SMTP. You will also identify the protocols used to encapsulate SMTP.

Sending and receiving e-mail is a simple operation. When you send e-mail, the e-mail is uploaded to a Simple Mail Transport Protocol (SMTP) server. E-mail is received from or downloaded from an Internet Message Access Protocol (IMAP) server, a Post Office Protocol (POP3) server, or an HTTP server, commonly referred to as a *Web e-mail server*. IMAP and POP3 are true e-mail protocols written expressly for e-mail communications. HTTP is not an e-mail protocol but rather a means to access your e-mail using a Web browser.

Look at the following screen capture of a typical Windows Live Mail configuration dialog box. Notice the choices for setting up an e-mail account. Three types of mail servers are listed for incoming e-mail: POP3, IMAP, and HTTP. The outgoing mail server uses SMTP to upload or send out e-mail. Port number 25 is associated with SMTP. Also, when you enter the name of the SMTP server, SMTP is typically incorporated into the name of the server such as smtp.ameritech.yahoo.com.

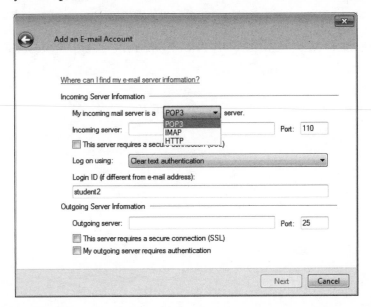

One server may be used for both uploading and downloading e-mail, or two separate servers can be used. Each server may use the same name or have two different names. For example, Comcast uses mail.comcast.net for its incoming mail server and smtp.comcast.net for its outgoing mail server.

In the following screen capture, you can see a typical POP e-mail connection sequence as it appears in Wireshark. The user is establishing a connection to the ISP e-mail account. Notice that there are 11 POP e-mail messages being downloaded. POP is used to download e-mail messages.

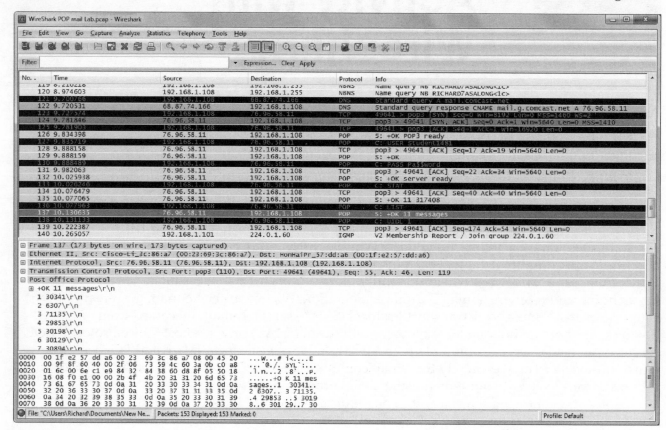

In the next screen capture, the SMTP protocol is used to upload an e-mail being sent to Student1@rmroberts.com. The exact series of packets will vary depending on the type of e-mail client being used as well as which e-mail service provider is accessed. When performing the lab activity, your series of e-mail packets in the capture will not match the packets presented in the screen captures.

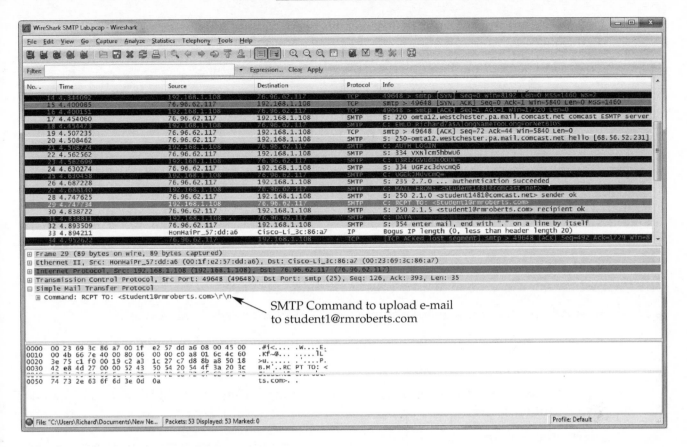

SMTP Command to upload e-mail
to student1@rmroberts.com

Equipment and Materials

❑ Windows XP or later computer with an Internet connection and Wireshark installed.
❑ E-mail account.

Note
You must have an e-mail account to perform this laboratory activity.

Procedure

1. _____ Report to your assigned workstation.

2. _____ Boot the computer and verify it is in working order.

3. _____ Establish a connection to the Internet.

4. _____ Open Wireshark. To limit the amount of background activity being captured, start the Wireshark capture just before sending the e-mail message in the next step.

5. _____ Create an e-mail message and send it to yourself.

6. _____ After the e-mail has been successfully sent, stop the Wireshark capture and review its contents. Answer the following questions. Record your answers in the spaces provided.

Which protocol was used to access and download the e-mail: POP, IMAP, or HTTP?

_____

Can you view the contents of the e-mail message? _____

7. _____ Start another capture and then send a short e-mail message to yourself or to any other e-mail address.

8. _____ After the e-mail has been successfully sent, stop the capture.

9. _____ Scan the capture for the protocols and packets used to send the e-mail. Answer the following question, writing your answer in the spaces provided.

   Which e-mail protocol was used to send the e-mail?

   _____

10. _____ You may run the laboratory activity again or until you feel comfortable with the results.

11. _____ Answer the review questions.

Review Questions

1. What are the three major e-mail protocols, not including HTTP?_____

2. Which e-mail protocol is designed to support e-mail uploads to the mail server? _____

3. Which e-mail protocols are designed to support downloading e-mail from the mail server?_____

   _____

4. Which protocol was designed to allow you to access e-mail using a Web browser and is not an exclusive e-mail protocol?_____

5. What port number is associated with IMAP?_____

6. Which port number is associated with POP3? _____

7. Which port number is associated with SMTP? _____

8. Which major protocols are used to encapsulate SMTP?_____

Laboratory Activity

62

Name_____ Date _____

Class/Instructor _____

Configuring FTP

After completing this laboratory activity, you will be able to:

■ Identify the URL heading for accessing an FTP site.

■ Differentiate between FTP site properties displayed in Windows Explorer and Computer Management.

■ Use Computer Management to install and configure the File Transfer Protocol (FTP) service.

Introduction

In this laboratory activity, you will install and configure the File Transfer Protocol (FTP) service for a peer-to-peer network. You will also create a document for the FTP server using a text editor, such as Notepad. Once the document is created, you will copy it to the FTP directory, C:\inetpub\ ftproot. The latest version of IIS FTP service associated with Server 2008 and Windows 7 is quite different from previous versions. The security features have been enhanced and the FTP service is disabled by default.

Although the FTP service requires that Internet Information Service (IIS) be installed, the FTP service is not installed by default when you install IIS. You will most likely need to install the FTP service in a similar fashion to the way you installed the Web service in the previous laboratory activity.

There are two ways to view FTP site properties just as there are two ways to view Web site properties. You can access the properties of the FTP site by using Windows Explorer or Computer Management. The results of these methods are different. When the FTP site or Web site is accessed through Windows Explorer, properties concerning the file system are displayed. When you view the properties of the FTP site or Web site through Computer Management, the properties of the service configuration and associated file properties are displayed. The main purpose of Computer Management is to view and configure a service. This will become more apparent after performing this laboratory activity.

The FTP service is a great way to provide access to documents in an office Intranet. Employees can easily access informational documents, such as policy books and office forms. To access the FTP site, you would use Internet Explorer and enter the IP address or name of the FTP server. You must replace the HTTP protocol in the URL with FTP. Look at the example in the following screen capture.

FTP protocol

As you see, the first part of the URL address is used to identify the protocol used for the communication. You may also use the port number as part of the address when accessing the site. The FTP port number is 21. For example, a complete address using the IP address of the FTP server and the FTP port number would be ftp://192.168.0.10:21.

There are known issues with the correct intended outcome of this lab activity. The FTP program and services were not intended to be used in a school environment. When multiple students share the same computer and complete the same FTP lab activity, unexpected results can occur. Fragments of the original lab activity configuration can remain and cause unexpected results in additional student labs. This lab is performed best on a computer that has never configured this lab before. Other known issues are as follows:

- You will need a local user account on the host to log on to the FTP site you create.

- You may need to set up share permissions for any folders and directories you add to the FTP site to allow access to users.

- The Windows Firewall blocks FTP access by default. You will need to reconfigure Windows Firewall to allow FTP incoming connections on the host.

- *FTP* and *Anonymous* are reserved words and cannot be used as an account name.

- FTP content, especially executable programs, are often blocked by Web browsers and antivirus programs.

If you continue to have problems accessing the FTP site, set up a typical share on the host computer and see if you can access it from a remote computer. If you can access the share, then most likely you have not configured the FTP site properly. If you cannot access the share, then most likely Windows Firewall or the share user permissions are preventing access to the computer remotely.

Equipment and Materials

❏ Two Windows 7 Professional or Windows 7 Ultimate computers configured as a peer-to-peer network.

Note
Windows 7 Home Premium does not support FTP.

Procedure

1. _____ Report to your assigned workstation.

2. _____ Boot the Windows 7 computers and verify they are in working order.

3. _____ Check if the File Transfer Protocol (FTP) Service is installed on one of the computers. If the FTP service is installed, you should see the C:\inetpub\ftproot directory listed in Windows Explorer as shown in the following screen capture.

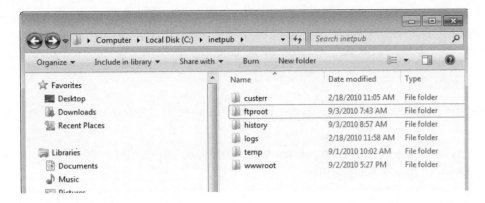

Also, Computer Management will display FTP sites that have been created. Note the Default Web Site and MyFTPsite entries in the following screen capture.

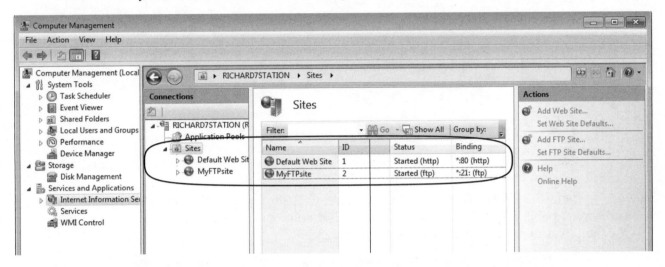

If FTP has not been installed, proceed to step 4. If it has been installed, proceed to step 5.

4. _____ To install FTP services on the workstation, select **Start | Control Panel | Programs | Turn Windows features on or off**. The **Windows Features** dialog box will display. Expand **Internet Information Services**. A list of the IIS services will display. Select the **FTP Server** option as well as **FTP Extensibility** and **FTP Service**. Click **OK**. The FTP service will be automatically installed.

5. _____ Open a text editor such as Notepad and create a document to install in the \Inetpub\ ftproot directory. For the contents of your document, enter, "This is a sample file for FTP demonstration." Save the file as FTP Demo File Document. Also, create a folder under \Inetpub\ ftproot called MyFTPsite. When you are finished, you will have a document under the \Inetpub\ ftproot and a folder.

6. _____ Set the permissions on the folder and document to allow everyone the right to read both.

7. _____ Open Computer Management to begin configuring the FTP site. It should look similar to that in the following screen capture.

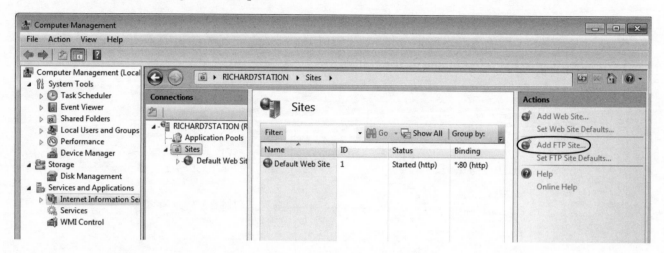

8. _____ Select the **Add FTP Site** to start the Add FTP Site wizard. This option is located in the right-most pane. The following dialog box will display prompting you for an FTP site name and for the physical path to the FTP content directory.

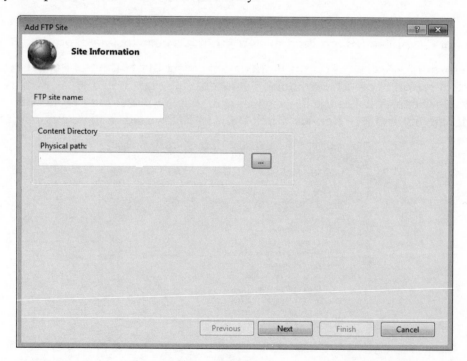

9. _____ Enter **MyFTPsite** in the **FTP site name** text box. In the **Physical path** text box, enter the location of the ftproot directory. You can use the browse button on the right side of the text box

to locate ftproot. The complete path should be similar to C:\inetpub\ftproot when located. Click **Next**. A dialog box similar to the following will display, prompting you for the FTP site IP address and security settings.

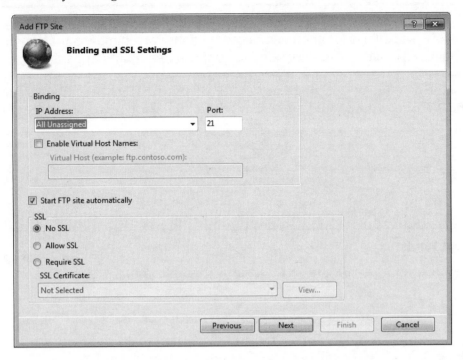

10. _____ The default setting in the **IP Address** text box is **All Unassigned**. Use the down arrow to reveal the IPv4 address of the host. The IPv4 address should be the same as the host address. Leave the **Start FTP site automatically** option enabled. This will start the FTP service automatically every time the host is booted. Change the default **SSL** option to **Allow SSL**. Click **Next**. A dialog box similar to the following will display.

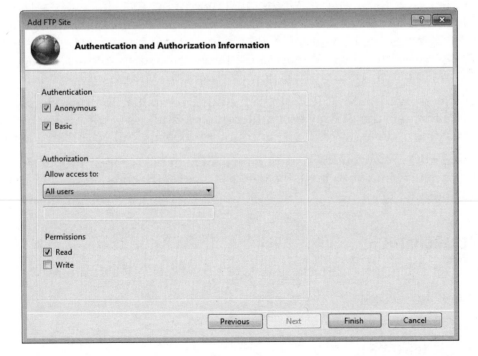

11. _____ Select the **Anonymous** and **Basic** options. In the **Permissions** section, select the **Read** option. Then, click **Finish** to create the new FTP site.

Note

A typical FTP site allows for anonymous connections, which means that when accessing an FTP site, you do not need to supply a user name or password.

---

12. _____ Test the new site by entering **ftp://** followed by the IPv4 host address, for example, **ftp://192.168.0.8**. The result should be similar to that in the following screen capture.

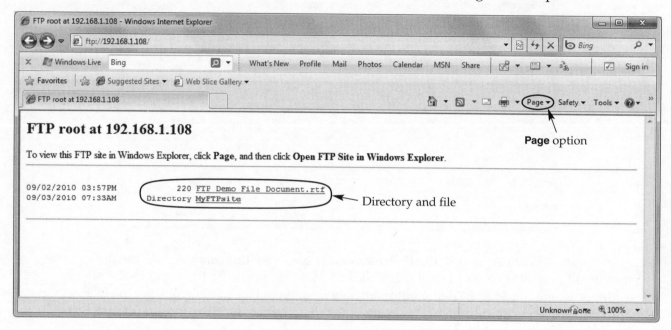

All contents, both the directories and individual files, of the FTP site will display. You may be prompted to enter a local user account name and password to access the directories and folder. Also, notice that a message is displayed telling you that you can view the FTP site in Windows Explorer. To view the Web site in Windows Explorer, you will need to select **Page | Open FTP Site in Windows Explorer**. This option is new starting with IIS version 7.

13. _____ Try accessing the new FTP site from the other computer. To do so, simply enter **ftp://** and the IPv4 address of the FTP host computer into the address bar. You may be prompted for a user account name and password. If you encounter problems, call your instructor for assistance.

14. _____ Answer the review questions and return all materials to their proper storage area. The instructor may want you to leave the new FTP site on the computer rather than remove it. Check with your instructor.

Review Questions

1. Which of the following is the correct example of a complete FTP URL address? _____

    A. HTTP://192.168.0.1:80

    B. HTTP://192.168.0.1:21

    C. FTP://192.168.0.1:80

    D. FTP://192.168.0.1:21

2. What two Windows utilities allow you to view FTP site properties? _____

_____

3. What is displayed when you view the properties of the FTP site through Computer
Management? _____

_____

_____

4. What is displayed when the FTP site is accessed through Windows Explorer? _____

_____

_____

5. Which option in Computer Management will start the Add FTP Site wizard? _____

_____

WINDOWS XP PROFESSIONAL OR LATER

Name_____ Date _____

Class/Instructor _____

Observing FTP Activity with Wireshark

After completing this laboratory activity, you will be able to:

- Identify protocols associated with FTP.
- Recall the purpose of the protocols associated with FTP.

Introduction

In this laboratory activity, you will use Wireshark to capture network activity associated with the File Transfer Protocol (FTP). You will first view the sample capture in the Wireshark Sample 13 file and inspect specific frame contents. Then, you will set up your own Wireshark capture.

Most FTP sites are configured for anonymous access. For this configuration, no user name or password is required. In the Wireshark captures, you will see that the user e-mail address is used as a password for the FTP site.

Near the end of the laboratory activity are several FTP sites that you can view if you have Internet access. Internet access is optional for this laboratory activity. You can still visit the sites using any computer that has Internet access, such as your home computer.

An interesting fact about connections made with FTP sites is that they are automatically included in the Windows Explorer directory structure listed under the Network folder after they are downloaded. Look at the following screen capture. Notice the FTP sites listed.

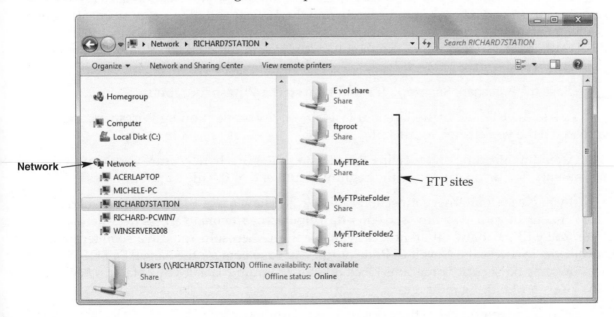

FTP is used for downloading content from the Internet, such as game software applications and user manuals. When you visit the Microsoft and Novell FTP sites in the lab activity, you will see some typical files available for download.

Equipment and Materials

❑ Two Windows Professional computers connected as a peer-to-peer network. (One computer must be running the FTP service with at least one file available for an FTP download. The other computer must have Wireshark installed.)
❑ Internet access (optional).
❑ Wireshark Sample 13 file.
Wireshark Sample 13 file location: _____

Procedure

1. _____ Report to your assigned workstation(s).

2. _____ Boot the Windows computers and verify they are in working order.

3. _____ Start Wireshark and then open the Wireshark Sample 13 file.

4. _____ Look at frame 5. Notice that the FTP process starts with a TCP request to the destination. The destination is using IP address 192.168.0.10 and port 21. By default, port 21 is associated with an FTP site.

5. _____ Now look at frame 9. Notice that the request has been made by "USER anonymous." In frame 10, the FTP server requests the anonymous user's e-mail address. Some sites request a user's e-mail address. Typically, the e-mail address for anonymous access is IEUser@ for no e-mail address or IEUser@<*your email provider*> when you do have an e-mail provider and a valid e-mail address. If you do not have a valid e-mail address, the e-mail address will be simply IEUser@. The e-mail address is also used as a password for accessing the FTP site.

6. _____ Inspect any of the FTP protocol frames. Notice that the protocol used to transfer the FTP protocol is TCP. The FTP protocol carries commands and information between the destination and source. The FTP protocol relies on the TCP, IP, and Ethernet protocols to deliver the contents. The TCP protocol contains the source and destination port numbers, the IP protocol contains the source and destination IP addresses, and the Ethernet protocol contains the destination and source MAC addresses.

7. _____ Close the Wireshark Sample 13 file and then start a Wireshark capture.

8. _____ Access the FTP site created in your last lab activity while running Wireshark and download the file you created for this site.

9. _____ After downloading and viewing the file, stop the Wireshark capture and inspect the frame contents. See if you can locate the beginning and end of the file transfer process.

10. _____ If you have an Internet connection available, see how a real FTP site reacts when a request is made. In your Web browser, enter **ftp://ftp.microsoft.com** to access the Microsoft FTP site. You will see many different files available from Microsoft. You can also enter **ftp://ftp.novell.com** to access the Novell FTP site or **ftp://ftp.suse.com** for the Novell SUSE FTP site. Some browsers and security programs block downloads from FTP sites by default. Watch the screen closely for warning messages.

12. _____ Return the computers to their original configuration.

13. _____ Answer the review questions.

Review Questions

1. What protocol contains the destination and source IP addresses? _____

2. What protocol contains the destination and source MAC address? _____

3. What protocol contains the FTP transfer commands? _____

4. What is the purpose of the FTP protocol? _____

   _____

   _____

5. What protocols does the FTP protocol rely on to deliver its contents? _____

   _____

Name_____ Date _____

Class/Instructor _____

Observing HTTP Activity with Wireshark

After completing this laboratory activity, you will be able to:

■ Recall the purpose of the HTTP protocol.

■ Recall the purpose of the DNS protocol.

■ Identify the protocols that support HTTP.

Introduction

In this laboratory activity, you will become familiar with the HTTP and DNS protocols and how they are used to locate and display Web server content. The DNS protocol provides a mechanism for converting domain names to assigned IP addresses. The DNS service is needed because packets are sent across the network using IP addresses, not domain names. There is no place in the address of a packet header for a domain name, only IP addresses.

After DNS resolves the host name to an IP address, HTTP is used to transmit the contents and HTML code from the Web site to the requesting computer. The Ethernet, IP, and TCP protocols encapsulate HTTP and provide the proper addressing to transfer information between the source and destination.

Equipment and Materials

❑ Two Window 7 computers connected as a peer-to-peer network. (One computer should have Wireshark installed.)

❑ Wireshark Sample 14 file.

  Wireshark Sample 14 file location: _____

❑ Wireshark Sample 15 file.

  Wireshark Sample 15 file location: _____

Procedure

1. _____ Report to your assigned workstation(s).

2. _____ Boot the computers and verify they are in working order.

3. _____ Start Wireshark and then open the Wireshark Sample 14 file.

4. _____ Look at frames 4 through 7. Notice that the Web browser attempted to make a connection to www.microsoft.com when the browser was started. A Web browser is configured to connect to a default Web site on startup. The computer on which this capture was taken is configured to automatically connect to www.microsoft.com when the

Web browser is opened. Since the computer used for the capture is not connected to the Internet, you see only the attempt to connect to the www.microsoft.com site, and not the actual transfer of Web page content.

5. _____ Now, look at frame 8. Notice the attempt to connect to a Web page that is located on another computer. Frames 8, 9, and 10 are a series of TCP packets used to establish a connection between the destination and source. After the connection has been established, the HTTP protocol supports the Web page transfer.

6. _____ Examine frame 12. This frame carries the contents and HTML coding of the Web page. The middle pane of the Wireshark capture displays the Web page source code. The bottom pane displays the Web page source code in ASCII code.

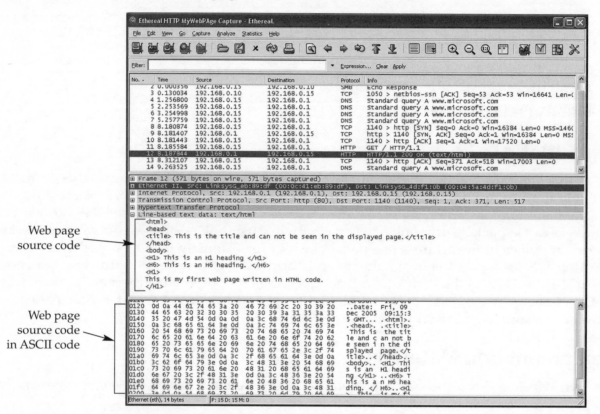

Web page source code

Web page source code in ASCII code

7. _____ In frame 12, look in the TCP packet and locate the port information. It will indicate port 80 for the source and port 1140 for the destination. The default port for Web server is port 80. The computer requesting the Web page can use most any available port to establish a connection with the Web server.

8. _____ Close the Wireshark Sample 14 file and then open the Wireshark Sample 15 file.

9. _____ Look at frames 1 and 2. You will see a DNS query asking for the address of www.google.com. Frame 2 responds to the DNS query with three IP addresses that can be used to access the Google Web site search engine.

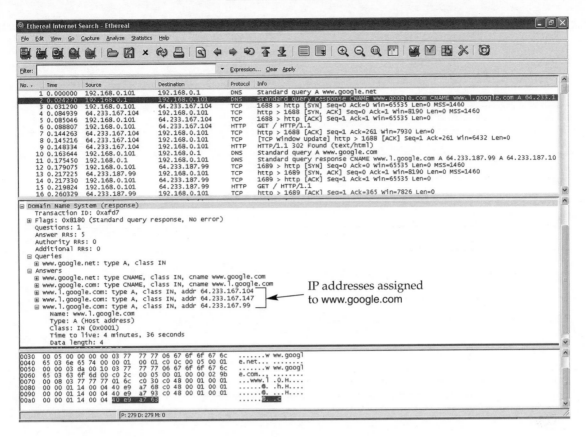

IP addresses assigned
to www.google.com

10. _____ Now, look at frame 31 and 32 and see if you can determine what Web site is being queried and what IP address is assigned to the Web site. Record this information in the space provided.

_____

_____

11. _____ Close the Wireshark Sample 15 file.

12. _____ If you have an Internet connection, start a Wireshark capture and then visit the www.rmroberts.com Web site. Stop the Wireshark capture and then inspect the contents of the frames. See if you can locate the DNS query and the IP address of the www.rmroberts.com Web site.

13. _____ Repeat step 12, this time accessing a different Web site. Verify the port address used by the Web site. Also, study which protocols are used to support the HTTP protocol.

14. _____ Answer the review questions.

Review Questions

1. What is used to transmit Web page contents and HTML code from the Web site to the requesting computer? _____

2. What protocol is used to match domain names to IPv4 addresses? _____

3. What protocols encapsulate HTTP and provide the proper addressing to transfer information between the source and destination? _____

Laboratory Activity

65

Name_____ Date _____

Class/Instructor _____

Configuring a Dial-Up Connection

After completing this laboratory activity, you will be able to:

■ Use the Internet Connection wizard to configure a dial-up connection.

■ Recall the protocols used to establish a dial-up connection.

■ Differentiate between an RJ-11 and RJ-45 connection.

Introduction

In this laboratory activity, you will practice configuring a telephone modem. There are many places in the United States and in the world that do not have Broadband Internet service available. When Broadband is not available, a telephone line connection usually is. As a technician, you must be familiar with common dial-up connection configuration settings.

This lab activity will guide you through the various dial-up connection options. There will be no need to have actual telephone line access, nor an actual Internet Service Provider (ISP) account to complete this lab activity. You may already have a telephone modem installed in a computer or an exterior type telephone modem that connects through a USB port. However, if you do not have a telephone modem, you can still complete this lab activity.

Installing a telephone modem using Plug and Play designed devices is quite simple. The actual physical installation will not be covered in this lab activity, only configuration settings. When installing a new or replacement modem, follow the manufacturer's instructions. The hardware is almost always detected and configured automatically. You will still need to provide information such as the ISP telephone number and user name and password to configure the dial-up connection.

Telephone modems are analog devices. This means the telephone signal sent from the computer across the telephone line is not digital but rather a varying electrical signal. The maximum rated throughput of a telephone modem is 56 k, but this speed is seldom achieved. Realistic speeds of 46 k or less and as little as 4 k can be found. The dial-up connection can be shared by two of more computers. When the dial-up connection is shared, the bandwidth is also shared. Telephone modems are still used to some extent to make remote connections to company networks by employees.

The connection from the telephone modem to the telephone line is made with an RJ-11 not an RJ-45 connector. The RJ-11 typically uses two or four wires with matching pin numbers. In contrast to RJ-11, RJ-45 uses eight wires and eight connection pins.

There are two protocols associated with a dial-up connection: Serial Line Interface Protocol (SLIP) and Point-to-Point Protocol (PPP). SLIP is obsolete today and seldom encountered. PPP is the standard dial-up protocol used today. After the connection is established using PPP, the TCP/IP suite of protocols are used to maintain data exchange. One of the weaknesses of PPP is that it lacks sufficient security features. An alternative to PPP is Point-to-Point Tunneling Protocol (PPTP), which uses tunneling techniques to make the exchange of packets secure. Tunneling will be covered in more detail later in the lab activities and in Chapter 15—Network Security.

Equipment and Materials

❏ Windows Vista or Windows 7 computer with an internal or external telephone modem installed.

❏ The following information provided from an ISP or your instructor. If you do not plan to actually configure a working connection, you may make up this information.

ISP dial-up number: _____

ISP user name: _____

ISP user password: _____

Procedure

1. _____ Report to your assigned workstation.

2. _____ Start the computer and verify it is in working order.

3. _____ Open the **Internet Properties** dialog box and then select the **Connections** tab. You can quickly access the **Internet Properties** dialog box by typing **Internet Options** into the **Search** box located off the **Start** menu.

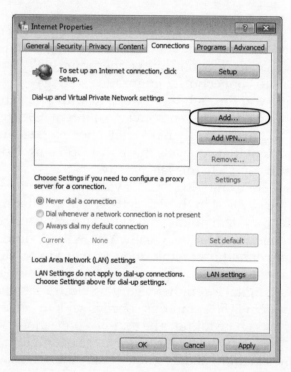

Quickly look at the main options available through the **Connections** tab dialog box. The three options for making dial-up connections are the following:

- **Never dial a connection**

- **Dial whenever a network connection is not present**

- **Always dial my default connection**

Never dial a connection is the default configuration. Also, notice that LAN settings do not apply to dial-up connections. This means that changes made with the dial-up settings do not affect your connection to the local area network.

4. _____ Click the **Add** button. A dialog box similar to one of the following will display.

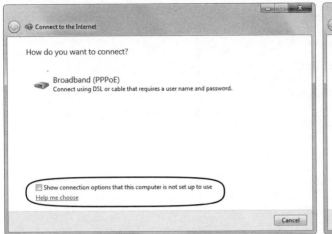
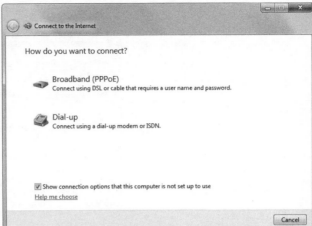

No Modem Installed   Dial-Up Connection Option Shown

If a dial-up modem is not installed or not detected by the operating system, you can select the option box to **Show connection options that this computer is not set up to use** to display the **Dial-up** option.

5. _____ Click the **Dial-up** option. The Internet Connection wizard will begin, and you will be prompted for the dial-up number, user name, and password provided to you by your ISP. You may also give the connection a meaningful name. This is useful if you will be using more than one dial-up connection.

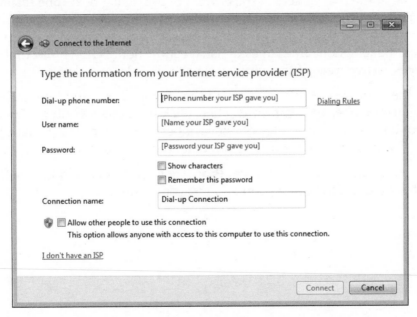

Notice that there is an option that will allow you to view the password characters as you are typing them. This is a handy feature if you are using a very complex password. Also, notice the option **Allow other people to use this connection**. This option would be used if you have a small local area network and want to share an Internet connection through a single computer. Do *not* enter the information at this step.

       Laboratory Activity 65

6. _____ Select the Dialing Rules link. The **Location Information** dialog box will display.

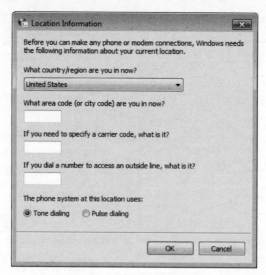

Adding information to this dialog box is optional and not necessary when making a local area connection. If you will be making a long distance call or if the default configuration is not in the United States, then you must make appropriate changes.

Besides changing the country/region you are in, you can also enter the area code you are in, a carrier code, and the number to access the outside line. Some switchboards require a "9" to be dialed to access an outside line.

Take special note of the two choices at the bottom of the dialog box: **Tone dialing** and **Pulse dialing**. Tone dialing is the default, and it is used in the United States today. Pulse dialing was the original method used with rotary dial telephones. These telephones sent pulses of electrical energy through the telephone lines to establish a connection. While pulse dialing is obsolete in the United States, many areas of the world still use this older technology.

7. _____ Close the dialing rules dialog box and then enter the required ISP information: dial-up phone number, user name, and password. Then, click the **Connect** button. The operating system will attempt to dial the configured telephone number. You will be given an option to skip dialing. Do so if you do not have a real account entered or a telephone line.

8. _____ When completed, open the **Internet Properties** dialog box and then select the **Connections** tab to reveal the connection you just configured.

Name _____

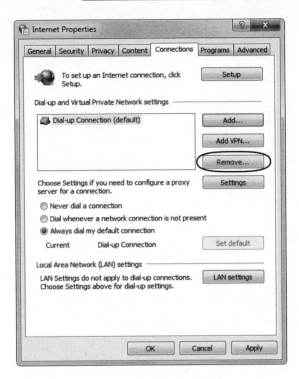

9. _____ Have your instructor inspect your lab activity.

10. _____ With the consent of your instructor, remove the dial-up connection by highlighting **Dial-up Connection** in the **Internet Properties** dialog box and clicking the **Remove** button. Then, return all materials to their proper storage area.

11. _____ Answer the review questions.

Review Questions

1. What three items are provided by the ISP and are necessary to make a dial-up Internet connection? _____

2. Can more than one computer station use the same dial-up connection? _____

3. Which two protocols are associated with establishing a dial-up connection? _____
   _____

4. What type of jack is found on a telephone modem and used to connect to the telephone line?
   _____

5. What type of electrical signal is used by a telephone modem? _____

6. What is the maximum advertised speed of a 56 k telephone modem? _____

7. How many conductors are used in a typical RJ-11 connection? _____

8. How many conductors are used in an RJ-45 connection? _____

Laboratory Activity

66

Name_____ Date _____

Class/Instructor _____

Routing and Remote Access Service (RRAS)

After completing this laboratory activity, you will be able to:

- Recall the purpose of each Routing and Remote Access Service (RRAS) option.
- Use the RRAS Setup Wizard to configure the Routing and Remote Access Service.
- Explain the Callback feature.

Introduction

In this laboratory activity, you will configure the Routing and Remote Access Service (RRAS), which is available in Windows Server 2008 and earlier Windows Server operating systems. Microsoft provides an RRAS Setup Wizard, which automatically walks a technician through RRAS configuration. RRAS allows a server to pose as a remote access server or as a network router.

When configured as a router, the server is used to connect various network segments or subnets. You will not configure the server as a router during this laboratory activity. You will only configure the server as a remote access server accessible by telephone.

The following figure shows one way a client might access a company server. A salesperson that is traveling across the United States might use a dial-up connection from a laptop to the home office to place an order, check e-mail, or access files on the server. The server has a telephone modem installed and configured to receive incoming calls. This modem is dedicated to remote access and is not used for Internet access.

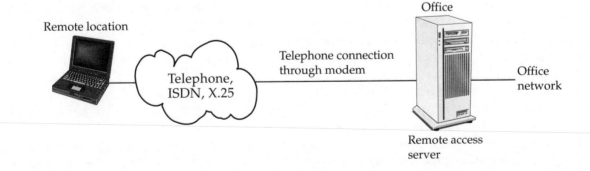

More than one telephone modem can be installed in a server to provide multiple access points to the server. Each modem is assigned a unique telephone number. Several manufacturers make a dial-up telephone modem bank. A dial-up telephone modem bank is a separate group of telephone modems that provide multiple access points to the server. Large, corporate network servers that have a high demand for remote access commonly use a modem bank.

A small-office server might have two modems installed in a single server: one for dialing out and the other for dialing in. The server may also be configured as a multiple connection location for Virtual Private Network (VPN) connections or may be configured as a Network Address Translation (NAT) server providing access to the Internet for multiple workstations through a modem or high-bandwidth connection.

After a server is configured for dial-in remote access, user profiles must be configured so that users can access the server using a dial-up connection. Look at the following screen capture of the dial-in properties for user Richard Roberts.

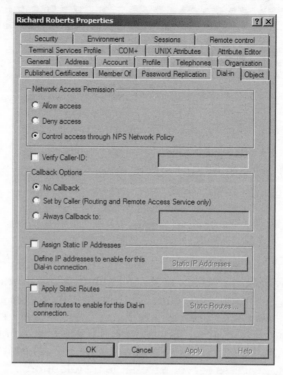

Take note of the **Allow access** option in the **Network Access Permission** section. By default, all users are denied access. By selecting the **Allow access** option, the user can dial in to the server from a remote location. Also, take note of the **Callback Options** section. A callback number can be entered next to the **Always Callback to** option. This enables a call back from a specified telephone number and thus enhances security because the user must call from the specified telephone number.

A new featured option for Windows Server 2008 is **Control access through NPS Network Policy**. NPS options allow security features to be enforced such as Network Access Protection (NAP). NAP is a new feature that requires the client computer have the latest updates installed before it can access the network. Another security feature is RADIUS. The RADIUS feature requires that the user who is connecting to the network from a remote location be Authenticated, Authorized, and Audited, and it is commonly referred to as *triple A* or simply *AAA*. To use the RADIUS service, the client computer's network adapter needs to be configured for the 802.11x. RADIUS and AAA are covered in Chapter 15—Network Security.

At the server, properties for the remote configuration can be set up to limit telephone calls to specific days and hours and for the maximum length of a connection. For example, all dial-in calls can be limited to a maximum of five minutes. This way, no one single user can monopolize the dial-in service.

The RRAS Setup Wizard provides a link to more information about RRAS. Also, extensive information is available through **Help and Support** accessed from the **Start** menu.

At the end of this laboratory activity, your instructor will most likely want you to uninstall the RRAS service. Be sure to check with your instructor before you begin the laboratory activity.

Equipment and Materials

❑   A Windows 2008 server with a modem installed.

Note
All features of the RRAS Setup Wizard may not be available for viewing without a modem installed, but you can still perform the lab activity.

Procedure

1. _____   Report to your assigned workstation.

2. _____   Boot the server and ensure it is in working order.

3. _____   Add the Network Policy and Access Services role to the server by opening Server Manager and selecting the **Add Roles** option. Select **Network Policy and Access Services** and click **Next**.

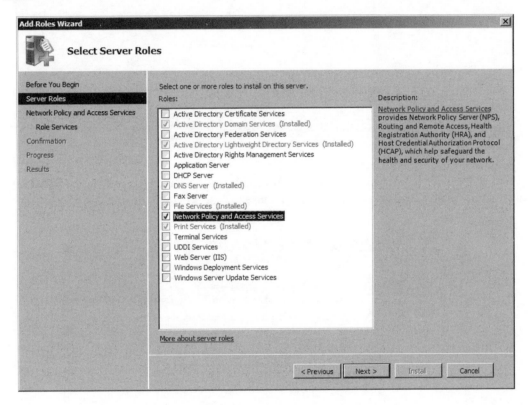

4. _____ In the **Select Role Services** screen of the Add Roles Wizard, select **Routing and Remote Access Services** and the services listed beneath this item as shown in the following screen capture. Click **Next** and then **Finish**.

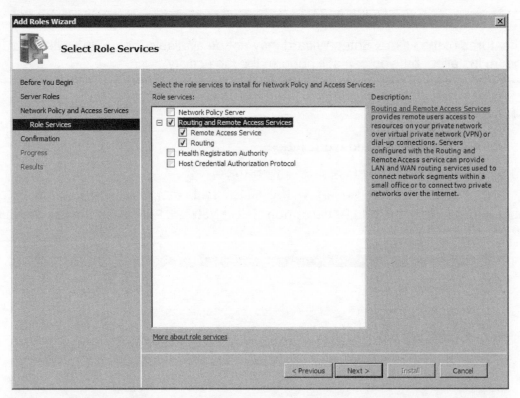

5. _____ To access the Routing and Remote Access Server Setup Wizard, open **Start |**
Administrative Tools | Routing and Remote Access. A screen similar to the following will appear.

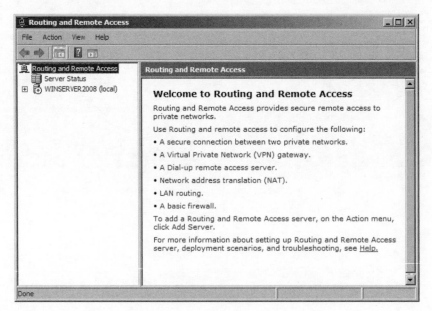

Read the **Welcome to Routing and Remote Access** screen to learn about the types of routing and remote access RRAS will allow you to configure.

6. _____ Right-click the server name located beneath **Routing and Remote Access** and then select **Configure and Enable Routing and Remote Access** from the shortcut menu.

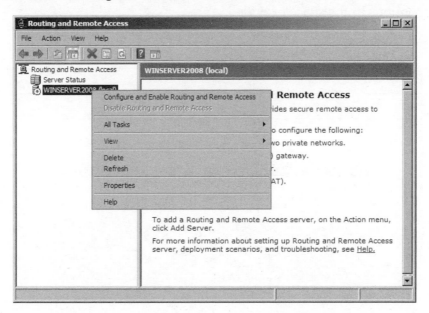

The RRAS Setup Wizard will display and look similar to that in the following figure. The RRAS Setup Wizard provides an easy to follow step-by-step process for setting up the server for remote access and routing.

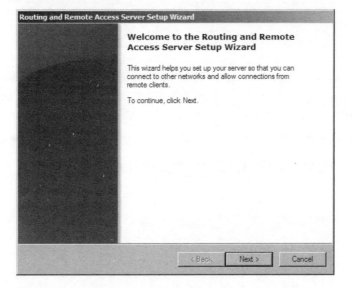

7. _____ Click **Next**. The RRAS Setup Wizard will display various configuration options, such as **Remote access (dial-up or VPN)** and **Network address translation (NAT)**. Record these five configuration options in the space provided.

_____

_____

_____

_____

_____

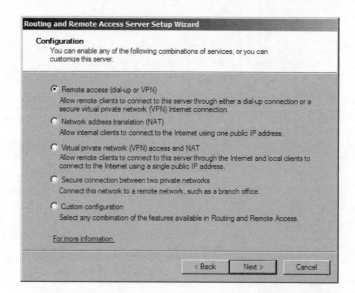

8. _____ Select **Remote access (dial-up or VPN)**. At the bottom of the screen is a For more information link that will provide more information about RRAS. Take a few minutes and explore this link, and then return to the current RRAS Setup Wizard screen.

9. _____ Click **Next**. You will be presented with two options: **VPN** and **Dial-up**. Select **Dial-up**.

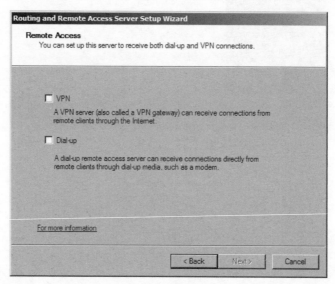

Notice the difference between the two remote access options. The VPN option allows the user to connect remotely to the server through the Internet and does not require a physical telephone line connection. Also notice that the other name used for *VPN server* is *VPN gateway*.

10. _____ Click **Next**. If you have more than one connection available from the server, the **Network Selection** screen will display and prompt you to select which connection to use. Choose the option that is associated with the telephone modem, not the network adapter.

If you have only one connection available from the server, the **IP Address Assignment** screen will display. The **IP Address Assignment** screen allows you to select the IP address assignments method. You can select either **Automatically** or **from a specified range of addresses**. To be able to use the **Automatically** option, you must have DHCP configured on this server or another server. If you are not using a DHCP server, you must manually assign IP addresses by selecting the **From a specified range of addresses** option. When using a specified range, you only need to reserve one or more IP addresses to be used by remote access clients.

11. _____ For this laboratory activity, select **From a specified range of addresses** option and then click **Next**. The **Address Range Assignment** screen will display.

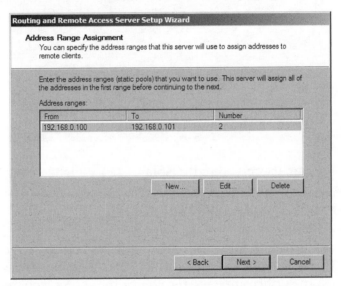

12. _____ To enter a range of IP addresses, click **New** and then enter the starting IP address and ending IP address. Alternatively, you can enter the starting IP address and then the number of IP addresses desired. In the following figure, notice that two IP addresses are reserved: 192.168.000.100 and 192.168.000.101.

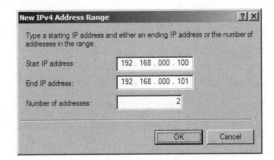

13. _____ Click **OK** and then click **Next**. The **Managing Multiple Remote Access Servers** screen will display. You will be asked if you want to set up this server to work with a RADIUS server. RADIUS is typically used on large networks that have more than one Wireless Access Point (WAP) for accessing the network system. For this laboratory activity, select **No, use Routing and Remote Access to authenticate connection requests**.

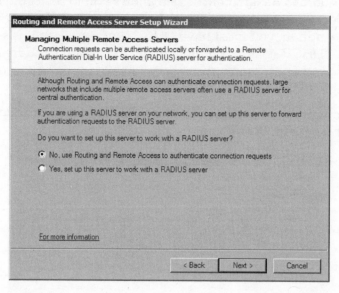

14. _____ Click **Next**. A summary screen will display. Click **Finish** to complete the RRAS configuration. If you have another telephone line available in the lab, you can test RRAS by dialing in on this line from a separate computer.

15. _____ In this step, you will delete the Routing and Remote Access Service from the server by deleting the server from the Routing and Remote Access utility. To remove RRAS from the server, open the Routing and Remote Access utility (**Start | Administrative Tools| Routing and Remote Access**). When the utility appears, right-click the server icon and then select **Delete** from the shortcut menu.

16. _____ After you have removed the Routing and Remote Access Service, answer the review questions.

Review Questions

1. How do you access the Routing and Remote Access utility? _____
   _____

2. A technician has just successfully configured remote dial-in access for a server, but no one can access the server. What might be the problem? _____
   _____
   _____
   _____

3. Where is the **Callback** option configured for a client? _____
   _____

4. What are the five configuration options available in the RRAS Setup Wizard? _____

_____

_____

_____

_____

_____

5. What are the two options for assigning an IP address to the dial-in clients? _____

_____

_____

Laboratory Activity

67

Name_____ Date _____

Class/Instructor _____

Creating a Virtual Private Network Connection

After completing this laboratory activity, you will be able to:

- Recall the characteristics of the Point-to-Point Tunneling Protocol.
- Recall the characteristics of the Layer 2 Tunneling Protocol.
- Use the Network and Sharing Center options to configure a VPN host and client.
- Use the **Network Connections** dialog box to verify a VPN connection.

Introduction

In this laboratory activity, you will install a Virtual Private Network (VPN) connection between two computers on a LAN. VPN connections are made to increase security or privacy when two computers are exchanging data. The two original tunneling protocols associated with VPN connections are Point-to-Point Tunneling Protocol (PPTP) and Layer 2 Tunneling Protocol (L2TP). Today, two additional security protocols are available for VPN connection support: Secure Socket Tunneling Protocol (SSTP) and IKEv2.

PPTP is part of the TCP/IP protocol suite. It allows TCP/IP, IPX/SPX, or NetBEUI packets to be encapsulated inside PPP using the Generic Route Encapsulation (GRE) protocol. PPTP incorporates authentication, encryption, and compression. The authentication ensures that only authorized persons can open the contents of the frames. The encryption ensures that if content is captured, the information inside will remain secure. The compression allows for large collections of data to be compressed and transported in a more efficient manner.

L2TP is a proprietary protocol and has been jointly developed by Cisco Systems and Microsoft. Its characteristics are similar to those of PPTP, but there are a few differences. The main difference is that L2TP supports data transmission across Frame Relay, ATM, X.25, and TCP/IP systems.

SSTP was first introduced in Windows Vista. It provides a mechanism to support PPP to be transported through Secure Sockets Layer (SSL), which is associated with HTTP SSL-type connections.

IKEv2 was first introduced in Windows 7 and Windows Server 2008. It allows for a continuous wireless network connection while moving between different Wireless Access Points. Before IKEv2, VPN connections would disconnect and need to be reestablished each time the connection was broken. With the introduction of IKEv2, this is no longer a problem.

Windows 7 has a configuration option that allows the network adapter and the operating system to automatically detect the proper security tunneling mechanism to apply. There is also an option to select a specific tunneling security method.

When creating a VPN connection, you must first configure a VPN host and then a VPN client. On completion, the client will connect to the host. The host allows a remote connection to the VPN client.

After completing the VPN connection, all activities that take place between the two computers are encrypted. In other words, if you open a share on the host from the client, the transaction is encrypted.

Configuring of a VPN is accomplished using a wizard. You simply respond to a series of dialog boxes and the configuration will be automatically created. You may also manually change configuration settings after the VPN has been created. The following list contains some common causes of VPN connection problems:

- A user account on the VPN host and VPN client has not been created.
- The user name and password have been incorrectly entered. (Check if the [Caps Lock] key has been accidentally enabled.)
- The network cable is unplugged.
- A firewall is blocking the connection. This is normally not a problem because the firewall in Windows 7 automatically configures itself for a VPN-type connection.
- Third-party security or antivirus software is preventing the connection.
- The Internet Connection Share (ICS) on the local network is causing the VPN connection to fail.
- A network switch, gateway, or router is blocking the VPN connection.

For additional troubleshooting help, Microsoft has a Web page for VPN error codes: http://support.microsoft.com/default.aspx?scid=kb;en-us;824864.

Equipment and Materials

❏ Two Windows 7 computers configured as a peer-to-peer network.

Note
A user account name and password must be established on both computers before starting the laboratory activity. A VPN connection relies on user authentication to complete the connection between the two computers.

Procedure

1. _____ Report to your assigned workstation(s).

2. _____ Boot the computers and verify they are in working order.

3. _____ Assign each computer a role, one as VPN host and the other as VPN client. Then, record the following information:
   - VPN host name: _____
   - VPN host IPv4 address: _____
   - VPN host IPv6 address: _____

   - VPN client name: _____
   - VPN client IPv4 address: _____
   - VPN client IPv6 address: _____

4. _____ At the VPN host, open the Network and Sharing Center and then select the **Change adapter settings** option.

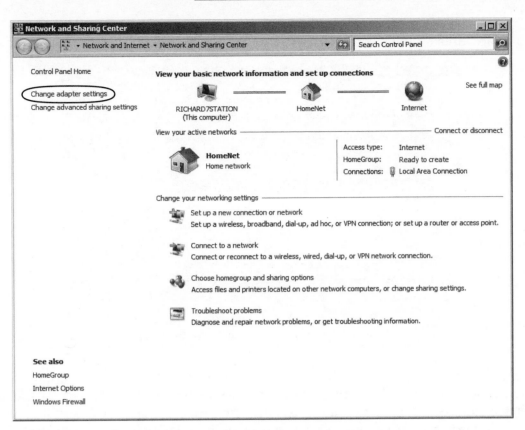

5. _____ Press the [Alt] key to reveal the menu bar. The menu bar is typically hidden from view.

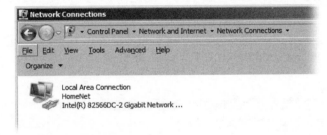

6. _____ From the menu bar, select **File | New Incoming Connection**. This will start a short series of dialog boxes to assist in configuring the VPN host.

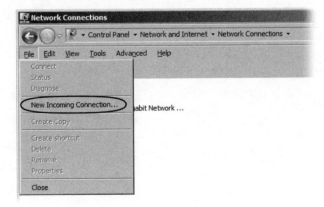

7. _____ The next dialog box will allow you to ether select existing user accounts or to create new user accounts for the incoming connection.

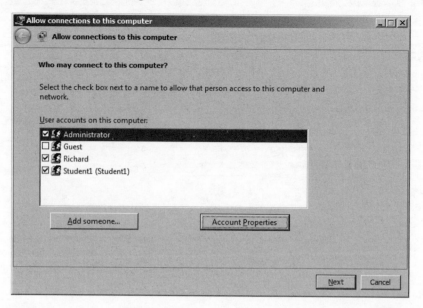

Only users in the list can be authenticated and allowed to connect to this computer. Notice the **Add someone** button, which can be used to create a user name and password. The **Account Properties** button allows you to change user account properties such as a forgotten password. One very important aspect about resetting a user account password is a user will no longer be able to access any files they have created on the computer. An administrator will need to intervene on behalf of the user to transfer any existing files to the user after the password is reset.

8. _____ The next dialog box to appear prompts you to select the VPN connection method. The options are **Through the Internet** and **Through a dial-up modem**. For this lab activity select **Through the Internet**.

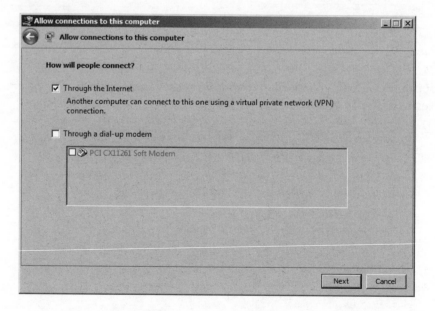

9. _____ The next dialog box will prompt you to select the appropriate network software to use to support the VPN connection. By default, Internet Protocol Version 6 (IPv6) is not enabled because IPv6 is not the default Internet protocol at this time. Accept the defaults and click **Allow access**.

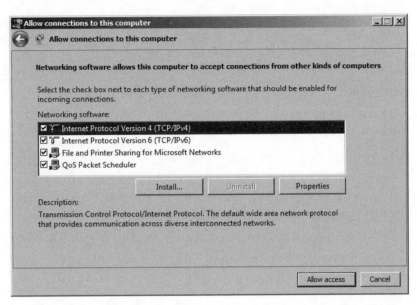

10. _____ The last dialog box to appear contains the name of the host computer. The name of the host computer is typically used to establish a connection from the client. You may also use IP address in some cases.

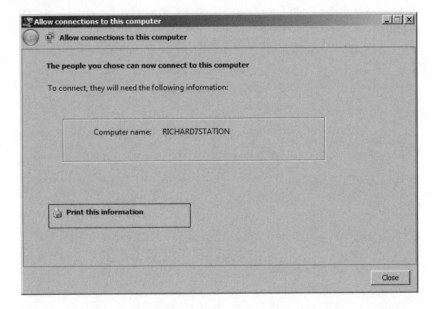

There is no need to print the information because you already recorded the name at the beginning of the lab activity. Click **Close**.

11. _____ To verify that the VPN host has been successfully completed, open the **Network Connections** dialog box. You should see the new VPN connection called "Incoming VPN Connection," in addition to Local Area Connection. If the Incoming VPN Connection is not viewable through the **Network Connections** dialog box, call your instructor for assistance.

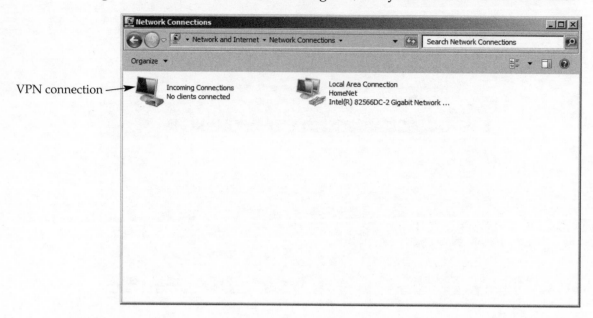

12. _____ At the VPN client, start the VPN client configuration by opening the Network and Sharing Center and then selecting the **Connect to a network** option.

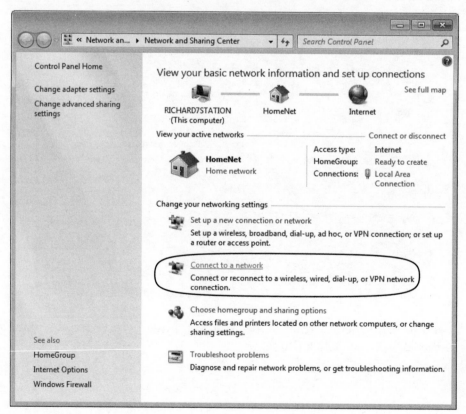

13. _____ In the next dialog box, select the **Connect to a workplace** option.

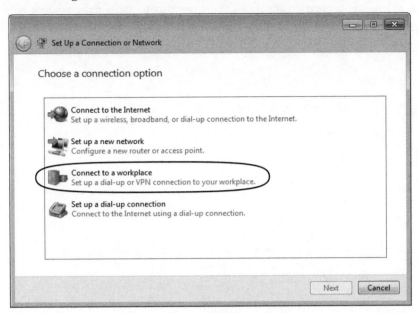

14. _____ Select the **Use my Internet connection (VPN)** option.

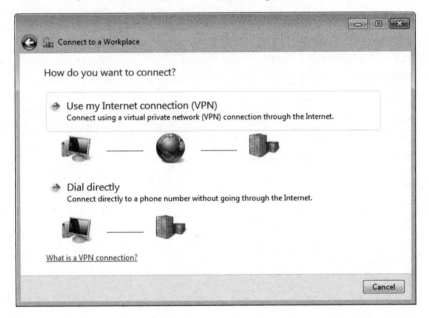

Laboratory Activity 67   479

15. _____ The next dialog box to appear prompts you for the VPN host name of address in IPv4 or IPv6 format. For this lab activity, use the VPN host name. You may repeat this portion of the lab activity later using the IPv4 address and then the IPv6 address to observe the results.

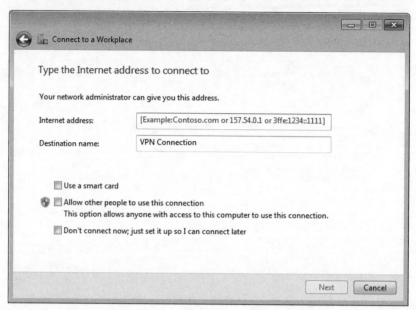

16. _____ The next dialog box to appear will prompt you for a user account name and password. You must have a user account on the VPN host. If not, create one now on the VPN host and then return to the VPN client to complete the connection. It is recommended not to select the **Remember this password** option because it is considered a security risk.

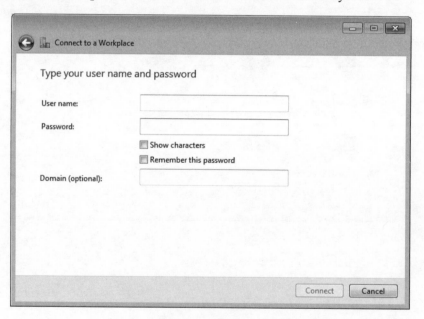

17. _____ You can verify a successful connection being established by opening the Network and Sharing Center. On the VPN host, the VPN connection will be indicated as "RAS (Dial-in) Interface," as shown in the following screen capture. The RAS connection will only appear after the VPN client has established a connection.

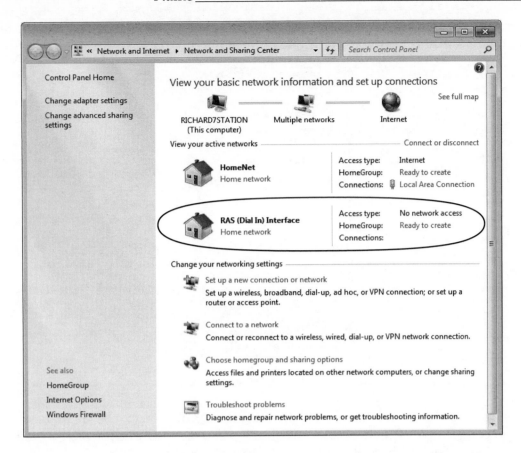

On the VPN client, the VPN connection will be indicated as "VPN Connection."

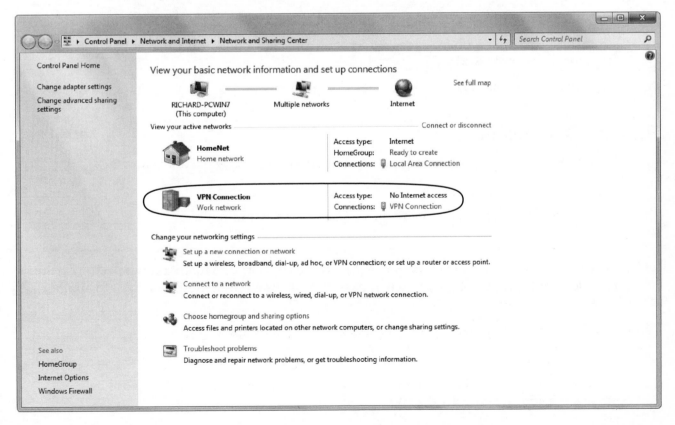

If you move your mouse over the **Network** icon located in the notification area of the taskbar, you will see a dialog box similar to the one in the following screen capture.

Network icon

Notice in the screen capture that more than one VPN connection can be created. For example, you could configure a VPN client for multiple VPN connections, one for each company network in various cities. Each VPN configuration created will appear as a separate VPN connection option. You can simply click the option to start the existing VPN connection process.

18. _____ Call your instructor to inspect your VPN connection.

19. _____ If time permits, you may create another VPN connection, this time using the host IPv4 address or the Host IPv6 address.

20. _____ Return all materials to their proper storage area and then answer the review questions.

Review Questions

1. What are the two original tunneling protocols associated with VPN connections? _____
   _____

2. What additional VPN protocols were introduced after the original two? _____
   _____

3. Which VPN protocol was developed by Microsoft to support and maintain wireless connections so they are not broken when passing from one Wireless Access Point to another Wireless Access Point? _____

4. Which VPN protocol utilizes Secure Sockets Layer (SSL) technology?_____
   _____

5. On which computer (VPN host or VPN client) must a user account and password be established before creating a VPN connection?_____
   _____

6. When does the VPN connection appear in the **View your active networks** section of the Network and Sharing Center? _____

_____

7. Can you have more than one VPN connection configured on a client workstation? _____

Laboratory Activity

68

Name_____ Date _____

Class/Instructor _____

WINDOWS 7

Observing VPN Activity with Wireshark

After completing this laboratory activity, you will be able to:

- Explain the basic connection process between a VPN client and host.
- Recall the role of the GRE protocol.
- Recall the role of the CHAP protocol as related to VPN.
- Recall the port numbers for PPTP, SSTP, and L2TP.

Introduction

In this laboratory activity, you will use Wireshark to view a sample capture containing a Virtual Private Network (VPN) communications. You will study the specific frames and data packets to see how VPN communicates. After studying the sample capture, you will generate your own capture and view its contents. Many of the protocols viewed in this lab activity will be better understood after completing Chapter 15—Network Security.

There are several tunneling protocols that can be used to support VPN connections. They are Point-to-Point Tunneling Protocol (PTPP), Layer 2 Tunneling Protocol (L2TP), and Secure Socket Tunneling Protocol (SSTP). The particular network environment and the Windows operating system determine which protocol is used.

The Point-to-Point Tunneling Protocol (PPTP) will be viewed in this lab activity as well as other protocols related to a VPN. PPTP uses port 1723 to establish a connection between a VPN client and host. PPTP is an encapsulation protocol that is based on the Point-to-Point Protocol (PPP) and the Generic Routing Encapsulation (GRE) protocol. PPP was originally designed to encapsulate other protocols and transport them across a telephone connection. It does not, however, offer any security.

Generic Routing Encapsulation (GRE) is designed to encapsulate a wide range of protocols beyond PPP. GRE encapsulates and encrypts the data carried inside a PPP packet. GRE does not encrypt IP header information, but rather hides it. The IP header contains the IP address of the destination and the source computers. The GRE header contains an alias IP address that is used in place of the assigned IP addresses. In this way, the original IP address is hidden during the tunneling operation. A tunnel is created, hiding not only the information inside the GRE packet, but also the "real" IP address of the destination and source. The GRE IP address is generally referred to as an *alias* or *virtual IP address*.

PPTP communication typically provides authentication through the Challenge Handshake Authentication Protocol (CHAP) or Microsoft Challenge Handshake Authentication Protocol (MS-CHAP). CHAP provides a mechanism for the verification of user passwords. The actual password is never exchanged inside packet contents; only a mathematical algorithm representing the password is exchanged. There will be more about CHAP in a later laboratory activity.

Please keep in mind that the term *Virtual Private Network* is generic in that it refers to any method of tunneling communications between two connections across a public or unsecured media. Other methods can be employed to accomplish the same task. For example, the Layer 2

Tunneling Protocol (L2TP) can be used, which incorporates all the same features as PPTP and also relies on the possession of a "certificate." L2TP uses either port 500 or port 4500 to maintain a connection between a client and host. Port 500 is associated with the Internet Key Exchange (IKE) encryption method, and port 4500 is associated with Network Address Translation (NAT) when translating network IP addresses. An Internet Key Exchange (IKE) or Internet Protocol Security (IPSec) certificate is used with L2TP. The certificate verifies the identity of both the source and the destination. There will be more about certificates later while studying security. PPTP can be used on computers with Windows 2000 or later.

Secure Socket Tunneling Protocol (SSTP) is the latest tunneling protocol applied to Windows VPN connections. SSTP uses the SSL or HTTPS protocol over port 443. SSTP encapsulates PPP to create a VPN. This protocol can only be used with Windows Server 2008, Window Vista, and Windows 7.

In this lab activity, you will first look at a Wireshark capture made with Windows XP and then you will view a Wireshark capture made with Windows 7. You will verify that PPTP is still used with Windows 7 even though newer VPN protocols have been introduced. You will also see where Windows 7 assigns a temporary IPv6 address to be used with VPN connections but still relies on IPv4 as the default VPN protocol. There are options for the VPN configuration that will allow you to specify either IPv4 or IPv6 as the address mechanism, or both. The default is IPv4.

Note

For a Windows XP VPN client, the DHCP server assigns it an alias IPv4 address. This is no longer the case in Windows 7. Windows 7 generates a temporary IPv6 address and an IPv4 APIPA alias address, typically starting with 169.254 in the first two octets. You will identify this address using the **ipconfig** command during this laboratory activity.

Equipment and Materials

❑ Two Windows 7 computers configured as a peer-to-peer network. One computer must have the Wireshark program installed.

❑ Wireshark Sample 16 file.
  Wireshark Sample 16 file location: _____

❑ Wireshark Sample 17 file.
  Wireshark Sample 17 file location: _____

Procedure

1. _____ Report to your assigned workstation(s).

2. _____ Boot the Windows computers and verify they are in working order.

3. _____ One computer should be configured as a VPN host and the other as a VPN client. If they are not, configure them now and record the IP address of each in the space provided.

   VPN host IPv4 address: _____

   VPN client IPv4 address: _____

4. _____ Start the Wireshark program and then open Wireshark Sample 16 file. This capture was created on a Windows XP computer.

5. _____ Look at frames 1 through 7. Notice that the basic connection between the VPN host and client is being established using TCP and then PPTP. PPTP is used to configure the basic

486   Networking Fundamentals Laboratory Manual

Copyright by Goodheart-Willcox Co., Inc.

connection, such as identify the media (telephone line, network cable, etc.), operating system and revision, and other characteristics of the connection. You may expand the contents of the packets to examine them more closely.

6. _____ Look at frame 8. PPP is identified as the main protocol used for the packet. On closer examination, you will see that the frame is composed of not only PPP, but also GRE. GRE is encapsulating the PPP packet.

7. _____ Look at frames 18, 19, and 20. You will see the sequence of CHAP events. CHAP is used for authentication between the VPN host and client.

8. _____ Now look at frame 37. The details of the packet contents should appear similar to the ones in the following screen capture.

```
36 0.079711   192.168.0.200   192.168.0.30    PPP CCP    Configuration ACK
37 0.080209   192.168.0.200   192.168.0.30    PPP IPCP   Configuration Nak
38 0.080804   192.168.0.30    192.168.0.200   PPP IPCP   Configuration Request
39 0.081108   192.168.0.200   192.168.0.30    PPP IPCP   Configuration Ack
40 0.115027   192.168.0.30    224.0.0.22      IGMP       V3 Membership Report
```

```
⊞ Frame 37 (64 bytes on wire, 64 bytes captured)
⊞ Ethernet II, Src: LinksysG_4d:f1:0b (00:04:5a:4d:f1:0b), Dst: LinksysG_eb:89:df (00:0c:41:eb:89:df)
⊞ Internet Protocol, Src: 192.168.0.200 (192.168.0.200), Dst: 192.168.0.30 (192.168.0.30)    ← Source and
⊞ Generic Routing Encapsulation (PPP)                                                           destination
⊟ Point-to-Point Protocol                                                                       IP addresses
      Protocol: IP Control Protocol (0x8021)
⊟ PPP IP Control Protocol
      Code: Configuration Nak (0x03)
      Identifier: 0x06
      Length: 16
   ⊟ Options: (12 bytes)                          ← Alias and DNS server
      IP address: 192.168.0.3                       IP addresses
      Primary DNS server IP address: 192.168.0.1
```

Notice that the assigned destination and source IP addresses are indicated in the Internet Protocol packet header contents. The alias IP address and the DNS server IP addresses are indicated in the PPP IP Control Protocol packet. The alias IP address for the source (DNS server) IP address 192.168.000.200 is 192.168.0.1, and the alias IP address for the destination IP address 192.168.0.30 is 192.168.0.3. Notice that the contents are encapsulated inside the GRE packet.

9. _____ During most of the remaining frames in the sample, a series of GRE and PPP protocols are exchanged. You will notice that many of the frames have been identified as compressed data and encapsulated PPP. You will also see the common background activity frames associated with a peer-to-peer network.

10. _____ Look at frames 196 and 197 at the end of the sample capture. They are an echo-request and an echo-reply used to verify that the VPN connection still exists. In the second column labeled **Time**, the lapse time is approximately 59.9 seconds. Approximately every 60 seconds an echo-request and echo-response is exchanged. A VPN connection can last an undetermined amount of time, but it needs to incorporate a mechanism to detect an open circuit or if one of the computers disconnects for some reason, such as a power failure. The echo-request and echo-response is used for this purpose. This is similar to the ping echo-request, except that the ICMP protocol is not used.

11. _____ Open file Wireshark Sample 17 and scan the protocols used to establish the PPTP connection. You will see that they are similar to the Windows XP sample capture. You will also notice that the VPN transactions using PPP and PPTP are carried out using IPv4 source and destination addresses even with a temporary IPv6 addresses being configured for the VPN.

12. _____ Close the sample capture and start your own capture of the VPN connection you have configured. Be sure that Wireshark is running before a connection is established. You may wish to wait a short period (one to two minutes) after booting the computers before starting Wireshark. This will keep a lot of activity from being included in the capture that is unrelated to the VPN connection when the computer is booted.

13. _____ After the VPN connection has been established, run the **ipconfig** command at each computer to inspect the assigned IP addresses. You will see a result similar to that in the following screen capture at the Windows 7 VPN client. Notice that the "PPP Adapter VPN Connection" section has two IPv6 addresses. One is the link-local address and the other is the default gateway address. These are only temporary IPv6 addresses that will be lost after breaking the VPN connection.

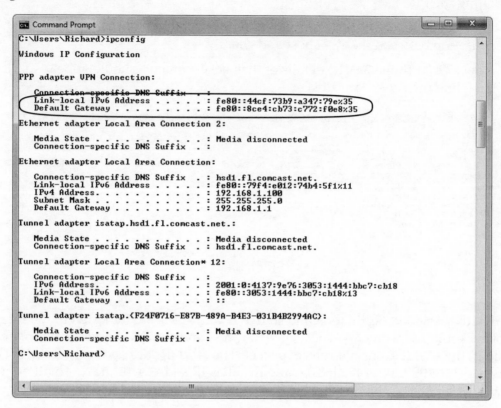

Look at the following screen capture from the Windows 7 VPN host computer. Notice that the Windows 7 VPN host has an IPv4 address of 169.254.0.23 and an IPv6 address of fe80::8ce4:cb73:c772:f0e8 listed under the PPP adapter RAS (Dial-in) Interface section. The IPv4 address is in APIPA form, which is automatically generated. It is not a DHCP assigned IPv4 address. The Windows 7 computer automatically generated the IPv4 and IPv6 address.

Read and record the assigned IPv6 addresses of the host and client and their corresponding alias in the spaces provided.

Host assigned IPv4 address: _____

Host assigned IPv6 address: _____

Client assigned IPv4 address: _____

Client assigned IPv6 address: _____

14. _____ Now, disconnect the VPN connection and then stop and view the contents of the Wireshark capture. Look for the key features discussed in the earlier steps of this laboratory activity. Notice that PPP and PPTP are still used to support VPN in Windows 7. Repeat the capture if necessary or until you are comfortable with the results.

15. _____ At the VPN client, use the **ipconfig** command to see if the PPP IPv6 temporary addresses have been lost since disconnecting the VPN connection.

16. _____ Return all materials to their proper storage area and then answer the review questions.

Review Questions

1. Describe what happens when a basic connection between the VPN host and client is being established. _____

   _____

   _____

2. What is the role of the Generic Routing Encapsulation (GRE) protocol? _____

   _____

3. What protocol is used to authenticate the client and host? _____

4. What port number is associated with PPTP? _____

5. What port number is associated with SSTP? _____

6. What port numbers are associated with L2TP? _____

Name_____ Date _____

Class/Instructor _____

Microsoft Remote Desktop

After completing this laboratory activity, you will be able to:

■ Select the appropriate Windows operating system for a Remote Desktop client and remote computer.

■ Use the **System Properties** dialog box to configure a remote computer.

■ Use the **Remote Desktop Connection** dialog box to configure a Remote Desktop client.

■ Use the **Start** menu, **Search** box, and command prompt to start Remote Desktop Connection.

■ Use Remote Desktop Connection to access a remote computer.

■ Check for common issues that might prevent establishing a Remote Desktop connection.

Introduction

In this laboratory activity, you will become familiar with the Remote Desktop feature. The Remote Desktop host feature is only available in the Professional, Ultimate, and Enterprise editions of Windows. The Remote Desktop client feature is supported by all Windows operating systems. The Remote Desktop client feature allows a user to access and run a remote computer just as if he or she were sitting at the remote computer's keyboard.

Note
Do not confuse Remote Desktop with Remote Assistance. The differences will become apparent after completing Laboratory Activity 70—Microsoft Remote Assistance.

The following illustration shows the various methods that can be used to connect two computers through Remote Desktop: LAN, dial-up, or Internet. Notice the operating systems indicated in the illustration. When establishing a connection through the Internet, Internet Explorer version 4.0 or later must be used. This type of connection will not be covered in this laboratory activity. The remote computer must use a Professional, Enterprise, or Ultimate edition of Windows starting with Windows XP or Windows Server 2000. The client can use any Windows operating system, including the Home editions.

Remote Computer

LAN, dial-up, Internet

Client Computer

Any Windows Professional, Ultimate, or Enterprise version

Any Windows operating system

The terms used to describe the two computers are *remote* and *client*. This can add to some confusion. In brief, the client (where the user is sitting) is used to take control of the remote (distant) computer. This type of arrangement is typically used to access your work computer from your home computer or to access your home computer from another computer such as laptop.

The Remote Desktop feature is designed to work on a persistent connection such DSL, ISDN, Broadband Cable, and wireless. The remote computer must also use a persistent IP address. If not, the client will not be able to find the remote computer. ISPs typically issue a temporary IP address.

This laboratory activity can be confusing because of all the options available in the **Remote Desktop Connection** dialog box. Before you begin this laboratory activity, quickly scan the following steps for setting up and establishing a Remote Desktop connection between two computers on a LAN.

At the designated remote computer:
1. Start Remote Desktop Connection on the remote computer.
2. Identify the users who may access the remote computer.
3. Leave the remote computer running.

At the designated client computer:
1. Start Remote Desktop Connection on the client computer.
2. In the **Remote Desktop Connection** dialog box, enter the computer name or IP address of the remote computer.

As a matter of security, only accounts that require a password for logging on can configure a Remote Desktop session and use it. If the remote computer you are using for this laboratory activity does not have a password-enabled login, you will need to open **Control Panel | User Accounts** and change the requirement forcing the user to use a password to log on to the computer. Setting up a password requires that you must be a member of the Administrator group. You are most likely already a member of the Administrator group, but may need to modify the user account to use a password.

While this is a relatively simple laboratory activity, there are many causes for this laboratory activity to fail. The computer you are using has been used in many laboratory activities. The typical default settings may no longer exist. You may need to check many different areas to solve a remote connection problem if experienced during this laboratory activity, such as the following:

■ Check all cable connectors.

■ Ping the localhost and the remote host.

■ Make sure TCP port 3389 is not blocked by a firewall. (Port 3389 is used to establish the remote connection.)

■ Check if the folder you are trying to access is shared.

■ Check if static IP addresses have been assigned to the computers. Pay particular attention to the subnet mask. (Not required for a peer-to-peer network using Windows 7.)

■ Check the media type. If you are performing this activity on a LAN, it must be identified as such in the **Remote Desktop Connection** dialog box under the **Experience** tab.

■ Check the Microsoft Management Console or Computer Management utility to see if the services that support Remote Desktop are running.

■ You may need to add *Administrator* to the list of users allowed to access the remote computer.

■ You must log on to the computer using a password, or you will not be able to establish a remote connection.

Note

The network administrator may have the Group Policy configured to prevent a Remote Desktop connection. This should not be the case in your network laboratory, but it can be the cause of connection failure in the real world.

You can access Remote Desktop Connection in several ways: through **Start | All Programs | Accessories | Remote Desktop Connection**, by entering "remote" into the **Search** box and then selecting the **Remote Desktop Connection** from the results list, and by entering "mstsc" in the **Search** box or at the command prompt. Entering "mstsc" will start the mstsc.exe program, which is the executive file for Remote Desktop Connection. MSTSC is the acronym for Microsoft Terminal Server Connection, which is the legacy program that Remote Desktop Connection is based on.

Equipment and Materials

❑ Two Windows 7 computers connected as a peer-to-peer network.
❑ Two 3 × 5 cards or equal. (The cards will be used to label the two computers as *Client* or *Remote*.)

Note
For the Remote Desktop client computer, you can use any Windows operating system, including the Home edition; however, if you are not using Windows 7, the screens may not exactly match those in this lab activity.

Procedure

1. _____ Report to your assigned workstation(s).

2. _____ Boot the computers and verify they are in working order.

3. _____ Identify each computer by its name and assign it as either the client or remote. Remember that the remote computer must have a Windows Professional, Ultimate, or Enterprise edition installed. Also, a user account should be created on the remote computer and must be configured to require a password for logging on to the remote computer.

Client computer name: _____

Remote computer name: _____

User account name: _____

User account password: _____

4. _____ At the remote computer, open **Control Panel | System and Security** and then select the **Allow remote access** option listed under the **System** section as indicated in the screen capture.

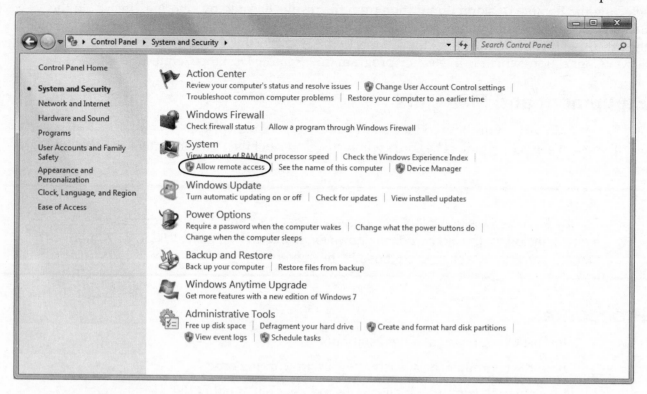

After selecting **Allow remote access** option, a dialog box will appear similar to the one in the following screen capture.

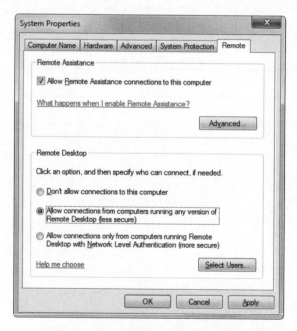

There are two major sections under the **Remote** tab: **Remote Assistance** and **Remote Desktop**. There are three options available under the **Remote Desktop** section.

The first option, **Don't allow connections to this computer**, will prevent remote connections. It is the most secure option.

Networking Fundamentals Laboratory Manual

Name _____

The second choice, **Allow connections from computers running any version of Remote Desktop (less secure)**, will allow any version of a Microsoft operating system to connect to the computer.

The third choice, **Allow connections only from computers running Remote Desktop with Network Level Authentication (more secure)**, only allows Windows 7 or later operating systems to connect to the computer. Earlier operating systems cannot connect to the remote desktop.

5. _____ For this lab activity, select the **Allow connections from computers running any version of Remote Desktop (less secure)** option.

6. _____ Click the **Select Users** button to view the default user list and to add additional users.

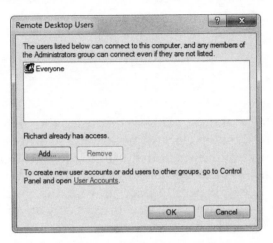

The default user list is *Everyone*. You can add additional or specific users by clicking the **Add** button. The *Everyone* group includes all users who have an account on the computer; hence, you can use any user account to access the computer. The *Everyone* group should be fine for this lab activity.

7. _____ Now at the client computer, open **Start | All Programs | Accessories | Remote Desktop Connection**. You can also start the Remote Desktop Connection by entering "remote" into the **Search** box and then selecting the **Remote Desktop Connection** from the results list. You can also enter "mstsc" in the **Search** box or at the command prompt. A dialog box similar to the following will display.

8. _____ Enter the name of the remote computer you wish to access. You can also enter the remote computer IP address, if known. Then, click the **Connect** button.

9. _____ Enter your credentials when prompted. The credentials are your account user name and password. The user name and password must match a user account on the remote computer.

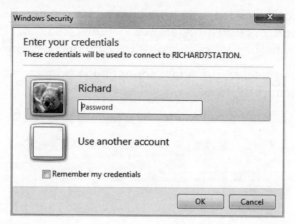

10. _____ A warning message will most likely be displayed the first time you run this lab activity. The Windows 7 Remote Desktop feature checks for a security certificate before allowing the connection. In a network environment that uses a Windows Server for authentication, there should be no warning message because a security certification will typically be available. However, if you are using a simple peer-to-peer network, the warning message will display because this type of network will not have a security certificate. If a warning message displays, click **Yes** to connect to the remote computer.

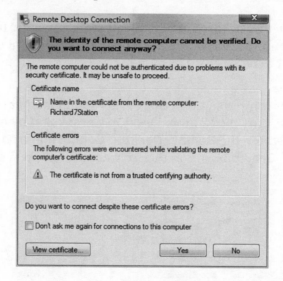

11. _____ After successful authentication, you will see the remote computer desktop.

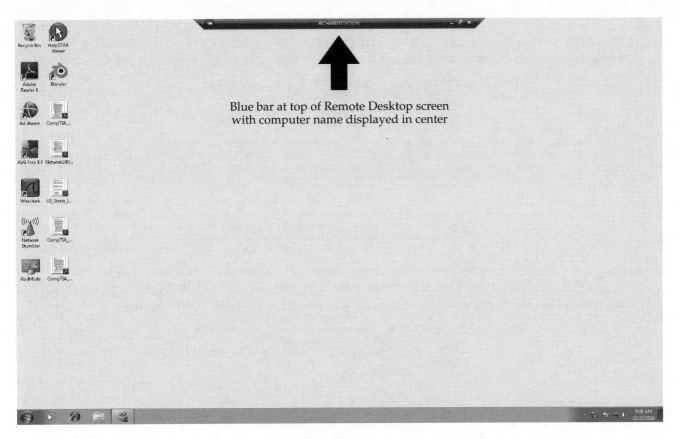

Blue bar at top of Remote Desktop screen
with computer name displayed in center

The remote computer name will appear in the middle of the blue bar at the top of the Remote Desktop computer screen. If you do not successfully connect to the remote computer, call your instructor for assistance.

12. _____ Take a few minutes to experiment with the remote computer's desktop. You should be able to open the **Start** menu and access programs and files on the remote computer.

13. _____ At the remote computer, access the **Start** menu. Any activity at the remote computer will break the Remote Desktop connection. At the client computer, you will see a message similar to that in the following screen capture, informing you that the Remote Desktop session has ended.

14. _____ Open the Remote Desktop Connection once more. You can do this by typing "remote" in the **Search** box or by accessing **Start | All Programs | Accessories | Remote Desktop Connection**. When the **Remote Desktop Connection** dialog box appears, click the **Options** arrow.

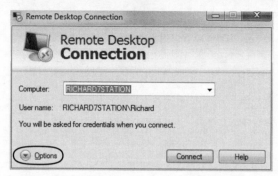

15. _____ A dialog box will display, allowing you to make changes to the Remote Desktop Connection configuration. Take a few minutes to explore the options available under each of the tabs. The following is a screen capture of all the available configuration options.

Notice that you can save your logon credentials so that you do not need to enter them each time you make a connection. The **Allow me to save credentials** option is deselected by default.

On the **Display** page, you can change the display settings to allow for better performance when using a low-bandwidth connection.

On the **Local Resources** page, you can configure local resources such as audio, keyboard key combinations, printers, and Clipboard.

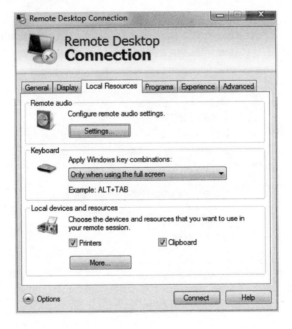

On the **Programs** page, you have an option to automatically start a program after a successful connection is established rather than starting the program through the **Start** menu.

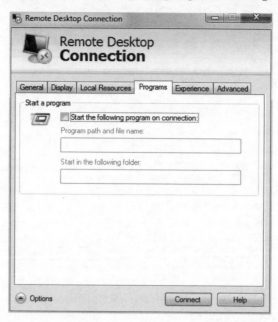

On the **Experience** page, you can select the type of connection ranging from low-speed dial-up to high-speed Broadband. You also have options to configure features that most affect computer performance over a limited-bandwidth connection.

The **Advanced** page provides options for configuring server authentication.

Clicking the **Settings** button produces the **RD Gateway Server Settings** dialog box for configuring the Remote Desktop (RD) Gateway server. RD Gateway server is new in Windows Server 2008.

A remote gateway server is a connection between two computers that run different protocols or different security methods. For example, the default security method for Remote Desktop Connection is using the Remote Desktop Protocol (RDP) and port 3389. The Remote Desktop Gateway server uses port 443 which utilizes Secure Sockets Layer (SSL), a security protocol that can be used to tunnel through most Internet Service Providers (ISP). This feature allows a computer to make a connection to a corporate network without the necessity of establishing a Virtual Private Network (VPN) connection.

The default setting in the **RD Gateway Server Settings** dialog box is **Automatically detect RD Gateway server settings**. You may need to manually intervene when another port number is required or the use of a smart card is needed to establish a secure connection.

Select the What is an RD Gateway server and how do I know if I need one? link to learn more about the RD Gateway.

16. _____ Close the **Remote Desktop Connection** dialog box and then take a few minutes to practice establishing a connection. Make sure you can open the connection by going through the **Start** menu, entering "remote" into the **Search** box, and entering the executable file name mstsc or mstsc.exe in the **Search** box or at the command prompt.

17. _____ Return all materials to their original storage area and then answer all review questions.

Review Questions

1. In a typical scenario using Remote Desktop Connection, the computer that is controlled is called the _____ computer. _____

2. In a typical scenario using Remote Desktop Connection, the computer used to control the other computer is called the _____ computer._____

3. What operating system can be used as the client computer? _____

4. What operating system must be installed as the remote computer? _____
   _____

5. JoAnne has her notebook computer with her while traveling for her company. She wants to connect to her home computer to look at some files. Which role will her notebook computer most likely be in this scenario—the client or the remote computer? _____

6. Which default port number is used to establish a Remote Desktop connection? _____

7. Which port number is used to establish an RD Gateway connection using SSL? _____

8. List nine different areas you should check to solve a remote connection problem?
   _____
   _____
   _____
   _____
   _____
   _____
   _____
   _____
   _____
   _____
   _____
   _____

9. Which operating system first introduced RD Gateway server?_____

10. What would you enter at the command prompt to start a Remote Desktop connection? _____
    _____

Laboratory Activity

70

Name_____ Date _____

Class/Instructor _____

Microsoft Remote Assistance

After completing this laboratory activity, you will be able to:

- Compare and contrast Remote Desktop and Remote Assistance.
- Summarize the roles of expert and novice.
- Recall the TCP port number used for Remote Assistance.
- Use Remote Assistance to request help from an expert or helper.

Introduction

In this laboratory activity, you will configure and use the Remote Assistance feature. This feature was first introduced with Windows XP. Remote Assistance is very useful for a technician performing network support. It allows a technician stationed at a help desk to access a user's computer, make changes to the system configuration, and perform other related repairs without leaving the help desk. Many repairs or modifications can be made from the help desk, thus eliminating the time it takes to go to the computer's location. The location of the computer can be as close as the same building or as far away as anywhere in the entire world.

When using Remote Assistance, you send an invitation to another user who has asked for help or assistance. Both computers must be using Windows Instant Messenger or an e-mail client that is MAPI compliant, such as Outlook, Outlook Express, or Windows Live Mail.

The overall process of using Remote Assistance is simple. The person who needs help is referred to as the *novice* while the person providing the help is referred to as the *expert* or *helper*. The term *expert* was used by Microsoft in earlier versions of Remote Assistance. Now, Microsoft uses the term *helper*. The novice starts the requests for help by starting the Remote Assistance program and then following the screen prompts. The novice chooses to use either e-mail or Microsoft Instant Messenger to send the invitation to the expert. The expert receives the invitation and opens the attachment, which starts the connection process. The expert must use a password to start the connection process to the novice's computer. The password should have already been provided, typically by telephone or by a separate, secure e-mail. The expert can chat with the novice, and at the same time, view the computer system. The expert cannot take control of the other computer unless the novice gives permission. When the session is over, the connection is terminated.

Note
The novice can terminate the session at any time by pressing the [ESC] key.

Windows 7 introduced a new Remote Assistance option called **Easy Connect**. The **Easy Connect** option allows two computers to connect without the need to send an e-mail. The novice's computer must be running Windows 7. The expert's computer can use Windows Vista or Windows 7. The novice starts a Remote Assistance session and the novice's computer automatically generates a password. The novice requests help from the expert by telephone, instant messaging, or some other method and requests that the expert start a Remote Assistance session. The novice gives the password to the expert so the expert can establish the Remote Assistance connection. After a short delay, the connection is established between the two computers.

The Remote Assistance executable file name is msra.exe (Microsoft Remote Assistance) and can be entered into the **Search** box located off the **Start** menu to start the Remote Assistance session. The executable file name can also be entered at the command prompt to start a Remote Assistance session.

Both Remote Assistance and Remote Desktop are based on the same Microsoft technology; however, they are very different. Look at the following table to compare Remote Assistance and Remote Desktop.

Remote Assistance	Remote Desktop
Requires two people—one who needs assistance (novice) and one who provides assistance (expert).	Requires one person who accesses and controls a remote computer.
Novice must use Instant Messenger or e-mail to invite the expert, unless the novice is using the **Easy Connect** option in Windows 7.	User can connect directly to the remote desktop. No invitation is needed.
Can use a temporary IP address.	Requires a persistent network connection such as DSL, ISDN, and a local area network connection, which provides a persistent IP address. Starting with Window 7, the **Easy Connect** option can be used so that a persistent connection is no longer required.
Uses an e-mail address to identify the expert.	Uses the computer name or IP address to identify the remote computer or uses the randomly-generated password key for Easy Connect access.
Available in all Windows editions, including the Home edition.	Only available in Windows Professional, Ultimate, and Enterprise editions, not Home edition.
Provides limited control over the novice computer.	Provides complete control over the remote computer.

The problems associated with Remote Assistance are similar to the problems associated with Remote Desktop.

- The e-mail must be MAPI compliant. If it is not, the e-mail client will not be able to properly process the request.
- Port 3389 must be open and not blocked by a firewall.
- Antivirus and Internet security third-party software, such as Norton, may interfere with the connection.
- The network administrator might have Group Policy configured to prevent Remote Assistance.
- Legacy hardware may block Easy Connect.

Note
There is a new restriction introduced in Windows 7. You can configure the Remote Assistance to only accept invitations from computers running Windows Vista or later operating systems. This provides better security then previous versions.

Equipment and Materials

❏ Two Windows 7 computers. (Windows Vista with the latest service pack may be used for the expert's computer.)

Note

The computers may be connected as a peer-to-peer, but they must both have access to the Internet for this lab activity to work correctly.

Procedure

1. _____ Report to your assigned workstation(s).

2. _____ Boot the computers and verify they are in working order.

3. _____ At the designated novice computer, start the session by typing "msra" into the **Search** box located off the **Start** menu and then selecting msra.exe from the top of the results list. You should see a dialog box similar to one of the two following screen captures. The dialog box that will match the one your computer depends on if the workstation has been used previously to configure a Remote Assistance request. If you have not used Remote Assistance to connect to an expert before, the dialog box will look like the following.

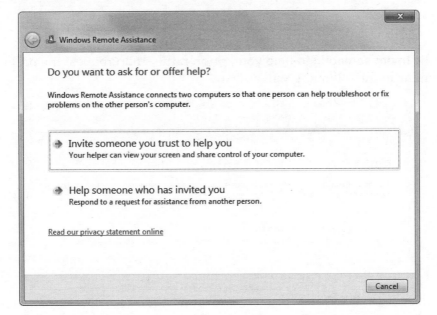

If you have used Remote Assistance to connect to an expert, the dialog box will look like that in the following screen capture. You will have an option to connect to the expert you connected to before. Notice that in the screen capture "Richard" was used for Remote Assistance in a previous configuration. You will also have the option to send an invitation to someone different.

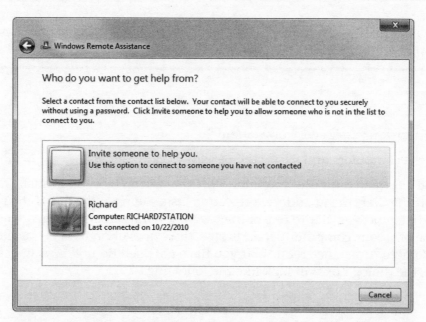

If you select the **Invite someone to help you** option rather than request the previous helper, a dialog box similar to the following will appear.

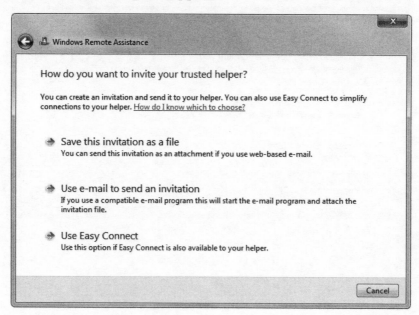

4. _____ Select the **Use Easy Connect** option. For this option, you do not need to use e-mail.

5. _____ The next dialog box to appear presents a randomly-generated Easy Connect password.

In an actual scenario, you would contact the expert to tell him or her the password. The expert would need to input the password to establish a Remote Assistance connection with the novice's computer. For this lab activity, write the password down and then go to the expert's computer.

6. _____ At the expert's computer, start the Remote Assistance program by typing "msra" into the **Search** box located off the **Start** menu and then selecting msra.exe from the top of the results list. A dialog box similar to the following will display.

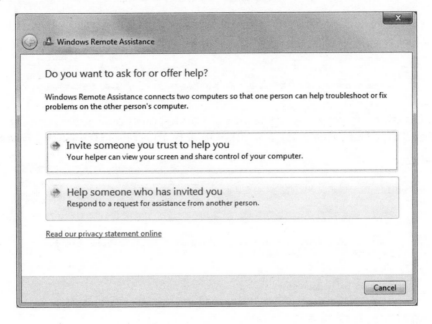

7. _____ Select the **Help someone who has invited you** option. The next dialog box to appear will be similar to the following. Again, the exact appearance of the dialog box will depend on if Remote Assistance has been provided previously from this computer. If it has, then the previous session will be retained and will appear in the list of options. Select the **Help someone new** option for this lab activity.

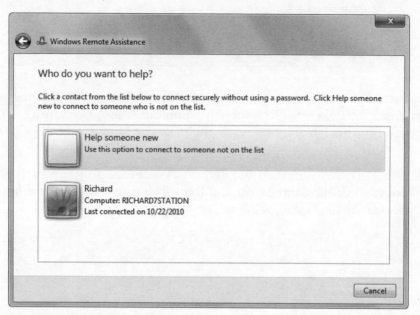

8. _____ The next dialog box to appear prompts you to select one of two options: **Use an invitation file** and **Use Easy Connect**. For this lab activity, select **Use Easy Connect**.

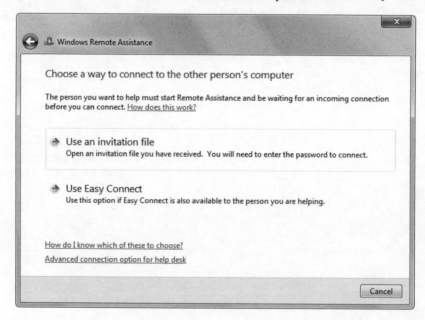

9. _____ After selecting Use Easy Connect, you will be prompted for the session password. Enter the password that you wrote down in step 5, which was generated by the novice's computer. It is not uncommon for there to be a delay of several minutes after entering the password. The password is forwarded across the Internet to verify the authorized expert/helper is allowed to connect to the remote computer.

10. _____ After a few minutes delay, the desktop of the novice's computer will appear similar to the one in the following screen capture. Notice that a notification appears in the middle of the screen informing the novice that the desktop is now being viewed by the expert/helper.

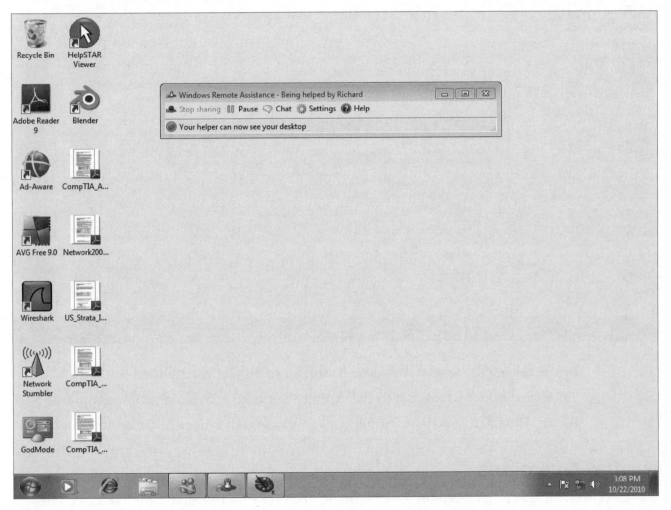

After selecting the **Chat** option at the novice desktop, a Chat window will open, allowing both the novice and expert/helper to exchange messages. However, Chat is not required. The novice and expert could simply use a cell phone to converse if they wish. For this lab activity, use the **Chat** option so that you will become familiar with it.

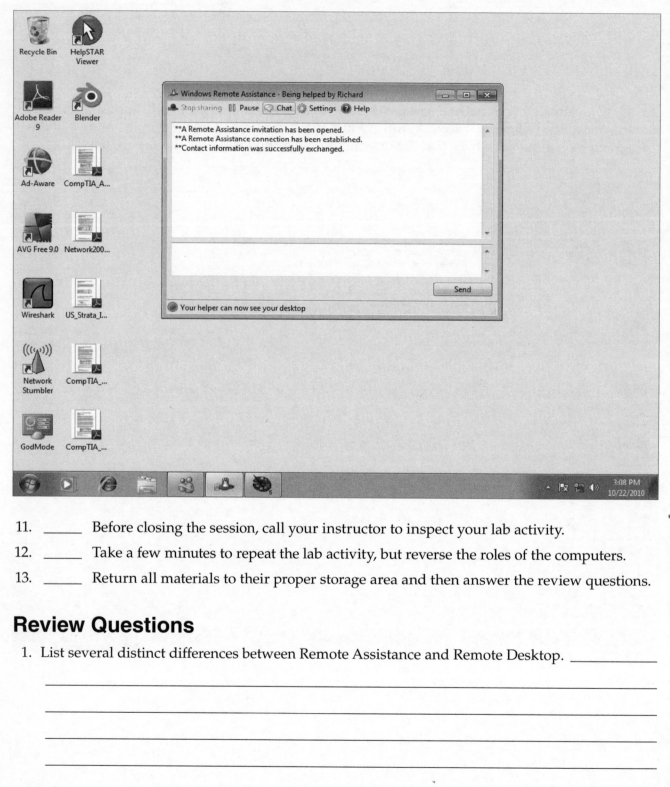

11. _____ Before closing the session, call your instructor to inspect your lab activity.

12. _____ Take a few minutes to repeat the lab activity, but reverse the roles of the computers.

13. _____ Return all materials to their proper storage area and then answer the review questions.

Review Questions

1. List several distinct differences between Remote Assistance and Remote Desktop. _____

_____

_____

_____

_____

_____

_____

2. The person who requests assistance is referred to as the _____. _____

3. The person who provides assistance is referred to as the _____ or _____. _____

   _____

4. What are the requirements for a Remote Assistance connection when not using the **Easy Connect** option? _____

   _____

5. Which TCP port is used for Remote Assistance?_____

6. How can the expert/helper and the novice exchange information? _____

   _____

7. How can Remote Assistance help you as a network technician?_____

   _____

   _____

   _____

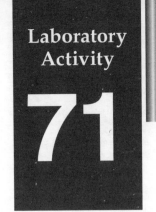

Laboratory Activity 71

Name_____ Date_____

Class/Instructor _____

Using the Tracert and Pathping Commands

After completing this laboratory activity, you will be able to:

- Compare and contrast the **ping**, **tracert**, and **pathping** commands.
- Use the **ping**, **tracert**, and **pathping** commands to test a network route.
- Recall the function of commonly used switches associated with **tracert** and **pathping**.

Introduction

In this laboratory activity, you will use the **tracert** and **pathping** commands to verify the media route between a host and client. The **ping** command, which you are already familiar with at this point in the course, only verifies a complete path from source to destination and provides very limited information.

The **tracert** command displays the complete path from source to destination, listing the number of "hops" along the path. Each hop is an intermediate connection along the path from source to destination. The intermediate connection typically represents a router. The **tracert** command provides information such as the IP address, time to each hop displayed in milliseconds (1/1000), and sometimes the name of each device encountered along the path.

The **pathping** command is an enhancement of the **ping** and **tracert** commands. Pathping first displays path information in a similar fashion as the **tracert** command. It then does an analysis of each hop along the path by sending a series of **ping** commands and performing calculations to display statistics about packet loss at each hop. The statistics can be used to identify problem areas along the path from source to destination. You can identify device failure along the intended path or areas of high traffic.

Look at the following screen captures which show a comparison of the **ping**, **tracert**, and **pathping** commands. In the following screen capture, a successful ping to www.comcast.net shows four successful echo request packets with the amount of time displayed in milliseconds for each.

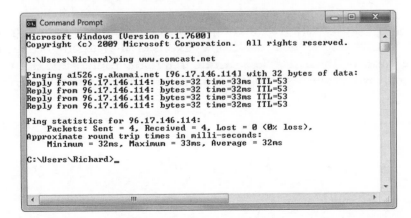

The next screen capture shows the results of the **tracert www.comcast.net** command. Notice that 13 hops were encountered. The number of milliseconds for each echo request is shown along with the IP address of each hop.

```
Command Prompt

C:\Users\Richard>tracert www.comcast.net

Tracing route to a1526.g.akamai.net [96.17.146.99]
over a maximum of 30 hops:

  1    <1 ms    <1 ms    <1 ms  192.168.1.1
  2     9 ms     9 ms     8 ms  73.17.116.1
  3    18 ms     8 ms     8 ms  ge-2-2-sr01.sebring.fl.westfl.comcast.net [68.86.199.77]
  4     9 ms     6 ms     7 ms  te-3-2-sr01.arcadia.fl.westfl.comcast.net [68.87.238.105]
  5    11 ms    10 ms     9 ms  te-9-4-ur01.portcharlott.fl.westfl.comcast.net [68.87.238.101]
  6    15 ms    13 ms    12 ms  te-8-2-ur01.northport.fl.westfl.comcast.net [68.87.238.65]
  7    13 ms     8 ms     8 ms  te-8-4-ar02.venice.fl.westfl.comcast.net [68.87.238.25]
  8     8 ms    12 ms    11 ms  te-9-3-ar01.venice.fl.westfl.comcast.net [68.87.238.17]
  9    28 ms    27 ms    30 ms  68.86.95.61
 10    32 ms    39 ms    42 ms  pos-3-12-0-0-cr01.atlanta.ga.ibone.comcast.net [68.86.86.221]
 11    33 ms    33 ms    32 ms  pos-0-7-0-0-cr01.miami.fl.ibone.comcast.net [68.86.86.65]
 12    34 ms    31 ms    32 ms  pos-0-1-0-0-pe01.nota.fl.ibone.comcast.net [68.86.87.106]
 13    30 ms    36 ms    31 ms  a96-17-146-99.deploy.akamaitechnologies.com [96.17.146.99]

Trace complete.

C:\Users\Richard>_
```

The next screen capture shows the immediate results of issuing the **pathping www.microsoft.com** command. The immediate results contain a list of the 13 hops but do not provide information about the amount of time to each hop. The information is not yet complete. As indicated in the screen capture, an additional 325 seconds (5 to 6 minutes) will be needed to perform additional echo requests so that a set of statistics about the route can be completed. The additional time is used to perform tests that calculate packet loss. These tests can indicate problems along the route, such as points of excessive network traffic.

```
Command Prompt - pathping www.comcast.net

C:\Users\Richard>pathping www.comcast.net

Tracing route to a1526.g.akamai.net [96.17.146.114]
over a maximum of 30 hops:
  0  Richard-PCwin7.hsd1.fl.comcast.net. [192.168.1.100]
  1  192.168.1.1
  2  73.17.116.1
  3  ge-2-2-sr01.sebring.fl.westfl.comcast.net [68.86.199.77]
  4  te-3-2-sr01.arcadia.fl.westfl.comcast.net [68.87.238.105]
  5  te-9-4-ur01.portcharlott.fl.westfl.comcast.net [68.87.238.101]
  6  te-8-2-ur01.northport.fl.westfl.comcast.net [68.87.238.65]
  7  te-8-4-ar02.venice.fl.westfl.comcast.net [68.87.238.25]
  8  te-9-4-ar01.venice.fl.westfl.comcast.net [68.87.238.13]
  9  68.86.95.65
 10  pos-3-12-0-0-cr01.atlanta.ga.ibone.comcast.net [68.86.86.221]
 11  pos-0-8-0-0-cr01.miami.fl.ibone.comcast.net [68.86.85.194]
 12  pos-0-0-0-0-pe01.nota.fl.ibone.comcast.net [68.86.87.102]
 13  a96-17-146-114.deploy.akamaitechnologies.com [96.17.146.114]

Computing statistics for 325 seconds...
```

The following screen capture shows the computed statistics for the **pathping** command, indicating the problem areas along the route. Packet loss is an indication of congestion usually caused by excessive traffic on the network. Be aware that many routers and firewalls are programmed to reject ICMP probes as a matter of security. This can also show packet loss.

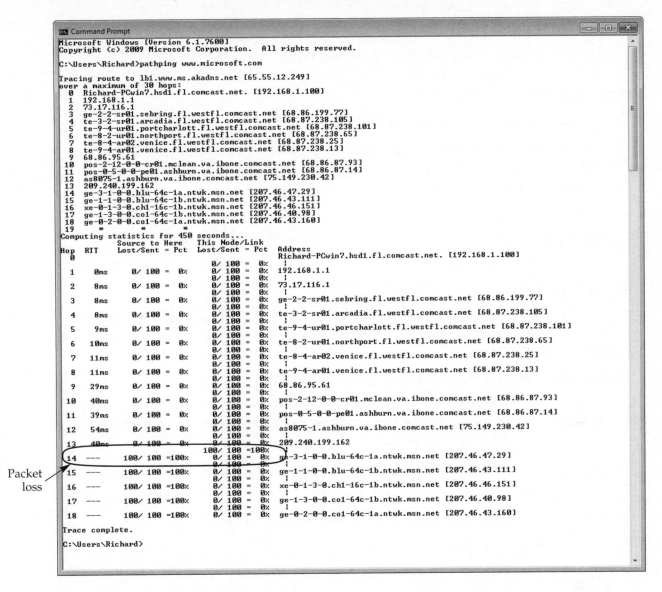

The **pathping** command is an excellent choice when testing a LAN consisting of a number of routers and you suspect that one or more are overloaded with network traffic. You could use the **pathping** command from the gateway to an internal workstation at the edge of the network to see the statistics generated on the local routers.

Commercial utilities are also available to perform a detailed analysis of routes between source and destination points. One such product is called *Ping Plotter* and is available for free at the time of this writing. You can conduct an Internet search for Ping Plotter and then add a copy to your software tool kit.

Ping, **tracert**, and **pathping** are encapsulated inside Internet Control Message Protocol (ICMP) packets. ICMP is a TCP/IP upper-layer protocol for transporting packets carrying error, control, and information messages.

The **ping** and **pathping** commands are also compatible with UNIX/Linux operating systems. The equivalent UNIX/Linux command for **tracert** is **traceroute**. These commands were developed to test TCP/IP-based communication systems; hence, any operating system that uses TCP/IP will also support the use of these commands.

Equipment and Materials

❑ Windows 7 computer with Internet access and Wireshark installed.

Procedure

1. _____ Report to your assigned workstation.

2. _____ Boot the computer and verify it is in working order.

3. _____ Access the command prompt and test the connection to one of the suggested Internet sites using the **ping** command. For example, **ping www.comcast.net**.

   ■ www.comcast.net

   ■ www.google.com

   ■ www.microsoft.com

   ■ www.RMRoberts.com

4. _____ Use the **tracert** command to view the hops from your computer to the destination—for example, **tracert www.comcast.net**. Answer the following question based on the result of the **tracert** command.

   How many hops were encountered? _____

5. _____ Use the **pathping** command to the same Internet site you used for the **tracert** command—for example, **pathping www.comcast.net**. Answer the following question based on the result of the **pathping** command.

   How many hops were encountered along the route? _____

6. _____ Use the **/?** switch to answer the following questions about the **tracert** command.

   Which switch can be used to change the default number of hops? _____

   Which switch is used to force an IPv6 ping? _____

7. _____ Use the **/?** switch to answer the following questions about the **pathping** command.

   Which switch is used to change the default number of hops? _____

   Which switch is used to force the use of IPv6? _____

8. _____ Use Wireshark to capture and study a set of packets generated by the **ping, tracert**, and **pathping** commands. This will give you insight into how the three commands are related and how they are different. After viewing the captured packets, look for the most common high-level protocol used. Also, take note of the number of packets used by each utility to carry out the command.

9. _____ After performing the Wireshark analysis, return all materials to their proper storage area.

10. _____ Answer the review questions.

Review Questions

1. Which command, **ping**, **tracert**, or **pathping**, provides the most detailed information about a connection path between a destination and a source? _____

2. Which command, **ping**, **tracert**, or **pathping**, requires the most amount of time to complete when gathering information about the route between the source and destination? _____

   _____

3. Which command, **ping**, **tracert**, or **pathping**, should you use when you simply want to confirm a complete path exists between the destination and source? _____

4. Which command, **ping**, **tracert**, or **pathping**, should you use if you want to quickly confirm the number of hops between the source and destination? _____

5. Which commands, **ping**, **tracert**, or **pathping**, are compatible with both Microsoft operating systems and Linux? _____

6. What UNIX/Linux command is comparable to **tracert**? _____

7. Which command is used to display packet losses at each hop? _____

8. Which command, **ping**, **tracert**, or **pathping**, simply sends out four echo request messages to verify route from source to destination? _____

9. Which TCP/IP upper-level protocol is designed to carry out the ping, tracert, and pathping echo request commands? _____

10. Which command, **ping**, **tracert**, or **pathping**, generates the most ICMP traffic when testing the path to the destination? _____

11. What switch is used to increase the number of hops for the **pathping** command? _____

    _____

12. Which command, **ping**, **tracert**, or **pathping**, would you use to locate a router suspected of causing packet exchange delays on your local network system? _____

Networking Fundamentals Laboratory Manual

Name_____ Date _____

Class/Instructor _____

Security Event Monitoring

After completing this laboratory activity, you will be able to:

- Use Event Viewer or Computer Management to open the security log.
- Interpret a failed security event.
- Identify the type of events that are recorded in the security log.
- Use Event Viewer or Computer Management to modify the security log configuration.

Introduction

In this laboratory activity, you will access and modify the security log configuration. The security log can be accessed directly through Event Viewer or through Computer Management. To open Event Viewer, enter **eventvwr.exe** in the **Search** box off the **Start** menu and select **Event Viewer** from the search results. The same executable command can be used for Windows XP and later operating systems. To open Computer Management, right-click **Computer** and then select **Manage** from the shortcut menu. When Computer Management opens, you will see Event Viewer listed as a folder in the left-hand pane.

Event Viewer Filter Current Log

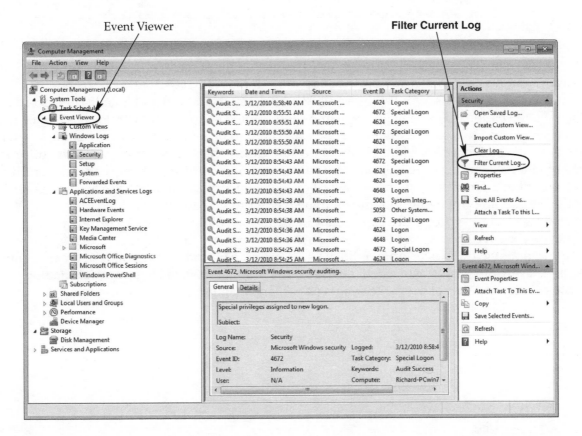

Event Viewer contains many different types of files. For example, the screen capture shows the list of events contained in the security log. A detailed set of information about the event can be viewed by simply double-clicking the selected event. An **Event Properties** dialog box will appear similar to the one in the following screen capture.

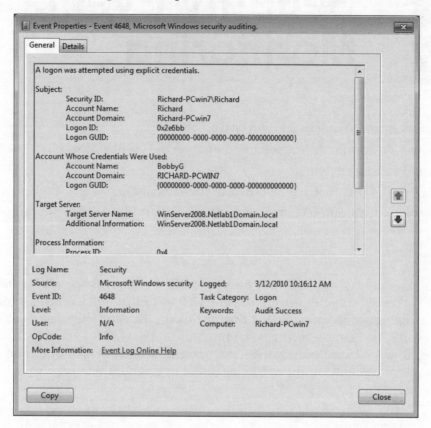

You can see the information gathered about an attempted logon using explicit credentials. The event took place on 3/12/2010 at 10:16:12 AM. The user account name entered for authentication was *BobbyG* and his credentials are located at account domain RICHARD-PCWIN7. BobbyG attempted to log on to the server WinServer2008.Netlab1Domain.local and failed. This record can be copied to the clipboard as a single event and then printed so the administrator has a hard copy to work from or to add to a security report. The event can also be e-mailed to an account for viewing as well. As you can see, Event Viewer is an important utility that can monitor user authentication. If a series of failed events occur using the same name, an administrator will know that either the user *BobbyG* is having a problem with his password or that someone is attempting to access the server using the *BobbyG* account name and guessing the password.

Certain security log properties can be modified, such as the size of the security log file. The entire file can be saved to a separate folder for storage or review. Look at the following screen capture and note the three overwrite options listed near the bottom of the **Log Properties–Security** dialog box: **Overwrite events as needed (oldest events first)**; **Archive the log when full, do not overwrite events**; and **Do not overwrite events (Clear logs manually)**.

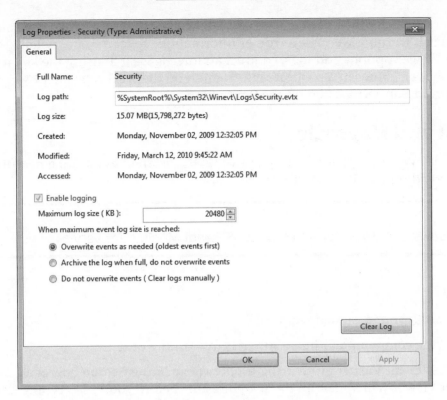

The default setting is **Overwrite events as needed (oldest events first)**. This means when the allotted amount of file space is used, the oldest event will be erased as new ones are generated. The **Do not overwrite events (clear log manually)** option is not often used because if the log reaches its limit, the computer will generate an error message or a blue screen and then lock the computer when a new event needs to be recorded. The server must then be restarted and the log manually cleared.

The entire log can contain an overwhelming number of events numbering into the tens of thousands. To overcome the extensive number of events collected in the log, the event can be filtered. Look at the following screen capture of the **Filter Current Log** dialog box.

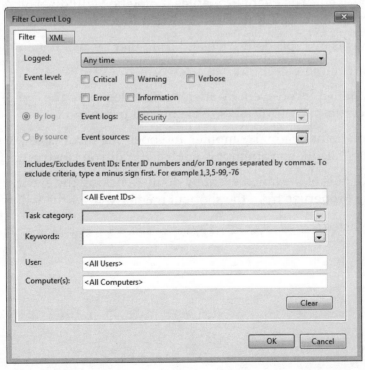

You can filter events by time period such as days, weeks, or hours. You can also filter events by level such as critical, warning, verbose, error, or information. To learn more detailed information about the Event Viewer options and logs, conduct an Internet search using the key terms "Microsoft TechNet Event Viewer." You can also locate information on the local computer by entering "Event Viewer" in Help and Support located off the **Start** menu.

Equipment and Materials

❏ Computer with Windows 7 or Windows Server 2008 installed as part of a peer-to-peer network. You will need administrative privileges.

Note
The Windows 7 and Windows Server 2008 Event Monitor are very similar.

Procedure

1. _____ Report to your assigned workstation.

2. _____ Boot the computer and make sure it is in working order.

3. _____ Access Event Viewer by entering **eventvwr.exe** in the **Search** box located off the **Start** menu. Event Viewer will appear in the search results before you finish typing the entire name.

4. _____ After Event Viewer opens, exit Event Viewer by selecting **File | Exit**.

5. _____ Now, access Event Viewer by selecting **Start**, right-clicking **Computer**, and selecting **Manage** from the shortcut menu. The Computer Management console will open. The Event Viewer is listed as a folder in the left-hand pane.

6. _____ Expand the Event Viewer folder so that you can see the five Windows log types: **Application**, **Security**, **Setup**, **System**, and **Forwarded Events**.

7. _____ Select **Security**. Look at the security events listed in the center pane of the window. If your system is new, there may be few events listed. Take note of what the latest event is by double-clicking the event. The **Event Properties** dialog box will display. When you are finished viewing the event details, click **OK** to close the **Event Properties** dialog box.

8. _____ Sort the events by type, date, user, and computer by clicking on the top of each column.

9. _____ Log off the computer.

10. _____ Generate a failed logon event by attempting to log on to the computer from a different computer in the peer-to-peer using a bogus name and password.

11. _____ Now, log on to the original computer and open the security log to see if the failed event was recorded. If the failed logon attempt is not listed, call your instructor for assistance.

12. _____ View the details of the failed event by double-clicking the event or by right-clicking the event and selecting **Properties** from the shortcut menu. Answer the following questions.

Is the bogus name listed? _____

What other information is listed in the **Event Properties** window? _____

_____

_____

_____

_____

_____

13. _____ Close the **Event Properties** window by clicking **OK**.

14. _____ Right-click the **Security** folder listed under the Event Viewer folder and then select **Properties**. Look at the options listed on the **General** page. Practice changing the log size and the overwrite options. When you are finished experimenting, click **Cancel** to exit the dialog box without saving any changes.

15. _____ Answer the review questions and then return the computer to the condition specified by your instructor.

Review Questions

1. What is the name of the executable file that will start the Event Viewer? _____

2. What are the three overwrite options for the security log? _____

_____

_____

_____

_____

3. What is the default overwrite option? _____

_____

4. What does the **Filter Current Log** option allow you to do? _____

_____

_____

_____

5. List the five Event Viewer logs. _____

_____

_____

Observing the TCP/IP Three-Way Handshake

After completing this laboratory activity, you will be able to:

■ Explain the packet exchange of a TCP/IP three-way handshake.

■ Recall the role of a flag.

■ Explain why TCP is considered a connection-oriented protocol.

Introduction

In this laboratory activity, you will capture and analyze a TCP/IP three-way handshake. TCP is a connection-oriented protocol, which means it establishes a connection between the source and destination. UDP packets do not establish a connection between the source and destination. UDP is a "best effort" packet delivery system.

To establish a connection, the TCP protocol sends a series of three packets; hence, the name "three-way handshake," which is used to describe the action. During this process, no security information is exchanged. The following are the three steps of the three-way handshake process.

1. The source host sends a packet with the SYN (synchronize) flag set to on. Basically, it is requesting to make a connection with the destination host.

2. The destination host responds with both a SYN and an ACK (acknowledgement) flag set to on. This is basically an acceptance of the connection from the destination host to the source host.

3. The source host sends an ACK back to the destination host, and the three-way handshake is complete.

SYN and ACK are flags contained inside the TCP packet. *Flag* is a programming term. It refers to an assigned bit in a specific location that is used to identify a condition. Typically, a bit represented by a binary 1 represents a true condition, and a bit represented by a binary 0 represents a false condition. Look at the following screen capture to see an example of flag conditions in a captured packet.

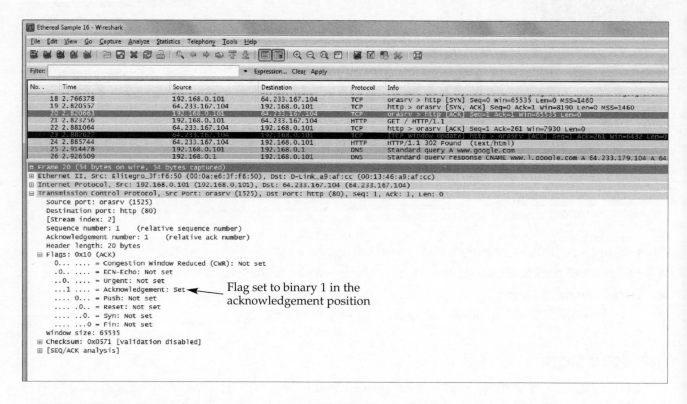

In the packet description section is an area identified as "Flags." Below the Flags heading, the binary position for acknowledgment is set to 1. This means the packet contains the acknowledgement flag required in the TCP handshake. The three-way TCP handshake is used whenever the TCP/IP protocol requires a connection to be maintained between two devices in a network.

In this laboratory activity, you will first open and view the contents of the sample Wireshark file. Then, you will make your own capture and examine it for the presence of the same three-way handshake.

Equipment and Materials

❑ Windows 7 computer with Internet access and Wireshark installed.
❑ Wireshark Sample 18 file.
   Wireshark Sample 18 file location: _____

❑ Wireshark Sample 19 file.
   Wireshark Sample 19 file location: _____

Procedure

1. _____ Report to your assigned workstation.

2. _____ Boot the computer and verify that it is in working order.

3. _____ Open the Wireshark Sample 18 file.

4. _____ Look at frames 18, 19, and 20. You will see that these frames contain the TCP three-way handshake used to establish a connection between a source host and destination host. The source host IP address is 192.168.0.101 and the destination host is 64.233.167.104.

5. _____ In frame 18, the first step in the process begins. Expand the contents of the packet and look at the flag. Notice that the SYN bit has been set to 1.

6. _____ In frame 19, you see the second step of the process in which the SYN and the ACK flag bits are set to 1.

7. _____ Frame 20 is the final or third step of the process. It contains the flag bit for ACK set to 1.

8. _____ Close the Wireshark Sample 18 file.

9. _____ Open the Wireshark Sample 19 file to see what the three-way handshake looks like in the IPv6 environment. The following screen capture shows the three frames of an IPv6 three-way handshake process.

Pay particular attention to the SYN and ACK series identified in the **Info** column. This is how you will locate the three-way handshake when you create your own Wireshark capture.

10. _____ Close the Wireshark Sample 19 file.

11. _____ Start a Wireshark capture and then access the Internet using Internet Explorer and open any page. The default home page will be sufficient to generate the needed capture.

12. _____ Stop the Wireshark capture and then search the capture for the TCP three-way handshake. When located, call your instructor to inspect your work.

13. _____ After your instructor views your capture, return the workstation to its original condition and return all materials to their proper storage area.

14. _____ Answer the review questions.

Review Questions

1. What is the purpose of the TCP three-way handshake? _____

   _____

2. Briefly describe the TCP three-way handshake process. _____

   _____

   _____

   _____

3. Which protocol is used for the TCP three-way handshake—TCP or UDP? _____

4. Which protocol is a" best effort" delivery protocol—TCP or UDP? _____

5. Why is TCP considered a connection-oriented protocol? _____

   _____

   _____

6. What is the purpose of a program flag? _____

   _____

   _____

   _____

   _____

7. True *or* False. The three-way handshake is only supported in IPv4. _____

WINDOWS 7

Name _____ Date _____

Class/Instructor _____

Wireless Encryption

After completing this laboratory activity, you will be able to:

- Summarize the security weaknesses related to wireless networks.
- Recall the purpose of a security key.
- Check if a wireless connection to an SSID has been made.

Introduction

Wireless media and devices are considered security risks because any wireless device within range may connect to a wireless network that is configured with default settings. The device default settings for the SSID and default administrator name and password can be commonly found by anyone who accesses the product information. This product information is typically available on the Internet or in the product information guide that accompanies the device when purchased. There are two things that you can do to dramatically increase the security of a wireless system:

- Change the default configuration.
- Enable encryption.

When using encryption, you must supply a security key also known as a *passphrase*. A security key is similar to a password. The security key must be the same for all wireless devices expected to connect to each other. By default, most wireless devices do not have any encryption enabled; thus, they are easily connected to by unauthorized persons. To provide good security, you must enable some type of encryption for the wireless devices.

This laboratory activity focuses on the WPA-Personal security type. Earlier wireless security was based on WEP, which is rarely encountered today except when using legacy hardware. Microsoft Windows 7 and most commonly encountered wireless devices support WPA-Personal security.

In this laboratory activity, you will configure encryption for the wireless devices on three computers. The three computers will be configured as an ad-hoc wireless network. When configuring the three computers, be sure to match the workgroup name, subnet mask, and network IP address. For example, all three computers should belong to the workgroup *Workgroup* and use the subnet mask 255.0.0.0 and one of the following IP addresses: 10.0.0.1, 10.0.0.2, or 10.0.0.3. Notice that the computers share the same network IP address: 10.

Each of the three computers must use the same SSID, encryption type, and security key. Using the same security key is referred to as *symmetric-key encryption*. The security key is a unique set of characters used to generate the encryption code that is used to encrypt the contents of the packets. The security key will be configured manually, but each computer must match. If the security key on a computer does not match the security key on the other computers, it will not be able to join the group. Security keys are typically made from ASCII or hexadecimal characters.

ASCII is represented by the entire alphabet *a–z* and *A–Z* and numbers *0–9*. The hexadecimal character set is limited to letters *a–f* and *A–F* and numbers *0–9*.

When making a connection to a wireless network using encryption, you may be required to provide the key when connecting for the first time. Providing a key is similar to providing a password when connecting to a shared network device for the first time.

Note

If this lab activity has been completed previously by another student using your assigned computer, the computer may already be configured for WPA-Personal and already have a wireless security key.

Before performing this laboratory activity, you may want to review your earlier lab experiences with wireless networking by rereading earlier wireless laboratory activities. This laboratory activity assumes that you can complete a default configuration of a wireless device.

A wireless device can be configured to connect to more than one SSID, but it can only connect to SSID at a time. In other words, a wireless-enabled device such as a laptop can be configured for many different wireless networks, both encrypted and not encrypted. The wireless-enabled laptop can only be a part of one wireless network at one time.

Microsoft's version of WPA has two types of encryption available: Advanced Encryption Standard (AES) and Temporal Key Integrated Protocol (TKIP). You must match the encryption type for each computer.

Note

Windows uses AES by default, but other encryption types may be available for your configuration because of the drivers loaded during the installation of your wireless network adapter.

Wireless networks are extremely difficult to work with. They can be very frustrating because of the conflict between the Windows operating system's wireless configuration and the manufacturer's wireless configuration. For assistance, you may want to view the Microsoft TechNet Wireless Networking site located at http://technet.microsoft.com/en-us/network/bb530679.aspx. To access this site, you can conduct a Google search using key terms "Microsoft Windows 7 Wireless networking."

Equipment and Materials

❏ Three Windows 7 computers connected as a peer-to-peer network.
❏ Three wireless devices: 802.11b, 802.11a, 802.11g, or 802.11n. (The devices must match or be compatible. A USB wireless device is recommended for this laboratory activity, but is not required.)

Name _____

☐ The following information provided by your instructor:

Account user name: _____

Account password: _____

SSID name: _____ (Each group of three computers in your class should use a unique SSID.)

WPA-Personal key: _____ (Suggested: 8 character ASCII key, such as 12345678)

Workgroup name: _____ (Suggested: *workgroup*)

Note

Some legacy devices do not support WPA-Personal encryption. If you are using a legacy wireless network device, you must use WEP encryption.

Note

This laboratory activity is based on the Microsoft 7 operating system wireless configuration software. If the device you are using must be configured with the manufacturer's software, the dialog boxes may not match the laboratory activity screen captures. Also, be aware that wireless network device drivers and Windows service packs can introduce newer versions of security software and encryption types. Service packs and drivers can cause choices different from those in the laboratory activity. You can proceed with the laboratory activity using the steps as a general guide. All wireless devices will contain similar configuration settings even if they are not an exact match.

Procedure

1. _____ Report to your assigned workstation(s).

2. _____ Boot the three computers and verify they are in working order.

3. _____ Label the three computers *Source*, *Destination*, and *Intruder*. This will help you while following the lab instructions.

4. _____ Each computer should have at least one matching user account. The user name and password should be the same for each computer user account to ensure that each computer can access the other.

   Note that in a lab environment, configuration changes can often cause problems concerning accessibility. When a share is set up on a computer, check the share permissions for the user to ensure that the user has access. The permissions should match on all three computers using similar shares. Also, check that each of the three computers are configured for a workgroup, not a domain.

5. _____ Consult the manufacturer's information before configuring the wireless devices. When the USB wireless device is first installed into a USB port, it will automatically be detected and the **Wireless Network Connection** icon will appear in the desktop notification area. The icon for the wireless device will be similar to the one in the following screen capture.

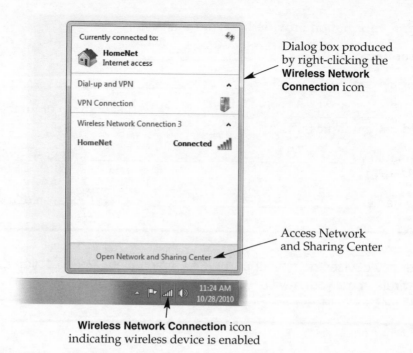

Dialog box produced by right-clicking the **Wireless Network Connection** icon

Access Network and Sharing Center

Wireless Network Connection icon indicating wireless device is enabled

Notice that the **Wireless Network Connection** icon is represented by an image for wireless signal strength. Clicking the icon will produce a dialog box similar to that in the previous screen capture. Notice that you can open the Network and Sharing Center by selecting the link at the bottom of the dialog box.

6. _____ Open the Network and Sharing Center. You should see information about the wireless connection similar to that in the following screen capture.

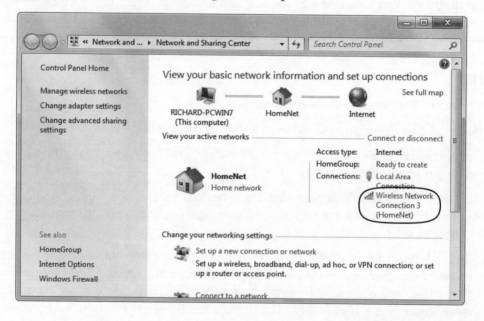

To view the properties for the wireless network, select **Wireless Network Connection** followed by the name of the local network—for example, **Wireless Network Connection 3 (HomeNet)**.

Do *not* select **Local Area Connection**, which is located immediately above the **Wireless Network Connection**.

After selecting **Wireless Network Connection**, a dialog box similar to the following will display.

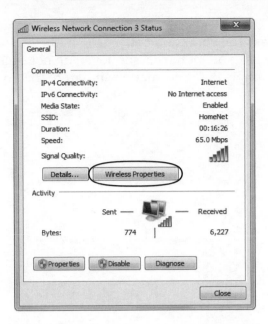

7. _____ Click the **Wireless Properties** button. A dialog box similar to the following will display.

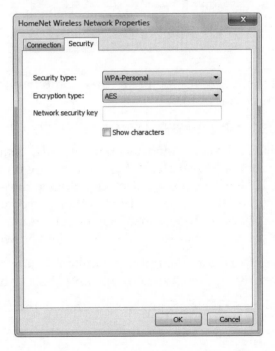

Under the **Security** tab is where you will select the security type, encryption type, and network security key. The network security key is also known as the *passphrase*.

For each computer, select WPA-Personal for the security type and AES for the encryption type. Use 12345678 for the security key. This will make all of the computers capable of connecting to each other in ad-hoc mode.

8. _____ Check if all three computers are configured with a matching SSID and security type. To do this, click the **Wireless Network Connection** icon in the notification area and then move the cursor over the dialog box and let the cursor hover; do not click the connection. This will produce a box listing the connection information similar to that in the following screen capture.

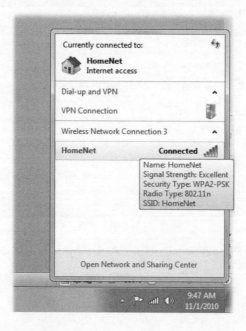

9. _____ After completing the configuration of all three computers, check if you can create a connection between the three computers.

10. _____ Call your instructor to inspect your laboratory activity thus far.

11. _____ Now, designate one of the computers as an intruder by changing the security key at the intruder computer so that it no longer matches the security key on the other two computers. For example, if you are using 12345678 as the security key, change the security key of one computer to 87654321. Try to connect the intruder to one of the other two computers. You should not be able to successfully connect because the security key no longer matches. However, all three computers will be able to see each other in the list of wireless networks.

12. _____ Take a few minutes to explore the options available under the **Security** tab. Try configuring a different security and encryption type and observe the results.

13. _____ Return the computers to their original configuration and then answer the review questions.

Review Questions

1. What is a security key?_____

_____

_____

2. Name two security weaknesses related to wireless networks._____

_____

3. What is the difference between an ASCII character set and a hexadecimal character set? _____

_____

_____

_____

4. Which items must match to support a wireless connection between computers? Indicate with a "Yes" or "No."

a. _____ SSID

b. _____ Security type

c. _____ Encryption type

d. _____ Security key

e. _____ IPv4 address

f. _____ IPv6 address

g. _____ MAC number

5. True *or* False. You can only configure a wireless computer for one SSID.

6. True *or* False. You can connect to more than one SSID group simultaneously.

7. You can see the available wireless network computer in the Network browser and there are packets being exchanged as indicated in the **Wireless Network Connection Status** dialog box, but you cannot successfully connect to it. You have a user account on each wireless network computer. What is *most likely* the problem?_____

_____

_____

Name_____ Date _____

Class/Instructor _____

NTFS Encrypting File System

After completing this laboratory activity, you will be able to:

- Use the **Advanced Attributes** dialog box to encrypt the contents of a file or folder.
- Identify which file types support file encryption.
- Summarize the effect on encryption when moving an encrypted file or folder.

Introduction

In this laboratory activity, you will encrypt an NTFS file or folder. File encryption is an essential part of data security. A computer can be compromised by unauthorized personnel. If a computer stores critical information, it is best to require a password for user log on and to encrypt the data. A computer may be accessed either directly or over a network. Files could be copied or opened by an intruder. A notebook computer containing customer lists, corporate information, sensitive e-mail information, bank account information, and other forms of sensitive information could be lost or stolen. A person might possibly open the files on the computer and reveal the contents.

The Windows Encrypting File System (EFS) requires NTFS to be installed on the partition where the file/folder is to be encrypted. EFS will not work on a FAT partition. Windows Home Edition does not support EFS. Only Windows Professional, Ultimate, and Enterprise editions as well as Windows Server support EFS.

System files and compressed files cannot be encrypted. Do *not* encrypt files such as those with the EXE, DLL, and COM extensions. These file types are critical to other programs. You should only apply encryption to data files.

Note

Microsoft has an encryption method referred to as "Bitlocker," which was first introduced in Windows Vista. Bitlocker is designed to encrypt an entire disk drive, including hidden files and operating system files. Windows 7 introduced "Bitlocker To Go," which is designed to encrypt removable drives and smart cards. Bitlocker is only available for Windows Vista and Windows 7 Ultimate and Enterprise operating systems.

To the user who encrypted the file/folder, encryption will be transparent. This means that the user will be able to open, modify, and copy an encrypted file/folder without having to decrypt the file/folder first. However, there are several copy rules concerning EFS files and folders to be aware of:

- When you copy or move an encrypted file/folder from one partition to another partition on the same computer and both partitions are NTFS, the file/folder remains encrypted.
- When you copy or move an encrypted file/folder from one partition to another partition and the destination partition is FAT32, the file/folder will no longer be encrypted.
- When you copy or move an encrypted file/folder to a NTFS partition on another computer, the file/folder remains encrypted.

It is important to note that the limited user will not be aware that there is an encrypted file/folder on the system. The encrypted file/folder will not appear in the limited user's Windows Explorer. A user with a user account equal to the user account that encrypted the file/folder will see that the file/folder is encrypted by its name appearing in green. However, the user will be denied access to the file/folder contents.

A command line encryption tool with the executable named cipher.exe can be run from the command prompt. The tool has been available since Windows 2000 but is seldom used today.

For more detailed information about using EFS, check the Microsoft TechNet support Web site. Simply conduct a Google search using the key words "Microsoft TechNet EFS." Look for "Microsoft" in the URL results. You can also find a lot of related information located in Help and Support located off the **Start** menu. When Help and Support opens, enter "EFS" into the **Search help** box.

Equipment and Materials

❑   Windows 7 Professional, Ultimate, or Enterprise computer.

Note

You may also perform this laboratory activity using Windows Vista Ultimate or Windows XP Professional. The Home editions do not support encryption.

Procedure

1. _____   Report to your assigned workstation.

2. _____   Boot the computer and verify that it is in working order. Be sure that at least two additional user accounts exist for this laboratory activity. One account should have access rights equal to your user account. The other account should have limited access. You may wish to use the account names *AdminEqual* and *LimitedUser* to help you identify the accounts.

3. _____   Create a new folder in the Documents folder called \Secret Folder.

4. _____   Encrypt the folder by right-clicking \Secret Folder and selecting **Properties** from the shortcut menu. The **Secret Folder Properties** dialog box will display. On the **General** page, click **Advanced**. The **Advanced Attributes** dialog box will display. Under the **Compress or Encrypt attributes** section, select the **Encrypt contents to secure data** option. Click **OK**. Click **OK** again to close the **Secret Folder Properties** dialog box.

5. _____   Now, create a short memo with the contents, "I have many secrets." Name the memo Secret Memo and save it to the \Secret Folder directory.

6. _____   Use the two accounts you created and the Secret Memo file to experiment and answer the following questions. Record your answers in the spaces provided. Use the simple file-sharing mode for this series of tests.

What color characters are used to represent the encrypted folder? _____

Can another equal user account view the contents of the encrypted file? _____

What happens when you drag or copy the encrypted memo into a different folder that is not encrypted? For example, what will happen if you drag or copy it into the \Shared Documents folder? _____

What happens when you compress an encrypted file? _____

Can another equal user account send the encrypted document to the Recycle Bin? _____

7. _____ When you have finished experimenting and answering the questions, answer the review questions.

8. _____ Return all materials to their proper storage area and return the computer to its original condition. Be sure to remove the user accounts, test folder, and file.

Review Questions

1. What does the acronym EFS represent? _____

2. What type of file should be encrypted? _____

3. What color is a file or folder name displayed in after it is encrypted?_____

4. What happens when you move or copy an encrypted file to a folder that is not encrypted? _____

   _____

   _____

5. What happens when a limited account user attempts to access an encrypted file? _____

   _____

   _____

6. What happens when a user with an equal user account attempts to access another equal user's encrypted file or folder?_____

   _____

7. Can a user with an equal account to the user who encrypted a file remove or delete that user's encrypted file?_____

8. Who can restore a file from the Recycle Bin? _____

9. What type of files can you not encrypt? _____

10. What text command can be used to encrypt files? _____

Name_____ Date _____

Class/Instructor _____

Configuring a Firewall

After completing this laboratory activity, you will be able to:

- Recall the role of Windows Firewall.
- Use the various options available to configure Windows Firewall.
- Identify the port number and protocol assignment of common TCP/IP services.
- Recall the function of the Windows Firewall security log.

Introduction

In this laboratory activity, you will become familiar with Windows Firewall, which was introduced with Windows XP and referred to as *Internet Connection Firewall*. In Windows XP service pack 2 and later, it was renamed to *Windows Firewall*. The workstation version of Windows Firewall is very similar to the server version.

A firewall is designed to prevent unauthorized access to or from a workstation through the Internet. It is a basic way of providing protection for a private network from Internet attacks.

Note

Originally, Microsoft recommended that the Windows Firewall should not be enabled on a workstation that is not serving as a gateway or as a stand-alone computer connected to the Internet. This was because Windows Firewall could create problems with network applications such as file sharing or VPN connections as well as with ICMP troubleshooting utilities such as ping and tracert. Today Microsoft has reversed the recommendation about using the Windows Firewall on individual workstations. Microsoft now recommends enabling Windows Firewall for all workstations in all types of settings such as Home, Public, and Domain. Windows Firewall is designed to automatically configure ports for most software applications and programs.

A firewall is designed to set restrictions for communications through the designated host or gateway. It can be set up to inspect each frame for the destination and source IP addresses, enable or disable services running on the host computer, create a log of network activities, and record items such as attempted log on to the network.

A firewall will help to prevent attacks by malicious software, such as worm programs, but it does not provide full protection. Most malicious software, such as worm and Trojan horse programs, are spread by e-mail attachments. Since e-mail ports are typically left open for communication, an attachment containing malicious software can gain access to the computer or network system.

The firewall settings will automatically change according to the type of network environment (Home, Work, Public, or Domain) that is selected during the network configuration. For example, when a Public location is selected, most incoming ports will be blocked. Also, most software applications recognized by Microsoft are also automatically configured through the firewall during the configuration process. For example, the firewall will automatically unblock port 110 during the configuration process of e-mail that uses a POP3 e-mail client.

Note
Microsoft recommends that you disable the firewall when using a third-party firewall system.

Equipment and Materials

❏ Windows 7 computer.

Procedure

1. _____ Report to your assigned workstation.

2. _____ Boot the computer and verify it is in working order.

3. _____ Open Windows Firewall by accessing **Control Panel | System and Security | Windows Firewall**. You should see a dialog box similar to the one in the following screen capture.

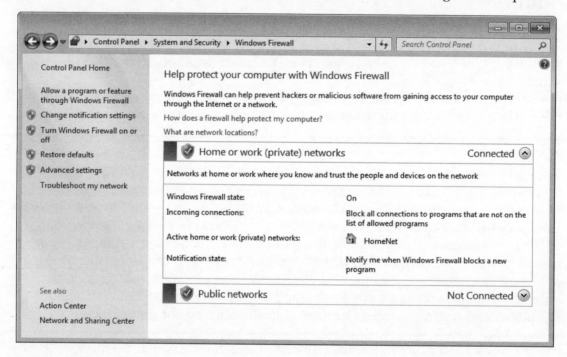

You will see the two major firewall locations listed as Home or work (private) networks and Public networks. Windows Firewall is automatically configured to match the type of network location and provide the best security for that location type without compromising functionality.

4. _____ Click the What are network locations? link and read the information provided to answer the following questions.

What are the four network locations? _____

Which type of network is controlled by a network administrator? _____

Name _____

For which two types of network is Network Discovery turned on by default? _____

_____

Is HomeGroup available for the **Public network** option? _____

5. _____ Close the **Windows Help and Support** dialog box. The Windows Firewall will still be open on your desktop. In the left pane of Window Firewall, you will see the two options **Change notification settings** and **Turn Windows Firewall on and off**. Selecting either will produce a dialog box similar to the one in the following screen capture.

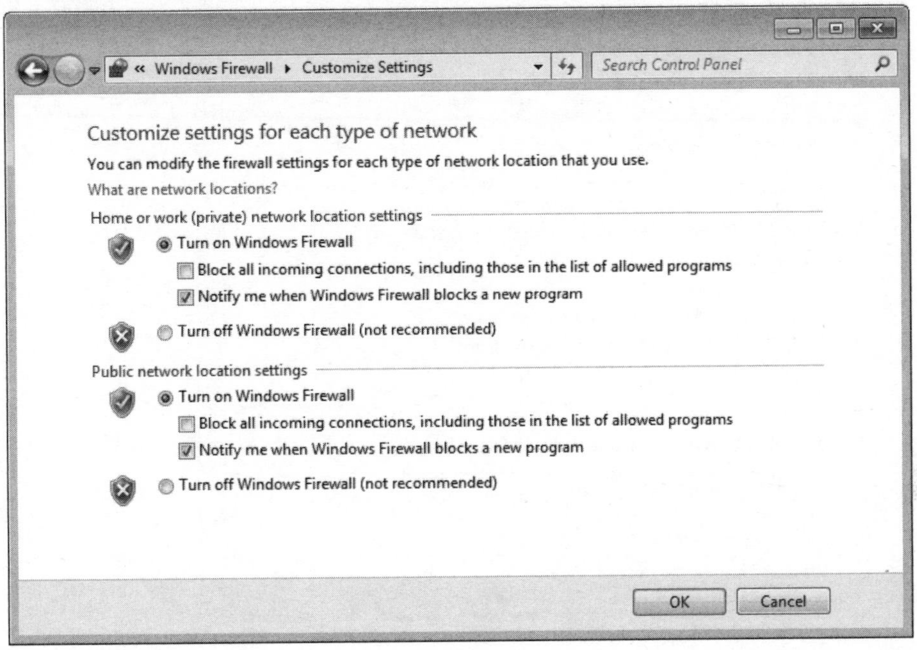

Notice the options available in the dialog box. The first set of options correlate to a Home or Work type of network location. The second set correlates to a Public type of location. The options for each are duplicated. This is where you turn the Windows Firewall on or off and also decide if you want to be notified when Windows blocks a new program.

6. _____ Close the dialog box. Window Firewall should still be in view.

7. _____ Notice the **Restore defaults** option in the left pane of Windows Firewall. Select this option to restore the default settings, and then write the message that appears in the dialog box in the space below.

_____

_____

8. _____ Use the left arrow to return to Windows Firewall or close the dialog box and open the Windows Firewall again.

9. _____ Select the **Advance settings** option. The **Windows Firewall with Advanced Security** console will display, similar to that in the following screen capture.

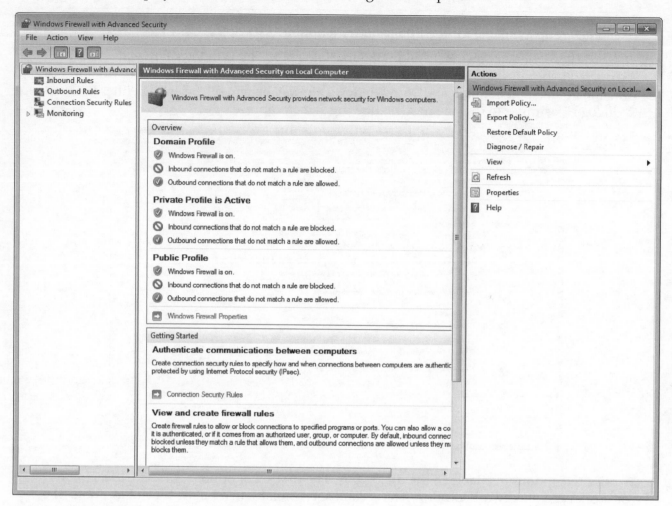

10. _____ In the left pane, select **Inbound Rules**. This will produce a list of all rules configured for Windows Firewall.

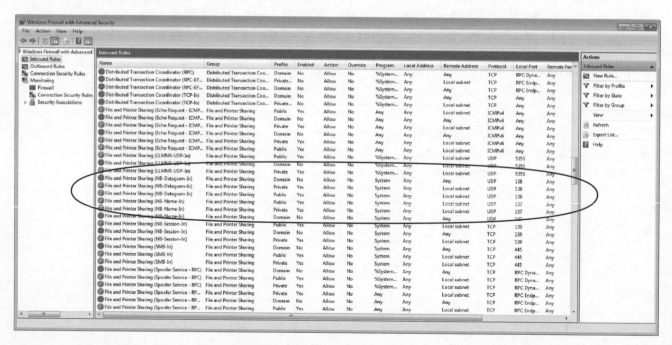

Rules are the actions associated with a specific port, protocol, service, and more. In the circled area in the previous screen capture, File and Print Sharing (NB-Datagram-In) is listed three times—once for each of the three types of locations: Domain, Private, and Public. The location type is listed in the **Profile** column.

The **Enabled** column lists Yes or No indicating if the firewall is enabled for this feature. When the inbound rule is enabled, a check mark in a green circle will appear to the left of the **Name** column. If the firewall is not enabled for the feature, a check mark in a gray circle is used.

Notice that the port number assigned is located in the **Local Port** column. In the screen capture, port number 138 is assigned to the three File and Print Sharing (NB-Datagram-In) entries.

11. _____ Take a minute and look at the column labels running from left to right across the chart of inbound rules. You can use the slide at the bottom to see any columns hidden from view.

12. _____ Locate the inbound rule "File and Printer Sharing (NB-Datagram-In)." Open it by right-clicking it and selecting **Properties** from the shortcut menu or by double-clicking it. A **Properties** dialog box will appear similar to the one in the following screen capture.

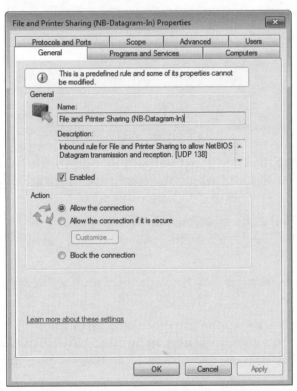

Under the **General** tab, you will see the name of the inbound rule as well as a brief description and options for changing the configuration of the rule. For example, you can enable or disable the rule. You can also modify the action by selecting the **Allow the connection**, **Allow the connection if it is secure**, or **Block the connection option**.

Pay particular attention to the fact that some of the properties for this inbound rule cannot be modified as indicated by the message in the yellow textbox. This means that by Microsoft design, certain services must have specific configuration features to work properly, and therefore, cannot be changed.

Clicking on the link labeled Learn more about these settings will open the Help and Support information associated with this dialog box.

13. _____ Select the **Advanced** tab. A dialog box similar to the following will display.

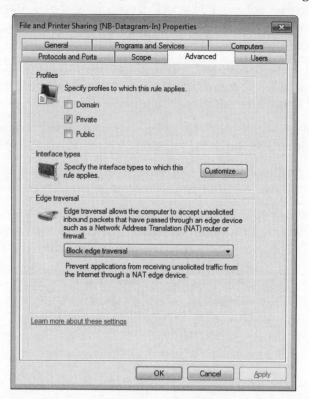

Notice how you can select the type of network location to enable for this rule. There is also an option that will allow you to select which interface type (network adapter) to apply this rule to when you have more than one network adapter installed.

The bottom section labeled **Edge traversal** allows you to configure how the rule should be applied when a network edge device is encountered on the network. An edge device is a NAT router or another firewall.

The Learn more about these settings link is available, which will provide more information about the configuration options.

14. _____ Take a few minutes to explore the other tabs associated with the dialog box so that you can see the various ways the inbound rule can be configured. For example, you can configure the inbound rule for specific users, computers, IP addresses, programs, and services.

15. _____ Identify which port number or numbers are associated with the following inbound rules and outbound rules.

Inbound Rules

■ File and Printer Sharing (SMB-In) _____

■ File and Printer Sharing (NB-Name-In) _____

■ Core Networking–Dynamic Host Configuration Protocol (DHCP-In) _____

■ Core Networking–Dynamic Host Configuration Protocol for IPv6 (DHCPv6-In) _____

■ FTP Server (FTP Traffic-In) _____

■ Remote Desktop (TCP-In) _____

■ World Wide Web Services (HTTP Traffic-In) _____

■ Windows Peer-to-Peer Collaboration Foundation (PNRP-In) _____

Outbound Rules

■ Core Networking–DNS (UDP-Out) _____

■ Core Networking–Dynamic Host Configuration Protocol (DHCP-Out) _____

■ Core Networking–Dynamic Host Configuration Protocol for IPv6 (DHCPv6-Out) _____

■ File and Printer Sharing (LLMNR-UDP-Out) _____

■ File and Printer Sharing (NB-Datagram-Out) _____

■ File and Printer Sharing (SMB-Out) _____

■ Network Discovery (SSDP-Out) _____

■ SNMP Service (UDP-Out) _____

16. _____ Close all open dialog boxes and then access Windows Firewall again.

17. _____ In the left pane, select **Allow a program or feature through Windows Firewall**. A dialog box similar to the following will display.

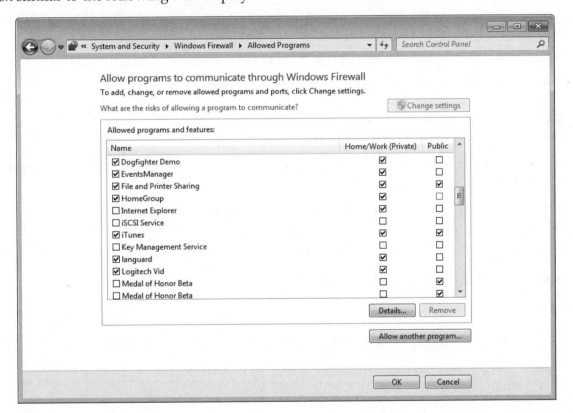

When programs are installed on a computer, they are typically identified by Windows Firewall and automatically configured to allow a connection to a remote port and to a local port. You will usually be prompted during the program installation and asked if you wish to permit the program to access the remote site or a local service. When allowed, the appropriate port numbers are assigned. The automatic configuration is not always successful, and you may need to manually configure a program. That is the purpose of the **Allow another program** button. This button will start a wizard that will allow you to configure a specific program or search for one using the **Browse** button. Click the **Allow another program** button and then take a minute to explore the **Add a Program** dialog box that displays. Only explore this dialog box. Do *not* actually allow another program to have access through Windows Firewall at this time.

18. _____ Close all open dialog boxes and return all materials to their proper storage area.

19. _____ Answer the review questions.

Review Questions

1. What is the purpose of a firewall? _____

    _____

2. What are the four network locations identified in Windows 7?_____

    _____

3. Which two network locations turn Network Discovery on by default? _____

    _____

4. Yes *or* No. HomeGroup is available for all network locations._____

5. Which two port numbers are associated with Core Networking—Dynamic Host Configuration Protocol (DHCP-In)?_____

6. Which port number is associated with FTP Server (FTP Traffic-In)? _____

7. Which port number is associated with Remote Desktop (TCP-In)? _____

8. Which port number is associated with World Wide Web Services (HTTP Traffic-In)?_____

9. Which port number is associated with Core Networking–DNS (UDP-Out)? _____

10. Which two port numbers are associated with Core Networking—Dynamic Host Configuration Protocol (DHCP-Out)? _____

11. Which two port numbers are associated with Core Networking—Dynamic Host Configuration Protocol for IPv6 (DHCP-Out)?_____

12. Which port number is associated with Network Discovery (SSDP-Out)? _____

13. Why are some of the inbound and outbound rules repeated two or three times?_____

    _____

    _____

Laboratory Activity

77

Name_____ Date _____

Class/Instructor _____

Digital Certificates

After completing this laboratory activity, you will be able to:

■ Recall the purpose of a digital certificate.
■ Identify sources of digital certificates.
■ Use Certificate Manager to view digital certificates located on a computer.
■ Use the Certificate Export Wizard to back up a digital certificate.

Introduction

Digital certificates are mainly used to establish identities prior to securely exchanging information. The typical uses of digital certificates are securing e-mail messages, securing remote server logons, verifying the integrity of a software program, and making a secure online purchase. There are several common sources of digital certificates found on a workstation or server. Some are loaded on to the computer when the operating system or software is installed. Some are loaded on to the computer during an SSL session on the Internet. Some have been purchased from a digital certificate company to be used for personal or company use.

Microsoft refers to the location of where certificates are stored as the *certificate store*. You can access the certificate store through the **Internet Properties** dialog box, which is accessed through **Control Panel | Network and Internet | Internet Options**. The **Internet Properties** dialog box will display. Select the **Content** tab and then click the **Certificates** button to access the certificate store. You can also access **Internet Properties** by entering "Internet options" in the **Search** box off of the **Start** menu.

Certificates on a workstation typically contain a public key that is used to exchange encrypted information with a company server that contains the private key. Certificates contain more than just a public encryption key. They usually contain the issuing authority name and validity dates.

In this laboratory activity, you will explore the certificate store and view information about the certificates. You will also back up a certificate.

Equipment and Materials

❑ Windows 7 computer.
❑ USB flash drive for certificate backup.

Note
The laboratory activity is very similar when using Windows Vista, but it is not an exact match.

Procedure

1. _____ Report to your assigned workstation.

2. _____ Boot the computer and verify it is in working order.

3. _____ There are two common ways to access a dialog box to view digital certificate information. One way is to enter "certmgr.msc" into the **Search** box located off the **Start** menu. You must include the ".msc" file extension or the program will not appear in the search list results. The certmgr.msc program will appear at the top of the list under **Programs**. After selecting certmgr.msc from the list, you will see the Certificate Manager console similar to the one in the following screen capture.

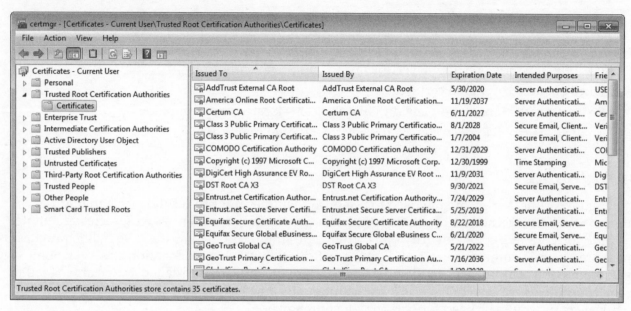

The Certificate Manager console contains a list of all digital certificates installed on the computer. Notice that the tree directory in the left pane is arranged by classifications, such as Personal, Trusted Root Certification Authorities, and more. This provides a quick and easy way to locate digital certificates by function or classification.

4. _____ Open the Certificate Manager console on your computer now by entering "certmgr.msc" into the **Search** box.

5. _____ Close the Certificate Manager console.

6. _____ The second common way to access a dialog box to view digital certificate information is through the **Internet Properties** dialog box. The **Internet Properties** dialog box can be accessed through **Control Panel | Network and Internet | Internet Options**. You can also enter "Internet" into the **Search** box and then select "Internet Options" located under **Control Panel** section of the **Search** results list. When the **Internet Properties** dialog box displays, select the **Content** tab and then click the **Certificates** button.

Name _____

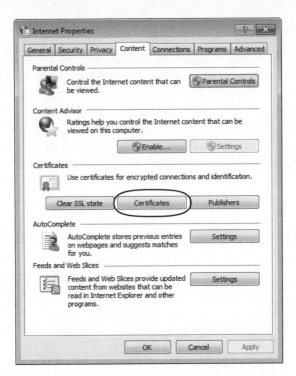

After clicking the **Certificates** button you will see the **Certificates** dialog box similar to that in the following screen capture.

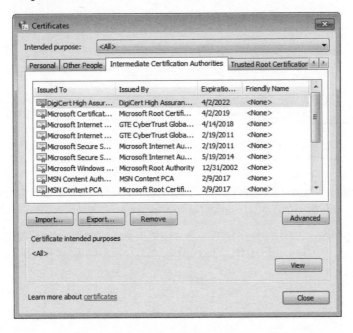

The classification of certificate is grouped by the dialog box tab system. You can select the type of certificate by selecting the corresponding tab. For example, to view any personal certificates installed on the computer, you would select the **Personal** tab.

7. _____ After opening the **Certificates** dialog box, take minutes to view all the tabs: **Personal**, **Other People**, **Intermediate Certification Authorities**, **Trusted Root Certification Authorities**, **Trusted Publishers**, and **Untrusted Publishers**. You will need to use the arrows located at the right of the tabs to view the hidden tabs.

Personal certificates belong to the computer's owner. Other People certificates are obtained from other people, such as people you correspond with using e-mail. Trusted Root Certification Authorities and Immediate Certification Authorities require some explanation. A Trusted Root Certification Authority is a recognized self-certified source of certificate. For example, VeriSign is a company that creates certificates for other companies and individuals; hence, it is a "Root" Certificate Authority. It originated the certificate. An Intermediate Certification Authority is a company that uses certificates that were created by a root Certificate Authority such as VeriSign. Trusted Publishers and Untrusted Publishers are typically software publishers. Under the **Untrusted Publishers** tab, do not be surprised to see two certificates listed as Microsoft Corporation certificates. These are not true Microsoft certificates, but actual forgeries used to send out e-mail announcements. After being originally discovered, they were immediately revoked and, thus, pose no danger.

8. _____ Select the **Trusted Root Certification Authorities** tab. A dialog box similar to the following will display.

9. _____ Click one of the items in the list and watch as the box labeled **Certificate intended purposes** located at the bottom of the dialog box changes.

10. _____ Select one of the certificates on the **Trusted Root Certification Authorities** tab and then click the **View** button. A dialog box that reveals details about that particular certificate will display.

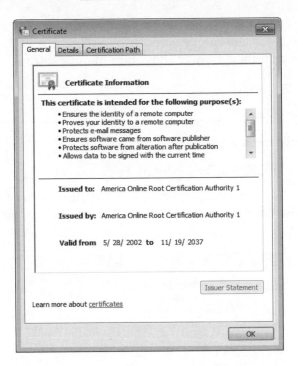

The purpose of the certificate is described and additional tabs are provided that allow you to view detailed information about the certificate. Take a few minutes to explore several certificates before moving on in the laboratory activity. When you are finished, close all open dialog boxes.

11. _____ Open the **Certificates** dialog box again and then select the **Personal** tab. A dialog box similar to the following will display.

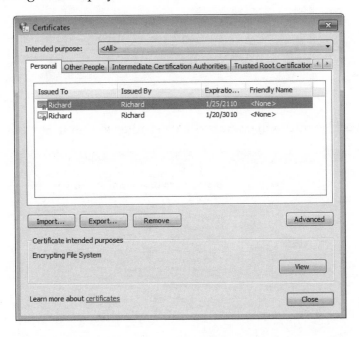

The Personal certificates are the computer owner certificates that were automatically generated when certain configurations were made on the computer. The Personal certificates on your computer will not necessarily match the ones in the screen capture. The screen capture shows two Personal certificates. The first was created when a file or folder on the computer was encrypted. The second was created when the computer joined a peer-to-peer network. Take a minute to explore the Personal certificates on your computer. You should have Personal certificates created from prior laboratory activities. Explore one of the Personal certificates located on the computer and then answer the following questions.

What is the certificate used for? _____

When will the certificate expire? _____

How many bits are used for the encryption? _____

Does the certificate use a public key or a private key? _____

12. _____ To back up a digital certificate, double-click the digital certificate or highlight it and click the **View** button. The **Certificate** dialog box will open. Select the **Details** tab and then click the **Copy to File** button.

The Certificate Export Wizard will open and look similar to that in the following screen capture.

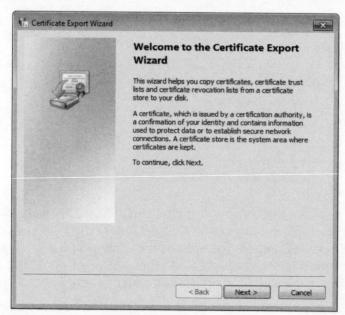

The wizard will prompt you with a series of dialog boxes asking for input concerning the backup of the certificate. Follow the wizard prompts and back up the Personal certificate to a USB drive. Call your instructor to inspect your work.

13. _____ Answer all review questions and then return all materials to their proper storage area.

Review Questions

1. What is the purpose of a digital certificate? _____
   _____
   ` _____

2. Where do certificates come from? _____
   _____
   _____
   _____
   _____
   _____

3. What is a certificate store? _____
   _____

4. Which type of key is typically stored on a workstation—public or private? _____

5. How do you make a backup of a certificate? _____

Laboratory Activity

78

Name_____ Date _____

Class/Instructor _____

SANS Organization

After completing this laboratory activity, you will be able to:
- ❑ Recall the purpose of the SANS organization.
- ❑ Summarize the Web content located at www.SANS.org.

Introduction

This laboratory activity will familiarize you with the SANS organization Web site. The acronym SANS represents SysAdmin, Audit, Network, Security. SANS was first established in 1989 as a research and educational organization mainly concerned with information technology security. The SANS Web site, located at www.SANS.org, contains the most up-to-date and in-depth security materials and training. Some materials are free, and some require purchase. There is an information security reading room that contains over 1,200 articles. There are step-by-step guides and security policy templates available and much more as you will see during this laboratory activity.

Equipment and Materials

- ❑ Windows XP or later computer with Internet access.

Procedure

1. _____ Report to your assigned workstation.

2. _____ Boot the computer and verify it is in working order.

3. _____ Access the SANS organization Web site home page at www.SANS.org.

4. _____ On the home page, locate and then open the About SANS link. Answer the following questions. Record your answers in the spaces provided.

   What is GIAC? _____

   _____

   What is the Internet Storm Center? _____

   _____

   _____

5. _____ Select the Resources link. You will see many of the resources available concerning security. Look for the Top 20 security vulnerabilities list. Scan the list.

6. _____ Now, select the SANS Security Policy Samples link, which is listed on the Resources page. Take a few minutes to explore the policy templates. The policy templates are outlines of policies that can be used by companies to create their own policy book for IT security. This is a fabulous resource for saving time when creating your own network security policy book.

7. _____ Select the Glossary of Security Terms link, which is listed on the Resources page. Answer the following questions. Record your answers in the spaces provided.

How is the term *Kerberos* defined? _____

_____

_____

_____

_____

_____

How is the term *IP Spoofing* defined? _____

_____

_____

_____

_____

How is the term *Public Key* defined? _____

_____

_____

_____

_____

8. _____ Select the Internet Storm Center link, which is listed on the Resources page.

What type of information is contained on the Internet Storm Center page? _____

_____

_____

_____

9. _____ Select the Malware FAQ link, which is listed on the Resources page.

What information is contained on the Malware FAQ page? _____

_____

_____

_____

_____

10. _____ Navigate the Web site for a few minutes to explore your own interests.

11. _____ Answer the review questions.

Review Questions

1. What does the acronym SANS represent?_____

_____

2. What is the primary function of the SANS organization?_____

_____

_____

Laboratory Activity

79

Name_____ Date _____

Class/Instructor _____

TCP/IP Filtering

After completing this laboratory activity, you will be able to:

■ Recall the names of the three IANA port number ranges.

■ Recall the role of port numbers in association with the TCP/IP suite.

■ Use the New Inbound Rule Wizard to filter TCP/IP connections by port number.

Introduction

In an earlier laboratory activity, you used Windows Firewall to explore how port numbers are used to filter TCP/IP connections. In this laboratory activity, you will filter TCP, UDP, and IP port activity using the New Inbound Rule Wizard.

TCP/IP filtering is used typically as a security feature to prevent certain software programs from communicating with a computer by blocking all packets to a specific port number. For example, you could stop all instant messaging on your computer by blocking port number 1863. Instant messaging has been identified as a potential security problem on private networks connected to the Internet.

The Internet Assigned Numbers Authority (IANA) is an organization responsible for overseeing the assigning of IP addresses, port numbers, and port number identification. You can see the complete set of port numbers identified by IANA at www.iana.org/assignments/port-numbers.

Packets contain address information, such as IP address and port number. The IP address is used to direct the packet to the correct host on the network, and the port number is used to identify which server or software program will receive the contents of the packet. Port numbers are used by the TCP/IP suite of protocols to establish connections for services and programs. A port number is used to match the software program or service to the information contained inside a network packet. For example, an HTTP packet uses port 80. This port number identifies that the contents are to be sent to the browser software program, such as Internet Explorer or Firefox.

Port numbers are assigned by the IANA organization so that a standard for using port numbers can be maintained. For example, you would not want two different software vendors using the same port number for their software programs when communicating over a network using TCP/IP. If two vendors used the same software for different purposes, there would be a conflict. One of the software programs would fail to work. At times, two software packages can be assigned the same port number as long as a method to prevent interfering with other software programs has been incorporated into the software.

The port numbers are divided into three ranges: well-known ports, registered ports, and dynamic and/or private ports. Well-known ports range from 0 to 1023, registered ports range from 1024 to 49151, and dynamic and/or private ports range from 49152 to 65535.

The well-known port numbers are assigned by IANA and are used for specific core network processes such as FTP, echo request, time, DHCP, DNS, and HTTP. The registered port numbers are registered to specific companies and organizations to support their software packages. For example,

Shockwave uses port 1626, and the games Half-Life and Counter-Strike use port 27010 for online gaming. At times, port numbers can create a conflict between two programs causing one to fail.

The dynamic and/or private range is not assigned, but rather it is used to provide connectivity on a temporary basis when required. The dynamic and/or private port numbers can be used by any software program and are not regulated.

Equipment and Materials

❑   Windows 7 computer with Internet access.

Procedure

1. _____ Report to your assigned workstation.

2. _____ Boot the computer and verify it is in working order.

3. _____ Access **Control Panel | System and Security | Windows Firewall | Advanced settings | Inbound Rules**. You will see a list of inbound rules similar to those in the following screen capture.

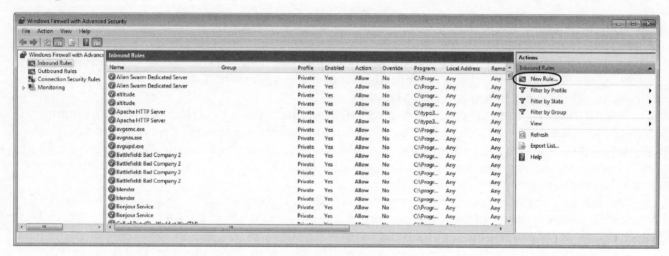

4. _____ Select the **New Rule** option located in the right pane to start the New Inbound Rule Wizard. There are four rule types to choose from: **Program**, **Port**, **Predefined**, and **Custom**.

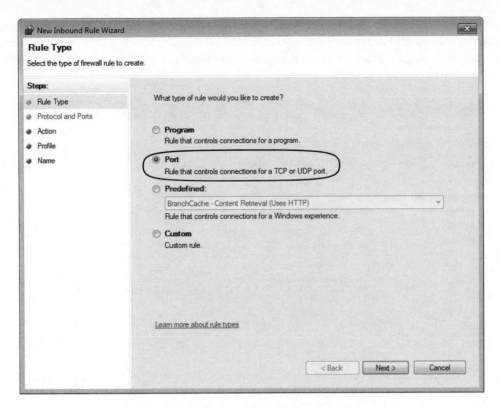

The **Program** option refers to software programs located on the computer. The **Port** option refers to port numbers associated with programs and services. The **Predefined** option refers to predefined inbound rule configurations. The **Custom** option refers to an inbound rule for a program or service not covered by any of the three other options—for example, an undetected software application.

5. _____ For this lab activity, select the **Port** option and then click **Next**. A dialog box similar to the following will display, prompting you to identify to which one of the two protocols, TCP or UDP, the rule is to apply. There is also an option to select all local ports and to specify a specific port or a range of ports.

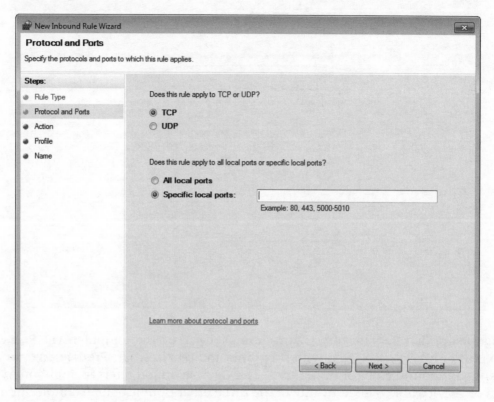

6. _____ Select **TCP** and **Specific local ports**. Enter "5000" in the **Specific local ports** text box and then click **Next**. A dialog box will display, prompting you to select a type of action associated with the port. The options displayed are **Allow the connection, Allow the connection if it is secure**, and **Block the connection**.

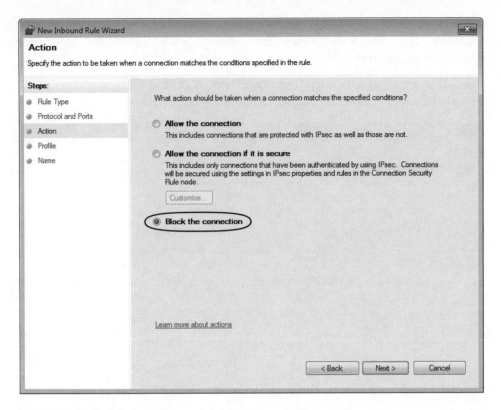

7. _____ Select **Block the connection** and then click **Next**. The next dialog box presents three profile options that relate directly to the type of network location: **Domain**, **Private**, and **Public**.

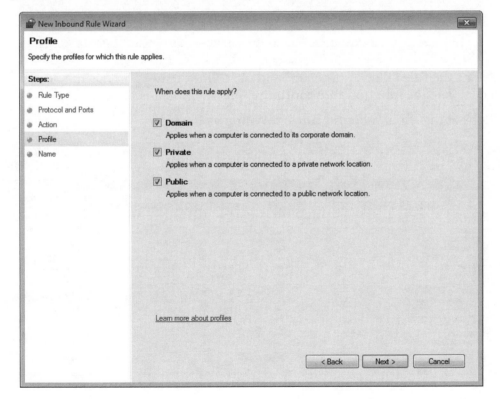

Notice that the three profiles correspond to the three network location types that are encountered when first setting up or modifying a network location. You can apply this rule to any combination of location types.

8. _____ Select all three locations and then click **Next**. A dialog box similar to the following will display, prompting you to name and describe the inbound rule.

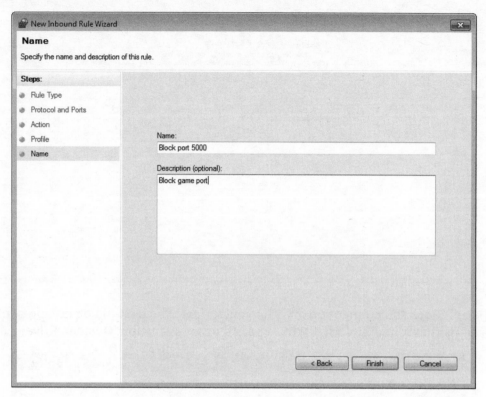

9. _____ Name the rule "Block port 5000" and use "Block game port" as the description. Click **Finish** to complete the inbound rule configuration.

10. _____ Look at the list of inbound rules in Windows Firewall.

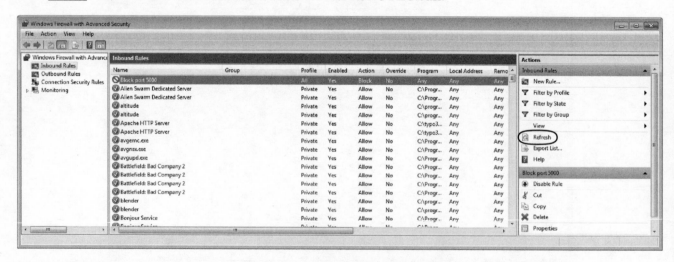

At the top of the list you will see "Block port 5000." If you closed and reopened Windows Firewall, the inbound rules will be listed alphabetically by default. You may need to scroll down the list to see the new rule you created. If the new inbound rule fails to appear in the list, select the **Refresh** option located in the right pane.

Note that the color of the icon for the inbound rule is red in contrast to the other inbound rules. A red icon indicates that the port is blocked, and green icon indicates that the port is open.

Using the slide control, you can view the hidden information about the rule, such as the actual assigned port number.

11. _____ Call your instructor to view the "Block port 5000" rule.

12. _____ Now, double-click the "Block port 5000" rule and then change the configuration to allow the port. Simply select the appropriate option corresponding to allow the connection.

13. _____ View the list of inbound rules once more. You should see that the "Block port 5000" rule has a green icon indicating that it is an allowed port connection.

14. _____ Remove the rule by right-clicking it and selecting **Delete** from the shortcut menu.

15. _____ Inspect the inbound rule list to verify the "Block port 5000" rule has been deleted.

16. _____ Return all materials to their proper storage area and then answer the review questions.

Review Questions

1. Which two protocols are typically associated with port number filtering? _____

2. What is the purpose of port filtering? _____

_____

_____

3. List the names of the three major port number groups and their corresponding port number ranges. _____

_____

_____

4. Which set of port numbers are not regulated? _____

5. What role do port numbers play in support of the TCP/IP protocol suite? _____

_____

_____

6. What are the three profile options that can be assigned to the filtered port? _____

_____

7. Who is in charge of regulating port number assignments? _____

8. What color icon is used to indicate that the port is blocked? _____

9. What color icon is used to indicate that the port is open? _____

Laboratory Activity

80

Name_____ Date _____

Class/Instructor _____

Wireshark OSI Model Exploration

After completing this laboratory activity, you will be able to:

- Use the Wireshark Network Protocol Analyzer to match protocols to the OSI model.
- Identify the protocols responsible for MAC address, IP address, and port numbers.
- Explain how protocols encapsulate data and other protocols.

Introduction

In this laboratory activity, you will use the Wireshark Network Protocol Analyzer to compare the relationship of specific protocols to the layers of the OSI model. You can typically determine the OSI layer a protocol aligns with by looking at its relative position in the hierarchy of protocols in the Wireshark program. Look at the following screen capture. Notice that the hierarchy of protocols is displayed in the middle pane of the Wireshark screen. Each frame that is selected displays its own hierarchy. The typical hierarchy lists at the top of the pane the protocol related to the bottom-most OSI layer.

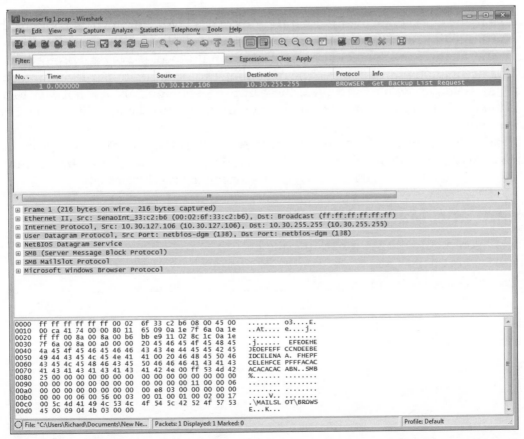

Clicking the box with a plus sign in it can reveal more information about each protocol listed in the hierarchy. This information may reveal items such as source, destination, MAC, and port addresses.

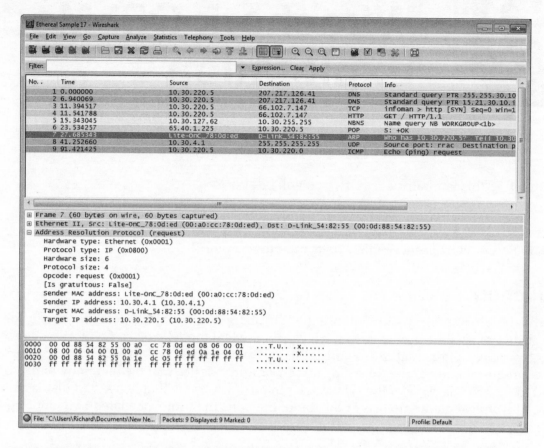

According to the OSI model, the Ethernet II protocol is a layer 2 protocol. It contains the MAC address of the destination and source. The Internet Protocol is a layer 3 protocol. It contains the IP address of the destination and source. The User Datagram Protocol is a layer 4 protocol. It contains the source and destination port numbers. The remaining protocols are upper-level protocols (layers 5, 6, and 7). Unless you know the function of these upper-level protocols, it is not easy to determine their location in the OSI model. Many protocols span more than one layer because they perform more than one function.

In this laboratory activity, you will open and inspect a Wireshark capture file (provided by your instructor) and identify to which OSI layer each protocol in the capture should be assigned. Layers 5, 6, and 7 are combined for this activity. Layer 1 does not exist for this activity.

Equipment and Materials

❏ Windows 7 computer with Wireshark installed.
❏ Wireshark Sample 20 file.

Wireshark Sample 20 file location: _____

Name _____

Procedure

1. _____ Report to your assigned workstation.
2. _____ Boot the computer and verify it is in working order.
3. _____ Start the Wireshark Network Protocol Analyzer utility.
4. _____ Open the Wireshark Sample 20 file.
5. _____ Place an X in the corresponding OSI model layer in the table and write out the protocol name for each protocol displayed in the capture.

Protocol	Layer 2	Layer 3	Layer 4	Layers 5, 6, 7	Protocol Name
Ethernet II					
ARP					
IP					
TCP					
UDP					
SMTP					
POP					
NBNS					
HTTP					
SMB2					
DNS					
LLMNR					
ICMP					
RIPv2					

6. _____ After completing the table, go on to answer the review questions.
7. _____ Return the computer to its original condition.

Review Questions

1. Which protocol was found at layer 2 throughout this lab activity? _____
2. Which protocols were found at layer 3 throughout this lab activity? _____
3. Which protocols were found at layer 4 throughout this lab activity? _____
4. Which protocols were not specifically identified, but are typically found at layers 5, 6, and 7?___

_____

5. What protocols are used to encapsulate the upper-level (5, 6, and 7) protocols?_____

6. Which protocol uses the MAC address to identify the location of the destination and source?___

_____

7. Which protocol uses the IPv4 address to locate the source and destination? _____

8. Which protocols use the port number to identify the source and destination? _____

9. Explain how protocol encapsulation provides all the required information for data packet delivery. _____

_____

_____

Laboratory Activity

81

Name_____ Date _____

Class/Instructor _____

Route Print Command

After completing this laboratory activity, you will be able to:

- Interpret a routing table.
- Recall the role of a default gateway.
- Use the **route print** command to view a routing table.

Introduction

In this laboratory activity, you will inspect the routing table of a typical computer and identify the default gateway router. Gateways are important for establishing TCP/IP connections between different network segments. A gateway is usually a router.

Network adapters are associated with a routing table. A routing table provides information about network connections to and from the network adapter based on IP addresses and subnet masks. The information contained in the routing table can be viewed by issuing the **route print** command from the command prompt.

To better understand the information in a routing table, first look at the results from the **ipconfig/all** command shown in the following screen capture. Notice that the network adapter is assigned the IP address of 192.168.1.100 with a subnet mask of 255.255.255.0. The default gateway for the workstation's network adapter is 192.168.1.1.

```
Command Prompt

C:\Users\Richard>ipconfig/all

Windows IP Configuration

    Host Name . . . . . . . . . . . . : Richard-PCwin7
    Primary Dns Suffix  . . . . . . . :
    Node Type . . . . . . . . . . . . : Hybrid
    IP Routing Enabled. . . . . . . . : No
    WINS Proxy Enabled. . . . . . . . : No
    DNS Suffix Search List. . . . . . : hsd1.fl.comcast.net.

Ethernet adapter Local Area Connection:

    Connection-specific DNS Suffix  . : hsd1.fl.comcast.net.
    Description . . . . . . . . . . . : Realtek PCIe GBE Family Controller
    Physical Address. . . . . . . . . : 00-26-18-FD-50-DA
    DHCP Enabled. . . . . . . . . . . : Yes
    Autoconfiguration Enabled . . . . : Yes
    Link-local IPv6 Address . . . . . : fe80::79f4:e012:74b4:5f1%11(Preferred)
    IPv4 Address. . . . . . . . . . . : 192.168.1.100(Preferred)
    Subnet Mask . . . . . . . . . . . : 255.255.255.0
    Lease Obtained. . . . . . . . . . : Thursday, November 11, 2010 10:01:08 AM
    Lease Expires . . . . . . . . . . : Saturday, November 13, 2010 1:12:12 AM
    Default Gateway . . . . . . . . . : 192.168.1.1
    DHCP Server . . . . . . . . . . . : 192.168.1.1
    DHCPv6 IAID . . . . . . . . . . . : 234890776
    DHCPv6 Client DUID. . . . . . . . : 00-01-00-01-12-80-D0-23-00-26-18-FD-50-DA
    DNS Servers . . . . . . . . . . . : 68.87.74.166
                                        68.87.68.166
    NetBIOS over Tcpip. . . . . . . . : Enabled

Tunnel adapter isatap.hsd1.fl.comcast.net.:

    Media State . . . . . . . . . . . : Media disconnected
    Connection-specific DNS Suffix  . : hsd1.fl.comcast.net.
    Description . . . . . . . . . . . : Microsoft ISATAP Adapter
    Physical Address. . . . . . . . . : 00-00-00-00-00-00-00-E0
    DHCP Enabled. . . . . . . . . . . : No
    Autoconfiguration Enabled . . . . : Yes

Tunnel adapter Local Area Connection* 12:

    Connection-specific DNS Suffix  . :
    Description . . . . . . . . . . . : Teredo Tunneling Pseudo-Interface
    Physical Address. . . . . . . . . : 00-00-00-00-00-00-00-E0
    DHCP Enabled. . . . . . . . . . . : No
    Autoconfiguration Enabled . . . . : Yes
    IPv6 Address. . . . . . . . . . . : 2001:0:4137:9e76:2cb4:3ee6:bbc7:cb18(Preferred)
    Link-local IPv6 Address . . . . . : fe80::2cb4:3ee6:bbc7:cb18%13(Preferred)
    Default Gateway . . . . . . . . . : ::
    NetBIOS over Tcpip. . . . . . . . : Disabled

C:\Users\Richard>_
```

In this case, the default gateway is a gateway router used to connect several workstations to the Internet through a Cable modem. Now, look at the following screen capture of a routing table generated by issuing the **route print** command. You will see both the IPv4 and the IPv6 routing information displayed. The routing table is divided into three major sections: Interface List, IPv4 Route Table, and IPv6 Route Table.

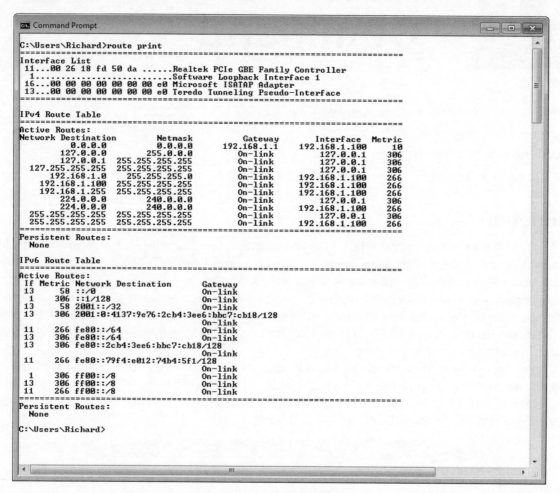

The Interface List contains information related to the network adapters installed in the local computer. The table displays the network adapter MAC address for the network adapter "00 26 18 fd 50 da Realtek PCIe GBE Family Controller." The routing table only shows the routes for the network-connected adapter.

You will also see that there are several interfaces with "00 00 00 00 00 00" as the assigned MAC address. These represent virtual network adapters used for IPv6 transition technologies such as Teredo and ISATAP. Both technologies are designed to tunnel IPv6 packets through IPv4 networks.

Now, look at the IPv4 Route Table section. This section displays a list of active routes associated with the network adapter. Most of this information was provided when the network adapter was configured. Notice that the table has five headings: **Network Destination**, **Netmask**, **Gateway**, **Interface**, and **Metric**.

- *Network destination* refers to a destination network address, not to a specific network adapter. For example, when the address 192.168.1.100 is assigned with a subnet mask of 255.255.255.0, the network address is 192.168.1.0.

- *Netmask* is similar to the subnet mask with the exception that all 0s are used to indicate the default gateway netmask, and all 255s are used to indicate the default broadcast netmask. Relatively new is the 240.0.0.0 multicast netmask.

- *Gateway* is the gateway.
- *Interface* is the local network adapter card.
- *Metric* is an assigned value for a particular route. The metric values are used to compare the various routes to take when more than one route exists. Typically, the lowest numeric metric is chosen first.

The first line in the IPv4 Route Table displays the destination of the route as 0.0.0.0. When the **Network Destination** column is filled with 0.0.0.0, it indicates the default route or default gateway. In the example, the row for this entry indicates that the default gateway is 192.168.1.1 and the local network adapter IP address is 192.168.1.100. You can use the following table as an aid for interpreting the table information concerning IPv4 network destinations.

Type	Netmask
Default route	0.0.0.0
Loopback	255.0.0.0
Multicast	224.0.0.0
Broadcast	255.255.255.255

The IPv6 Route Table section is relatively new. It provides IPv6 routing information for the local network adapter. Since IPv6 has not yet been fully implemented, the information is limited.

The IPv6 Route Table has four headings: **If** (interface), **Metric**, **Network Destination**, and **Gateway**. In the IPv4 Route Table, the default route or default gateway is indicated by "0.0.0.0." In the IPv6 routing table, the default route or default gateway is indicated by "::/0."

Some computer motherboards are equipped with two network adapters. For example, a computer configured as an Internet Connection Server (ICS) has one network adapter to connect to the Internet and another network adapter to connect to network. When a computer is equipped with more than one network adapter, it is referred to as a *multihomed computer*.

Failure to connect to the proper default gateway can result in network communication failure and or unusual communication results. The default gateway in a typical network setting is usually a router. A router can maintain a table of routes that are either automatically updated or manually entered. When values are manually entered into the routing table, they are referred to as *static values* or *static addresses*. When routers update their table values automatically, they use protocols designed specifically for that purpose. The protocols communicate with joining routers and exchange information about other network locations. These routing tables are used to make decisions as to what is the best route to take when delivering a packet across a WAN.

Equipment and Materials

❑ Windows 7 computer with Internet access.

Procedure

1. _____ Report to your assigned workstation.

2. _____ Boot the computer and verify it is in working order.

3. _____ Open the command prompt and enter the **ipconfig/all** command.

4. _____ Record the following information:

Host name: _____

IPv4 address: _____

IPv4 subnet mask: _____

Default gateway: _____

IPv6 address: _____

IPv6 default gateway: _____

5. _____ At the command prompt enter the **route print** command.

6. _____ Identify the IPv4 default gateway. Look for 0.0.0.0. in the **Network Destination** column.

   Does the default gateway in the IPv4 Route Table match the default gateway identified by **ipconfig/all** command? _____

   How is the IPv6 default gateway address identified? _____

7. _____ At the command prompt enter **route/?** to see more information about the **route** command.

8. _____ Return all materials to their proper storage area and then answer the review questions.

Review Questions

1. What is the role of the default gateway? _____
   _____
   _____

2. What command is used to display the routing table? _____

3. What information is contained in the first line of an IPv4 Route Table? _____
   _____

4. What does the netmask of 0.0.0.0 indicate? _____
   _____

5. What other information is contained in the IPv4 Route Table besides the default gateway IP address and the local network adapter IP address? _____
   _____

6. What would be the result of using the wrong gateway IP address when configuring a network adapter? _____
   _____

7. What is a metric? _____
   _____

8. How is the default IPv6 gateway indicated? _____
   _____

9. What is the IPv4 multicast netmask? _____

10. What is the IPv4 broadcast netmask? _____

WINDOWS XP OR LATER

Name_____ Date _____

Class/Instructor _____

LANguard Network Security Scanner

After completing this laboratory activity, you will be able to:

- Carry out proper procedures to download and install GFI LANguard.
- Use GFI LANguard to determine if the latest patches and service packs are installed on a system.
- Use GFI LANguard to identify network client and server potential security problems.
- Use GFI LANguard to inventory workstations, servers, and other network devices.

Introduction

In this laboratory activity, you will download and install a third-part utility called GFI LANguard Network Security Scanner. GFI LANguard is a software utility designed to check for potential security problems and scan for needed maintenance items, such as software patches and service packs. Identifying missing network operating system patches and updates are critical in keeping the network system secure and in working order.

GFI LANguard checks and identifies many security vulnerabilities and recommends corrective actions. The security items include open ports, open shares, passwords that do not meet minimum security requirements, and programs that run automatically, such as Trojans. GFI LANguard also checks for USB devices such as wireless adapters, Wireless Access Points, hard drives, and cameras that might be connected to the network and considered a violation of the company security policy. As you can see, GFI LANguard is a versatile utility that conducts an in-depth check of the network.

GFI LANguard not only identifies missing patches and service packs, it can be configured to install them from one location. It can also install third-party software patches and updates. GFI LANguard also identifies and inventories most of the devices connected to the network, including the type of operating systems installed, MAC and IP addresses, domain names, and user names.

The highlights of GFI LANguard are presented in this laboratory activity. To achieve a more detailed and comprehensive understanding of GFI LANguard, you need to read the user manual, which is in PDF form. It can be downloaded for free from the GFI Web site. Using the GFI LANguard is very simple. You simply select the type of scan you wish to perform, such as **Quick Scan** or **Full Scan**.

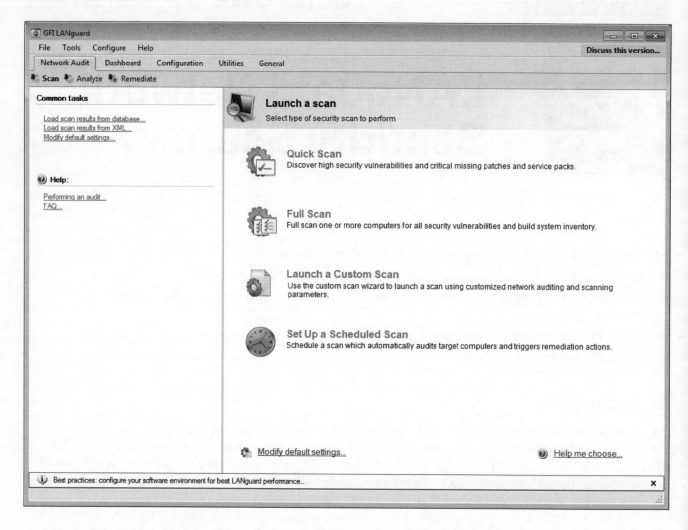

The next dialog box to appear prompts you to select the target to scan. The options are **Scan this computer**, **Scan another computer**, or **Scan the entire domain/workplace**. You can also configure a custom scan and even schedule an automatic scan.

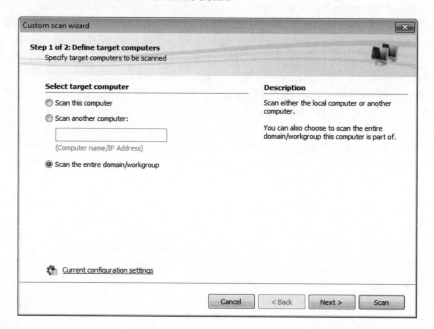

After selecting the target, you will be prompted to select credentials for the scan. This is shown in the following screen capture.

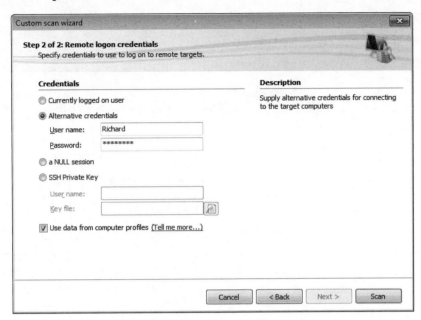

The credential options are **Currently logged on user**, **Alternative credentials**, **a NULL session**, and **SSH Private Key**. Using the **Alternative credentials** or **Currently logged on user** option allows you to detect missing patches and see vulnerabilities.

The **a NULL session** option allows you to see the network or selected target the same way a hacker would view the network. It is used to test network vulnerability to unauthorized personnel. The **SSH Private Key** option is required for connections to UNIX and Linux systems.

After selecting a credential option, you will need to press the **Scan** button to start the scan. The approximate amount of time to complete the scan will be presented along with a progress bar.

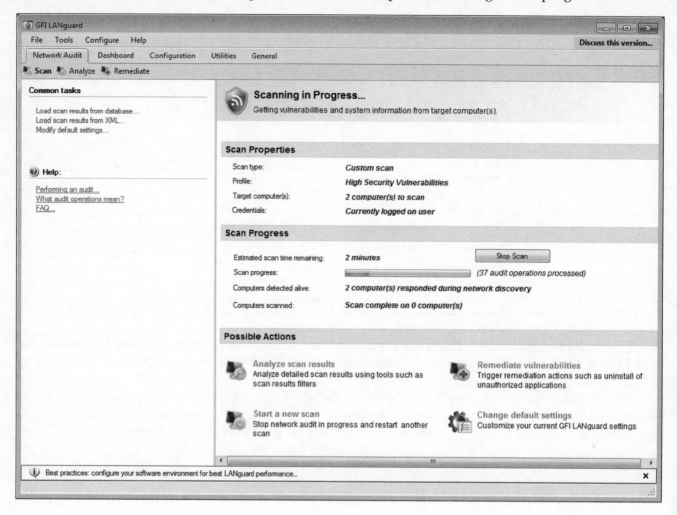

After the scan is completed, the results will be displayed similar to that in the following screen capture.

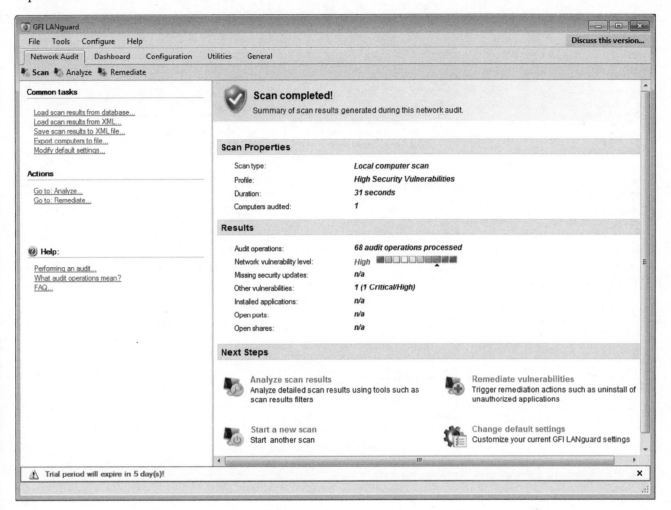

A more detailed view of scan results will be displayed when the **Analyze** option is selected under the **Network Audit** tab.

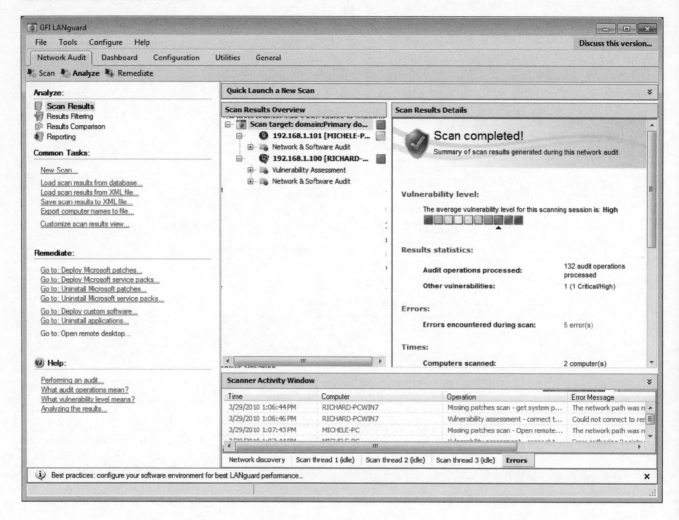

The scan results are displayed by IP address, and an overall vulnerability level is displayed as well.

Equipment and Materials

❑ Computer with Windows XP or later. Must be part of a peer-to-peer or client/server network.
❑ The following information provided by your instructor:

Administrator user name: _____

Password: _____

Note
Your instructor may supply you with a copy of GFI LANguard. This lab activity is based on GFI LANguard version 9.

Procedure

1. _____ Gather all required materials and report to your assigned workstation.

2. _____ Boot the computer and verify it is in working order.

3. _____ If you already have a copy of GFI LANguard, skip to step 6. If not, create a LANguard folder on your computer. This is where you will download the GFI LANguard program and documentation.

4. _____ Locate GFI LANguard on the Internet by either conducting an Internet search using the keywords "GFI LANguard" or going to www.GFI.com and accessing the GFI LANguard download page.

5. _____ After locating GFI LANguard, download the trial copy, the accompanying manuals, and the quick start or installation guide. You will need to refer to the installation guide when installing GFI LANguard on your computer. Make sure it is GFI LANguard that you download. GFI has many different software utilities that allow you to scan the network and check for vulnerabilities and maintenance items.

6. _____ Read the instructions carefully before installing GFI LANguard.

7. _____ After reading the instructions, install GFI LANguard.

8. _____ Use GFI LANguard to scan the network using your credentials (user name and password). Review the results.

9. _____ Run the scanner a second time with the NULL session credentials. Again, review the results.

10. _____ Take a few minutes to look over the tools available under the **Tools** menu.

11. _____ Remove the GFI LANguard utility if requested by your instructor.

12. _____ Answer the review questions. You may use the GFI LANguard manual to assist you with the review questions.

Review Questions

1. What four types of scan options are available in GFI LANguard? _____
_____
_____

2. What kind of information does the **a NULL Session** option reveal? _____
_____

3. What does the **Alternative credentials** option allow you to do? _____
_____
_____

4. What type of information can be revealed by GFI LANguard? _____
_____
_____

5. How would you determine which devices needed patches and had security vulnerabilities if you did not use a program like GFI LANguard? _____

_____

_____

_____

Laboratory Activity

83

Name_____ Date _____

Class/Instructor _____

Performing a System Backup and Restore

After completing this laboratory activity, you will be able to:

■ Use Windows Backup and Restore to backup files.

■ Use Windows Backup and Restore to restore files.

Introduction

In this laboratory activity, you will use the Windows Backup and Restore utility in Windows 7. Windows Server 2008 uses the Windows Server Backup utility, which is customized to meet the server role. However, backup terminology for all Microsoft operating systems is similar, even though it changes somewhat for each generation of operating system to better match the latest technology.

Backing up system and user files are a critical part of maintaining a network system. In this laboratory activity, you will create a folder on the hard disk drive to use as the location for the files you back up. In a real scenario, you would most likely use an internal drive, external drive, CD/DVD disc, USB flash drive, or network storage location. Backing up to a location on the default hard disk drive is not recommended because if the hard disk drive fails, you will lose the backup. Although, you could have two separate hard drives installed and use the second hard disk drive as a backup location. The most common backup location for networked computers is a network attached storage (NAS) device. Tape is no longer the main choice of media for backups.

Note

The automatic backup function requires internal disk storage, external disk storage, or a network storage location to be used. Automatic backups will not be successfully performed for media such as CD/DVD discs or USB flash drives because they must be present at the time of the automatic backup, which is unlikely. If the CD/DVD disc or USB flash drive is not present, the automatic backup will not occur.

RAID 2 and RAID 5 systems perform a similar function as a backup. The difference is that RAID systems are continuous backup systems, which mean they always have the very latest copy of system and data files. Traditional backup systems are not continuous and can result in lost data.

There are several types of backups identified by Windows Backup and Restore: system image, system repair disc, and file. A *system image* is an exact copy of a hard drive, including all system settings, programs, and files. It can be used to recover the entire operating system as well as all user files. A *system repair disc* contains all of the required files to repair the operating system but does not back up user files such as documents. Selecting the **Set up backup** option will start the Windows Backup wizard, which allows for a default and a custom backup of user data files.

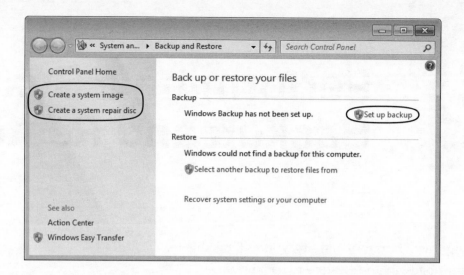

The default backup, which is selected with the **Let Windows choose (recommended)** option, backs up user data stored on the desktop, in default Windows folders, and in libraries. The **Let me choose** option allows you to indicate which files to backup and is referred to as a *custom backup*.

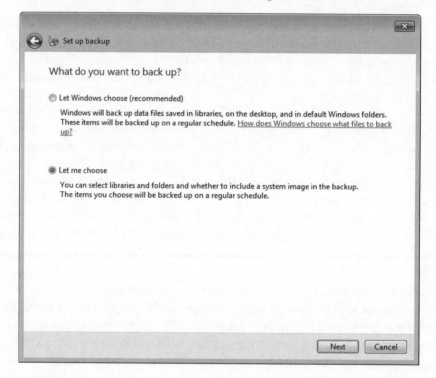

Once the default or custom backup is created, Backup and Restore will perform automatic backups, the first of which will be a full backup followed by incremental backups. By default, automatic backups are scheduled for every Sunday at 7:00 PM.

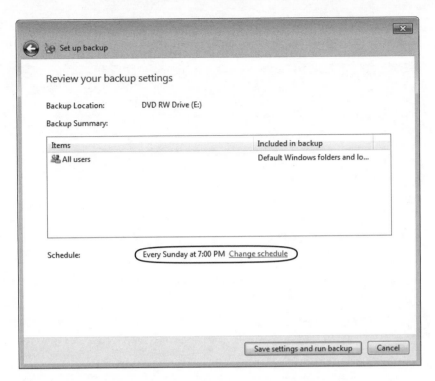

By selecting the **Change schedule** option, you will be allowed to change the date and time and how often you want Backup and Restore to perform an automatic backup. You can also deselect the **Run backup on a schedule (recommended)** option, to perform a one-time backup.

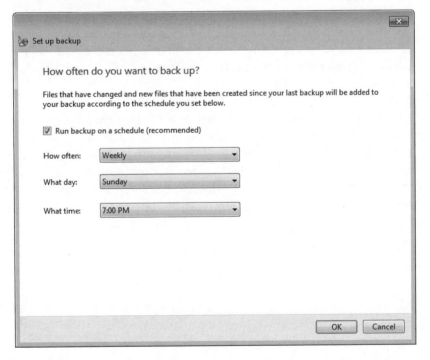

During the file backup operation, Windows 7 automatically creates a folder named after the backup location computer. Beneath that folder, it creates a folder with the name "Backup Set" followed by the date and time—for example, Backup Set 11-12-150809. This represents the entire "set" or collection of backup events by date and time. Within the set are individual backup events or backups. In the following screen capture, notice that there are two backup events or backups made on two different dates. The last backup named "Backup Files 2010-11-13 073114" was created on 2010-11-12 at 7:31:14. You can always identify the backup by date and time. The first backup in the set is always a full backup. After the first backup, Windows 7 creates incremental backups.

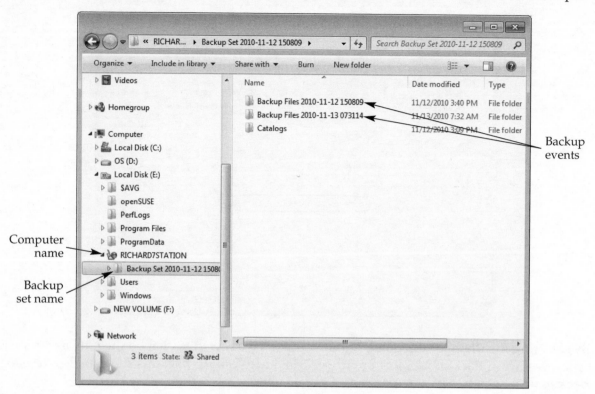

A *full backup* copies all files you select and clears the archive attribute, indicating that the files have been copied. An *incremental backup* copies files that have been created or changed since the last full or incremental backup. It then clears the archive attribute, indicating that the files have been copied.

The file attribute called *archive* is represented by the letter *A*. It is used to identify if a file needs to be backed up. This was the original way Microsoft identified files that are ready for an incremental backup. Microsoft still uses the file attribute *A*, but it also uses additional information to determine if a file should be backed up, such as date and time. The date and time is used to make copies of files for the Shadow Copy feature. The Shadow Copy feature makes a copy of a file each time it is opened, changed, and closed. You can select an earlier version of a file such as a document or picture that was edited. In the following screen capture, notice the four versions of a folder titled New Network Lab Activities. Any of the four versions of the folder can be restored.

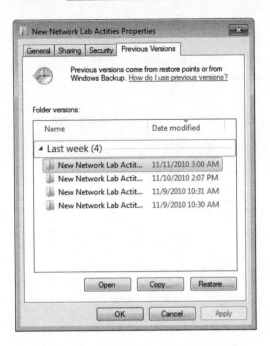

The fastest way to back up a large amount of files is to perform a full backup followed by incremental backups. An incremental backup is the fastest backup method because it only copies the files that have changed or have been created since the previous backup. However, when restoring files, the incremental backup takes more time because it requires the full backup to be restored first, followed by each incremental backup. The backups must be restored in the order they were originally backed up. You can find extensive information about the Backup and Restore in Windows Help and Support.

Equipment and Materials

❏ Windows 7 computer. (You may use Windows Vista, but it will not exactly match the screen captures in this activity.)

❏ The following information provided by your instructor:

Backup location: _____

Save or delete the backup after completing the laboratory activity? _____

Note
The backup location will indicate if you need additional materials to perform this laboratory activity. For example, the backup location can be USB-connected external hard disk drive.

Procedure

1. _____ Gather the required materials and then report to your assigned workstation.

2. _____ Boot the computer and verify it is in working order.

3. _____ Create a folder on drive C called Practice Backup Folder. If your instructor has provided you with a different backup location or media, create the Practice Backup Folder at that location. The folder will serve as the destination for the files you back up.

4. _____ To access Backup and Restore, select **Start | Control Panel | System and Security | Backup and Restore**. You can also enter "backup" in the **Search** box. Backup and Restore will be listed under the **Programs** section of the results. Backup and Restore can also be accessed through **Start | All Programs | Maintenance | Backup and Restore**. The Backup and Restore dialog box will appear and look similar to that in the following screen capture.

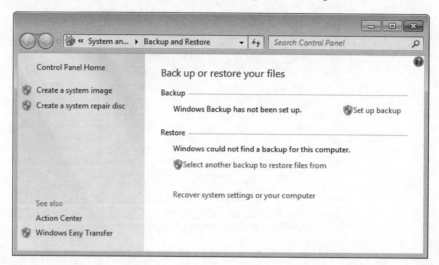

If the Backup and Restore program has been previously run, the dialog box will appear similar to the one in the screen capture below.

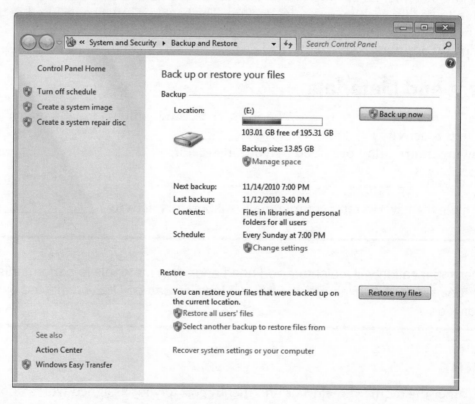

As you can see, the location, size of the backup, date and time, contents, and schedule are displayed. The following options are available.

- **Create a system image:** Creates an exact copy of a hard drive, including all system settings, programs, and files. The system image can be used to recover the entire operating system as well as all user files.

■ **Create a system repair disc**: Creates a disc with all of the required files to repair the operating system. It does not back up user files such as documents.

■ **Set up backup**: Starts the Windows Backup wizard, which allows for a default and a custom backup.

■ **Select another backup to restore files from**: As implied, allows the user to restore files from a location other than the default location.

■ **Recover system settings or your computer**: Uses System Restore to recover system settings.

5. _____ Select the **Set up backup** option and then follow the screen prompts. If a backup set has already been created, you can create a new backup set by selecting the **Change settings** option and following the prompts. When you've completed the backup configuration, the backup will begin. Depending on the size of the files to be backed up, the backup process could take quite a while.

6. _____ After completing the backup, call your instructor to inspect your laboratory activity.

7. _____ Now, open Windows Explorer to inspect the location of the backup files. The backup files are located at C:\Practice Backup Folder unless a different location was specified by your instructor.

8. _____ Perform a restore operation by clicking the **Restore my files** button in the Backup and Restore utility. If the wrong location is displayed or you wish to use a different location, you can choose the **Select another backup to restore files from** option. Depending on the size of the backup, restoring the files can take quite a while.

9. _____ After you have finished the laboratory activity, return all materials to their proper storage area. Delete or save the backup folder you created as indicated by your instructor.

10. _____ Answer the review questions.

Review Questions

1. What is the archive attribute used for? _____
_____

2. What does a full and incremental backup do to the archive attribute after backing up a file?
_____
_____

3. Why should you *not* save the backup on the default hard disk drive? _____
_____

4. Which Backup and Restore option allows you to create an exact copy of a hard drive, including system settings, programs, and files? _____

5. Which Backup and Restore option uses System Restore to recover system settings? _____
_____

6. What backup storage locations does Backup and Restore require for automatic backups? _____
_____

7. What is the default day and time Backup and Restore performs system backups? _____
_____

8. How does Backup and Restore identify backup sets in Windows 7?_____

_____

_____

_____

9. What type of backup does Windows 7 Backup and Restore perform after the first backup is made?_____

Laboratory Activity

84

Name_____ Date _____

Class/Instructor _____

Downloading and Installing an Antivirus Program

After completing this laboratory activity, you will be able to:

- Test the antivirus software program using the EICAR test file.
- Use AVG Internet Security to scan a specific folder or file.

Introduction

In this laboratory activity, you will download and install the 30-day trial version of AVG Internet Security. You may also use one of the following Web sites from which to download and install a trial version of antivirus software. This laboratory activity is based on AVG Internet Security, but other antivirus software will produce similar results and closely match the laboratory activity.

- AVG: www.avg.com.
- F-Secure: www.f-secure.com.
- Symantec: www.symantec.com.
- McAfee: www.mcafee.com.
- Trend Micro: www.trendmicro.com.
- Panda Security: www.pandasecurity.com.
- Computer Associates: www.ca.com.
- Kaspersky Lab: www.kaspersky.com.
- Sophos: www.sophos.com.

You will need a copy of the European for Computer Antivirus Research (EICAR) test files located at www.eicar.org. The EICAR test files are an industry standard used to test the antivirus software configuration. The EICAR test files simulate an actual computer virus. You will use these files to test the antivirus software after it is installed and configured on your computer. The EICAR test files will be treated like a real threat to the computer or network.

The EICAR test files come in several versions. Each version represents a more difficult detection level starting with the eicar.com file—the easiest to detect—and progressing to the eicarcom2.zip—the hardest to detect. All virus scanners should be able to detect eicar.com.

Equipment and Materials

- ❑ Windows XP SP2 or later computer with Internet access.
- ❑ Downloaded copy of AVG Internet Security. (Be sure you download the 30-day trial version. Read the download page carefully.)
- ❑ Downloaded copy of the EICAR test files.

Note

The computer may already have an antivirus software package installed. The antivirus software package, if installed, will detect the EICAR test files when you attempt to download them. If you have problems downloading the EICAR test files, you may need to temporarily disable the antivirus software on the computer or network. You must have your instructor's permission to disable the antivirus software, even if on a temporary basis.

Procedure

1. _____ Report to your assigned workstation.

2. _____ Boot the computer and verify it is in working order.

3. _____ Download and install the 30-day trial version of AVG Internet Security located at www.avg.com. Be sure to download the AVG manual in PDF file format. The manual contains all the information you will need to install and configure this software package. It also has information about the EICAR test files.

4. _____ Create a folder on the desktop titled EICAR. You will use this folder for the downloaded copies of the EICAR test files.

5. _____ Download a copy of the EICAR test files from www.eicar.org. There are several formats to choose from: TXT, COM, and ZIP. You may have difficulty downloading the COM file if your network or Internet access is protected by an antivirus software program. You may need to download the TXT file or the ZIP file instead. The COM file is detected by most antivirus programs as a malicious code. The antivirus program will block attempts to download this file. Be sure to read the information and instructions located at the EICAR Web site.

6. _____ Scan the EICAR folder on the desktop where you have installed the EICAR test files. Most antivirus software will perform a scan when you right-click the EICAR folder and select the scan option in the shortcut menu. The name of the scan option will vary according to the antivirus software program installed. The antivirus software should detect the test files. Do *not* delete or quarantine the EICAR test files until you call your instructor to inspect your antivirus configuration.

7. _____ Answer the review questions. You may use the download of the PDF version of the *AVG Internet Security User Manual*, which is located on the AVG Web site under the Support Center | Download | Documentation link. Do *not* print a hard copy of the guide without first obtaining your instructor's permission.

8. _____ Return the computer to its original configuration.

Review Questions

1. What are the EICAR test files? _____

_____

_____

_____

2. What is the default configuration setting in AVG Internet Security for handling an infected file when first detected? _____

   _____

3. Where does AVG Internet Security send an infected file that cannot be healed? _____

   _____

4. What are the scan options for AVG Internet Security? _____

   _____

5. What may be done to an infected file once it is sent to the AVG Virus Vault? _____

   _____

6. Can you check e-mail with the AVG Internet Security program? _____

Notes

Networking Fundamentals Laboratory Manual

Name_____ Date _____

Class/Instructor _____

Obtaining Malware Information

After completing this laboratory activity, you will be able to:

- Use the Internet to obtain information about malware.
- Compare information about malware from different sources.
- Recall where you can find up-to-date information about the latest security threats.

Introduction

In this laboratory activity, you will obtain descriptions of several known types of malware. You will use a number of different sources so that you can compare information from each Web site. You will also locate a list of the most common threats at this time.

An excellent source for information is the Web site of the antivirus software you are using. Another excellent source of information is the www.sans.org Web site and organization. The SANS Institute has a listing of the latest threats to security. You should always check the SANS Institute Web site and antivirus vendor Web sites for information on the latest security threats. Microsoft also provides security information, which is located at http://technet.microsoft.com/en-us/security/default. aspx.

It is interesting to note that not all antivirus software manufacturers use the same name for a particular malicious software program. For example, one particular virus may have several names associated with it. Look at the following list of names that are used by various software companies to identify the same virus. Multiple names can cause a great deal of confusion when researching information about a particular virus.

Software Company	Malware Identification Name
Computer Associates	Win32.DIWreck
Kaspersky	Trojan-Downloader.Win32.Vidlo.p
McAfee	Downloader-ACS
Sophos	Troj/Vidlo-P
Trend Micro	TROJ DLOADER.RY
CME	CME-402

Your assignment for this laboratory activity is to answer questions about various malicious software programs using the list of antivirus software vendors and the SANS Institute Web site.

Equipment and Materials

❏ Windows XP or later computer with Internet access.

Procedure

1. _____ Report to your assigned workstation.

2. _____ Boot the computer and verify it is in working order.

3. _____ Use the Internet to research how each malicious software program listed in the following table is classified (Trojan, hoax, etc.), its characteristics, and how it is spread. Also identify the source of your information.

Malicious Software	Classification	Characteristics	How it Spreads	Information Source
W32.Spacefam				
Backdoor.Cybot				
Mal/GIFIframe-A				
Exploit.JS.Gumblar				

4. _____ Use the SANS Institute Web site and various antivirus Web sites to determine the top five current security threats. Record your answers in the space provided.

_____

_____

_____

_____

_____

Review Questions

1. Where can you find information about the latest threats to security? _____

_____

Laboratory Activity

86

Name_____ Date _____

Class/Instructor _____

Advanced Boot Options

After completing this laboratory activity, you will be able to:

- Recall the function of each **Advanced Boot Options** menu option.
- Interpret the ntbtlog.txt boot log file.
- Use the **Advanced Boot Options** menu.
- Recall which programs and system features are accessible in safe mode.

Introduction

In this laboratory activity, you will explore the various options available from the **Advanced Boot Options** menu, commonly referred to as the *Safe Mode startup menu*.

A successful startup of a Windows server or workstation is complete when the user successfully logs on to the system. Before a successful logon occurs, the system can fail for numerous reasons. One of the first tactics used to determine and correct the problem is to invoke the **Advanced Boot Options** menu by pressing and holding the [F8] key during the POST, just before the system logon screen appears. The **Advanced Boot Options** menu will look like that in the following screen capture.

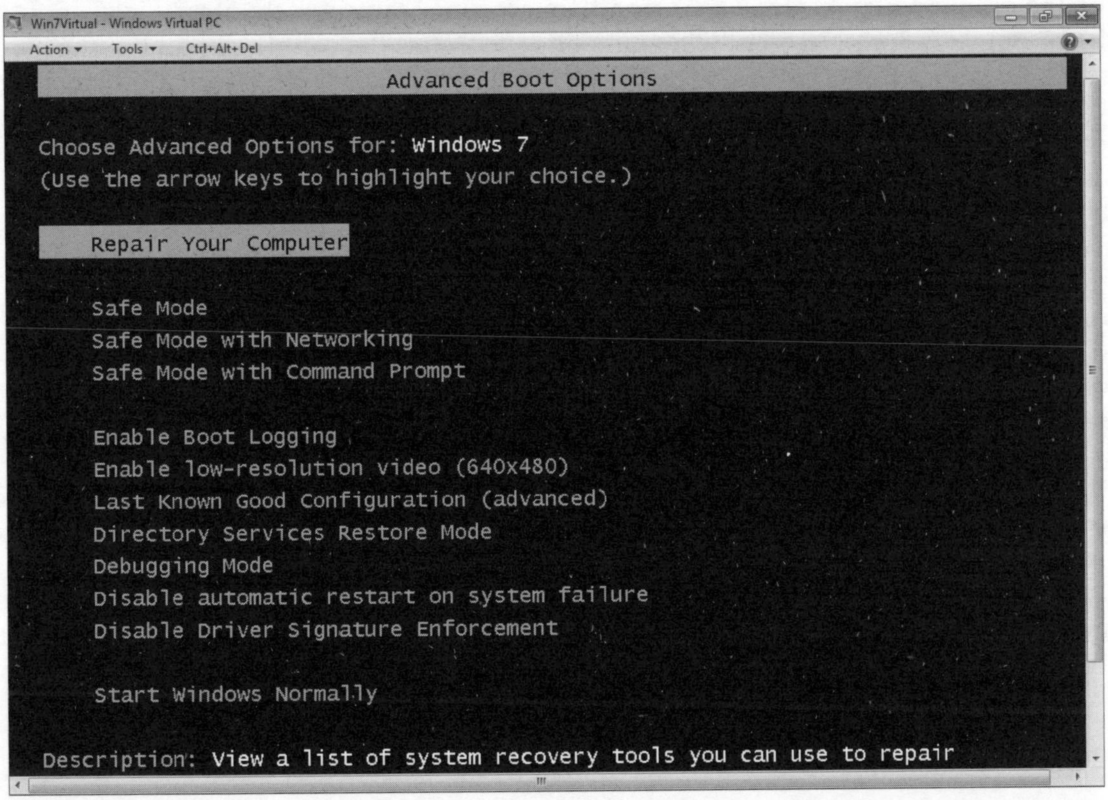

Repair Your Computer generates a dialog box with a menu of common repair tools such as Startup Repair, System Restore, System Image Recovery, Windows Memory Diagnostic, and Command Prompt. The **Repair Your Computer** option was first introduced in Windows 7.

Note

The **Repair Your Computer** option is not available in the **Advanced Boot Options** menu list for Windows Server 2008 at the time of this writing, but may be released as part of a service pack.

Safe Mode starts with only 1 MB of memory and a minimal set of drivers. A low-resolution GUI is available to the user. If the computer successfully starts in safe mode but not in normal mode, the cause of the problem is most likely a newly installed driver or software program, a corrupt driver, a service in conflict with a software program, or a corrupt registry. You can typically access all the standard utilities while in safe mode to troubleshoot and fix the problem. For example, you can access and run the System Configuration Utility and then eliminate suspect drivers, files, or services until you isolate the problem.

Safe Mode with Networking is the same as safe mode but with a connection to the network. This is a good way to determine if the startup problem is caused by the network connection or not.

Safe Mode with Command Prompt is similar to safe mode, but it uses a command prompt in place of the GUI.

Enable Boot Logging creates a log file containing information about which services and drivers were loaded during the boot operation. The log file is ntbtlog.txt and is saved in the C:\Windows directory.

Enable low-resolution video (640 x 480) allows you to use the legacy VGA resolution when you are experiencing a video problem.

Last Known Good Configuration is used to restore the computer to the most recent configuration that worked. It does this by restoring the system registry from the last successful system boot and log on. Be careful when using the **Last Known Good Configuration** option. If you receive an error message indicating a problem and then successfully log on to the computer, the **Last Known Good Configuration** option will not correct the error. If an error message is encountered, you should shut down the computer before successfully logging on. Then, start the computer and use the [F8] key to access the **Advanced Boot Options** menu options and select **Last Known Good Configuration**. This will reset the registry to the last "successful log on" registry settings.

Directory Services Restore Mode is only available on servers or computers acting as a server. It is used to repair or restore Active Directory.

Debugging Mode allows debugging information to be sent over the COM 2 port. A device must be attached to the COM port to receive the debugging information. This option is used most often by programmers. It is also incorporated into diagnostic software packages.

Disable automatic restart on system failure prevents Windows from restarting when an error is detected, resulting in a continuous startup loop.

Start Windows Normally starts the computer in normal mode.

When determining the cause of a system failure, always think about the last thing that occurred that could have caused the failure. One of the most common causes of a system failure is the installation of a new driver or software program. If a system fails to complete the startup process after installing a new hardware device and device driver or after installing a new software program, you should attempt to start the computer in safe mode. If you can start the system in safe mode, then chances are the last action performed is the cause of the failure. Typically, if the system starts in safe mode, then the hardware is functioning correctly and the offensive item is a driver, software program, or a corrupt file in the system registry.

Equipment and Materials

❑ Windows 7 computer.

Note

Versions of Windows earlier than Windows 7, including Windows Server 2008, do not have a matching set of Advanced Boot Options available.

Procedure

1. _____ Report to your assigned workstation.

2. _____ Boot the computer and verify it is in working order.

3. _____ Start the computer in safe mode by pressing and holding the [F8] key during the POST, just before the system logon screen appears. This can be tricky on some computers and may require several attempts before you are successful. You may wish to repeatedly press [F8] during the POST until the **Advanced Boot Options** menu appears. If you have difficulty accessing the menu, call your instructor.

4. _____ After the **Advanced Boot Options** menu appears, select the **Safe Mode** option.

5. _____ Attempt to access the various utilities listed below and record your findings as *Yes* or *No* with *Yes* meaning you can access and use the feature and *No* meaning you cannot.

   _____ Device Manager

   _____ Command Prompt

   _____ System Configuration Utility (msconfig.exe)

   _____ Notepad

   _____ Control Panel

   _____ Windows Explorer

   _____ System Information (msinfo32.exe)

   _____ Computer Management

   _____ Event Viewer

6. _____ Reboot the computer and access the **Advanced Boot Options** menu. Try each option in the menu. To gain experience in accessing the **Advanced Boot Options** menu, reboot the computer after trying each option. You need not use the **Repair Your Computer** option because it will be covered in detail in the next laboratory activity.

7. _____ Open and view the contents of ntbtlog.txt located in the C:\Windows\ntbtlog.txt directory. If you have trouble locating the file, try using the **Search** option to find it. Be sure to include the file extension .txt in the search. The file will contain a series of loaded drivers followed by a list of drivers that did not load. Look at the following example.

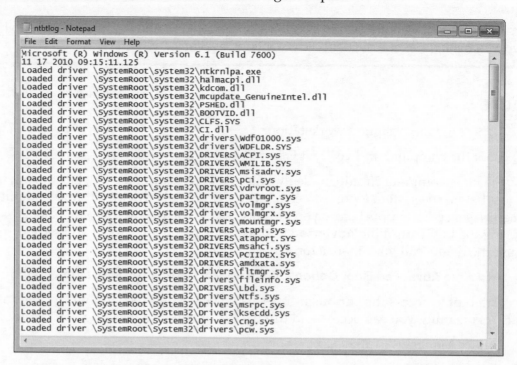

The boot log is a simple text file opened in Notepad by default. It can provide you with a clue as to which driver caused the problem. Scan the list of drivers loaded and not loaded and then close the file. The list of drivers is typically very long.

8. _____ Return the computer to its original configuration and then answer the review questions.

Review Questions

1. Which function key is used to access the **Advanced Boot Options** menu? _____

2. What is one of the most common reasons for system boot failure? _____

_____

3. What determines a successful boot operation? _____

_____

4. Can you access Computer Management from safe mode? _____

5. Can you access the System Configuration Utility from safe mode? _____

6. When will the **Last Known Good Configuration** option have no effect on repairing a problem?

_____

7. Where is the boot log file typically located? _____

8. What information is contained in the ntbtlog.txt file? _____
    _____

9. Which **Advanced Boot Options** menu option would you select to restore the system registry?
    _____

10. What repair tools are available after selecting the **Repair Your Computer** option from the
    Advanced Boot Options menu? _____
    _____

11. Which Windows operating system first introduced the **Advanced Boot Options** menu option,
    Repair Your Computer? _____

Networking Fundamentals Laboratory Manual

Laboratory Activity

87

Name_____ Date _____

Class/Instructor _____

Windows Recovery Environment

After completing this laboratory activity, you will be able to:

■ Recall how to access the Windows Recovery Environment.

■ Summarize the function of each Windows Recovery Environment option.

■ Test the system memory with Windows Memory Diagnostic.

■ Use the Windows Recovery Environment command prompt.

Introduction

Windows XP and Windows Server 2003 were the last computer operating systems that supported the Microsoft Recovery Console. The Recovery Console provides a command prompt for accessing files and folders on a failed computer. It allows commands to be entered in an attempt to repair the system.

Windows Vista, Windows 7, and Windows Server 2008 use the Windows Recovery Environment (WinRE). The Windows Recovery Environment incorporates a **Command Prompt** option that works in similar fashion to Recovery Console. It also has many other recovery options. Look at the options in the following screen capture of the **System Recovery Options** menu.

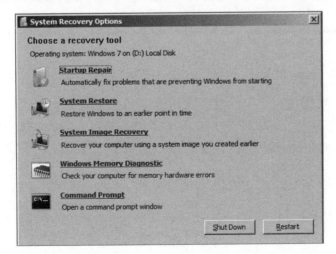

The **System Recovery Options** menu provides a set of tools that will repair some of the most commonly encountered computer problems. The following is a list of the tools and a short description of each.

System Recovery Tool	Description
Startup Repair	Automatically repairs damaged or missing required startup files.
System Restore	Restores operating system files to an earlier point in time but does not change personal files such as e-mail, documents, and pictures.
System Image Recovery	Recovers the system using a system image disc created earlier.
Windows Memory Diagnostic	Checks the system memory for errors.
Command Prompt	Produces a command prompt, which allows you to run command-line tools. Commonly used when the GUI is unavailable.

WinRE can also be accessed by using the installation DVD for Windows 7, Windows Vista, and Windows Server 2008. At the time of this writing, WinRE can be accessed through the **Advanced Boot Options** menu only for Windows 7. You can expect the WinRE feature to be available in Windows Server 2008 with the release of a future service pack.

Note

In this laboratory activity, you will access WinRE **Advanced Boot Options** menu.

Equipment and Materials

❑ Windows 7 computer.

Note

The Windows Recovery Environment (WinRE) can only be accessed through the **Advanced Boot Options** menu in Windows 7.

Procedure

1. _____ Report to your assigned workstation.

2. _____ Boot the computer and verify it is in working order. Then, shut down the computer.

3. _____ Start the computer and hold down the [F8] key during the POST to access the **Advanced Boot Options** menu.

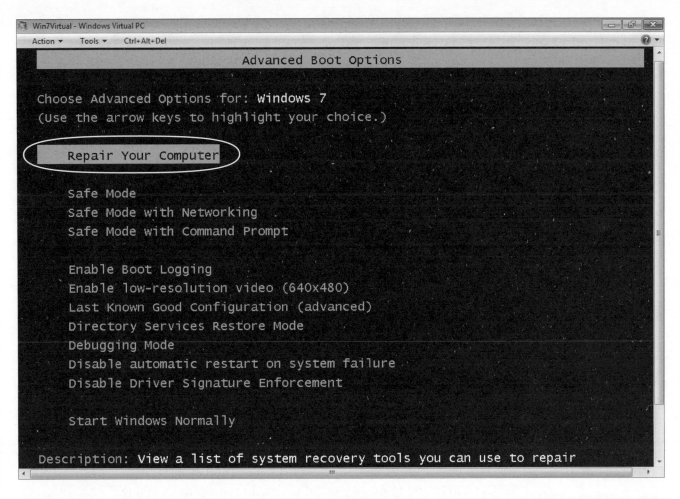

Note

The **Repair Your Computer** option can be disabled on a networked computer by the system administrator. If this option fails to appear in the **Advanced Boot Options** menu, call your instructor for assistance.

4. _____ Select the **Repair Your Computer** option. You will be prompted to select the language and then an administrator user account name and password as shown in the following two screen captures.

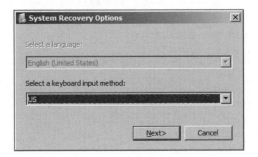
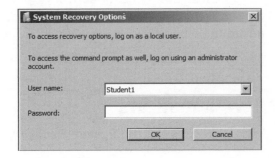

5. _____ Select **English (United States)** and **US** options and then the appropriate user account name and password. After the user name and password have been entered, the **Systems Recovery Options** menu should appear similar to the one in the following screen capture.

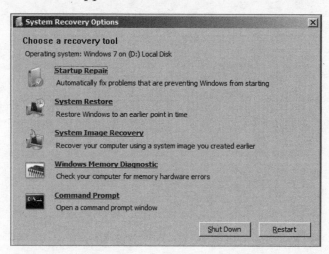

6. _____ Now, you will try each of the options in the **System Recovery Options** menu. Simply follow the online message dialog boxes for each and observe the actions. Be aware that the memory test takes a long time. You may wish to cancel the test before it is completed.

   a. _____ Select the **Startup Repair** option. Observe the actions. You will need to select the language, administrator user account name, and password.

   b. _____ Select the **System Restore** option. Start the process and observe, but do *not* select a restore point.

   c. _____ Select the **System Image Recovery** option. You do not need an image disc to observe the dialog box contents. Simply cancel the process after viewing the initial dialog box.

   d. _____ Select the **Windows Memory Diagnostic** option. The diagnostic process takes a long time to complete and could possibly use up all of your laboratory time. You can exit Windows Memory Diagnostic before it completes by pressing the [Esc] key. Windows Memory Diagnostic requires a system restart.

   e. _____ Select the **Command Prompt** option. Run the following commands from the command prompt and observe the results: **dir, time, arp -a, tree, exit**. After entering the **exit** command, you will be returned to the **System Recovery Options** dialog box.

7. _____ Close the **System Recovery Options** dialog box by clicking the **Restart** button. The computer will boot to Windows 7 and should be in the same working order as before you started the laboratory activity. If not, call your instructor for assistance.

8. _____ Return all materials to the proper storage area and then answer the review questions.

Review Questions

1. What two ways can the **System Recovery Options** menu be accessed in Windows 7?_____

_____

_____

2. Which option in the **System Recovery Options** menu restores your computer to an earlier time?

    _____

3. Which option in the **System Recovery Options** menu automatically repairs damaged or missing required startup files? _____

4. What does WinRE represent? _____

5. What command closes the command prompt and returns you to the GUI? _____

Networking Fundamentals Laboratory Manual

WINDOWS 7

Name_____ Date _____

Class/Instructor _____

Create a System Repair Disc

After completing this laboratory activity, you will be able to:

- Recall the appropriate use of a system repair disc.
- Differentiate between a system image and a system repair disc.
- Create a system repair disc for Windows 7.
- Use a system repair disc to recover an operating system that fails to boot because of corrupt or missing required files.

Introduction

In this laboratory activity, you will create either a 32-bit or 64-bit Windows 7 system repair disc. The Windows 7 system repair disc is used to quickly repair a Windows 7 operating system that has failed to boot because of corrupt, damaged, or missing required files. The Windows 7 system repair disc differs from a system image in that the system image contains all the files and folders contained on the disk drive; whereas, the system repair disc contains only the files necessary to repair the operating system boot process. The system repair disc does not contain copies of any additional files such as documents, pictures, and music. It does not format the default system partition. The system repair disc is the best choice for a quick recovery. Using a system image to recover a system could take a great deal of time.

You can create either a 32-bit or 64-bit system recovery disc; however, the recovery disc type must match the computer system type. You may use either a recordable CD or DVD to make the system repair disc. Approximately 140 Mb of space is required to make the system repair disc. At the time of this writing, a USB storage device is not an option. Maybe after a future service pack, the USB storage device will be an option.

Equipment and Materials

- ❏ Windows 7 computer.
- ❏ Recordable CD or DVD.

Procedure

1. _____ Report to your assigned workstation.

2. _____ Boot the computer and verify it is in working order.

3. _____ Insert a recordable CD/DVD into the appropriate drive.

4. _____ Access the Create a system repair disc wizard through **Start I Control Panel I System and Security I Backup and Restore** and then by selecting the **Create a system repair disc** option. You can also access the **Create a system repair disc** option through **Start I All Programs I Maintenance I Create a System Repair Disc**.

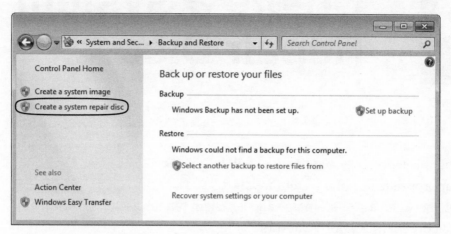

5. _____ The first dialog box to appear requests that you select the appropriate drive to use for creating the system repair disc.

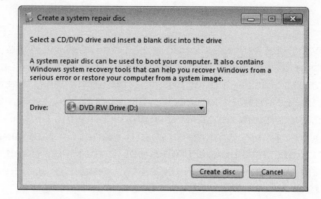

After selecting the appropriate drive, click the **Create disc** button. The wizard will start and display the progress of the operation.

6. _____ When the system repair disc is created, a dialog similar to the following will display, prompting you to label the disc as "Repair disc Windows 7 32-bit" or "Repair disc Windows 7 64-bit."

7. _____ View the contents of the system repair disc with Windows Explorer. The contents should look similar to that in the following screen capture.

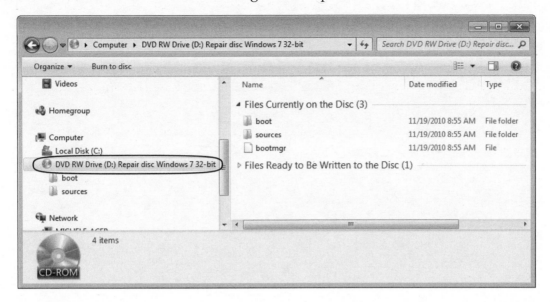

There will be two main folders labeled "boot" and "sources" as well as a file named bootmgr. The system repair disc contains all the files necessary to repair the boot operation for Windows 7.

8. _____ With your instructor's permission, use the system repair disc to simulate repairing your computer. To do this, leave the system recovery disc in the drive. Reboot the computer and observe the process. You may need to change the boot order in the system BIOS so that the CD/DVD drive is configured as the first boot device.

9. _____ Return all materials to their proper storage area and then answer the review questions.

Review Questions

1. What is the purpose of the Windows 7 system repair disc? _____

_____

_____

_____

2. What is the difference between a system image and a system repair disc? _____

_____

_____

_____

3. Can you recover a 64-bit operating system using a 32-bit disc?_____

4. What is the complete path to **Create a System Repair Disc** from the **Start** menu? _____

_____

5. What type of storage media can be used to make a system repair disc?_____

6. Choose the correct major section of Control Panel where Backup and Restore is found. _____

   A. Hardware and Sound

   B. System and Security

   C. Programs

   D. Ease of Access

Laboratory Activity

89

Name_____ Date _____

Class/Instructor _____

Windows 7 Action Center

After completing this laboratory activity, you will be able to:

■ Recall how to access the Action Center.

■ Recall the common functions associated with the Action Center.

■ Use the Action Center to diagnose Internet and networking problems.

Introduction

This laboratory activity will familiarize you with the Action Center and focus on the links that assist with solving Internet and networking problems. The Action Center was first introduced with Windows 7. It is a centralized utility that list problems that were automatically detected by the operating system and possibly corrected. It also provides the **Recovery, Troubleshooting, View Performance Information, Change User Account Control settings, Backup and Restore, Windows Update**, and **Windows Program Compatibility Troubleshooter** options. The following screen capture shows the Action Center and two problems that have been identified on a particular computer.

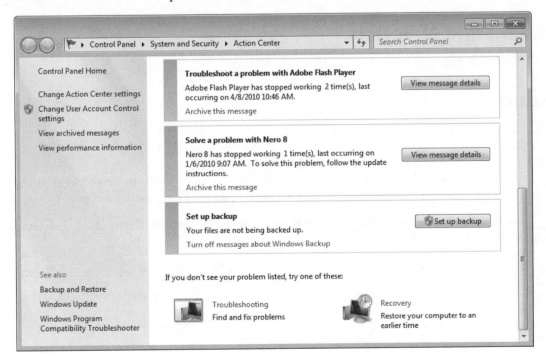

Notice that one of the problems is with Adobe Flash Player and another is with Nero 8. After problems are discovered, they are often corrected at a later date through operating system updates.

A quick way to access the Action Center is by clicking the **Action Center** icon (flag) located in the notification area of the taskbar. In the following screen capture, notice that recent messages associated with the Action Center are displayed as well as the **Open the Action Center** option.

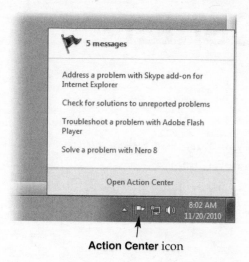

Action Center icon

If you hover the mouse pointer over the **Action Center** icon, a brief notification concerning the type of and number of messages will display, such as "Solved PC issues: 2 messages."

You can also access the Action Center by entering "action" in the **Search** box or through **Control Panel | System and Security | Action Center**.

In this lab activity, you will explore many of the features provided by the Action Center. Since you are using a computer that most likely has no real problems, the test you run will not find any problems nor recommend any corrective actions to take.

Equipment and Materials

❑   Windows 7 computer.

Procedure

1. _____ Report to your assigned workstation.

2. _____ Boot the computer and verify it is in working order.

3. _____ Locate the **Action Center** icon in the notification area of the taskbar or open the Action Center through **Control Panel | System and Security | Action Center**.

4. _____ Select the **Troubleshooting** option located at the bottom of the screen. A dialog box similar to the following will display.

Name _____

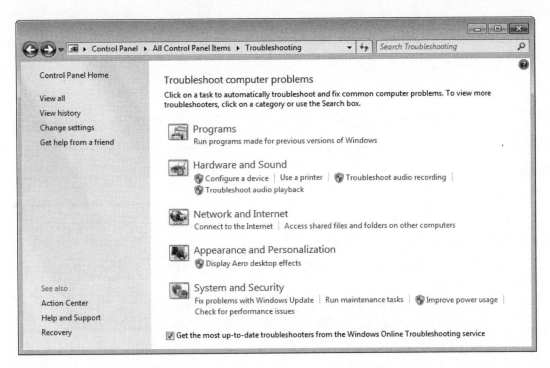

Notice that there are five major areas listed under **Troubleshooting computer problems**: **Programs, Hardware and Sound, Network and Internet, Appearance and Personalization,** and **System and Security.**

5. _____ Select **Network and Internet**. A dialog box similar to the following will display.

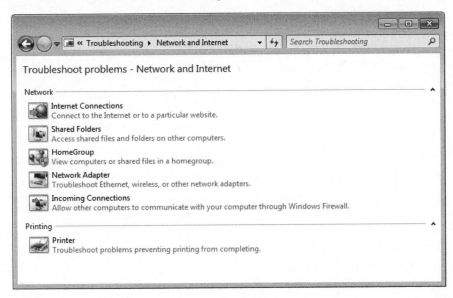

Notice that there are five troubleshooting areas listed in the **Network** section: **Internet Connections, Shared Folders, HomeGroup, Network Adapter,** and **Incoming Connections.** Take a few minutes to explore each of these troubleshooting areas.

6. _____ Close all dialog boxes and then reopen the Action Center.

7. _____ Select the **View performance information** option located in the left pane of the Action Center. The **Performance Information and Tools** dialog box will display. List the scores for each item listed below.

Processor: _____

Memory (RAM): _____

Graphics: _____

Gaming graphics: _____

Primary hard disk: _____

8. _____ Click the arrow in the upper-left corner of the **Performance Information and Tools** dialog box to return to the Action Center.

9. _____ In the Action Center, select **Change Action Center settings**. A dialog box similar to the following will display.

This is where you can change the configuration settings related to Action Center messages. Look at the various message types that can be enabled or disabled.

10. _____ Select the How does Action Center check for problems link and read the information provided.

11. _____ Close all open dialog boxes.

12. _____ Answer the review questions.

Review Questions

1. List three ways you can access the Action Center. _____

_____

_____

_____

_____

Name _____

2. What are the five major areas listed under **Troubleshoot computer problems**? _____

_____

_____

_____

3. What are the five areas listed under the **Network** section of the **Network and Internet** dialog box?

_____

_____

_____

4. Without opening the Action Center, how can you quickly see if there are any new messages concerning PC problems? _____

_____

Name_____ Date _____

Class/Instructor _____

System Configuration Utility

After completing this laboratory activity, you will be able to:

■ Recall how to access the System Configuration utility.

■ Carry out a "selective startup" troubleshooting procedure.

Introduction

In this laboratory activity, you will explore the function of the System Configuration utility. The System Configuration utility is an essential troubleshooting tool. It is very similar in operation for Windows XP, Windows Server 2003, and later operating systems.

The System Configuration utility will help you solve many different problems usually caused by software programs, drivers, or corrupt configuration files. This utility uses the process of elimination to narrow down a list of all possible software, drivers, and configuration settings to find which is causing the problem.

The System Configuration utility is started by selecting **System Configuration** or **msconfig.exe** from the **Search** results list. The **System Configuration** utility dialog box will look similar to the one in the following screen capture.

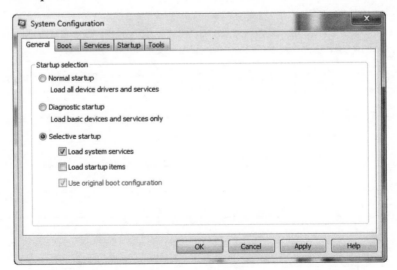

The **General** page provides a means to first eliminate all unnecessary items. The **Services** and **Startup** pages allow you to add the items one at a time to the boot process. For example, you would normally select the **Diagnostic startup** option on the **General** page. This will force the system to start in similar fashion as in safe mode. If you are able to reboot the system without the failure occurring, the problem is related to a system service or a program that is loading during startup. You can then select the **Selective startup** and **Load system services** options and reboot the system. If the failure reoccurs, the problem is related to a startup item. If the failure does not reoccur, the problem is related to a system service. Once you've determined the problem area, you can narrow down the cause of the system failure by adding items to the boot process one at a time from the **Services** page or **Startup** page and then rebooting. When the failure reoccurs after introducing a specific item to the boot process, you have found the problem service or startup item.

Using the System Configuration Utility to troubleshoot a system failure can be a very time-consuming task, but it is well worth the effort if it prevents reformatting the disk drive, reinstalling the operating system, and adding files from the latest system backup.

Equipment and Materials

❑   Windows Vista or Windows 7 computer.

Procedure

1. _____   Report to your assigned workstation.

2. _____   Boot the computer and verify it is in working order.

3. _____   Open the System Configuration utility by entering "msconfig.exe" into the **Search** box located off the **Start** menu.

4. _____   In the **System Configuration** dialog box, select the **Diagnostic startup** option to load only basic drivers and services required for the boot operation. Click the **Apply** button. You will be prompted to restart the computer for the change to take effect. Do so now.

5. _____   Now, select the **Selective startup** option and deselect **Load system services** and **Load startup items**. Reboot the system and observe the effect.

6. _____   Select **Load system services** or **Load startup items** and then reboot the system.

7. _____   For the option **Load system services** or **Load startup items** that you left deselected, go to its related page, **Services** or **Startup**, and reintroduce items to the boot process one at a time until all items have been selected.

8. _____   Return the System Configuration utility to a non-diagnostic mode by selecting the **Normal startup** option and rebooting the computer. Observe the effect.

9. _____   Now, explore the System Configuration tabs to see what type of files and configuration information is located under each.

10. _____   Select the **Tools** tab and then record in the space provided the tools that are available for troubleshooting.

_____

_____

_____

_____

_____

_____

_____

11. _____   Practice using the System Configuration utility until you feel comfortable with using it.

12. _____ Return all materials to their proper storage area. Be sure the computer is not left in diagnostic mode.

13. _____ Answer the review questions.

Review Questions

1. Which options are available for a selective startup? _____

   _____

   _____

2. Explain how you would use the System Configuration utility to troubleshoot a startup problem? _____

   _____

   _____

3. Place a check mark by the tools that are available under the **Tools** tab?

   a. _____ System Restore

   b. _____ Internet Protocol Configuration

   c. _____ Display Configuration

   d. _____ Event Viewer

   e. _____ Firewall Configuration

   f. _____ Registry Editor

   g. _____ Modem Configuration

   h. _____ Task Manager

   i. _____ Remote Assistance

   j. _____ Remote Desktop

WINDOWS VISTA OR LATER

Name_____ Date _____

Class/Instructor _____

Using the Netstat Command

After completing this laboratory activity, you will be able to:

■ Recall the function of the **netstat** command.

■ Identify the screen display results for each **netstat** command switch.

■ Use the **netstat** command as a diagnostic tool.

Introduction

This laboratory activity is designed to familiarize you with the **netstat** command. The **netstat** command displays the active TCP and UDP protocols and port connections. In this laboratory activity, you will use the **netstat** command and several common switches to view active port connections. The following is a screen capture of the **netstat** command results. The command was issued while the computer was connected to the Internet and conducting a search.

Notice that the **netstat** command was issued without any command switches. As you can see, the protocol (**Proto** column), local computer IP address and port number (**Local Address** column), address the port is connected to (**Foreign Address** column), and the connection status (**State** column) are displayed. The following table lists common **netstat** command switches and their function.

Switch	Results
/?	Displays help.
-a	Displays all active TCP and UDP connections and ports.
-e	Displays Ethernet statistics.
-f	Displays Fully Qualified Domain Names (FQDMs) for foreign addresses.
-n	Displays addresses and port numbers in numerical form but does not resolve names.
-p proto	Displays results by specific protocol. For example, **netstat -p icmp** will display results for the ICMP protocol.
-s	Displays statistics for protocols and can be used with the **-p** switch to display statistics for a specific protocol.
-r	Displays the contents of the routing table.
-o	Displays the Process ID (PID) in addition to the protocol. The PID identifies running programs in a similar fashion to the way Task Manager identifies running processes.

Many software utilities such as packet analyzers display the same information in a GUI form as **netstat**. You need to be familiar with the **netstat** command to perform a quick spot-check when more sophisticated utilities are not available. Also, be aware that the **netstat** command can be part of a CompTIA Network+ exam question. You should be familiar with the command if you plan to take the exam.

Equipment and Materials

■ Windows Vista or Windows 7 computer with an Internet connection.

Note
This lab activity can be run without an Internet connection, but the results of the **netstat** command will be limited.

Procedure

1. _____ Report to your assigned workstation.

2. _____ Boot the computer and verify it is in working order.

3. _____ Access the command prompt. Enter **netstat /?** and observe the results.

4. _____ Type and enter the **netstat** command using a variety of uppercase and lowercase letters to determine if the command is case-sensitive. Write your conclusion in the space provided.

_____

_____

_____

5. _____ Issue the **netstat** command using the **-a** switch and observe the results.

6. _____ Issue the **netstat** command using the following switches and observe the results of each: **-e, -r, -f,** and **-s**.

7. _____ Issue the **netstat** command again using each of the switches **-a, -e, -r, -f, -s** after establishing an Internet connection to a Web site. Observe the results.

8. _____ Carefully study each of the **netstat** command switches and be sure you can identify the display results for each.

9. _____ Answer the review questions before shutting down the computer.

Review Questions

1. Is the **netstat** command case-sensitive? _____

2. What is the purpose of the **netstat** command? _____

   _____

3. What effect does the **-e** switch have on the **netstat** command output? _____

   _____

4. What effect does the **-r** switch have on the **netstat** command output? _____

   _____

5. What effect does the **-f** switch have on the **netstat** command output? _____

   _____

6. Which **netstat** command switch produced the following results? _____

```
Command Prompt                                                              - □ ✕

C:\Users\Richard>
Interface Statistics

                        Received              Sent

Bytes                 3476380205          310311437
Unicast packets         11088942           13455249
Non-unicast packets       876510             253725
Discards                       0                  0
Errors                         0                  4
Unknown protocols              0

C:\Users\Richard>_
```

7. Which **netstat** command switch produced the following results? _____

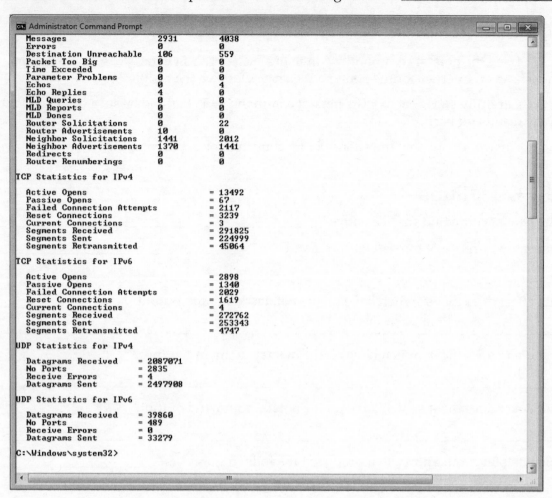

8. Which **netstat** command switch produced the following results? _____

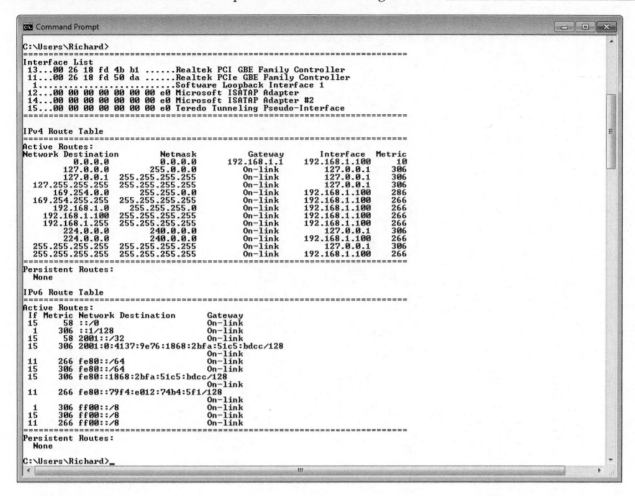

9. Which **netstat** command switch produced the following results? _____

```
Administrator: Command Prompt
Copyright (c) 2009 Microsoft Corporation.  All rights reserved.

C:\Windows\system32>

Active Connections

  Proto  Local Address          Foreign Address        State
  TCP    0.0.0.0:135            Richard-PCwin7:0        LISTENING
  TCP    0.0.0.0:162            Richard-PCwin7:0        LISTENING
  TCP    0.0.0.0:445            Richard-PCwin7:0        LISTENING
  TCP    0.0.0.0:514            Richard-PCwin7:0        LISTENING
  TCP    0.0.0.0:1170           Richard-PCwin7:0        LISTENING
  TCP    0.0.0.0:2869           Richard-PCwin7:0        LISTENING
  TCP    0.0.0.0:3389           Richard-PCwin7:0        LISTENING
  TCP    0.0.0.0:5357           Richard-PCwin7:0        LISTENING
  TCP    0.0.0.0:7787           Richard-PCwin7:0        LISTENING
  TCP    0.0.0.0:49152          Richard-PCwin7:0        LISTENING
  TCP    0.0.0.0:49153          Richard-PCwin7:0        LISTENING
  TCP    0.0.0.0:49154          Richard-PCwin7:0        LISTENING
  TCP    0.0.0.0:49155          Richard-PCwin7:0        LISTENING
  TCP    0.0.0.0:49156          Richard-PCwin7:0        LISTENING
  TCP    0.0.0.0:49181          Richard-PCwin7:0        LISTENING
  TCP    127.0.0.1:5354         Richard-PCwin7:0        LISTENING
  TCP    127.0.0.1:10110        Richard-PCwin7:0        LISTENING
  TCP    127.0.0.1:27015        Richard-PCwin7:0        LISTENING
  TCP    127.0.0.1:27015        Richard-PCwin7:49164    ESTABLISHED
  TCP    127.0.0.1:39123        Richard-PCwin7:0        LISTENING
  TCP    127.0.0.1:49164        Richard-PCwin7:27015    ESTABLISHED
  TCP    192.168.1.100:139      Richard-PCwin7:0        LISTENING
  TCP    192.168.1.100:49388    192.168.1.1:5431        TIME_WAIT
  TCP    192.168.1.100:49389    192.168.1.1:5431        TIME_WAIT
  TCP    192.168.1.100:49390    192.168.1.1:5431        TIME_WAIT
  TCP    192.168.1.100:49391    192.168.1.1:5431        TIME_WAIT
  TCP    192.168.1.100:49392    192.168.1.1:5431        TIME_WAIT
  TCP    192.168.1.100:49393    192.168.1.1:5431        TIME_WAIT
  TCP    192.168.1.100:49394    192.168.1.1:5431        TIME_WAIT
  TCP    192.168.1.100:49395    192.168.1.1:5431        TIME_WAIT
  TCP    192.168.1.100:65395    cs:25999                ESTABLISHED
  TCP    [::]:135               Richard-PCwin7:0        LISTENING
  TCP    [::]:445               Richard-PCwin7:0        LISTENING
  TCP    [::]:2869              Richard-PCwin7:0        LISTENING
  TCP    [::]:3389              Richard-PCwin7:0        LISTENING
  TCP    [::]:5357              Richard-PCwin7:0        LISTENING
  TCP    [::]:49152             Richard-PCwin7:0        LISTENING
  TCP    [::]:49153             Richard-PCwin7:0        LISTENING
  TCP    [::]:49154             Richard-PCwin7:0        LISTENING
  TCP    [::]:49155             Richard-PCwin7:0        LISTENING
  TCP    [::]:49156             Richard-PCwin7:0        LISTENING
  TCP    [::]:49181             Richard-PCwin7:0        LISTENING
  TCP    [::]:49182             Richard-PCwin7:0        LISTENING
  TCP    [fe80::79f4:e012:74b4:5f1x11]:49153   Richard-PCwin7:49252   ESTABLISHED
  TCP    [fe80::79f4:e012:74b4:5f1x11]:49252   Richard-PCwin7:49153   ESTABLISHED
  TCP    [fe80::79f4:e012:74b4:5f1x11]:49309   Michele-PC:49156       ESTABLISHED
  UDP    0.0.0.0:162            *:*
  UDP    0.0.0.0:500            *:*
  UDP    0.0.0.0:514            *:*
  UDP    0.0.0.0:1434           *:*
  UDP    0.0.0.0:3544           *:*
  UDP    0.0.0.0:3702           *:*
  UDP    0.0.0.0:3702           *:*
  UDP    0.0.0.0:3702           *:*
  UDP    0.0.0.0:3702           *:*
  UDP    0.0.0.0:4500           *:*
  UDP    0.0.0.0:5355           *:*
  UDP    0.0.0.0:50913          *:*
```

10. Which **netstat** command switch produced the following results? _____

```
Command Prompt
C:\Users\Richard>

Active Connections

  Proto  Local Address          Foreign Address        State
  TCP    127.0.0.1:27015        Richard-PCwin7:49164    ESTABLISHED
  TCP    127.0.0.1:49164        Richard-PCwin7:27015    ESTABLISHED
  TCP    192.168.1.100:49162    192.168.1.1:5431        TIME_WAIT
  TCP    192.168.1.100:49163    192.168.1.1:5431        TIME_WAIT
  TCP    192.168.1.100:49165    192.168.1.1:5431        TIME_WAIT
  TCP    192.168.1.100:65395    cs.xfire.com:25999      ESTABLISHED
  TCP    192.168.1.100:65397    a96-17-75-40.deploy.akamaitechnologies.com:http  CLOSE_WAIT
  TCP    192.168.1.100:65398    a96-17-75-40.deploy.akamaitechnologies.com:http  CLOSE_WAIT
  TCP    192.168.1.100:65399    a96-17-75-8.deploy.akamaitechnologies.com:http   CLOSE_WAIT
  TCP    192.168.1.100:65401    a96-17-75-8.deploy.akamaitechnologies.com:http   CLOSE_WAIT
  TCP    192.168.1.100:65402    cds49.mia9.msecn.net:http  CLOSE_WAIT
  TCP    192.168.1.100:65403    a96-17-75-42.deploy.akamaitechnologies.com:http  CLOSE_WAIT
  TCP    192.168.1.100:65517    192.168.1.1:5431        TIME_WAIT
  TCP    192.168.1.100:65520    192.168.1.1:5431        TIME_WAIT
  TCP    192.168.1.100:65521    192.168.1.1:5431        TIME_WAIT
  TCP    192.168.1.100:65523    192.168.1.1:5431        TIME_WAIT
  TCP    192.168.1.100:65524    192.168.1.1:5431        TIME_WAIT
  TCP    192.168.1.100:65525    192.168.1.1:5431        TIME_WAIT
  TCP    192.168.1.100:65528    a72-246-45-82.deploy.akamaitechnologies.com:http  ESTABLISHED
  TCP    192.168.1.100:65531    wwwco1vip.microsoft.com:http  ESTABLISHED
  TCP    [fe80::79f4:e012:74b4:5f1x11]:49153   Richard-PCwin7.hsd1.fl.comcast.net.:49252   ESTABLISHED
  TCP    [fe80::79f4:e012:74b4:5f1x11]:49156   [fe80::8c62:b6aa:704d:22b1x11]:58325   ESTABLISHED
  TCP    [fe80::79f4:e012:74b4:5f1x11]:49252   Richard-PCwin7.hsd1.fl.comcast.net.:49153   ESTABLISHED
  TCP    [fe80::79f4:e012:74b4:5f1x11]:65422   Michele-PC:49156       ESTABLISHED

C:\Users\Richard>_
```

Name_____ Date _____

Class/Instructor _____

Using the Nbtstat Command

After completing this laboratory activity, you will be able to:

■ Use the **nbtstat** command for verifying NetBIOS name resolution.

■ Recall the purpose of the **nbtstat** command.

■ Recall the purpose of common command line switches used with the **nbtstat** command.

■ Use the **net view** command to view a list of local area network computers.

Introduction

In this laboratory activity, you will explore the use of the **nbtstat** command. The **nbtstat** command is used to help troubleshoot NetBIOS name resolution problems. NetBIOS name resolution is still supported on current Windows operating systems in the effort to support legacy operating systems. NetBIOS names are used to support communication with an operating system that uses NetBIOS names such as Windows 98 or earlier and legacy hardware devices.

Note
Network computers and devices prior to Windows 2000 required NetBIOS names for communication. Starting with Windows 2000, NetBIOS names were only required to communicate with older operating systems.

Networks based on TCP/IP use a service called *NetBIOS over TCP/IP* to resolve NetBIOS names to IP addresses. Typically, a network device queries the WINS server through a broadcast to locate a NetBIOS named device. NetBIOS name resolution can also be achieved through the use of the lmhosts file, host file, and DNS server queries. A quick way to see the NetBIOS names assigned to devices in a local area network is with the **nbtstat** command.

Note
TCP/IP networks use DNS names for device identification. IPv6 resolves computer names and IPv6 addresses automatically in a local area network.

The **net view** command will also be introduced during this lab activity. The **net view** command is used to display a list of local area network computers, domains, workgroups, and resources. To view a list of computers in the local network, simply enter **net view** at the command prompt.

The following screen capture shows the **net view** command used to list the computers on the local network. It also shows **nbtstat** with the **-n** switch. The **nbtstat -n** command lists the NetBIOS names that are associated with the local host adapter.

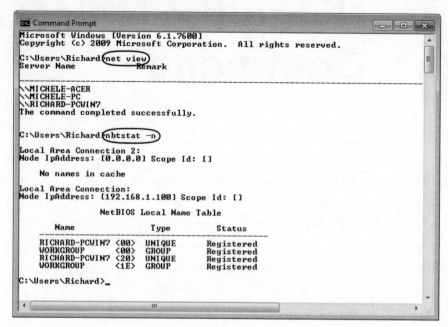

DNS names use 63 characters to identify network devices; NetBIOS uses 15 characters. When 63-character names are used and a NetBIOS name is required to provide compatibility with operating systems based on NetBIOS names, the 63-character names are automatically truncated.

Note

To view a complete list of NetBIOS suffixes, conduct an Internet search using the key terms "Microsoft article 163409" or "Microsoft NetBIOS name suffix".

Look at the following screen capture of the **WINS** page of the **Advanced TCP/IP Settings** dialog box taken from a Windows 7 computer. Notice the options for LMHOSTS lookup and for NetBIOS settings.

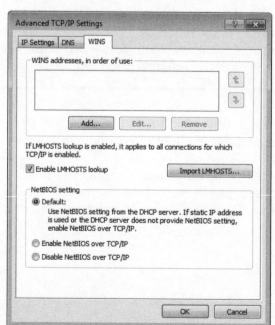

Windows Internet Name Service (WINS) is based on NetBIOS names. NetBIOS names are fine for older operating systems that communicated only on local area networks, but they cannot be used to communicate over the Internet because they are not routable. Routers rely on IP addresses for routing packets across the Internet. To enable NetBIOS named devices to be identified and routed over the Internet, they must be matched to IPv4 addresses. Look at the NetBIOS setting section of the **Advanced TCP/IP Settings** dialog box. The default setting uses the DHCP server to resolve NetBIOS names to IP addresses or enables NetBIOS over TCP/IP. When NetBIOS over TCP/IP is enabled or selected, the NetBIOS information is encapsulated and carried by the TCP/IP protocols.

You can disable NetBIOS over TCP/IP when using a server that supports DNS name registration and resolution. Disabling NetBIOS resolution reduces the number of NetBIOS broadcasts used to resolve device names on the local area network. If NetBIOS name resolution is required by the local area network, at least one network device must have NetBIOS over TCP/IP enabled.

The **nbtstat** command is not case sensitive, but the switches are. Look at the **nbtstat** command syntax and command switches for the Windows 7 operating system in the following screen capture. The **nbtstat** commands can be used to verify that the network adapter is indeed registering its NetBIOS name and that it is able to communicate with other computers using the NetBIOS name.

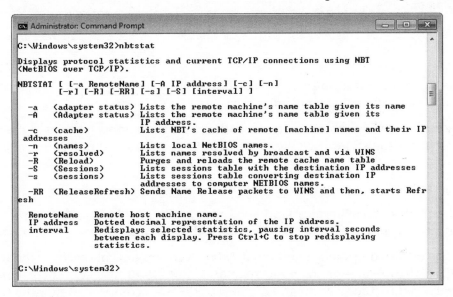

Note
The **nbtstat** command is a test item on the CompTIA Network+ exam. Be sure you are familiar with the command and the display generated by the command. The **nbtstat** and **netstat** command questions can be very confusing. As a help, remember that **nbtstat** generates information about the assigned NetBIOS names, and **netstat** generates network statistics in relation to the TCP/IP protocol suite.

Equipment and Materials

❑   Two Windows 7 computers connected as a peer-to-peer network.

Note
A Windows XP or Windows Vista computer can be substituted for this lab activity.

Procedure

1. _____ Report to your assigned computer(s).

2. _____ Boot the computers and verify they are in working order.

3. _____ Fill in the workgroup name, IPv4 address, and MAC address for each computer. This will help you to better understand the information displayed by the commands and command switches.

Workgroup name: _____

Computer 1 name: _____

IPv4 address: _____

MAC address: _____

Computer 2 name: _____

IPv4 address: _____

MAC address: _____

4. _____ Open a command prompt as the administrator by right-clicking the **Command Prompt** menu item and selecting **Run as administrator**.

5. _____ Enter the **net view** command to view all computers connected to and running on the local area network. You should see the name of both computers. If not, call your instructor for assistance.

6. _____ Enter **nbtstat** at the command prompt and observe the results.

7. _____ Enter the **nbtstat help** command and observe the results. You should see a list of information similar to that displayed by the **nbtstat** command.

8. _____ At one of the computers, enter the **nbtstat -A** command followed by the IP address assigned to that computer—for example, **nbtstat -A 192.168.10.10**. Then, enter the **nbtstat -A** command followed by the IP address assigned to the other computer. Enter the same commands at the other computer.

9. _____ At one of the computers, enter the command **nbtstat -a** followed by the computer name—for example, **nbtstat -a Computer 1**. At the other computer, do the same but using the name of that computer.

10. _____ Now, use the **nbtstat -n** command to display a list of all NetBIOS names for the local host adapter. For each entry, you should see a 15-character NetBIOS name followed by a 16th character, such as <00>, that identifies the device; the type of name, such as "unique" or "group"; and the status, such as "registered." If you do not see this information, call your instructor for assistance.

11. _____ Now use the **nbtstat -c** command to generate a list of NetBIOS names stored in the cache. If no names are displayed after issuing the command, use **net view**, **ping**, or the network browser to generate names in the cache. The names can remain in the cache typically up to 10 minutes. If you do not see the other computer name in the cache, call your instructor.

12. _____ After successfully seeing the list of names in the cache, you will purge the cache. Use the **nbtstat -R** command to purge the NetBIOS name cache. Use the **nbtstat -c** to verify that the cache has been purged. No network computer names should appear in the display.

13. _____ Now use the **nbtstat -r** command to view all previous NetBIOS names resolved by broadcasts. You should see all the past names that were in the cache.

14. _____ Practice using the **nbtstat** command with the various switches until you are familiar with the purpose of each.

15. _____ Before shutting down the computers, answer the review questions.

Review Questions

1. What does the **net view** command display? _____

   _____

2. What information is revealed by the **nbtstat -n** command? _____

   _____

3. What command generated the following display? _____

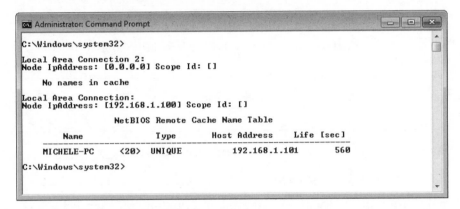

4. What command generated the following display? _____

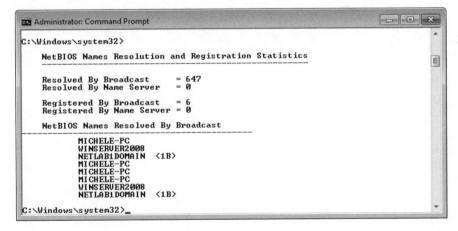

5. What command generated the following display?_____

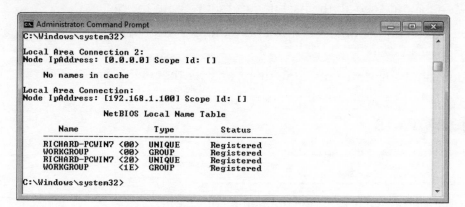

```
Administrator: Command Prompt
C:\Windows\system32>

Local Area Connection 2:
Node IpAddress: [0.0.0.0] Scope Id: []

    No names in cache

Local Area Connection:
Node IpAddress: [192.168.1.100] Scope Id: []

                 NetBIOS Local Name Table

        Name                Type         Status
        ---------------------------------------------
        RICHARD-PCWIN7 <00>  UNIQUE       Registered
        WORKGROUP      <00>  GROUP        Registered
        RICHARD-PCWIN7 <20>  UNIQUE       Registered
        WORKGROUP      <1E>  GROUP        Registered

C:\Windows\system32>
```

6. Which **nbtstat** switch would you use to purge the NetBIOS name cache?_____

7. How would you fill the NetBIOS name cache with NetBIOS names if it was empty?_____

_____

8. When is NetBIOS over TCP/IP required for a network adapter in a Windows XP computer?

_____

9. How many characters are used in a NetBIOS name? _____

_____

10. How many characters can be used in a DNS name for a device? _____

11. What does the acronym WINS represent?_____

12. What is the main difference between the **nbtstat** and **netstat** commands?_____

_____

_____

Name_____ Date _____

Class/Instructor _____

System Information

After completing this laboratory activity, you will be able to:

■ Recall when to use the System Information utility.

■ Use the System Information utility to identify system hardware and software configuration information.

Introduction

In this lab activity, you will explore the System Information utility, also known as *msinfo32.exe*. This utility is very handy for finding detailed information about a computer's hardware and software configuration. Look at the following screen capture of the System Information utility.

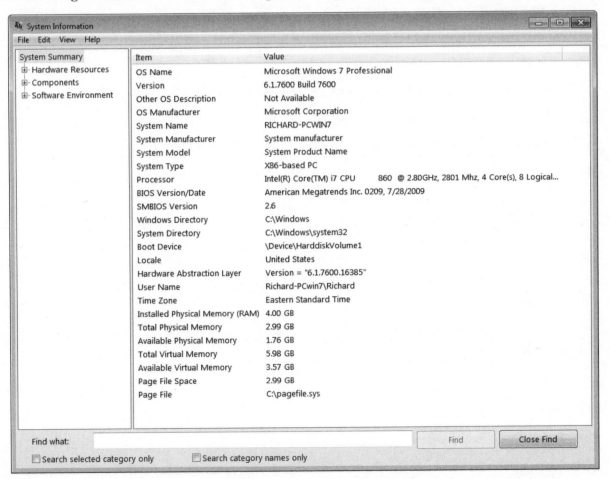

In the left pane of the screen, three major categories of system information are listed: Hardware Resources, Components, and Software Environment. The right pane displays the details for these categories. In this laboratory activity, you will use the System Information utility to identify the system hardware and software configuration information on your lab computer.

Equipment and Materials

❑   Windows Vista or Windows 7 computer.

Procedure

1. _____ Report to your assigned workstation.

2. _____ Boot the computer and verify it is in working order.

3. _____ Access the System Information utility by entering "msinfo32" in the **Search** box located off the **Start** menu and selecting msinfo32.exe from the list. Look at the System Summary information and answer the following questions about the computer.

   What operating system is installed? _____

   What is the last service pack installed? _____

   What is the system BIOS name and version? _____

   Where is the /System directory located? _____

   What is the size of the physical memory? _____

   What is the size of the page file? _____

   What is the size of the virtual memory? _____

4. _____ Now look at the Hardware Resources information and answer the following question.

   What is the assigned network adapter IRQ? _____

5. _____ Look at the Components information and answer the following questions.

   What is the brand and model of the CD or DVD drive? _____

   What is the brand of the display adapter? _____

   To what resolution is the display set? _____

   How many bits per pixel is the display set to? _____

6. _____ Look at the Network information listed under Components. Fill in the following information.

   Adapter type (Probably Ethernet 802.3): _____

   Adapter brand: _____

   IP address: _____

   Subnet: _____

   DHCP enabled (*Yes* or *No*): _____

   DHCP server IP address: _____

Name _____

MAC address: _____

Gateway: _____

7. _____ Look at the Software Environment information and answer the following questions.

Approximately how many system drivers are installed? _____

Approximately how many drivers are signed? _____

Approximately how many services are running? _____

Approximately how many modules are loaded? _____

Approximately how many programs are loaded at startup? _____

What other Windows utility provides similar information about the software environment such as running programs and services? _____

8. _____ Take a few minutes to explore the Summary Information utility and its menu items.

9. _____ Answer the review questions.

Review Questions

1. How is the System Information utility accessed? _____

_____

2. When would you *most likely* use the System Information utility? _____

_____

_____

Laboratory Activity

94

Name_____ Date _____

Class/Instructor _____

Online Help for Network Problems

After completing this laboratory activity, you will be able to:

■ Identify sources for network troubleshooting information.

■ Carry out Internet searches for network troubleshooting information related to a specific device, application, or operating system problem.

■ Use network troubleshooting information found through Internet searches to solve network problems.

Introduction

This laboratory activity will familiarize you with various sources for network troubleshooting information. Many students and professionals spend too much time trying to solve a problem using trial and error. Chances are, you are not the first person to encounter the problem. Many users may have already experienced the problem, and a cause and a solution may have been posted on the Internet at the software or hardware provider's Web site or on other Web sites.

Before spending an extraordinary amount of time troubleshooting a network problem, you should conduct an Internet search based on the symptoms exhibited by the system. An hour or more spent on the same problem means you really need to perform an Internet search. However, the exact process of troubleshooting and the amount of time you spend troubleshooting will depend on your supervisor. Some organizations have a step-by-step procedure to follow. If the cause and solution to the problem are not uncovered through the procedure, the technician forwards the problem to a more experienced technician.

A good source of troubleshooting information is the operating system's or software product's Web site. For example, when troubleshooting Microsoft operating systems and software products, you would use the Microsoft Web site or Microsoft's TechNet Web site. Microsoft's TechNet Web site is designed especially for technicians and administrators.

The TechNet Web site has a vast system of resources for PC and network support. The TechNet home page can be found at http://technet.microsoft.com/default.aspx or by using the key words "Microsoft TechNet" in a Google search. You can access Microsoft's extensive Knowledge Base articles through this page as well as many other links. TechNet also offers a subscription to copies of beta software, patches, and drivers.

For the Novell SUSE Linux operating system, you should use the Novell Support Web site. Conduct a search using the key words "Novell Support." You may also enter www.novell.com/support into the address bar of your Web browser.

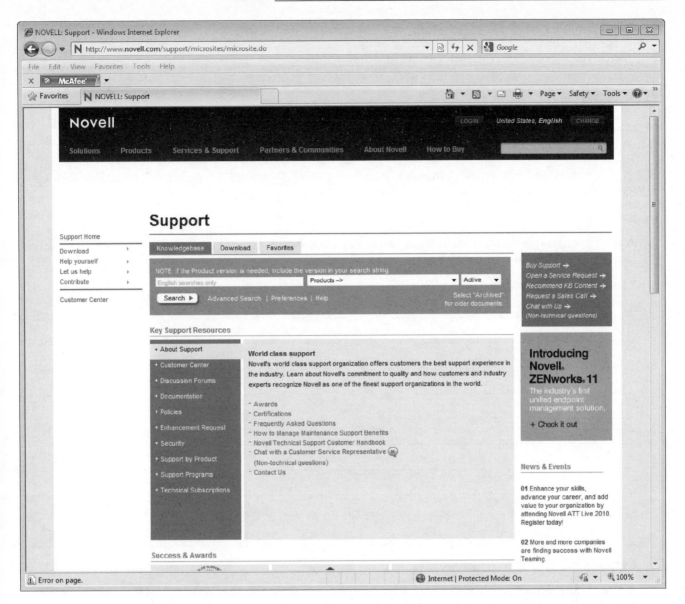

The Google and Firefox search engines are an extremely valuable tool for gathering troubleshooting information. The following are also good sources of troubleshooting information: www.windowsnetworking.com/articles_tutorials/trouble and http://compnetworking.about.com/od/homenetworktroubleshooting/Home_Network_Troubleshooting.htm.

You may find it difficult to describe the problem using terms that correctly identify the symptoms. Through experience, you may want to assemble a list of key words to use in future searches.

You may also wish to review the Microsoft Knowledge Base article 242450: "How to Query the Microsoft Knowledge Base Key Words and Query Words." You may conduct a search using the key terms "Microsoft 242450" to locate the article.

There are a lot of information sources on the Internet today. When conducting searches for troubleshooting problems, include the terms that relate directly to the manufacturer. For example, for a Microsoft operating system, include the terms "Microsoft," "TechNet," the operating system version, and the symptom.

Equipment and Materials

❏   Windows XP or later computer with Internet access.

Procedure

1. _____ Report to your assigned workstation.

2. _____ Boot the computer and verify it is in working order.

3. _____ Solve the following computer/network problems using the resources mentioned in this laboratory activity. Also, provide the source of the information.

Symptom:

A user complains that a workstation immediately reboots after shutting down. The workstation is running Windows Vista and is connected to a client/server network.

Problem and Solution:

_____

_____

_____

_____

_____

_____

_____

Source:

_____

Symptom:

A user complains of a blue screen with a cryptic test message that reads, "A fatal exception 0D has occurred at 0028:c0038f07 in VXD VMCPD(01) + 00002DB." The workstation is running Windows Vista.

Problem and Solution:

_____

_____

_____

_____

_____

_____

_____

Source:

_____

Symptom:

A user complains that she cannot play a media file that she received through e-mail. The error message reads, "The server could not be found. (Account: account name, POP server: 'mail', Error Number: 0x800ccc0d)" She is using Windows 7 and Microsoft Outlook 2010.

Problem and Solution:

_____

_____

_____

_____

_____

_____

_____

_____

Source:

_____

Symptom:

When trying to activate Windows 7, the error "0xC004F061" occurs.

Problem and Solution:

_____

_____

_____

_____

_____

_____

_____

_____

_____

Source:

_____

Review Questions

1. Why should you do an Internet search for a computer or network problem before spending an extraordinary amount of time troubleshooting the problem? _____

_____

_____

_____

2. What is the Microsoft TechNet Web site and who is its intended audience?_____

_____

_____

_____

Name_____ Date _____

Class/Instructor _____

Designing a Small Network

After completing this laboratory activity, you will be able to:

- Construct a simple materials list.
- Design a simple project timeline.
- Produce a price bid for the installation of a small office network.

Introduction

In this laboratory activity, you will design a small network system for a business office. You will decide on the workstations, network equipment, network media, and software. Your assignment is to carefully review the requirements as specified in the scenario and then construct a materials list, which includes prices for materials and labor. You will also calculate a profit figure. You will use the Internet for locating project items and obtaining prices.

Equipment and Materials

❑ Computer and printer. (The computer must have Internet access to conduct the research for the project. The printer is necessary to provide equipment specifications and pricing.)

Scenario

RMRoberts Inc. is setting up a brand new office for its Web design business. The office will consist of 16 workstations with the capability of supporting Web design functions. The office will require high-speed Internet access. Each person in the office will require a laser black and white printer. One full-color printer, centrally located, will be shared by all workstations. Each workstation must have a Microsoft operating system, Microsoft Office Professional software, and

Microsoft Expression Web Suite software installed. Also needed are office cubical dividers that will accommodate network and electrical wiring. The following figure illustrates what the final office design should look like as well as the office dimensions. Notice that the office has a drop ceiling.

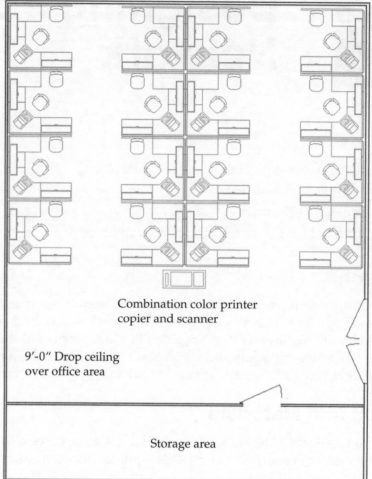

Combination color printer copier and scanner

9'-0" Drop ceiling over office area

Storage area

Scale 1/4" = 1'-0"

In summary, the materials should include the following:

- Microsoft operating system and Microsoft Office Professional for 16 workstations.
- Microsoft Expression Web Suite for 16 workstations.
- Server(s).
- Network devices, such as hubs, switches, or routers.
- Network media.
- 16 laser black and white printers.
- 1 full-color printer.
- Office cubicle dividers.

Procedure

1. _____ Select appropriate computer workstations; any needed servers, hubs, switches, or routers; and network medium, such as copper wire, wireless, or fiber-optic for the network system. Be prepared to defend your selection of materials.

2. _____ Configure a detailed list of materials, material costs, a time line for installing all hardware and software and providing at least one day of training for all office personnel on the system. A materials list must provide the following items:

■ Item name.

■ Manufacturer.

■ Part number.

■ Individual price.

■ Total cost.

■ Shipping cost.

■ Approximate delivery time.

3. _____ Submit the following items to your instructor:

■ Materials list.

■ Materials costs.

■ Labor cost.

■ Profit.

■ Timeline.

■ Hard copy of all prices and equipment specifications found in your Internet search.

4. _____ For extra credit, download a free demo version of Microsoft Visio or an equal drawing software program and make a drawing of the network system matching the proposal.

Project Tips

■ Keep the system simple. Do *not* try to create an elaborate system.

■ Sketch the network system before attempting to start a materials list.

■ Less expensive materials may not necessarily be the best way to go.

■ Feel free to be creative.

Laboratory Activity

96

Name_____ Date _____

Class/Instructor _____

Establishing a Baseline

After completing this laboratory activity, you will be able to:

■ Recall the reasons for establishing a network baseline.

■ Use the Wireshark Network Protocol Analyzer to establish a baseline.

■ Analyze statistical content commonly gathered in a baseline.

Introduction

In this laboratory activity, you will use Wireshark Protocol Analyzer to explore a network baseline and to interpret statistics associated with a baseline. Establishing a baseline of network activity will prove to be a valuable network troubleshooting and maintenance tool.

A baseline is a reference of statistical information used for comparison and to establish trends. The baseline is established for the first time after a network has been created. After the initial creation of a network system, a baseline is reestablished whenever a major change has taken place that might affect network performance. Changes that can affect network performance are the addition or replacement of workstations, new or replaced servers and equipment, new or modified network segments, and upgrading or replacing server and workstation operating systems.

A baseline should be established periodically to project a network's future needs. You can monitor network traffic and predict the need of additional segments, servers, data storage, and more.

Wireshark has an assortment of useful items under the **Statistics** menu for recording baseline information. Look at the following screen capture of the Wireshark **Statistics** menu.

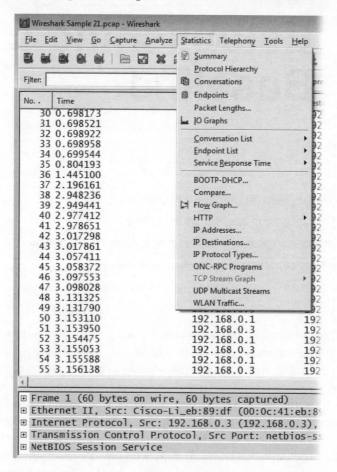

The following table lists some of the common **Statistics** menu items you will explore during this laboratory activity. There is a great deal more detailed information in the Wireshark user guide available from the Wireshark Web site.

Statistics Menu Options	Description
Summary	A general summary of network information and statistics during a specific time period.
Protocol Hierarchy	A hierarchal display of all protocols captured during a specific time period.
Conversions	A display of traffic between two end points.
End Points	A display of traffic by addresses.
IO Graphs	A graphical display of the amount of traffic over a specific period of time.

Equipment and Materials

❑ Windows XP or later computer with Wireshark installed.
❑ Wireshark Sample 21 file.

Wireshark Sample 21 file location: _____

❑ Wireshark Sample 22 file.

Wireshark Sample 22 file location: _____

Note

The computer must be apart of a peer-to-peer or client/server network to generate network traffic.

Procedure

1. _____ Report to your assigned workstation.

2. _____ Boot the computer and verify it is in working order.

3. _____ Start Wireshark and then open the sample Wireshark Sample 21 file. Look at the information in the **Summary** dialog box accessed through **Statistics | Summary**. The dialog box should look similar to the following.

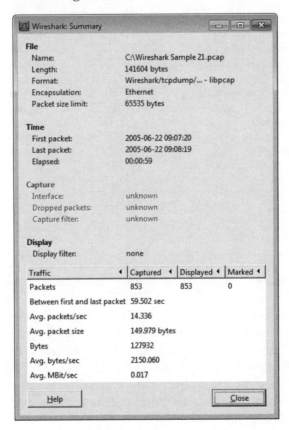

The **Summary** dialog box presents a summary of general network statistics such as the total time elapsed during the capture, total number of packets captured, average number of packets per second, average packet size, total number of bytes, average number of bytes per second, and average number of megabytes per second.

4. _____ Close the **Summary** dialog box.

5. _____ Access **Statistics | Protocol Hierarchy**. A dialog box similar to the following will display.

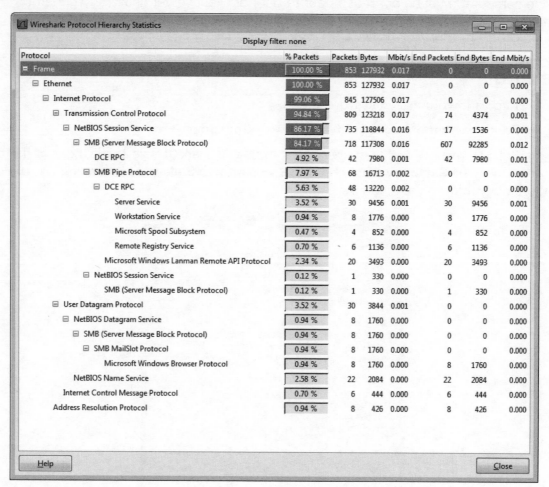

Protocol	% Packets	Packets	Bytes	Mbit/s	End Packets	End Bytes	End Mbit/s
⊟ Frame	100.00 %	853	127932	0.017	0	0	0.000
⊟ Ethernet	100.00 %	853	127932	0.017	0	0	0.000
⊟ Internet Protocol	99.06 %	845	127506	0.017	0	0	0.000
⊟ Transmission Control Protocol	94.84 %	809	123218	0.017	74	4374	0.001
⊟ NetBIOS Session Service	86.17 %	735	118844	0.016	17	1536	0.000
⊟ SMB (Server Message Block Protocol)	84.17 %	718	117308	0.016	607	92285	0.012
DCE RPC	4.92 %	42	7980	0.001	42	7980	0.001
⊟ SMB Pipe Protocol	7.97 %	68	16713	0.002	0	0	0.000
⊟ DCE RPC	5.63 %	48	13220	0.002	0	0	0.000
Server Service	3.52 %	30	9456	0.001	30	9456	0.001
Workstation Service	0.94 %	8	1776	0.000	8	1776	0.000
Microsoft Spool Subsystem	0.47 %	4	852	0.000	4	852	0.000
Remote Registry Service	0.70 %	6	1136	0.000	6	1136	0.000
Microsoft Windows Lanman Remote API Protocol	2.34 %	20	3493	0.000	20	3493	0.000
⊟ NetBIOS Session Service	0.12 %	1	330	0.000	0	0	0.000
SMB (Server Message Block Protocol)	0.12 %	1	330	0.000	1	330	0.000
⊟ User Datagram Protocol	3.52 %	30	3844	0.001	0	0	0.000
⊟ NetBIOS Datagram Service	0.94 %	8	1760	0.000	0	0	0.000
⊟ SMB (Server Message Block Protocol)	0.94 %	8	1760	0.000	0	0	0.000
⊟ SMB MailSlot Protocol	0.94 %	8	1760	0.000	0	0	0.000
Microsoft Windows Browser Protocol	0.94 %	8	1760	0.000	8	1760	0.000
NetBIOS Name Service	2.58 %	22	2084	0.000	22	2084	0.000
Internet Control Message Protocol	0.70 %	6	444	0.000	6	444	0.000
Address Resolution Protocol	0.94 %	8	426	0.000	8	426	0.000

You will see a detailed breakdown by protocol of all packets captured. The **Protocol Hierarchy** menu item can be used to identify network activity or to spot some unusual or suspicious activity. For example, a high percentage of Address Resolution Protocol (ARP) requests could indicate an intruder probing the network for IPv4 and MAC addresses or indicate a defective hardware device or software program. In the Wireshark Sample 21 file, you will see that the total ARP percentage is less than 1% of the total packets. A low percentage of ARP requests is normal.

6. _____ Close the **Protocol Hierarchy Statistics** dialog box.

7. _____ Access **Statistics | Conversations**. Look at the following three screen captures. The first is of the **Conversations** dialog box with the **Name resolution** option disabled. The second screen capture shows the **Conversations** dialog box with **Name resolution** enabled. In the third screen capture, the **IPv4:6** tab is selected.

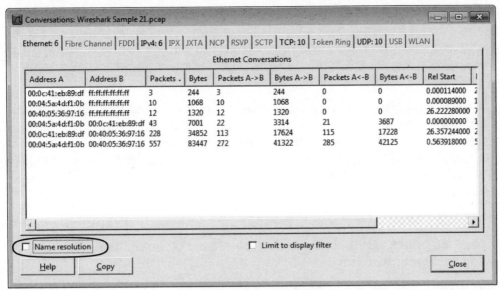

Name Resolution Disabled

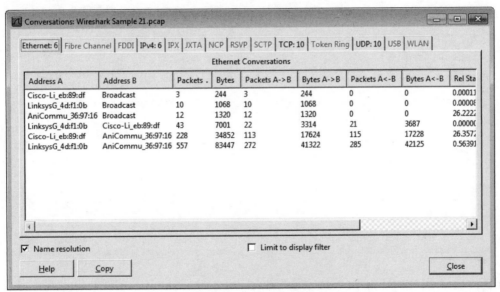

Name Resolution Enabled

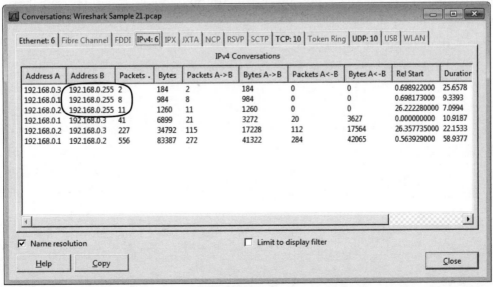

IPv4:6 Selected

The **Conversations** dialog box displays the traffic between various nodes on the network. The default tab selected is **Ethernet:6**. The number 6 indicates that six nodes are referenced by IP address. Source IP addresses are listed under column **Address A**, and destination addresses are listed under column **Address B**. Notice that broadcasts are considered IP addresses. Broadcasts are listed in the previous dialog box as 192.168.0.255.

The **Conversations** dialog box is very handy for locating an IP address that is sending an unusual amount of broadcast traffic. A high amount of broadcast traffic can indicate a problem such as a defective device, improper configuration, virus, or security breach. The **Conversations** and the **Endpoints** menu items allow you to display the information related to only Ethernet, IPv4, TCP, or UDP. Also, notice that in addition to these four protocols, traffic can be selected by additional protocols, such as Fibre Channel, FDDI, and IPX.

8. _____ Close the **Conversations** dialog box.

9. _____ Access **Statistics | Endpoints**. The **Endpoints** dialog box will display and look similar to the following screen capture.

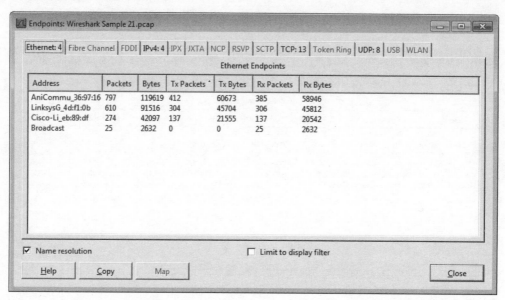

The **Endpoints** dialog box displays network activity by each network device. This is an excellent way to determine where most of the network traffic is being generated. This can be helpful when identifying sources of high-volume traffic on the network. A switch can then be used to create segments to reduce the network traffic.

10. _____ Close the **Endpoints** dialog box.

11. _____ Access **Statistics | IO Graphs**. A dialog box similar to the following will display.

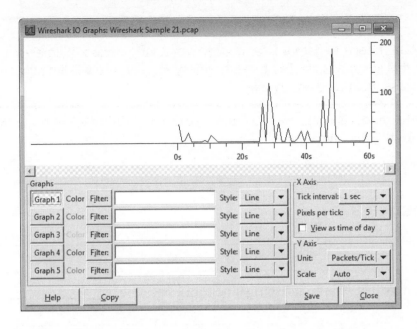

The **IO Graphs** dialog box displays network traffic as a graph. You can make changes to the way the data appears in the graph. The X axis and Y axis control are in the lower-right corner of the dialog box. The X axis is the horizontal axis and represents the time. The Y axis is the vertical axis and represents the network volume typically in packets or bytes. You can modify the display by filtering specific protocols and displaying them in a different color. This is controlled on the lower-left corner of the dialog box with the **Graph 1** through **Graph 5** buttons.

12. _____ Close the **IO Graphs** dialog box and Wireshark Sample 21 file.

13. _____ Open the Wireshark Sample 22 file and see if you can determine the network problem by looking at the statistics. Answer the following questions.

What type of protocol makes up the majority of the capture? _____

Which network device address is generating the most broadcasts? _____

What is the total lapse time of the capture? _____

How many bytes per second were transmitted? _____

Which are the top three devices generating traffic? _____

_____

What do you think is indicated by the statistics? _____

_____

_____

_____

_____

14. _____ Create a capture over a time period of five minutes. Generate traffic conditions by accessing shares on another computer or by accessing the Internet and conducting a search or download. After five minutes have elapsed, stop the capture and prepare a report for your instructor. The report should list the network devices in the local area network and the amount of traffic generated by each protocol. Identify which device is generating the most traffic.

Note

A true baseline needs to gather information over a long period of time. In a typical lab setting, this is impossible. For this laboratory activity, you will limit the time to five minutes, unless instructed otherwise.

15. _____ After the report is complete, you may use the remaining time in the class period to experiment with the **Statistics** menu.

16. _____ Answer the review questions.

Review Questions

1. What is a baseline?_____

_____

2. What changes may justify reestablishing a network baseline?_____

_____

_____

_____

_____

_____

3. Which Wireshark **Statistics** menu item will provide a listing of the amount of data exchanged between two devices in a network? _____

4. Which Wireshark **Statistics** menu item will display a list of all devices on the network? _____

_____

Creating a CompTIA Network+ Certification Study Guide

After completing this laboratory activity, you will be able to:

■ Use the Internet to locate and download a copy of the CompTIA Network+ Certification objectives.

■ Use the CompTIA Network+ Certification objectives to create a study guide.

Introduction

In this laboratory activity, you will download a copy of the CompTIA Network+ Certification exam objectives and then create your own study guide. The objectives can be found at the CompTIA Web site www.CompTIA.org. After downloading a copy of the exam objectives in PDF format, you can save a copy of the objectives as a text file. This will allow you to manipulate the contents to copy sections of the original content and paste them into a Word document to create a student study guide. It also allows you to create ample space for notes pertaining to each topic.

You will fill in the Network+ Certification study guide using information from your textbook and laboratory manual, the Internet, and any other source you think is appropriate. Check with your instructor for additional sources.

There are many different Network+ Certification study guides available commercially and for free. The problem with a ready-made study guide is that it typically does not help you actively learn the material. As a student, you are well aware that you learn a topic by reading, doing worksheets, writing reports, and doing other mental exercises that help you process and retain the information. You would most likely read a ready-made study guide once and then not review it. Your retention would be approximately equal to reading a text or a list of terms and definitions. To retain information, you must make some effort. For example, answering review questions and filling out worksheets will better enable you to retain the information than if you simply read the information. A study guide that you prepare for yourself will better prepare you for the exam and will help you identify the areas you feel inadequately prepared for.

Equipment and Materials

❑ Windows XP or later computer with Internet and printer access and Microsoft Word.

Note
A printer is not absolutely necessary for this laboratory activity. The finished product can be transferred to storage media such as a flash drive or CD/DVD.

Procedure

1. _____ Report to your assigned workstation.

2. _____ Boot the computer and verify it is in working order.

3. _____ Access the CompTIA Web site and locate the latest version of the Network+ Certification exam objectives.

4. _____ Download a PDF version of the objectives. Also, download a copy of any sample test questions that might be available.

Note

Sample test questions are not always available for CompTIA Certification exams on the CompTIA Web site.

---

5. _____ After successfully downloading a copy of the CompTIA Network+ Certification exam objectives, take a minute to look them over.

6. _____ Open the PDF file of the CompTIA Network+ Certification exam objectives and then access **File | Save as Text** as shown in the following screen capture.

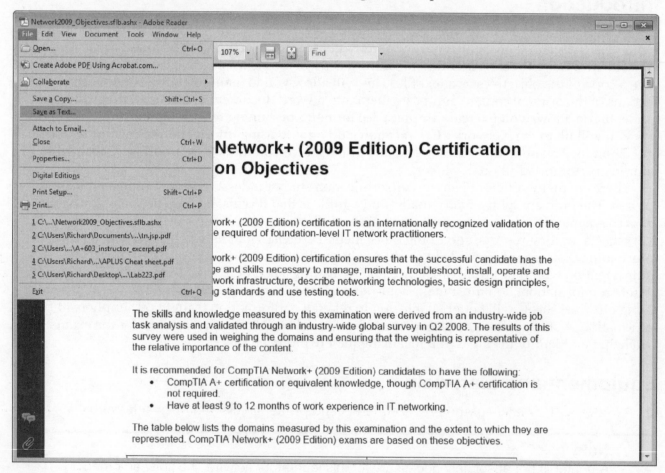

7. _____ Open the CompTIA Network+ Certification exam objectives text file. You can use most any word processing software to open this file. In this lab activity, Microsoft Word is used.

8. _____ After opening the text file of the CompTIA Network+ Certification exam objectives, select the area of the file you wish to copy—for example, the Domain 1 section and all of its topics.

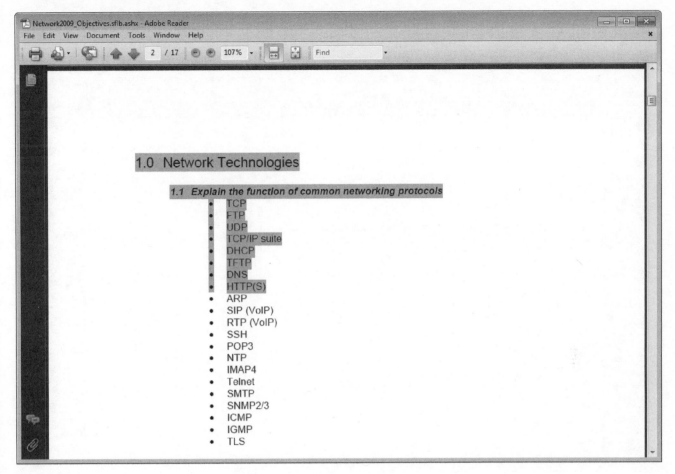

You can select the section of text you wish to copy by dragging the mouse pointer over the appropriate area while pressing the left mouse button. The selected area of text will be highlighted. Right-click the highlighted area and then select **Copy** from the shortcut menu.

9. _____ Open a new Microsoft Word document and paste the copied section into the new document by right-clicking a blank area and selecting **Paste** from the shortcut menu.

10. _____ Save the new document before making any changes. You might wish to name the file *"Your Name* Network Study Guide Domain 1" where *"Your Name"* is your actual name. This will identify your work should your instructor want you to turn in a copy of your completed study guide for a grade.

11. _____ Now, you will format the text in the document to create a useful study guide. Create spaces for your notes or for drawings. Look at the example in the following screen capture.

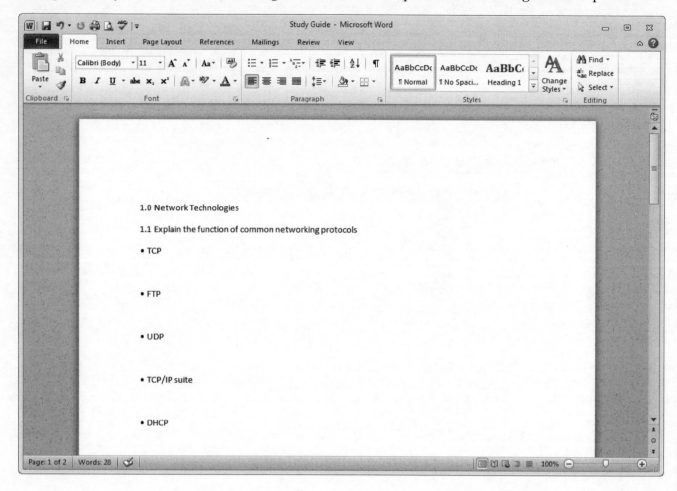

Notice that spaces have been added. You can use the mouse and the [Enter] key to create spaces in the study guide. Save your study guide often when creating the spaces.

12. _____ When you are finished, call your instructor to inspect your work.

13. _____ When you receive your instructor's approval, you may print your study guide and begin filling in the blank areas with notes pertaining to the objectives.

Laboratory Activity

98

Name_____ Date _____

Class/Instructor _____

Evaluating Test Information and Practice Test Sources

After completing this laboratory activity, you will be able to:

■ Use the Internet to locate several Web sites containing free CompTIA Network+ Certification exam questions.

■ Evaluate your readiness for the CompTIA Network+ Certification exam by taking practice quizzes.

Introduction

In this laboratory activity, you will visit some recommended Web sites containing sample CompTIA Network+ Certification exam questions. You will also conduct a search for more sites.

You are finishing the course of study and should be preparing to take the CompTIA Network+ Certification exam. You have created a study guide in a previous laboratory activity. Now, you will visit several Web sites to take some sample Network+ Certification quizzes to see if you are ready for the real exam. This lab activity contains a list of Web sites that have some good examples of test questions. There are many more Web sites with practice test questions.

You must not become too discouraged when taking a sample exam on the Internet. Many of the sample exam questions you encounter are more difficult to answer than those on the actual CompTIA Network+ Certification exam. It is likely that some Web sites deliberately present a series of difficult questions to make you believe you are not ready. The idea is to encourage you to buy the test bank and study guide they are selling. You do not need to purchase a study guide or a test bank. If you applied yourself throughout the course of study, completed all review and practice questions, attended class regularly, completed all laboratory activities, and completed your own study guide, you will be well prepared for the real exam.

When taking a sample exam, a score of 60% to 70% is excellent. Do not expect a higher score such as 90% to 100%. As stated earlier, these test questions are typically very difficult compared to those on the CompTIA Network+ Certification exam.

The following table contains a list of recommended Web sites containing sample CompTIA Network+ Certification exam questions. While every Web site was checked for accuracy at the time of this writing, Web sites often change their URL address and their offers for free test questions. Many good Web sites have come and gone over the past few years.

www.proprofs.com	Contains practice questions, a study guide, forum discussions, and exam tips. A free registration is required to be able to access the best materials. This Web site is very extensive. To locate this site's Network+ practice exam, it may be better to conduct an Internet search using the key terms "ProProfs Network+."
www.pagesbydave.com	Contains Network+ and A+ Certification practice questions.
www.simulationexams.com	Contains test materials for many different technology exams.
www.RMRoberts.com	Be sure to check out the latest free Network+ Certification practice tests on the author's Web site!
www.certification.about.com	Free practice tests for Network+ and more. No registration is required.
www.bestsamplequestions.com	At the time of this writing, this Web site contains over 275 free sample test questions for the Network+ Certification exam. It also includes sample test questions for the A+ Certification exam.

Equipment and Materials

❏   Windows XP or later computer with Internet access.

Procedure

1. _____ Report to your assigned workstation.

2. _____ Boot the computer and verify it is in working order.

3. _____ Access and review the Web sites listed in the table in the introduction.

4. _____ After reviewing the Web sites, you may conduct your own search using key words such as "CompTIA Network+ Certification free practice test."

5. _____ Meet with other students in your class to share your Internet findings. This would be a good time to form a study group to better prepare for the exam.

Writing a Résumé

After completing this laboratory activity, you will be able to:

■ Create a résumé.

■ Recall the headings to include in a résumé.

■ Recall the personal information you should *not* include as part of a résumé.

Introduction

In this laboratory activity, you will prepare a résumé. A résumé is a vital part of acquiring employment. Your résumé should contain the following headings and related information:

■ Education.

■ Employment.

■ Job skills.

■ References.

Before coming to class to perform this laboratory activity, gather information regarding your education, employment, job skills, and references. You will need to know the schools you have attended and the years you have attended them. List your education history as far back as High School. Include any special training you have had. Gather the names and addresses of the places at which you have worked and the start and end dates of your employment there. Also, make note of the various job skills you have mastered.

Note
At the interview, you should be prepared to provide a copy of any special training certificates, special recognitions, or degrees you have received.

At least four people should be selected as references. Be sure to obtain their permission before listing them on your résumé. Include contact information for each person, such as his or her name, phone number, and address.

The résumé must be typed and printed on quality paper. Microsoft Word includes three résumé templates: Professional Résumé, Contemporary Résumé, and Elegant Résumé. The templates can help you to professionally format your résumé. The templates also contain sample information. In this laboratory activity, you will examine the sentence structure of the sample sentences before entering your own information. You will create your sentences in a similar fashion. To enter your information, you simply highlight the sample text and then type in your information.

When creating a résumé, do *not* list your social security number. You do not want your social security number and personal information on the same document. Your social security number will be requested after you are hired for a position. Do *not* include a copy of your driver's license in the résumé for the same reason as the social security number. Your driver's license may be requested after you are hired. Do not post your résumé online at a Web site that charges fees. Do *not* post your résumé online at a nationally recognized Web site unless you are willing to relocate to another geographical area.

Equipment and Materials

❑ Windows XP or later computer with Internet access, printer access, and Microsoft Word or comparable word processing software.

Procedure

1. _____ Gather any notes you have made on references, employment, education, and job skills, and then report to your assigned workstation.

2. _____ Boot the computer and verify it is in working order.

3. _____ Open Microsoft Word.

4. _____ Access the **File** menu and select **New**.

5. _____ Click the **Other Documents** tab. You will see several icons representing templates. Select one of the résumé document icons: **Professional Resume**, **Contemporary Resume**, or **Elegant Resume**, or any other résumé template that your word processing program may display. The résumé will open and contain sample information.

6. _____ Read through the sample information in the Experience section. Notice that the sentences start with a verb, such as *managed* and *developed*. The sentences are also short and to the point and describe the most important tasks performed at the company. You will create similar sentences for your Employment section. Now look at the sentences under Education. Notice that the degree is listed followed by the title of the degree. Honors are listed below.

7. _____ Create the headings Education, Job Skills, Employment, and Reference by highlighting the sample headings and typing in the desired heading. Be sure to enter Education and Employment over the headings that contain fields for dates. For Job Skills and References, you can use the format of the heading styles Interests and Tips, or you can use the headings that contain fields for names and dates. You will be able to enter any information into the fields. Delete any unused headings along with sample information that is not used. Do not delete any of the sample information under your headings.

8. _____ Enter your information in the appropriate fields by highlighting the sample text and then typing in your information. List your employment and education history in descending order, from the most recent employment to your oldest employment.

9. _____ When you are finished, read through your résumé and spell check your work.

10. _____ If instructed to do so, print your document and give it to your instructor, or save your document to a storage device, such as a flash drive.

11. _____ Answer the review questions.

Review Questions

1. List four headings to include in a résumé. _____

   _____

   _____

   _____

   _____

2. What documentation should you be prepared to present at an interview? _____

   _____

   _____

   _____

   _____

3. What personal information should you *not* include as part of the résumé? _____

   _____

   _____

   _____

   _____

Networking Fundamentals Laboratory Manual

Laboratory Activity

100

Name_____ Date _____

Class/Instructor _____

Conducting a Job Search

After completing this laboratory activity, you will be able to:

■ Recall possible sources of job information.

■ Execute a job search to locate an entry-level network technician position.

Introduction

In this laboratory activity, you will conduct a job search for an entry-level position as a network technician. You will collect information pertaining to at least three jobs in your local area or in close proximity to your hometown. Some possible sources of job information are the following:

■ Local newspapers.

■ Government institutions.

■ Large employers.

Most local newspapers have Web sites with employment information. Conduct a search using the keywords "*your local newspaper* network technician employment" or simply "*your local newspaper* employment.*" Substitute the name of your local newspaper for "*your local newspaper.*"

Government institutions, such as local school districts, colleges, and government offices, and large employers, such as local manufacturers and hospitals, typically post jobs on their Web site. Most jobs are acquired through acquaintances, such as other students, instructors, friends, neighbors, and business contacts.

While conducting your online search, gather information to turn in for this laboratory assignment. Print copies of possible job opportunities matching your skill set. Be prepared to turn in to your instructor a copy of each eligible job or the three best possibilities.

Equipment and Materials

❑ Windows XP or later computer with Internet and printer access.

Procedure

1. _____ Report to your assigned workstation.

2. _____ Boot the computer and verify it is in working order.

3. _____ Conduct a job search and identify at least three jobs that you could apply for. Use sources such as the local newspaper, professional journals, and the Internet.

4. _____ Turn over to your instructor a copy of each job for which you may be eligible.

5. _____ Answer the review questions.

Review Questions

1. List three possible sources of job information. _____

   _____

   _____

   _____

2. List at least three examples of government institutions in which to find a job as an entry-level network technician. _____

   _____

   _____

   _____

Laboratory Activity

101

Name_____ Date _____

Class/Instructor _____

Researching Network Administrator Job Requirements

After completing this laboratory activity, you will be able to:

■ Identify the characteristics, experiences, and training requirements wanted by employers for most network administration positions.

■ Identify any additional training that may be needed to meet the requirements.

Introduction

In this laboratory activity, you will conduct an Internet search for the requirements of a network administrator position. You will also determine any additional training you may need to meet the requirements.

Equipment and Materials

❑ Windows XP or later computer with Internet access.

Procedure

1. _____ Report to your assigned workstation.

2. _____ Boot the computer and verify it is in working order.

3. _____ Look for job opportunities for network administrators. Conduct an Internet search using the keywords "IT Position Network Administrator," "Wanted Network Administrator," or similar variations. You may need to include your state name in the search to narrow down the results. The job can be for Microsoft, Linux, or UNIX operating systems. Keep a copy of at least five network positions and list the following requirements of the job applicant.

Special certificates:

_____

_____

Education:

_____

_____

Minimum experience:

_____

_____

4. _____ Repeat the activities in step three for a software programmer.

Special certificates:

_____

_____

Education:

_____

_____

Minimum experience:

_____

_____

5. _____ Repeat the activities in step three for a network engineer.

Special certificates:

_____

_____

Education:

_____

_____

Minimum experience:

_____

_____